Ethical, Legal and Social Aspects of Health Care for Migrants

Numerous important issues arise in relation to the health of, and health care for (and by), migrants. Much of the commentary on the migrant 'crisis' and health care has focused on the allocation of resources, with less discussion of the needs of, and provision for, migrants. Presenting a comparative perspective on the UK and Germany, this volume increases knowledge of a broad spectrum of challenges in health care provision for migrants.

'Migration' is deliberately understood in its broadest sense and includes not only migrant patients but also migrant health care professionals. The book's content is diverse, with insights from health care ethics, health care law, along with clinical perspectives as well as perspectives from the social sciences. The collection provides normative reflections on current issues and presents data from empirical studies. By informing researchers, politicians and health care practitioners about approaches to challenges arising in health care provision for migrants, the collection seeks to inform the development of adequate and ethically appropriate strategies.

Katja Kuehlmeyer, Dr. rer. biol. hum., is Research Associate at the Institute of Ethics, History and Theory of Medicine at LMU Munich. She works on various topics at the intersection of psychology, health and ethics.

Corinna Klingler, MSc, has recently finished her doctoral research on integration of migrant physicians in Germany and is currently working on translational bioethics as a postdoctoral researcher at the QUEST Center of the Berlin Institute of Health.

Richard Huxtable, LLB, MA, PhD, is Professor of Medical Ethics and Law and Director of the Centre for Ethics in Medicine, University of Bristol, UK. He works primarily on ethics and law at the end of life, surgical ethics, and clinical ethics support.

Law and Migration

Series Editor: Satvinder S. Juss, King's College London, UK

Migration and its subsets of refugee and asylum policy are rising up the policy agenda at national and international level. Current controversies underline the need for rational and informed debate of this widely misrepresented and little understood area.

Law and Migration contributes to this debate by establishing an edited volume series to encourage discussion and help to inform policy in this area. The series provides a forum for leading new research principally from the Law and Legal Studies area but also from related social sciences. The series is broad in scope, covering a wide range of subjects and perspectives.

Bureaucracy, Law and Dystopia in the United Kingdom's Asylum System
John R. Campbell

Children's Rights and Refugee Law
Conceptualising Children within the Refugee Convention
Samantha Arnold

Law and Asylum
Space, Subject, Resistance
Simon Behrman

Ethical, Legal and Social Aspects of Health Care for Migrants:
Perspectives from the UK and Germany
Edited by Katja Kuehlmeyer, Corinna Klingler and Richard Huxtable

Environmental Change, Forced Displacement and International Law from legal protection gaps to protection solutions
Isabel M. Borges

For more information about this series, please visit:
www.routledge.com/Law-and-Migration/book-series/LAWANDMIG

Ethical, Legal and Social Aspects of Health Care for Migrants

Perspectives from the UK and Germany

Edited by
Katja Kuehlmeyer, Corinna Klingler and Richard Huxtable

Routledge
Taylor & Francis Group
LONDON AND NEW YORK

First published 2019
by Routledge
2 Park Square, Milton Park, Abingdon, Oxon OX14 4RN

and by Routledge
52 Vanderbilt Avenue, New York, NY 10017

First issued in paperback 2020

Routledge is an imprint of the Taylor & Francis Group, an informa business

British Library Cataloguing-in-Publication Data
A catalogue record for this book is available from the British Library

Library of Congress Cataloging-in-Publication Data
A catalog record for this book has been requested

ISBN 13: 978-0-367-58247-0 (pbk)
ISBN 13: 978-1-138-05654-1 (hbk)

Typeset in Galliard
by codeMantra

Contents

List of tables and box

Tables

Box

Notes on contributors

Editors

Richard Huxtable, LLB, MA, PhD, is Professor of Medical Ethics and Law and Director of the Centre for Ethics in Medicine, University of Bristol, UK. He works primarily on ethics and law at the end of life, surgical ethics, and clinical ethics support.

Corinna Klingler, MSc, has recently finished her doctoral research on integration of migrant physicians in Germany and is currently working on translational bioethics as a postdoctoral researcher at the QUEST Centre of the Berlin Institute of Health.

Katja Kuehlmeyer, Dr. rer. biol. hum., is Research Associate at the Institute of Ethics, History and Theory of Medicine at LMU Munich. She works on various topics at the intersection of psychology, health and ethics.

Authors

Barbara Abdallah-Steinkopff is working as Psychotherapist at REFUGIO Munich, Germany, a centre for counselling and treatment for refugees and victims of torture. She is furthermore providing education and training in different institutions concerning psychotherapy of post-traumatic stress disorders, intercultural psychotherapy and cooperation with interpreters in the psychotherapy of refugees.

Carolin Bader is Advisor for domestic missions at Ärzte der Welt/Doctors of the World Germany, responsible for quality and strategy with regards to content and at the intersection to advocacy, media and communication. She has a background in cultural anthropology, sociology and gender studies.

Cormac Devlin has just completed his undergraduate degree in Law at Jesus College in the University of Cambridge, UK. He is particularly interested in immigration law and its intersection with health care policy and LGBT+ issues.

Christiane Falge, Prof. Dr., is Professor of Health and Diversity at the University of Applied Health Sciences, Bochum, Germany. She conducted her PhD at the Max Planck Institute for Social Anthropology in Halle.

Yasmin Ghazala Farooq, Ph.D., is Lecturer in Social Statistics at the University of Manchester, UK. She completed her PhD at the University of Manchester, UK in 2014. Her research interests include migration, identity, ethnicity, race and health inequalities. Her doctoral research focussed on the migration and identity experiences of overseas-trained South Asian doctors in the UK.

Monika Führer, Prof. Dr., is Pediatrician specialized in oncology, hematology and palliative medicine, Professor for Pediatric Palliative Medicine and head of the Pediatric Palliative Medicine Centre at LMU Munich, Germany. Her research interests are advance care planning and end-of-life decisions, social support and meaning in life in Pediatric Palliative Care.

Sabine Fürst is Head of Domestic Programs at Ärzte der Welt/Doctors of the World Germany since 2014, overseeing all projects in Hamburg, Stuttgart, Munich and Berlin. She worked for many years in international development cooperation in South Africa and Sudan, among others.

Lea Gelfert is a student of Political Sciences and Sociology and has worked as assistant for Ärzte der Welt/Doctors of the World Germany since April 2017.

Kerstin Hein, Dr. Phil, has a degree in Psychology from the Universidad Diego Portales in Santiago de Chile and a doctoral degree in Psychology and Sociology from LMU Munich, Germany. She is currently research coordinator at the Centre for Paediatric Palliative Medicine at LMU Munich and a parent trainer at REFUGIO Munich, Germany.

Hiranthi Jayaweera, Dr., is Research Associate at the School of Anthropology, University of Oxford, UK. She has long-standing research and policy interests in migrant health, in the UK, Europe and globally, and has written and presented extensively on this topic.

Lucy Jones is Director of Programmes at Doctors of the World UK, leading the programmes team and policy and advocacy work since 2013.

Markus Kaltenborn, Prof. Dr., is teaching Public Law at the Faculty of Law of Ruhr-University Bochum, Germany. He is Director of the Institute of Development Research and Development Politics (IEE) at Ruhr University Bochum. His main areas of research are Health Law, Social Security Law, the Law of Development Cooperation and Human Rights Law.

Sabine Klotz studied Polictical Science at the Frierich-Alexander University Erlangen-Nürnberg. She is currently working as a coordinator of the graduate program "Human Rights and Ethics in Medicine for the Ederly" at the Friedrich-Alexander Universität Erlangen Nürnberg, Germany.

Antje Lindenmeyer, Dr., is Lecturer in Qualitative Methods at the University of Birmingham. Her main field of research is the experience of health, illness and health care. She has a strong interest in the impact of migration on these experiences including health care encounters and everyday practices.

Ilhan Ilkilic, MD, PhD, has studied medicine, philosophy, Islamic science and oriental philology in Istanbul, Turkey and Bochum and Tübingen, Germany. He is currently Director of the Department of History of Medicine and Ethics at the Istanbul University Faculty of Medicine and Director of the Institute for Health Sciences of Istanbul University, Turkey.

Georg Marckmann, Prof. Dr., MPH, is Professor of medical ethics and Director of the Institute of Ethics, History and Theory of Medicine at LMU Munich, Germany. He studied medicine and philosophy at the University of Tübingen, Germany, and received a master's degree in Public Health from Harvard School of Public Health, Boston, MA, USA. His main research interests include ethical issues in end-of-life care, clinical ethics consultation, distributive justice in health care, and public health ethics.

Anna Miller is Policy and Advocacy Manager at Doctors of the World UK, overseeing programmes to strengthen the right to health care in the UK. She has a background in policy and campaigning work on the right to justice, housing and health care.

Amrei Müller, Dr, is currently a Leverhulme Trust early career researcher at the School of Law, Health & Human Rights Unit, Queen's University Belfast, United Kingdom. Her research interests lie in the area of human rights law and international humanitarian law, in particular the right to health, the protection of access to health care in times of armed conflict and the law of the European Convention on Human Rights.

Piret Paal, Dr., is researcher and facilitator for WHO Collaborating Centre in Nursing Research and Education, Institute of Nursing Sciences and Practice at the Paracelsus Medical University Salzburg. She is a member of steering groups on spiritual and palliative care education at the European Association of Palliative Care.

Oliver Razum, Prof. Dr., is full Professor and Dean of the School of Public Health, Bielefeld University, Germany. He also heads the Department of Epidemiology & International Public Health. His main research field is social epidemiology with a particular focus on the health of immigrants, and on the role of contextual factors in the production of health inequalities.

Penelope Scott, Ph.D., is guest researcher at the Institute of Sociology, LMU Munich, Germany. She has researched and published in the field of ethnic minority and im/migrant health in the UK and Germany.

Arianne Shahvisi, Ph.D., is Lecturer in Ethics at the Brighton & Sussex Medical School, UK. She received her Ph.D. from the University of Cambridge, UK in 2013. She has research interests in the philosophy of science and applied ethics, with current projects focusing on reproductive ethics and social epistemology.

Sarah Steele, Dr., is the Deputy Director of the Intellectual Forum at Jesus College in the University of Cambridge, UK. She is also a Senior Research Associate, focusing on themes and problems of interest to communities across the world at the interface of public health and law, and an Affiliated Researcher at the Department of Politics and International Studies.

Hella von Unger, Prof. Dr., is Professor of Sociology at LMU Munich, Germany. Her areas of expertise are qualitative methodologies, participatory research and research ethics in particular concerning research on health and illness, migration and ethnicity.

Judith Wenner is researcher at the Department of Epidemiology and International Public Health at the School of Public Health, Bielefeld University, Germany. She works on health inequality, access to health care and migration. Currently she is conducting a study on access to health care for refugees.

Foreword

Satvinder S. Juss

One of the most tantalizing myths of our time is that Europe's migration crisis is the result of the large number of their arrivals. It is true that in 2013 the figure stood at 1.3 million, but that upsurge was because of the Syrian war. The truth is closer to home. Public hostility to immigrants has been caused by a breakdown in trust, and in social disengagement, as well as the political disaffection, which arose exactly a decade ago, after the global financial crisis in 2008. Two distinct consequences arose from this. First, there was the unleashing of populist forces on both the far left and the far right, so that leaders from across the political divide were able to rise, such as the Labour Party's Jeremy Corbyn in the UK and Pablo Iglesias from the anti-austerity *Podemos* party in Spain, to Matteo Salvini, the leader of the Anti-Immigrant League, and Luigi Di Maio of the Five Star Movement in Italy. Second, and more worryingly, there arose a flagrant and unashamed attack on the liberal ideal from within the liberal order itself as demonstrated by the election to power of populists such as Donald Trump and Victor Orban with an outright rejection of the time-honoured liberal values of tolerance, diversity, and human rights that had begun to take shape.

It is this which shaped public hostility to migrants. Not the immigrants themselves who just became an easy scapegoat. In fact, all the evidence is that in countries where there are high levels of institutional trust, low levels of corruption, sound economies and most importantly a high level of social cohesion – which does include immigrants as well – there is markedly less anti-immigrant sentiment. In short, dislike of immigrants has little to do with the immigrants themselves. This is why this study by leading experts in the field of health care for migrants is so timely and important. The authors, Katja Kuehlmeyer, Corinna Klingler and Richard Huxtable, do not just make it clear that the exclusion of specific migrant groups from public health care is ethically unacceptable (noting that several public health ethicists eschew such restrictions critically) but they even pose the question whether a restrictive policy actually saves costs, thus rendering this study indispensable to today's financially strapped policy-makers.

It is often forgotten that in one of the most defining decisions in the UK,[1] concerning a 30-year old Ugandan asylum seeker threatened with expulsion had a "tragic complication" in the words of the Judge in the country's apex court, Lord Nicholson, in that she "suffer(ed) from advanced HIV/AIDS ('full blown AIDS', in the old terminology)."[2] When she arrived in the UK "she was very poorly" and "within hours she was admitted to Guy's Hospital"[3] in London, where, "as a result of modern drugs and skilled medical treatment over a lengthy period, including a prolonged course of systematic chemotherapy," she was "now much better."[4] However, as a failed asylum seeker, Lord Nichols recognised her, "cruel reality" that if she "returns to Uganda her ability to obtain the necessary medication is problematic" so that, "her position will be similar to having a life-support machine switched off."[5]

Whilst recognizing that, "[a]s everyone knows, the prevalence of AIDS worldwide, particularly in southern Africa, is a present-day human tragedy on an immense scale",[6] Lord Nichols was clear that the European Convention of Human Rights 1950 did "not require contracting states to undertake the obligation of providing aliens indefinitely with medical treatment lacking in their home countries."[7] In short, for those seeking to remain in a host country, "[i]f their applications are refused, the improvement in their medical condition brought about by this interim medical treatment, and the prospect of serious or fatal relapse on expulsion, cannot make expulsion inhuman treatment ..."[8] In so deciding the UK's apex court reversed the decision of the fact-finding tribunal of first instance, which had found in favour of the Ugandan asylum seeker and urged that she be not removed from the jurisdiction.

Another judge, Lord Hope, also was all too acutely aware that such a decision would have "profound consequences" for this Ugandan asylum seeker, because "[t]he prospects of her surviving for more than a year or two if she is returned to Uganda are bleak" so that "she will face an early death after a period of acute physical and mental suffering."[9] He was clear, nevertheless, that "[t]he function of a judge in a case of this kind, however, is not to issue decisions based on sympathy." Rather, "judges must examine the law in a way that suppresses emotion of all kinds" because "[t]he position that they must adopt is an austere one." This is because ultimately the question at hand was "about the extent of the obligations under Article 3 of the European Convention on Human Rights" and "about the treaty obligations of the contracting states" and whether "the contracting parties would have accepted and agreed to be bound by" an obligation to treat, perhaps indefinitely, the sick and ailing who happen to reach our shores from aboard or arrive at our airport terminals with no right to remain. No one, looking at the anxious scrutiny displayed by the judges and language deployed by them, can fail to be struck by how difficult they found the decision to be made in this case. And, lest it be thought that the decision was wrong in law, it was entirely upheld by the European Court of Human Rights in Strasbourg[10] some three years later. Yet, what this seminal immigrant medical health case demonstrates, however, the limits of the law specifically and of public policy more generally in the two most advanced economies of the European Union, namely, the UK and Germany, which the authors of this volume set out to examine, when it comes to the provision of medical health.

It is often said about the western conception of human rights that they are 'negative' rights in that they enjoin the State from refraining from interfering with, and impinging upon, the integrity of the individual, thereby making for the efficient running of the Capitalist system. Western rights are not generally 'positive' so as to require the alleviation of poverty of the masses as that would require the expenditure of money and resources. States, so the argument runs, do not willingly inflict poverty on their people (though the decade long European Union policy of 'austerity' makes one wonder!), but they do willingly torture their citizens, which is why it is correct to envision rights in this 'negative' sense. This, however, overlooks the fact that the right to vote, upon which western democracy is predicated, is very much a 'positive' right in that it entails costs on the part of the State every time people go to the polls.

It is against the background of such ambiguities and uncertainties that this laudable tome by Katja Kuehlmeyer, Corinna Klingler and Richard Huxtable aptly titled, *Ethical, Legal and Social Aspects of Health Care for Migrants,* is both so welcome and so timely, written with the erudition, expertise and objectivity, which policy-makers, state officials and lawyers will benefit from. What the authors do is to consider migrants' health, their need for and uptake of public health care, and their health care entitlements. Their focus is on Germany and the UK because both countries have a longstanding experience of migration, both have to deal with issues relating to immigrant and immigrant-sensitive health; both have had to deal with having to regulate migrants' access to and uptake of health care; and both are increasingly conscious of the need to ensure the provision of culturally sensitive health care in societies that are now pluralistic. Although many books have been usefully written on the rights of migrants, this is one of the few to focus on the pressing question of the health needs of immigrants. The authors tell us why this is so vitally important when they explain (at p. 3) that

> [p]eople value their health for various reasons but, foremost, health has an instrumental value, as it is a prerequisite to pursuing 'the innumerable projects of life that we are all involved with'" and not least because, "All humans are vulnerable to suffering...

Given this premise they are, *"convinced that, ethically, there is in principle no good reason for treating (literally and figuratively) migrants and non-migrants differently at least with regard to health care. Inadequate treatment of migrants can be variously conceived as a failure of solidarity, injustice, or a violation of human rights, such as the right to health*" (at p. 5) thus making the reading of this volume by a wider readership ever more compelling. This is because few immigration works are as well focused as this one on the ethics of the debate.

Yet this is exactly what has been done in the case-law. Notwithstanding the fact that some two decades ago Lord Hope urged that judges must "not to issue decisions based on sympathy" and Lord Nicholls concluded that the European Convention of Human Rights 1950 did "not require contracting states to undertake the obligation of providing aliens indefinitely with medical treatment ..." the issue is being revisited again by the courts. This is a telling reminder that ultimately it is the humane approach to the resolution of social and political problems that triumphs. In December 2016 the Grand Chamber of the European Court of Human Rights, in a case brought against the Belgium government,[11] decided to impose a much lower threshold than had been imposed in 2005 in the case of the Ugandan asylum seeker. In terms, it made it clear that,

> The Court considers that the 'other very exceptional cases' within the meaning of the judgment in *N. v. the United Kingdom* (§ 43) which may raise an issue under Article 3 should be understood to refer to situations involving the removal of a seriously ill person in which substantial grounds have been shown for believing that he or she, although not at imminent risk of dying, would face a real risk, on account of the absence of appropriate treatment in the receiving country or the lack of access to such treatment, of being exposed to a serious, rapid and irreversible decline in his or her state of health resulting in intense suffering or to a significant reduction in life expectancy. The Court points out that these situations correspond to a high threshold for the application of Article 3 of the Convention in cases concerning the removal of aliens suffering from serious illness.[12]

In a further twist, however, in 2017 an expert UK domestic immigration tribunal[13] held that the Grand Chamber decision was not one which is open to the Tribunal to apply by reason of its being contrary to judicial precedent, given that the UK's apex court had already decisively determined the matter in 2005 in a way that was binding to UK domestic courts and tribunals. In 2018 the Court of Appeal issued its decision on the matter,[14] concerning the case of a Zimbabwean AIDS sufferer this time whose condition was controlled by an anti-retroviral ("ARV") treatment he received in the UK involving medication called Eviplera, but who was subject to deportation on account of his criminal activities in the UK, which is worth setting out in detail:

> So far as the ECtHR and the Convention are concerned, the protection of Article 3 against removal in medical cases is now not confined to deathbed cases where death is already imminent when the applicant is in the removing country. It extends to cases where "substantial grounds have been shown for believing that [the applicant], although not at imminent risk of dying, would face a real risk, on account of the absence of appropriate treatment in the receiving country or lack of access to such treatment, of being exposed to a serious, rapid and irreversible decline in his or her state of health resulting in intense suffering or to a significant reduction in life expectancy" (para. [183]). This means cases where the applicant faces a real risk of rapidly experiencing intense suffering (i.e. to the Article 3 standard) in the receiving state because of their illness and the non-availability there of treatment which is available to them in the removing state or faces a real risk of death within a short time in the receiving state for the same reason. In other words, the boundary of Article 3 protection has been shifted from being defined by imminence of death in the removing state (even with the treatment available there) to being defined by the imminence (i.e. likely "rapid" experience) of intense suffering or death in the receiving state, which may only occur because of the non-availability in that state of the treatment which had previously been available in the removing state.

The Court of Appeal has made it clear, however, that the issue of medical health provision remains as doggedly intractable as ever so that there are currently in the UK "a significant number of other cases involving claims by foreign nationals to resist removal from the UK by invoking Article 3 on medical grounds which are already in the system,"[15] and where reliance is placed on the latest Grand Chamber decision of the European Court of Human Rights. Furthermore, it has even been said that "similar new claims based on application of Article 3 on medical grounds may be brought forward at any time." Although "all courts below the Supreme Court" in the UK "will be bound" by the early decision of 2005, nevertheless, "claimants may contend that they have grounds for saying that their cases are covered by the new guidance" given by the Grand Chamber in 2016" and moreover, even argue that, "any question of their removal from the UK should be stayed until the Supreme Court has decided to modify domestic law (potentially decisively in their favour) by reference to that guidance."[16] What a state of affairs, one might well argue!

One answer for lawyers, as we move to a reconsideration of a new legal paradigm in health care provision for migrants, may be to argue for a place for legal psychology, as I argued in a book in 1997.[17] Legal psychology is the scientific study of human behaviour in relation to the law and it consists of those theories that describe, explain and predict human behaviour by reference to law. By contrast, psychological jurisprudence consists of those theories that describe, explain and predict Law by reference to human behaviour. Legal psychology applies the science of psychology to law. Legal psychology is a science because it applies the scientific method of systematic observation, description and measurement to the study of behaviour that is legally relevant. By contrast, law relies primarily on logic as a foundation of knowledge. The basic function of psycho-logical research is to challenge the specific behavioural assumptions implicit in the law.

In this volume, Katja Kuehlmeyer, Corinna Klingler and Richard Huxtable have argued for the health care needs of immigrants to be recognized. It is, they explain, widely known that they face informal barriers when they are in need of health care and that they struggle to navigate a new health care system due to their relative lack of knowledge about it and difficulties in accessing it. There is also a reference to 'intercultural opening' with respect to the practice in Germany, (which other countries could do well to emulate), which seeks at the institutional level to strategically address and actively promote the users' understanding of the health care system and provide information that is comprehensible and accessible. Health care professionals, in turn, should not assume that their patients have uniform ideas about whether or how they want to be treated in a hospital or in an outpatient care service. They argue that people will differ in terms of their ages, their different social strata, their lifestyles, their faith-based values, and their religious commitments – such is the dynamic interplay. The authors argue that like 'migrant', 'culture' is a concept that has many meanings, but it is foremost a dynamic rather than a static notion. And that yet, it is not always clear how an appreciation of 'culture' might prove helpful in better understanding and then addressing any conflict that has arisen.

In my own work as a lawyer in 1997, I called for a 'cultural jurisprudence.' I wrote that 'the law is a cultural agent whose instrumental role cannot be ignored'.[18] I argued that cultural jurisprudence aims, 'through promotion of the values of individual autonomy, integrity of the fact-finding process, community safety, efficiency and economy, to enhance respect for the authorities, by making laws and practices of those authorities more culturally sensitive and competent ...'[19] In fact, as a concept cultural jurisprudence is 'prescriptive so that the law should protect and respect the cultural rights and expectations of a diverse community.'[20] To this end social science information should be utilized so that the values of equity, parity and justice can be more accurately secured in any increasingly diverse and multicultural society. At the time, a noted jurist, Sir Louis Blom-Cooper, who wrote the Foreword to my book, while commending such radical thinking, described this as a 'futuristic approach.'[21]

Some 20 years later, this compendium on the, *Ethical, Legal and Social Aspects of Health Care for Migrants,* by Katja Kuehlmeyer, Corinna Klingler and Richard Huxtable makes a captivating case for culturally sensitive and inclusionary health care provision for migrant communities. It is a model which policymakers should be able to apply in other area of public regulation as well. It is an idea whose time has come.

Satvinder Singh Juss, Ph.D (Cantab) FRSA, is a Professor of Law at King's College London, a Barrister-at-Law practising from 3 Hare Court, Temple, London, and a Deputy Judge of the Upper Tribunal (IAC). He is a former Human Rights Fellow at Harvard Law School, Boston, MA, USA.

Notes

1 *N v. Secretary of State for the Home Department* [2005] UKHL 31 (5 May 2005).
2 ibid., at para 1.
3 ibid., at para 2.
4 ibid., at para 3.
5 ibid., at para 4.
6 Ibid., at para 9.
7 ibid., at para 15.
8 ibid., at para 17.
9 ibid., at para 20.
10 N. v. THE UNITED KINGDOM - 26565/05 [2008] ECHR 453 (27 May 2008).
11 *Paposhvili v. Belgium* [2016] ECHR 1113.
12 ibid., at para 183.
13 *EA & Others (Article 3 medical cases – Paposhvili not applicable)* [2017] UKUT 445 (IAC).
14 *AM (Zimbabwe)* [2018] EWCA Civ 64 at para 38.
15 ibid., at para 32.
16 ibid., at para 33.
17 Satvinder Juss, Disretion & Deviation in the Administrationb of Immigration Control (Modern Legal Studies, Sweet & Maxwell, London, 1997) at pp. 22–23.
18 ibid., at p. 14.
19 ibid., at pp. 16–17.
20 ibid., at p. 19.
21 ibid., at p. vii.

Preface

A new field has emerged at the interface of research on migration, health and ethics. For researchers in an emerging field it is important to find platforms where they can meet and build a community, allowing ideas to spread, be scrutinized, refined (or rejected) and finally established. Seeking to provide such a platform, the editors of this book organized an international and interdisciplinary workshop in Munich in March 2016. A diverse group of nearly 30 early career and established researchers from various disciplines, as well as health care practitioners and staff of the municipality and of non-governmental organisations, met at the Institute of Ethics, History and Theory of Medicine at LMU Munich, Germany. During the week, they discussed the ethical, legal and social aspects of health care provision for migrants. This workshop laid the groundwork for this book, which we hope will further facilitate the exchange of ideas.

Two of the editors of this volume, Katja Kuehlmeyer and Corinna Klingler, organized the workshop jointly with Dennis Odukoya and with the support of Professors Georg Marckmann, Hella von Unger, Oliver Razum and the third editor of this volume, Richard Huxtable. The workshop was organized in collaboration with the Munich Competence Centre for Ethics at LMU Munich. The workshop and subsequent publications were kindly funded by the German Ministry of Education and Research from 2015 to 2018 (01GP1483).

The discussions and most of the presentations during the workshop focused on either Germany or the UK or a comparison of the two. The two countries served as exemplar cases for reflection on the multitude of questions that arise in health care in diverse societies. The two national contexts allowed for relevant comparison, given their different historic backgrounds and dissimilar health care systems. Furthermore, the workshop focused on four major topics in health care provision for migrants: (1) terminology and knowledge production, (2) access to public health care, (3) responsibility for overcoming barriers to health care and (4) value pluralism. Two participants, Peter West-Oram and Nora Gottlieb, described the program and their experiences vividly in their conference report, which was published in 2017 (West-Oram & Gottlieb 2017).

This book encompasses some of the results of the workshop, which were further shared in a special issue in *Bioethics*, published in 2018. The two volumes are complementary and do not overlap. Contributions from further experts in law, mental health, palliative care and anthropology were sought to expand and enrich the analyses in this book.

This volume aims to increase knowledge about a broad spectrum of issues that relate to health care provision for migrants and seeks to stimulate further discussion. Discourses on this topic are not situated in any one discipline, as they include various voices from diverse fields such as philosophy, theology, social sciences and law, as well as from health care-related disciplines like medicine, nursing or psychology. Other disciplines that enrich this field of inquiry include public health and health policy, plus those disciplines contributing to the larger field of migration studies, such as political science and anthropology. This book therefore strives to capture various perspectives on the topic. The contributions thus come from various academic disciplines and also from researchers at various career stages. Theoretical and normative reflections on current issues are also featured, although much of the focus is on data from empirical studies.

We hope that the volume will be useful not only for researchers in this emerging field, but also for advocates and policymakers across Europe (and potentially elsewhere). The contributions provide arguments for and against different approaches or their suitability to various contexts, which might help advocates to push for the adoption or abolition of particular models. We furthermore hope that it encourages self-reflection amongst those directly engaging with migrants and migration, which might initiate further progress. The topics with which our book is concerned are politically contentious and there is the possibility that the points of view expressed may not be acceptable to every reader. We do not share every viewpoint that is presented in this book, but we have made an effort to ensure that the contributors substantiated their positions with robust and thorough argumentation and evidence, where available.

Munich, Berlin and Bristol, October, 2018
Katja Kuehlmeyer, Corinna Klingler and Richard Huxtable

Reference

West-Oram, P. & Gottlieb, N. 2017, 'International workshop: health care provision for migrants: comparing approaches to ethical challenges in Germany and the United Kingdom,' *Clinical Ethics*, vol. 12, no. 2, pp. 76–81.

Acknowledgements

We are grateful for the project funding from the German Federal Ministry of Education and Research (01GP1483) and the (much appreciated) support from Drs Svenja Krebs and Mathias von Witsch, as well as from Kathleen Heckert at the German Aerospace Center. We are grateful to Danielle Kuban at the Institute of Ethics, History and Theory of Medicine at LMU Munich who facilitated the project administration at LMU Munich. Katja and Corinna are appreciative of the advice received from the supporting senior researchers Professors Georg Marckmann, Hella von Unger, Oliver Razum and Richard Huxtable during the organization of the workshop. We sincerely thank Dennis Odukoya for his efforts in the organization of the workshop and the initial preparation of this book. Corinna and Katja would also like to thank (former) colleagues such as Silke Ohlmeier, Dr Sandra Thiersch, Marion Frobenius and Sigrid Detschey for their support behind the scenes during the workshop week. We feel indebted to all participants and expert speakers who enriched the discussions during the workshop and beyond and thereby contributed to the development of this book. We furthermore express our gratitude to our honourable series editor Prof. Satvinder Juss, and to Alex Buckley, Senior Editorial Assistant at Routledge, who helped us to improve this book through their editing and who supported us in coordinating the publication of the book. In addition, we were fortunate to be supported by anonymous language editors at Taylor and Francis Language Editing Service and Dr Dorothee Wagner von Hoff, who translated one of the manuscripts from German to English. Last but not least, we want to express our gratitude to Simon Böhm, who helped immensely with the formatting of the manuscripts and with preparations for the book's submission.

List of abbreviations

ADA	Argumentative discourse analysis
AIDS	Acquired Immune Deficiency Syndrome
AOK	Allgemeine Ortskrankenkasse
AsybLG	Asylbewerberleistungsgesetz
BAGFW	Bundesarbeitsgemeinschaft der Freien Wohlfahrtspflege
BAMF	Bundesamt für Migration und Flüchtlinge
BMBF	Bundesministerium für Bildung und Forschung
BMI	Body mass index
BVerfG	Bundesverfassungsgericht
CAT	Convention against Torture
CDU	Christlich Demokratische Union Deutschlands
CERD	Committee on the Elimination of Racial Discrimination
CESCR	Committee on Economic, Social and Cultural Rights
CFR	Charter of Fundamental Rights of the European Union
CHD	Coronary heart disease
CMW	Committee on the Protection of the Rights of All Migrant Workers and Members of their Families
CSU	Christlich-Soziale Union in Bayern
CVD	Cardiovascular disease
DCI	Defence of Children International
DLR	Deutsches Zentrum für Luft- und Raumfahrt
DOTW	Doctors of the World
ECDC	European Centre for Disease Prevention and Control
ECHR	European Convention on Human Rights
EEA	European Economic Area
ECtHR	European Court of Human Rights
EHIC	European Health Insurance Card
ESC	European Social Charter
ESCRev	Revised European Social Charter
EU	European Union
FCGS	Female cosmetic genital surgery
FEANTSA	European Federation of National Organisations working with the Homeless

FGA	Female genital alteration
FGM	Female genital mutilation
FIDH	International Federation of Human Rights Leagues
FRA	Fundamental Rights Agency
GMS1	Product code for a form to register with a family doctor in the UK
GP	General practitioner
HIV	Human immunodeficiency virus
HUMA	A network to promote access to health care for asylum seekers and undocumented migrants in the European Union
HUS	Haemolytic uraemic syndrome
HRC	Human Rights Committee
IAHR	Institute of Applied Health Research
ICCPR	International Covenant on Civil and Political Rights
ICERD	International Convention on the Elimination of All Forms of Racial Discrimination
ICESCR	International Covenant on Economic, Social and Cultural Rights
ICRMW	International Convention on the Protection of the Rights of All Migrant Workers and Members of Their Families
IOM	International Organisation for Migration
IQWiG	Institut für Qualität und Wirtschaftlichkeit im Gesundheitswesen
IRiS	Institute for Research into Superdiversity
LGBT	Lesbian, Gay, Bisexual and Transgender
LMU	Ludwig-Maximilians-Universität
MdM	Médecins du Monde
MERS	Middle Eastern Respiratory Syndrome
MIPEX	Migrant Integration Policy Index
NCDs	Non-communicable diseases
NGO	Non-governmental organization
NHS	National Health Service
OBE	Order of the British Empire
OHCHR	Office of the United Nations High Commissioner for Human Rights
OP-ICESCR	Optional Protocol to the International Covenant on Economic, Social and Cultural Rights
PCH	Pontocerebellar hypoplasia
PEG	Percutaneous endoscopic gastronomy
PET	Positron emission tomography
PHE	Proliferative haemorrhagic enteritis
PTSD	Post-traumatic stress disorder
RM-VA	Refugees' and Migrants' Vulnerability Assessment
SARS	Severe acute respiratory syndrome
SGB	Sozialgesetzbuch
SKAD	Sociology of Knowledge Approach to Discourse Analysis
SPPHC	Specialized Paediatric Palliative Home Care

SPD	Sozialdemokratische Partei Deutschlands
SPZ	Sozialpädiatrisches Zentrum
SRH	Special Rapporteur on the Right to Health
STD	Sexually transmitted diseases
TB	Tuberculosis
TCA	Thematic and Content Analysis
UDHR	Universal Declaration of Human Rights
UHC	Universal health coverage
UK	United Kingdom
UN	United Nations
UNESCO	United Nations Educational, Scientific and Cultural Organization
UNHCR	United Nations High Commissioner for Refugees
UNICEF	United Nations Children's Fund
VVG	Versicherungsvertragsgesetz
WHO	World Health Organisation

Introduction – ethical, legal and social aspects of health care for migrants

Perspectives from the UK and Germany

Katja Kuehlmeyer, Corinna Klingler and Richard Huxtable

I.1 Introduction

International migration is a significant contemporary issue, albeit one with a long history.[1] We live in an age of globalisation, which encourages and sometimes demands international workforce mobility. Yet people migrate across state borders for many reasons, amongst them people who want to improve their living conditions and those of their offspring, as well as people who are or feel forced to leave 'their' country and seek safety in foreign countries, departing from areas that are characterised by political instability or war. Other people choose to move from one state to another to be with their families, although that means moving to an unfamiliar destination. While there are various issues that arise and need to be discussed in relation to migratory movements, the chapters in this volume focus on migrants' health, their need for and uptake of public health care, and their health care entitlements. The volume also looks at health care provision, with some chapters discussing the perspectives of (migrant) health care providers.

Throughout this book, we understand the term 'migrant' deliberately in its broadest sense and the volume therefore encompasses a variety of migrants. It includes people that leave their country of origin to settle somewhere else temporarily and those that leave for longer periods, those that are forced to depart and those that choose to enter, as well as those that enter or remain in destination countries with the state's permission to do so and those who enter or stay without such permission.

The focus of the chapters, whether individually or in comparison, is on Germany and the UK. Both countries have a long-standing but quite different history of migration. Since these countries (at least, currently) are part of the European Union (EU), we will start our introduction by reflecting on the recent political climate in the EU with regard to migration and by positioning this volume and ourselves in the current ethical discourse. We then explain why we chose our two case countries and, thereafter, describe some of the challenges that arise for an immigration country (such as Germany or the UK) in the public health care provision for a diverse population that includes migrants. We will focus on three important questions: (1) how to conduct migrant- and migration-sensitive health surveillance and research, (2) how to regulate migrants' access to and uptake of health care and (3) how to ensure culturally sensitive health care provision, which appropriately seeks to navigate pluralism.

In this introductory discussion, we initially seek to outline the ethical dimensions of these issues, before providing an overview of the structure of this volume and the overarching issues that the different parts and chapters address.

I.2 The current political climate in the EU

In recent years, the regulation of immigration to European countries has been a major focus of attention in politics and the media across Europe. Germany's chancellor Angela Merkel has declared that the 'continuance of Europe' – by which she no doubt means the continuance of the EU – 'depends on the handling of migration' (DPA 2018).[2] Meanwhile, Great Britain's Prime Minister Theresa May is preparing for the so-called Brexit, which will remove the UK from the EU. The question of migration, its costs and national control over immigration from EU countries were particularly prominent issues during the 2016 referendum that led up to the (currently ongoing) Brexit negotiations (The Migration Observatory 2018). While the tone and specificities of the issues discussed seem new, the underlying theme of the discourse within the EU is old: the political construction of immigration, especially immigration from outside of the EU, is framed (and increasingly so) as a question of security, which involves reference to the presumably destabilising effects of migration and its dangers to public order (Huysmans 2000). The political climate has resulted in steadily increasing political efforts to limit the number of migrants who enter European countries. These efforts are directed at different immigrants, among them people who seek asylum in European countries. We find the recent developments to be extremely worrying, in which we believe we are not alone. We strongly object to policies, aimed at discouraging further migration attempts, which leave people in distress at sea (literally), without rescue (Steinhilper & Gruijters 2017). In the health care context, which is our focus in this volume, we analogously reject policies that deny an individual access to health care for questionable reasons, such as a country's wish to avoid appearing to be a 'welfare magnet' to potential immigrants (Zentrale Ethikkommission 2013). Our rejection is grounded in a strong belief in, and support for, solidarity, justice and universal human rights, as we make explicit in the next section.

I.3 Solidarity, justice and a human right to health

People value their health for various reasons but, foremost, health has an instrumental value, as it is a prerequisite to pursuing 'the innumerable projects of life that we are all involved with' (Duncan 2010, p. 321). All humans are vulnerable to suffering. They should be able to relate to, and respond compassionately to, the experience of suffering and appreciate how illness can generate not only physical, psychological or emotional challenges, but also an existential threat to a person and his or her family.

There is, of course, a rich literature on how, ethically, we – whoever we are – should respond to suffering and ill health. Various pertinent concepts and values arise, amongst them solidarity, justice and human rights, all of which are relevant to ethical debates about the health care of migrants. Solidarity permits different interpretations but basically can be understood as our commitment to support (particularly, vulnerable or dependent) others, even if this involves some cost to ourselves, on the basis that we recognise that these others are not so different from ourselves (Ter Meulen 2017; West-Oram, Buyx & Prainsack 2016). Justice also permits of various (substantive) definitions and accounts (Daniels 2008; Rauprich, Marckmann & Vollmann 2005; Venkatapuram 2011). Using Aristotle's widely accepted formal account, justice can at least be understood in terms of treating equals equally and unequals unequally (Aristotle, Ross and Brown 2009). There are also pertinent human rights arguments to consider, in particular arguments for the human right to health, a right which (as later chapters explore) can also find legal expression (Clapham & Robinson 2009; Wolff 2012; Müller, Chapter 5 and Kaltenborn, Chapter 6 in this book).

Academics lead lively debates about what these different concepts mean and entail, which will no doubt continue. In fact, most of the tensions in current debates result from different interpretations of these concepts. However, they nevertheless appear to share a concern with recognising and seeking to respect or protect our fellow humans, or at least those who can be considered our 'equals'. From a political perspective, whether migrants are the 'equals' of non-migrants, and thus deserving of the same entitlements, is a vexed question. Ethically, however, we are convinced that there is no compelling argument for distinguishing migrants from non-migrants, at least in relation to the provision of health care. Certainly, there is also ongoing debate about these questions, for example, about migrants' access to health care (Cole 2007; Wild, Zion & Ashcroft 2015). Discussion also continues about what the different values imply for health care provision, including for migrants. For example, there is disagreement about the duties entailed by particular rights, as well as more specific questions about what state duties are implied by the human right to health in relation to migrants (Chetail & Giacca 2009; Müller, Chapter 5 in this book; Wolff 2012).

We cannot hope to resolve these major questions here, but we think it is important to transparently state our shared position.[3] Essentially, we are convinced that, ethically, there is *in principle* no good reason for treating (literally and figuratively) migrants and non-migrants differently at least with regard to health care. Inadequate treatment of migrants can be variously conceived as a failure of solidarity, injustice or a violation of human rights, such as the right to health. Whatever the precise ethical basis for such a normative position, we believe that governments should ensure that (at least) all human beings under their jurisdiction have adequate access to health care and other services essential for their health. In short, a state should not disregard people in the vulnerable situation of sickness, merely on the basis that they happen to be migrants.

I.4 The two case countries: Germany and the UK

The chapters in this volume relate to either the German or the UK context or compare data from both contexts. Despite some similarities, the German and the UK contexts differ with regard to their historical backgrounds, the organisation of the respective health care systems, the regulation of immigration, and the migrant populations. The characteristics of migrants in the two countries have changed within the last 30 years. 'Britain's immigrant and ethnic minority population', for example, 'has conventionally been characterized by large, well-organized African-Caribbean and South Asian communities of citizens originally from Commonwealth countries or formerly colonial territories' (Vertovec 2007, p. 1024). Germany encouraged labour migration after the Second World War, which led to the recruitment of so-called guest workers from countries such as Italy, Spain, Greece, Turkey and former Yugoslavia (Bundesanstalt für Arbeit 1970). The country also received German 're-settlers', who return-migrated to Germany in the 1990s after the collapse of the Soviet Union (Razum & Wenner, Chapter 1 in this book). The way we display this information already points to the differences in the predominant discourses in these two countries: whereas in the UK researchers mostly refer to ethnicity-related categories, in Germany, the categories employed to capture migration refer to migrants' countries of origin or nationality. For example, the census included questions referring to the 'migration background' of a person, a category that applies to a person with at least one parent who was born with a nationality other than German (Statistisches Bundesamt 2017, p. 41). More recently, though, British migration patterns were characterised by 'super-diversity', a term that since its creation has carried various meanings, including a reference to increasing complexities in the categorisation of migrants (Lindenmeyer, Chapter 11 in this book; Vertovec 2007, 2017).

Turning to the organisation of health care systems, both countries have public health care systems in place. Health care in the UK is generally funded by taxation and provided via the National Health Service (NHS), a public health service created in 1948, which is free at the point of use. As is explained in forthcoming chapters, migrants can access (at least some) health care services in the UK free of charge, although there is a complex web of policy and regulation, which in part limit (some) migrants' rights of access and entitlement (Steele & Devlin, Chapter 7 in this book). Germany's health care system is insurance-based and primarily financed by employers and employees via payroll deductions. It is also mostly free of charge at the point of use. The health care entitlements of asylum seekers are limited to a certain degree, at least within the first 15 months of their stay (Kaltenborn, Chapter 6 in this book). Because of their different contexts, Germany and the UK are excellent case studies for describing and analysing the backgrounds of, and reasons for, both different and similar approaches to public health care provision for migrants, as well as the challenges associated with such provision.

I.5 Challenges in the provision of public health care for migrants

Public health care provision is often beset by challenges, as, for instance, difficult decisions about the allocation and distribution of scant health care resources have to be made. Health care systems are tasked with serving diverse populations and this can exacerbate the difficulties. Three particularly important areas of difficulty in the context of migration are: (1) migrant- and migration-sensitive health care surveillance and research, (2) the regulation of access to and uptake of health care and (3) culturally sensitive health care, which recognises – and is able to navigate – pluralism.

I.5.1 Migrant- and migration-sensitive health care surveillance and research

While health care surveillance is an important requisite to monitoring and targeting public health interventions, in many countries, there appears to be a dearth of robust data about migrants' health risks, health problems and their need for health care services. This lack of information might be because migrants are not always identifiable in routine data collection, as no (conclusive) migrant-relevant categories are included, or because certain migrant groups are systematically excluded from such data collection. Reasons for their exclusion can be formal (e.g., people with the legal status of 'asylum seeker' are not included per se), or informal or practical, because certain groups have difficulties with speaking the language of the receiving country or in filling out written questionnaires. Research appears to be particularly needed with regard to the complex relationships between ethnicity (or other relevant categories) and health care usage (Bhopal 2007; Knipper & Bilgin 2010; Jayaweera, Chapter 2 in this book) and with regard to the influence of migration on people's health (Razum et al. 2004, 2008; Razum & Wenner, Chapter 1 in this book). In Germany, an almost complete absence of health data from asylum seekers has been observed (Razum et al. 2016). This is problematic as such data are needed to make visible the specific health risks and needs of particular groups, develop targeted programs and ensure there is suitable and adequate health care for all, including migrants (Butler et al. 2007; Razum et al. 2016). An exception might be the monitoring of infectious diseases, where migration-relevant data has been included in the obligatory reporting (Beermann et al. 2015). Yet, while it seems important to have these data to allow for the targeted screening and diagnosis of transmittable diseases, to start adequate treatment, and to ensure the protection of those who might be in close contact to the infected person, the data can be framed in a problematic way. Public health publications can present migrants as *at risk* of infectious diseases and in need of treatment, but they can also frame the issue predominantly as one of migrants posing *a risk* to others, such as those in the receiving country (Scott, von Unger & Odukoya 2017). They might thereby support a discourse fostering fear and isolation of migrants.

This suggests that the invisibility of health-related differences between migrants and non-migrants is not the only problem in public health research and surveillance since the framing and interpretation of findings can potentially also have adverse consequences. Researchers and policy-makers might, for example, further contribute to a culturalised understanding of health needs. This means that, depending on how particular findings are collected, interpreted and presented, certain health needs might be associated with cultural differences, when they might be better explained by a combination of various factors – including socio-economic status (Knipper & Bilgin 2010; Razum et al. 2008). We want to stress that this does not mean that we believe migrant populations should be excluded from research. On the contrary, in our opinion, the inclusion of migrants should be promoted by additional resource investment, which can support the use of methods that are suitably adapted for, and targeted at, such individuals and groups (Schenk & Neuhauser 2005). It does, however, mean that findings should be interpreted and presented with care. Researchers should be particularly sensitive with regards to the possible construction and reconstruction of stereotypes, which might intensify the negative perceptions of migrants and thereby foster a distinct form of social exclusion and subordination, that is, research should avoid an exclusionary 'othering' of migrants (Roberts & Schiavenato 2017). Without attention to such issues, research risks fostering segregation and obstructing migrants from integrating into the destination country.

In this regard, it might be of particular importance to reflect on the categories used in health research or surveillance[4] (Scott & von Unger, Chapter 9 in this book). Since the term 'migrant' can refer to many different groups of people, the explanatory and predictive power of observed differences between 'migrants' and 'non-migrants' – where those terms are used – can and should always be questioned (Knipper & Bilgin 2010). In Germany, the census asks for 'migration background'. As we explained above, other categories can and have been used, such as 'ethnicity' or 'nationality'. All such categories are socially construed. They introduce a difference between, for example, 'migrants' and 'non-migrants' – sometimes also referred to as the 'autochthonous' population – between 'us' and 'them'. Such terms are accordingly not naturally given and researchers should transparently reflect on whether and how they choose migration-relevant categories and the possible – negative as well as positive – consequences of including specific categories in their research.

I.5.2 Access to health care

Governments and health administrations across Europe are preoccupied with the maintenance of sustainable and effective, as well as cost-effective, health systems. While, in most countries, migrants can obtain *some* health care, questions remain about migrants' entitlements. Different European countries choose different forms of regulation, which partly depend on the architecture of their health care systems and partly on the political climate at the relevant time. Many of these countries do not grant all migrant groups the same health care entitlements as the remainder of their population (Trummer & Krasnik 2017).

The justifications given for limitations on access to health care primarily refer to the costs of care and resource scarcity.

Germany, for example, limits the spectrum of health care that is accessible to asylum seekers within their first 15 months in the country to the necessary treatment of acute health problems and painful conditions (Kaltenborn, Chapter 6 in this book). Health care provision for this group is managed in a parallel system, which is organised by the municipalities, and which differs from the public or private health insurance arrangements that exist for the majority of German residents. There are many vexing questions that arise in this context, particularly whether such an exclusionary policy can be considered ethically defensible. We have already pointed out that we do not think that exclusion of specific migrant groups from public health care is ethically acceptable and several public health ethicists also view these restrictions critically (Wild, Zion & Ashcroft 2015). Where so many of the counterarguments refer to the costs of care, it is essential to ask: does such a restrictive policy actually save costs? On the basis of their detailed data analysis, public health researchers have doubted this (Bozorgmehr & Razum 2015; Trummer & Krasnik 2017). Similar questions arise in relation to other migrant groups, such as those who have no legal right to stay in Germany or other countries. In practice, they appear likely only to seek treatment in extreme emergency situations, since they generally fear that any engagement with health services might lead to them being reported to immigration services and perhaps then expelled from the country of current residence (Jones et al., Chapter 3 in this book).

Meanwhile, it is widely known that migrants in addition face informal barriers when they are in need of health care. As we noted above, many migrants struggle to navigate a new health care system due to their relative lack of knowledge about it and difficulties in accessing it (Suphanchaimat et al. 2015). In various contexts, migrants have therefore expressed a need for navigational assistance in the form of information and orientation, which can help them to identify and embark on pathways to health care (Green et al. 2014). Here too, then, questions arise about fair access to, and fair distribution of, health care resources.

In Germany, the concept of 'intercultural opening' refers to measures at the institutional level which seek strategically to address these issues (Droste et al. 2015). Intercultural opening demands, among other things, that health care institutions and their workforces actively promote their users' understanding of the health care system and provide information that is comprehensible and accessible. Health care systems across the world should at least recognise this widely known phenomenon and – we would argue – be responsive to it. As such, we would suggest there is a case, not only for addressing (and avoiding) formal barriers, but also for seeking to reduce informal barriers.

I.5.3 Culturally sensitive health care

In many health care systems, 'respect for patient autonomy' is accepted as a fundamental action-guiding principle (Beauchamp & Childress 2013). Although understandings of autonomy and of its relative importance vary across the world, its value is recognised in Germany and the UK (Gilbar & Miola 2015; Huxtable 2013). The principle implies that health care professionals working in these countries should not assume that their patients have uniform ideas about whether or how they want to be treated in a hospital or in an outpatient care service. The recognition and accommodation of diversity requires approaches to health care that centre on the patient (and sometimes on his or her family), rather than services that are provider-driven (Hodgkin & Taylor 2013). Differences between service providers' and recipients' values, beliefs and conceptual paradigms can clearly complicate communication and shared decision-making. Such complications are not specific to encounters between migrant patients and non-migrant professionals because people will differ in many respects, for example, because they are of different ages, come from different social strata, cultivate different lifestyles or have plural faith-based values or religious commitments (Michl, Potthast & Wiesing 2008). These sorts of characteristics, as well as their dynamic interplay, can influence people's experiences and shape their needs and belief systems. However, difficulties might well be aggravated in situations where (for example) a patient and a doctor (or a family and a health care team) have difficulties in expressing themselves in a shared language or have been socialised in different environments or cultures.

Like 'migrant', 'culture' is a concept that has many meanings, but it is foremost a dynamic rather than a static notion. This can mean that a person's or a group's culture does not always stay the same; it can change over time or be understood differently by different people and can be expressed in different ways. Culture influences patients and their relatives in how they understand medical knowledge, how it comes to be valued, and when and how it is adopted and applied (Napier et al. 2014). Culture can be used as an analytical concept or a lens to interpret and analyse situations where conflict arises. Yet it is not always clear how an appreciation of 'culture' might prove helpful in better understanding and then addressing any conflict that has arisen. This can be illustrated by a case in which families and providers disagree over who should be informed about an unfavourable prognosis: the family, so as to protect the patient, or the patient, so as to respect his or her autonomy (Ilkilic 2008). In such situations, it might be difficult to find common ground and arrive at a consensus or even a compromise. While it might help in resolving a conflict – at least in some situations – to identify it as one based on cultural differences, using culture as a lens to view certain encounters also has its drawbacks. As we noted previously, there is a risk of stereotyping patients and misunderstanding patients' wishes and desires as cultural where they are really caused by, for example, socio-economic factors. That might, again, lead to implementing approaches to conflict resolution that are unsuitable. Culture as an analytical tool should accordingly be employed with care (Kleinman & Benson 2006; Knipper 2015).

Navigating plural perspectives and values can be challenging and any effort to do so seems to require, at base, appropriate communication, which might necessitate cultural interpreters who should be aware of the ethical dimensions of their work (Kliche et al. 2018). Generally, health care providers should be prepared to engage in a mutual exchange with their patients (and, where appropriate, relevant others) about their values and interpretations of 'health' and 'health care'. Such an exchange also involves reflecting on one's own personal and professional values and understandings (Peters et al. 2014). Even if a shared understanding of the values that should guide health care decisions in a particular case proves elusive, at the very least, the procedural aspects of shared-decision-making should be made explicit and the relevant stakeholders (including the patients) should agree to them (Elwyn et al. 2012; Shay & Lafata 2014). We need further theoretical reflection, in order to identify justifiable strategies for managing these various cultural and ethical challenges.

Having set out these considerations, we now move to provide an overview of the volume, its parts and its chapters. The different contributions elaborate in different ways on one or more of the issues discussed.

I.6 The book's parts and chapters

I.6.1 Part I: Migrants' health in Germany and the UK

In the first part, the book provides a descriptive overview and normative reflection on migrants' health in Germany and the UK. This part provides and critically discusses data from public health (care) surveillance and research in both countries. It includes chapters focusing on migrants who are or feel excluded from public health care and gives information on the wider circumstances and consequences of their exclusion.

In Chapter 1, Oliver Razum and Judith Wenner propose a life-course approach to framing the issue of migrant health, which they suggest can improve our understanding of why migrants face health risks and how they develop health needs that differ from those of the remainder of a population. Despite a large body of empirical research on health disparities, Germany is still struggling to address these issues and improve the equitable delivery of health care. The authors argue that this struggle is related to hidden 'normative agendas' in the field of public health (implicit 'mind frames' that define what ought to be). These agendas constrain the work of public health researchers and experts who work in the field of migrant health. The authors argue that such constraints should be overcome, so that solutions can be found, which better recognise the current diversity (or, rather, diversities) of Germany's population.

In Chapter 2, Hiranthi Jayaweera explores what is known about the health of migrants in the UK, similarly putting migration into a biographical and social context. Jayaweera points out the limitations of the current health care surveillance approaches, in that the UK prioritises ethnicity over immigration variables. On the basis of the data that is available to her, she describes the heterogeneous migrant groups in the UK, who have different health needs and statuses. Jayaweera then sets out some of the key gaps in available data, which prevent a comprehensive understanding of migrant health outcomes and needs. She notes the growing diversity of migrants in the UK and analyses what the distinguishable groups of migrants share and how they differ. Furthermore, her chapter provides a reflection on access to and uptake of health care by migrants, which, as we described earlier, can be hindered by various regulatory and informal barriers.

The latter point returns in Chapter 3, in which Lucy Jones, Anna Miller, Sabine Fürst, Carolin Bader and Lea Gelfert provide a description of the health data collected in Médecins du Monde's Health Care and Advocacy Programmes in London and Munich in 2014. The clinics provide health care for patients who would not otherwise have access to public health care and social support services. They provide health care to anyone who requires it, on an anonymous and confidential basis. Participants give their data only if they wish to do so voluntarily. The chapter usefully enhances what is known about the health of migrants in both countries. By collecting data from both of the clinics, the authors provide much-needed information about those who regularly fail to feature in most of the health statistics in both countries. The authors reflect on the role of their organisation in bearing witness to the life circumstances of those who are, or feel, excluded from public health care provision.

In Chapter 4, Christiane Falge provides data on people who face informal barriers to health care, which she explores through the lens of the concept of 'cosmopolitan sociability'. She describes the results of three studies conducted at City Lab Hustadt (near Bochum, Western Germany). The City Lab is a 12-year research base, which seeks to advance collaborative, health-related knowledge production. In the participatory research undertaken at the lab, academics develop their research instruments together with community researchers, with whom they also discuss their results. Furthermore, they make efforts to develop measures that will improve health conditions locally. Falge vividly describes ethnographic fieldwork involving, for example, a Syrian family with a child who suffers from renal insufficiency, a chronic, incurable condition. The result is a thick description of barriers to health care, among them financial struggles, a lack of knowledge of health care entitlements and a power asymmetry between health care providers and migrant patients. She points out that, despite the struggles, being a migrant is actually perceived as a useful resource by the study participants, which unfolds through the local community. Hence, migrants build a network, through which they support one another. A sense of belonging together locally is identified as the most important prerequisite for a functioning network.

I.6.2 Part II: Migrants' access to health care

The second part is dedicated to describing and discussing how access to health care for different migrant groups is regulated in Germany and the UK, as well as at the international level. It focuses on the right to health and its realisation in (inter-)national legislation and its status within the German discourse about asylum seekers' health entitlements.

In Chapter 5, Amrei Müller discusses health care access within the framework of international and European human rights law. She describes the tension between human rights and citizens' rights as a fundamental feature of the current international legal order. This tension lies between, first, the requirement to protect human rights through membership of political communities and thus through domestic democratic institutions within national borders and, second, the universalist call of many regional and international human rights treaties on states to 'secure' the human rights of everyone. Müller focuses on two areas where migrants' right to health, as set out in European and international human rights law, plays an important role: first, in limiting the rights of states to decide which non-citizens enter and remain in their territories; and, second, in requiring states to grant non-citizens who find themselves within its borders the same access to health facilities, goods and services as the citizens. Müller's chapter describes efforts to give the notion of 'progressive realisation' a clearer direction, by adopting the 'minimum core' approach. Under this approach, the Committee on Economic, Social and Cultural Rights (CESCR) defines 'minimum essential levels of each of the rights' set out in the International Covenant on Economic, Social and Cultural Rights (ICESCR), which the states must ensure as a matter of the highest priority. Of course, what the levels should be and how these might best be secured remain important normative questions.

After the description of the tensions between international human rights legislation and its adoption by the EU and individual national states, the volume moves to look in detail at the relevant laws governing access to – including payment for – health care in the UK and Germany.

First, in Chapter 6, Markus Kaltenborn focuses on the health care entitlements of asylum seekers in Germany, while also touching on the entitlements of other migrant groups. With regard to the Act on Benefits for Asylum Applicants (Asylbewerberleistungsgesetz), Kaltenborn describes how asylum seekers and refugees are entitled to a wide range of basic health services. In direct comparison to other groups in German society, however, this group is disadvantaged, because their health care benefits are restricted in several respects. He also draws on international legal rights documents, concluding that this disparate treatment is not in line with the principle of non-discrimination, which is one of the core human rights demands.

In their complementary chapter, Sarah Steele and Cormac Devlin explore the increasingly complex legislation and regulations that govern entitlement to and charges for NHS care in England. Their chapter begins with a definition of the crucial category 'ordinary resident', that is, those to whom much of the NHS health care is provided free of charge. They then focus on the exemptions to free care, and trace how a policy directed at charging health tourists has now developed into a comprehensive regime that involves the progressive expansion of chargeable services. It has become a legal framework that is constantly changing in the face of increasing political desires to appear a 'hostile environment for migrants'. The chapter concludes by critically reflecting on the consequences of the current regulations.

In the last chapter in this part, Sabine Klotz provides insights into her analysis of the public discourse surrounding health care policy for asylum seekers in Germany between 2012 and 2015. Back then, it was suggested that asylum seekers be issued an electronic card (German: Gesundheitskarte), which would afford them some, albeit not full, access to health care while reducing bureaucratic hurdles encountered while accessing health care services. After recapitulating the legal regulation of asylum seekers' health care entitlements at that time, she describes three discourses that dominated the public discussions: the status quo discourse, the cost–benefit discourse and the human rights discourse. She describes in depth how representatives of different political parties and other stakeholders adopted different discourses, including an analysis of the points of agreement and disagreement between them. Finally, she notes how the policy was ultimately not adopted across Germany, perhaps due to the persistence of disagreement about their underlying concepts and values.

I.6.3 Part III: (Re)Constructing migrants in health research

The chapters in the third part offer insights into hidden structures, agendas or schemata that underlie thinking about migrants and discuss how they influence health research about and with migrants. This part provides reflections on the categorisation of migrants, on 'othering' through research and on the complex interactions between migrant study participants and migrant community researchers.

In Chapter 9, Penelope Scott and Hella von Unger provide an analysis of 'ethnicity' and further migration-related categories, which are the constituent elements of classification systems that are used in public health reporting. They argue that categorisations in public health research can be seen as discursive practices that demonstrate the biopolitical function of public health and the sociality of scientific knowledge. They advance their argument by reference to examples of categories found in UK and German health reporting on the communicable disease HIV/AIDS. In so doing, the authors critically examine the theoretical and methodological principles underpinning the construction of categories.

In Chapter 10, Piret Paal provides insights from research about palliative care, an advancing medical field that primarily provides care for patients with life-limiting illnesses. Paal critically discusses how some of the recent research initiatives in palliative care in Germany have placed their focus on the 'migrant issue'. While the author herself conducts research on migrants in Germany, she criticises some research approaches by reference to arguments from feminist theories. From her perspective, just as women were marginalised in the last century, migrants are being marginalised today. Drawing on examples from her own qualitative research, Paal offers insights into the biographies of people, which do not focus on their country of origin or their ethnic background. She ends with the plea that shared humanity should be the basis of encounters in health care and that differentiation between 'us' and 'them' should be overcome.

In Chapter 11, Antje Lindenmeyer shares experiences from an exploratory study into the health histories of recent migrants to the UK and her analysis is guided by the concept of 'superdiversity'. This concept was coined by Steven Vertovec (2007) and arose from the observation of an increasing diversity of migrants with regard to, for example, their countries of origin, languages and immigration statuses. The study followed a participatory approach where data on the health of migrants were collected in collaboration with community researchers. The research team faced many challenges in ensuring their study met the requirements of the local research ethics board, without losing sight of such values as anonymity and confidentiality. Lindenmeyer reflects on the proximity, as well as on the perceived differences, between the community researchers and the participants, with reference to shared language, ethnicity, religion or nationality and their impact on the data acquisition.

I.6.4 Part IV: Navigating pluralism in health care

The final part of our book reflects on different approaches to navigating pluralism in health care, in an era in which populations within particular territories are increasingly culturally diverse. This part discusses pluralism in various areas, such as mental health, body alteration, workforce migration and paediatric palliative care.

The first chapter in this part, Chapter 12 by Kerstin Hein and Barbara Abdallah-Steinkopff, proposes a socially and culturally sensitive approach to the provision of mental health care for asylum seekers and refugees in Germany, especially with regard to counselling and psychotherapy. Culturally sensitive care is not a new concept, but the authors acknowledge its utility in the context of mental health care for asylum seekers and refugees, richly describing the possible misunderstandings that can arise in encounters between patients and health care providers. They especially stress the importance of considering the social circumstances and personal living conditions of asylum seekers and refugees, since these might be the cause of, or an aggravating factor in, the mental health problems they may experience. Taking this observation seriously should lead health care professionals in mental health to incorporate networks of helpers that are able to provide social support services, in addition to medical care.

Chapter 13 boldly confronts a quite different phenomenon that of 'female genital mutilation' – or, as the author prefers, 'female genital alteration'. In this chapter, Arianne Shahvisi describes UK legislation around female genital alteration in its broader social and political context and compares it to the banning of the burkini on French beaches in 2016. While both are professed to stem from concerns about gender inequality, the author interrogates this motivation, and argues that this claim is undermined by its neglect of 'intersectionality'. She argues that both policies can be seen as a form of 'ethnocentrism'. Shahvisi specifically examines the caveat within UK legislation, which holds that non-medical female genital alteration is acceptable, except in cases in which the motivation is cultural, in that it involves a custom or a ritual. Her critical examination ends with a plea to allow women themselves to decide about the continuation or abolition of such practices.

The next two chapters turn to research on elite migrants, looking at migrant health care practitioners. Each specifically looks at doctors working in the UK and Germany, who were born and trained in other countries, but immigrated to either of the two countries to practice medicine. While Yasmin Farooq's study focuses on South Asian doctors working in the UK, Corinna Klingler and Georg Marckmann examine a diverse group of doctors in their first years of professional practice in Germany.

In Chapter 14, Yasmin Farooq draws on contemporary social policy debates on community cohesion in Britain to analyse the situation of migrant physicians. In her empirical study, she reflects on the integration of overseas-trained doctors, who work as General Practitioners in three geographically diverse UK locales. She explores such issues as migration, identity and sociocultural integration. She describes this elite group as existing somewhere between privilege and marginalisation. Her study thereby highlights how identities are more plural than discourses of belonging often allow.

The study by Corinna Klingler and Georg Marckmann, reported in Chapter 15, analyses the various challenges that doctors face when they must navigate through an unfamiliar health care system. The chapter focuses on possible support structures for easing integration into a new health care system. The approaches that were mentioned during their interviews with migrant doctors ranged from work shadowing, organising joint social activities to loan schemes that would facilitate participation in preparatory courses whilst allowing doctors to sustain themselves and their family. Not all of the participants were in favour of targeted support measures. With their results, the authors wish to provide information for policy-makers on the opportunities for, and risks of, implementing support structures for migrant doctors, which could stimulate similar reflections in the case of migrant patients.

The final chapter encompasses different contributions from various authors, all focused on the (anonymised and fictionalised) case of Josip. The introduction, by Katja Kuehlmeyer and Monika Führer, describes the case of Josip, a critically ill infant who suffered from pontocerebellar hypoplasia. After being discharged from hospital, he received Specialized Paediatric Palliative Home Care (SPPHC) from a care team in Munich, Germany. His family had migrated from Croatia to Germany and his mother was his main caregiver. She was capable of communicating with the care team. The child's illness posed several psychosocial challenges to the family and some attendant ethical challenges. During a home visit with a Croatian guest doctor, the father – who was unable to converse in German – opened up and provided indications of mistrust and misunderstanding. When an emergency arose while the mother was away from the home, a decision was required about whether Josip should be actively treated or whether only comfort measures should be provided.

Following the outline of the case are three independent commentaries from researchers working in clinical ethics, which reflect on the ethical, legal and social implications of the case and offer some recommendations for addressing similar, future cases. In his commentary, Ilhan Ilkilic argues that the child's best interests should be the focus of (ethically defensible) decision-making.

However, he acknowledges the barriers that prevent effective communication about Josip's best interests in this case, emphasising the important influence of cultural values and moral diversity. Richard Huxtable also refers to the ethical and legal significance of the child's best interests, and offers three general prescriptions, which he relates to Josip's case. First, he argues that clinicians should focus on the case before them, second, he suggests that health services should be attentive to, and have some method for navigating, pluralism, and, third, he suggests that everyone involved in a case like this should ensure that there is effective communication. Both authors argue for the availability (and utility) of clinical ethics consultation services, which should be able to assist in cases of value conflict. In the third commentary, Georg Marckmann defends a particular model of clinical ethics support, which is based on 'principlism'. Marckmann notes that principlism has a strong universalist tendency, but is not universal in a strict sense, and that it can assist in the resolution of cases like that of Josip. He, therefore, applies the model to the case of Josip. Following the commentaries, the authors of the introduction describe how the SPPHC team in fact resolved the situation.

I.7 Concluding remarks

In conclusion, we hope to have brought together a wide-ranging collection, which nevertheless focuses clearly on many of the important issues arising in relation to the health of, and health care for (and by), migrants. We also hope that readers will enjoy the collection as much as we have enjoyed reading the contributions and participating in the rich discussions that occurred in the preceding workshop. Ideally, the chapters will prove helpful for those working (theoretically or practically) towards addressing – or even resolving – some of the problems that have been identified.

We are aware that many of the arguments raised and opinions expressed in this book might not be well received in the current political climate. However (or precisely for that reason), we judge this collection to be of considerable importance. It can enrich the ongoing debates, by providing a variety of different personal and disciplinary perspectives on the issues at stake. We hope that the volume can furthermore do its part in refocusing the debate from one of exclusion to one of adequate inclusion.

Notes

1 'International migration' refers to the movement of a person or a group across state borders from one geographical territory to another, for temporary or permanent settlement.

2 This was quoted in a newspaper article printed in *Die Zeit* online on July 4 2018, which was drawn from the Deutsche Presse Agentur (DPA).

3 Transparency, and reflexivity, is common in the social sciences, in which researchers reflect openly on how their positions – including any biases – are formed and informed. There has been a call for similar openness on the part of researchers working in bioethics, although such self-reflection still appears less common in this field (Ives and Dunn 2010). For our part, we would note that our work (and thus socialisation) within the field of bioethics is likely to have attuned us to – or accentuated our

existing commitments to – the need to value, respect and protect the rights and/or interests of others. Furthermore, we are all academics, who have lived and worked in places other than our countries (or even towns and cities) of origin; we have, therefore, some modest experience of migration, whether for longer or shorter periods.

4 As we noted above, 'migrant' is a heterogeneous category, which can encompass different groups of people, such as those who have recently moved between countries, those who are settled in their destination country, and those of different nationalities or ethnicities, who have long been settled in the relevant country or are even only the children of those that have moved between countries.

References

Aristotle, Ross, W.D., & Brown, L. 2009, *Nicomachean Ethics*, Oxford University Press, Oxford.

Beauchamp, T.L., & Childress, J.F. 2013, *Principles of Biomedical Ethics*, Oxford University Press, New York, Oxford.

Beermann, S., Rexroth, U., Kirchner, M., Kühne, A., Vygen, S., & Gilsdorf, A. 2016, 'Asylsuchende und Gesundheit in Deutschland: Überblick über epidemiologisch relevante Infektionskrankheiten', *Deutsches Ärzteblatt*, vol. 113, no. 4, pp. 1717–1720.

Bozorgmehr, K., & Razum, O. 2015, 'Effect of restricting access to health care on health expenditures among asylum-seekers and refugees: A quasi-experimental study in Germany, 1994–2013', *PLoS ONE*, vol. 10, no. 7, p. e0131483. doi:10.1371/journal.pone.0131483.

Bhopal, R.S. 2007, *Ethnicity, Race, and Health in Multicultural Societies. Foundations for Better Epidemiology, Public Health, and Health Care*, Oxford University Press, Oxford.

Butler, J., Albrecht, N.J., Ellsäßer, G., Gavranidou, M., Habermann, M., Lindert, J. et al. 2007, 'Migrationssensible Datenerhebung für die Gesundheitsberichterstattung Arbeitsgruppe Gesundheitsberichterstattung des Arbeitskreises, Migration und öffentliche Gesundheit', *Bundesgesundheitsblatt - Gesundheitsforschung – Gesundheitsschutz*, vol. 50, no. 10, pp. 1232–1239.

Bundesanstalt für Arbeit, *Ausländische Arbeitnehmer 1969*, Beilage zur ANBA Nr. 8/70 vom 28. August 1970, viewed 3 August 2018, https://statistik.arbeitsagentur.de/Statistikdaten/Detail/196912/anba/auslaenderbesch/auslaenderbesch-d-0-pdf.pdf

Chetail, V., & Giacca, G. 2009, "Who cares? The right to health of migrants", in A. Clapham & M. Robinson (eds.), *Realizing the Right to Health*, Swiss Human Rights Book, Vol. 3, Rüffer & Rub, pp. 224–234.

Clapham, A., & Robinson, M. (eds.) 2009, *Realizing the Right to Health*, Swiss Human Rights Book, Vol. 3, Rüffer & Rub, Zürich.

Cole, P. 2007, 'Human rights and the national interest: Migrants, healthcare and social justice', *Journal of Medical Ethics*, vol. 33, no. 5, pp. 269–272.

Daniels, N. 2008, *Just Health: Meeting Health Needs Fairly*, Cambridge University Press, New York.

DPA. 2018 'Merkel: Bestand Europas hängt am Umgang mit Migration', *Die Zeit online*, 4 July 2018, viewed 4 July 2018, www.zeit.de/news/2018-07/04/merkel-bestand-europas-haengt-amumgang-mit-migration-180704-99-10232.

Droste, M., Gün, A.K., Kiefer, H., Koch, E., Naimi, I., Reinecke, H. et al. 2015, *Das kultursensible Krankenhaus: Ansätze zur interkulturellen Öffnung*, Beauftragte der Bundesregierung für Migration, Flüchtlinge und Integration, Berlin, viewed 5 May 2018, www.bundesregierung.de/Content/Infomaterial/BPA/IB/Das_kultursensible_Krankenhaus_09-02-2015.html?view=trackDownload.

Duncan, P. 2010, 'Health, health care and the problem of intrinsic value', *Journal of Evaluation in Clinical Practice*, vol. 16, no. 2, pp. 318–322.

Elwyn, G., Frosch, D., Thomson, R., Joseph-Williams, N., Lloyd, A., Kinnersley, P. et al. 2012, 'Shared decision making: A model for clinical practice', *Journal of General Internal Medicine*, vol. 27, no. 10, pp. 1361–1367.

Gilbar, R., & Miola, J. 2015, 'One size fits all? On patient autonomy, medical decision-making and the impact of culture', *Medical Law Review*, vol. 23, no. 3, pp. 375–399.

Green, G., Davison, C., Bradby, H., Krause, K., Morente Meijias, F., & Alex, G. 2014, 'Pathways to care: How superdiversity shapes the need for navigational assistance', *Sociology of Health & Illness*, vol. 36, no. 8, pp. 1205–1219.

Hodgkin, P., & Taylor, J. 2013, 'Power to the people: What will bring about the patient centred revolution?' *BMJ*, vol. 347, p. f6701. doi:10.1136/bmj.f6701.

Huxtable, R. 2013, 'For and against the four principles of biomedical ethics', *Clinical Ethics*, vol. 8, no. 2–3, pp. 39–43.

Huysmans, J. 2000, 'The European Union and the securization of migration', *Journal of Common Market Studies*, vol. 38, no. 5, pp. 751–777.

Ilkilic, I. 2008, Kulturelle Aspekte bei ethischen Entscheidungen am Lebensende und interkulturelle Kompetenz', *Bundesgesundheitsblatt - Gesundheitsforschung - Gesundheitsschutz*, vol. 51, no. 8, pp. 857–864.

Ives, J., & Dunn, M. 2010, 'Who's arguing? A call for reflexivity in bioethics', *Bioethics*, vol. 24, no. 5, pp. 256–265.

Kleinman, A., & Benson, P. 2006, 'Anthropology in the clinic: The problem of cultural competency and how to fix it', *PLoS Med*, vol. 3, no. 10, p. e294. doi:10.1371/journal.pmed.0030294.

Kliche, O., Agbih, S., Protzer, U.A., Eulerich, S., Klingler, C., Neitzke, G. et al. 2018, 'Ethische Aspekte des Dolmetschens im mehrsprachig-interkulturellen Arzt-Patienten-Verhältnis', *Ethik in der Medizin*, vol. 30, pp. 205–220, https://link.springer.com/article/10.1007%2Fs00481-018-0488-6

Knipper, M. 2015, 'Verstehen oder Stigmatisieren? Die Krux mit der "Kultur" in Medizin und Public Health', *Public Health Forum*, vol. 23, no. 2, pp. 97–99.

Knipper, M., & Bilgin, Y. 2010, 'Medizin und ethnisch-kulturelle Vielfalt: Migration und andere Hintergründe', *Deutsches Ärzteblatt*, vol. 107, no. 3, pp. A76–A79.

Napier, A.D., Ancarno, C., Butler, B., Calabrese, J., Chater, A., Chatterjee, H. et al. 2014, 'Culture and health', *Lancet*, vol. 384, no. 9954, pp. 1607–1639.

Michl, S., Potthast, T., & Wiesing, U. (eds.) 2008, *Pluralität in der Medizin: Werte – Methoden – Theorien*, Verlag Karl Alber, Freiburg, München.

Rauprich, O., Marckmann, G., & Vollmann, J. (eds.) 2005, *Gleichheit und Gerechtigkeit in der modernen Medizin*, Paderborn, Mentis.

Razum, O., Geiger, I., Zeeb, H., & Ronellenfitsch, U. 2004, 'Gesundheitsversorgung von Migranten', *Deutsches Ärzteblatt*, vol. 101, no. 43, pp. A2882–A2887.

Razum, O., Zeeb, H., Meesmann, U., Schenk, L., Bredehorst, M., Brzoska, P. et al. 2008, *Schwerpunktbericht der Gesundheitsberichterstattung des Bundes: Migration und Gesundheit*, Robert Koch-Institut, Berlin.

Razum, O., Bunte, A., Gilsdorf, A., Ziese, T., & Bozorgmehr, K. 2016, 'Zu gesicherten Daten kommen', *Deutsches Ärzteblatt*, vol. 113, no. 4, pp. A130–A133.

Roberts, M.L.A., & Schiavenato, M. 2017, 'Othering in the nursing context: A concept analysis', *Nursing Open*, vol. 4, no. 3, pp. 174–181.

Shay, L.A., & Lafata, J.E. 2014, 'Understanding patient perceptions of shared decision making', *Patient Education and Counseling*, vol. 96, no. 3, pp. 295–301.

Schenk, L., & Neuhauser, H. 2005, 'Methodische Standards für eine migrantensensible Forschung in der Epidemiologie', *Bundesgesundheitsblatt - Gesundheitsforschung – Gesundheitsschutz*, vol. 48, no. 3, pp. 279–286.

Scott, P., von Unger, H., & Odukoya, D. 2017, 'A tale of two diseases: Discourses on TB, HIV/AIDS and im/migrants and ethnic minorities in the United Kingdom', *Social Theory & Health*, vol. 15, no. 8, pp. 261–284.

Statistisches Bundesamt. 2017, *Statistisches Jahrbuch 2017: Bevölkerung, Familien und Lebensformen*, Statistisches Bundesamt, Destatis.

Steinhilper, E., & Gruijters, R. 2017, *Border deaths in the Mediterranean: What we can learn from the latest data,* viewed 3 August 2018, www.law.ox.ac.uk/research-subject-groups/centre-criminology/centreborder-criminologies/blog/2017/03/border-deaths.

Suphanchaimat, R., Kantamaturapoj, K., Putthasri, W., & Prakongsai, P. 2015, 'Challenges in the provision of healthcare services for migrants: A systematic review through providers' lens', *BMC Health Services Research*, vol. 15, p. 390. doi:10.1186/s12913-015-1065-z.

The Migration Observatory at the University of Oxford COMPAS (Centre on Migration, Policy and Society). 2018, *Migration and Brexit*, University of Oxford, Oxford, viewed July 21 2018, http://migrationobservatory.ox.ac.uk/projects/migration-and-brexit/

Ter Meulen, R. 2017, *Solidarity and Justice in Health and Social Care*, Cambridge University Press, Cambridge.

Trummer, U., & Krasnik, A. 2017, 'Migrant health: The economic argument', *The European Journal of Public Health*, vol. 27, no. 4, pp. 590–591.

Venkatapuram, S. 2011, *Health Justice: An Argument from the Capabilities Approach*, Polity Press, Cambridge, Malden.

Vertovec, S. 2007, 'Super-diversity and its implications', *Ethnic and Racial Studies*, vol. 30, no. 6, pp. 1024–1054.

Vertovec, S. 2017, 'Talking around super-diversity', *Ethnic and Racial Studies.* doi:10.1080/01419870.2017.1406128.

West-Oram, P.G.N., Buyx, A., & Prainsack, B. 2016, 'Solidarity in bioethics', in *eLS (Encyclopedia of Life Sciences)*, John Wiley & Sons, Ltd, Chichester.

Wild, V., Zion, D., & Ashcroft, R. 2015, 'Health of migrants: Approaches from a public health ethics perspective' *Public Health Ethics*, vol. 8, no. 2, pp. 107–109.

Wolff, J. 2012, *The Human Right to Health*, Norton & Company, London/New York.

Zentrale Kommission zur Wahrung ethischer Grundsätze in der Medizin und ihren Grenzgebieten bei der Bundesärztekammer (Zentrale Ethikkommission). 2013, 'Versorgung von nicht regulär krankenversicherten Patienten mit Migrationshintergrund', *Deutsches Ärzteblatt*, vol. 110, no. 18, pp. A899–A903.

Part I

Migrants' health in Germany and the UK

1 Health of migrants and ethnic minorities in Germany

Reflecting on normative agendas

Oliver Razum and Judith Wenner

1.1 Introduction

Immigrants to European countries experience health risks and develop health needs that may differ from the risks and needs of the majority population of country receiving the immigrants. Additionally, immigrants may face specific barriers to accessing health care. These barriers apply both to migrants seeking protection and asylum (here called refugees) and to those seeking work and economic opportunities (here called immigrants with legally 'regular' residence status). We show in Part 1 of this chapter (Section 1.2) that a life course perspective can help to better understand the resulting health-related diversity, or heterogeneity, of today's societies in Europe. In Part 2 (Sections 1.3–1.5), we illustrate how health services address this heterogeneity using the example of migrants and refugees in Germany, with a particular emphasis on entitlement restrictions and access barriers to health care. Based on the insights from the life course approach and on empirical data, we demonstrate that public health research and practice are not 'neutral'. In other words, public health is not free of underlying normative agendas ('mind frames' that define what ought to be). We present such normative agendas that often constrain public health research work or practice in immigrant health and that researchers and practitioners are often not aware of. A life course approach can serve as a tool to expose such hidden normative agendas in immigrant health, such as by demonstrating the need to consider health needs arising beyond national borders.

1.2 A life course approach to migrant health

Michael Marmot, one of today's most distinguished social epidemiologists, is also one of the fathers of what we call a life course perspective in migrant health research. More than 40 years ago, he and a colleague published a seminal paper comparing the coronary heart disease (CHD) risk of Japanese people in Japan (this is the 'Ni' for Nippon in this so-called Ni-Hon-San study), Japanese people who had migrated to Honolulu/Hawaii (the 'Hon'; still somewhat close to their country of origin), and Japanese people in San Francisco (the 'San'). The researchers found a risk gradient, with the lowest CHD risk in Japan, intermediate risk in Hawaii, and the highest risk for immigrants to California – except for those immigrants who maintained their former 'Japanese' lifestyle (Marmot & Syme 1976). These findings indicate that migrants bring risks from their countries of origin ('risks' is here used in an epidemiological sense, also comprising 'good' risks or protective effects). In other words, past exposures in the country of origin are relevant for the present and future health risks and advantages immigrants experience in their receiving country. As becomes obvious from Marmot and Syme's work, health-related risks may change during the migration process, for example, due to more or less pronounced acculturation (adaptation to the culture of the receiving country) or other social processes.

Since this seminal paper, a life course approach has been established in epidemiology, albeit not with a particular focus on migrants (Ben-Shlomo & Kuh 2002; Kuh et al., 2003). It postulates critical periods of risk during the life course or the accumulation of risks as crucial for the development of chronic disease. When extended to migration processes, this approach can help to understand why migrants from less well-off countries experience a higher incidence of diseases that are determined by exposures during childhood relative to the majority population of the new home country (Razum & Twardella 2002). One such example is stomach cancer, which is more common amongst adults who had been exposed to *Helicobacter pylori*, a germ transmitted under poor hygienic conditions. Conversely, immigrants from poorer countries tend to have a lower risk of diseases such as colorectal and breast cancer because their exposure to a 'Western' lifestyle has been shorter (Arnold, Razum & Coebergh 2010).

In addition, exposures during migration can be highly relevant to health. It is only by looking beyond our national borders that an additional and major public health risk for refugees is revealed: unsafe escape routes. The International Organisation for Migration (IOM) provides an extreme but timely example. IOM collates data on deaths of refugees while trying to escape to Europe in their so-called Missing Migrants Project (International Organization for Migration 2017). In addition to the many avoidable deaths (more than 3,130 in the Mediterranean in 2017), there is substantial psychological and bodily trauma, which in all likelihood will affect the health of refugees later in the life course.

The aspects of the life course approach described thus far do not yet convey a complete picture of factors determining the health of immigrants relative to the majority population of their new home country. There are also the social determinants of health (Marmot et al. 2012); they operate on all population members irrespective of migration status, but some of these determinants are more commonly found amongst the immigrant population. Examples include low income and low educational attainment. Other determinants, such as low integration and racism, are specific to immigrants and their descendants (Spallek, Zeeb & Razum 2011). Finally, entitlement and access to health services and outcomes of treatment play an obvious role (Razum & Bozorgmehr 2016; Razum & Wenner 2016). We will return to this aspect shortly.

The life course approach provides an analytical perspective that helps explain health-related heterogeneity within countries. Moreover, adopting it corresponds with a change in the normative agenda. Taking a life course perspective means acknowledging determinants of health and public health challenges that lie outside of the borders of a specific nation state as equally relevant to those that lie within. This constitutes a paradigm change: much of public health research and action occurs entirely within the nation-state, which sociologists criticise as constituting a fixed 'container' of social relations. The nation-state container frequently and without sufficient reflection serves as the primary unit of analysis (Wimmer & Glick Schiller 2002). Public health researchers and practitioners often ignore – or fail to acknowledge – this limitation of their perspective. However, one must be clear about the *setting* in which to conceptualise or conduct migrant health research and about the normativity involved in such a decision. Staying within, or transcending, the nation-state container are two different normative perspectives that lead to substantially different research questions and designs and subsequently to different public health interventions.

1.3 Health of immigrants: it takes long to change normative agendas

For the second part of this chapter, we turn to the issue of health care provision. We introduce a second pair of normative positions: Should *all* population groups in a country enjoy equal entitlements and access to health care? The underlying normative position would treat health, and access to health care, as a ***universal human right***, a position in line with article 25.1 of the United Nations' Universal Declaration of Human Rights (UN 1948). Or should only persons with legally 'regular' residence status have full entitlement to health care? Applying this criterion would exclude refugees during the first 15 months of their stay. Limiting entitlement and access to health care according to residence status demotes health from a *human* right to a *citizen's right*, as Gorik Ooms aptly puts it (Ooms 2016). This second normative position, health as a citizens' right, reflects the current legal situation in Germany (which we describe in more detail shortly); hence, it might seem a natural starting point for public health research.

Depending on which of the two normative positions a public health researcher has adopted (knowingly or unknowingly), his or her research will take a markedly different direction. When defining health as a citizens' right, a researcher would acknowledge differences in access to health care between established citizens and refugees as necessary realities, and as being of no particular research interest – even providing a rationale to exclude from research people who do not have legally 'regular' residence status. When defining health as a human right, however, investigating access barriers and their health consequences becomes a priority. If such differences indeed exist, they should be decried as unacceptable inequities and eliminated.

We will illustrate this issue with empirical data. Germany is an immigration country. Without the various migration movements since the 1950s, Germany's population today would be much smaller (a projected 71 million instead of 82 million people) and considerably older (Mediendienst Integration n.d.).

In 2014, 8.2 million non-German nationals resided in the country, comprising approximately 10% of the population. A much larger proportion of the population, 21% (equivalent to 17 million people), has a migration background: they either immigrated themselves or are the offspring of immigrant parents. Approximately 2.9 million have a Turkish background, and 3.1 million are ethnic German 'resettlers' or their offspring, who return migrated to Germany mostly in the 1990s after the collapse of the Soviet Union (Statistisches Bundesamt 2015). For better readability, we here use the umbrella term immigrants with legally 'regular' residence status (as opposed not to refugees but to the group of persons without legal residence status) for these groups, although not all members immigrated themselves, to distinguish them from refugee migrants.

Immigrants with legally 'regular' residence status have the same entitlements to health care as the non-immigrant majority population via statutory health insurance. However, they face language-related and cultural access barriers to care (Razum et al. 2008). Acknowledging these barriers, and attempting to remove them, is a relatively recent achievement. Even years after labour migration started in the late 1950s, immigrants were called 'guest workers', assuming that they were only temporary members of German society (Bade 2017; Razum, Karrasch & Spallek 2015; Yano 2001). 'Guest workers' were ascribed specific diseases, implying that they do not fit in our health care system – the disparaging term 'Morbus Bosporus' applied to Turkish patients complaining of pain is the most blatant example (Bermejo et al. 2012). For many decades after the onset of labour migration to Germany, there was no research agenda to identify possible deficiencies of the health care system and resulting poor health outcomes amongst immigrants – a blatant example of a missed opportunity (Razum et al. 2008).

A change in the normative agenda occurred slowly. The political agenda change became visible in Germany with the report of the Süssmuth commission of 2001: 'Shaping immigration – promoting integration' (Zuwanderung gestalten – Integration fördern) (Süssmuth 2001). For the first time, Germany actually called itself an 'immigration country', thereby officially acknowledging a long-established fact.

It was only approximately that time that the first health report dedicated to immigrant health was commissioned by the Robert Koch Institute, Germany's national institute public of health. The report finally appeared in 2008 (Razum et al. 2008). In other words, it took decades after the onset of labour migration until it became more widely noticed amongst public health researchers (and unacceptable amongst politicians) that important data were lacking – such as data to establish whether access to health care was equitable for a numerically large and potentially disadvantaged subgroup of Germany's population, and what the health consequences were.

Since then, there has been progressively more public health research confirming that immigrants face cultural and language barriers towards care. The field of in-patient rehabilitative care provides a good example. Process and outcome data on rehabilitation are routinely collected for administrative purposes, so a secondary data analysis would have been possible for a long time. However, analyses comparing immigrants (here defined by their nationality due to limitations of the data set) to non-immigrants were conducted only relatively recently. They show that immigrants with a legally 'regular' residence status have a lower chance of access, after adjusting for sociodemographic variables. Those who do manage to access rehabilitation services experience 20% higher odds of rehabilitation failure (expressed as the inability to work for 3 hours or more in the previous job) compared to non-immigrants and are also less satisfied with the care they receive. These differentials cannot be explained by lower socio-economic status or by worse health before rehabilitation, as far as these factors can be adjusted for. Language barriers, culturally unacceptable treatment procedures and staff not trained in managing diversity have been shown to contribute to these differentials (Brzoska et al. 2010, 2016).

Access barriers can be overcome, provided they are identified in the first place – which requires that researchers actively look for them. This has occurred in the past years, and providers and politicians have worked hard since to make health services more culturally sensitive (Droste et al. 2015). Public health research indicates that the respective measures contribute to improvements, as the Berlin perinatal study shows (David et al. 2014, 2015). In this study, primary data were collected covering 7,100 consecutive births in three maternity hospitals of Berlin. Almost 60% of the women enrolled had a migration background, reflecting the existing diversity that is the 'normality' not only in this large German city but in many health care settings in the EU (Cattacin & Chimienti 2007). Participation in antenatal care and delivery outcomes were equally good or better amongst immigrant women compared to non-immigrant women. This showed in various measures such as a lower frequency of caesarean sections and of preterm deliveries but also in better health indicators of newborns. Only a small group of women at high risk with a short duration of stay in Germany could not be reached adequately.

In summary, it took decades after the onset of work migration to Germany until a normative agenda was widely accepted that grants immigrants with a legally 'regular' residence status the same entitlements and access to health care as non-immigrants. Currently, researchers in universities and in public health institutions such as the Robert Koch Institute share this view. There is public health research in line with this agenda, such as investigating differentials in access to care. If such differentials are found, they are perceived as unfair, and efforts are made to eliminate them. Still, not all political parties agree with this agenda change.

1.4 Health of refugees: persisting normative agendas

The situation is substantially different for persons entering Germany not as immigrants with a 'regular' residence status but as refugees seeking protection. In 2015, the number of such refugees reaching Germany and other European countries increased substantially, fuelled by armed conflicts in the near and

Middle East. More than 1 million people entered Germany in 2015, and close to 477,000 claimed asylum. This figure was not unprecedented: in 1992, 436,000 persons claimed asylum, but after restrictive measures were implemented, this number declined quickly to approximately 150,000 per annum and then to less than 30,000 per annum in 2008 (Mediendienst Integration n.d.). Little if any action was taken to prepare society in general and health services in particular, to appropriately respond to future refugee movements, which was clearly a missed opportunity (Pries 2016). In 2016, when the number of asylum claims reached almost 750,000, restrictive measures were again implemented, this time by reaching an agreement with Turkey to stop refugees from moving on to Germany and other north-western European countries and by setting up a European Border and Coast Guard Agency, leading to a substantial decline in numbers and at the same time also a 'reframing of solidarity in Europe' (Bozorgmehr & Wahedi 2016).

German health services, with the support of numerous volunteers, responded adequately to the acute health needs of the large numbers of refugees arriving in 2015 (Nicolai, Fuchs & von Mutius 2015). However, efforts to adapt the health care system for the refugees' longer term needs often had to start from scratch since there had been so little preparation and coordination in the previous decades (Bozorgmehr et al. 2016a, b). Refugees not only face language and cultural access barriers similar to immigrants with a legally 'regular' residence status; in addition, Germany restricts their entitlement to health care (see, e.g., Kaltenborn, Chapter 6 in this book p. 102). According to Article 4 of the Asylum Seekers' Benefit Act, introduced in 1993, they are entitled to care only for acute conditions and during pregnancy and childbirth for the first 15 months of their stay in Germany (Razum & Bozorgmehr 2016).

Unlike immigrants with a legally 'regular' residence status, refugees seeking protection encounter additional, specific access barriers during the first 15 months; depending on their place of residence in Germany, they must obtain a health voucher issued by non-medical staff before being able to access care. Some federal states have introduced an electronic health card for refugees, which makes the health vouchers unnecessary. However, entitlement restrictions remain in place even with the electronic health card, except in the city states of Bremen and Hamburg (Wächter-Raquet 2016). Article 6 of the Asylum Seekers' Benefit Act offers an escape route from the entitlement restrictions – provided the physicians treating refugees know how to interpret it and take the effort to apply for an exception from Article 4 for their patients. Ultimately, entitlement and access to care are contingent on the city or county a refugee is assigned to, and on the commitment of the treating physician (Razum, Wenner & Bozorgmehr 2016). Refugees cannot even seek information from a friend residing in the neighbouring town to ask how to access health services because procedures could be completely different there.

Before 1993, refugees received health care similar to immigrants with a legally 'regular' residence status and citizens in need of welfare transfers. However, this changed due to a new law after the collapse of Yugoslavia and the influx of

438,000 refugees in 1992 (Classen 2011). However, for the following 20 years after legal restrictions on entitlements were introduced, public health research was largely limited to collecting prevalence data on infectious diseases (often with the idea to protect the majority population) and on psychological trauma (Frank et al. 2017). There was hardly any health systems research investigating, for example, the health consequences of the entitlement restrictions that were put in place, or the continuity of treatment for cases of infectious diseases found during screening on arrival (Bozorgmehr et al. 2016a, b). The normative agenda underlying this constrained view of research priorities was apparently one that considered health a citizens' right (rather than a human right).

Health systems research might have yielded relevant findings to improve health care provision to refugees already since the 1990s had this need occurred to more than a small minority of public health researchers. The respective research is being conducted only now after larger numbers of public health researchers explicitly adopted an agenda considering health as a human right for refugees in Germany. The findings often contradict previously held assumptions. For example, proponents of entitlement restrictions used to defend their position with cost considerations, arguing that offering similar entitlements to refugees as those enjoyed by members of the majority population insured in the statutory health insurance would simply not be affordable (a line of argument also forwarded by Brexit supporters in the UK (McKee & Galsworthy 2016)). This argument turns out to be flawed, not only for ethical but also for economic reasons. Bozorgmehr and Razum (2015) analysed health expenditures for refugees over a 20-year period of 1994–2013 by comparing periods with and without entitlement restrictions. They demonstrated that restricting entitlement to care is actually *more* expensive than granting regular access for refugees. The total cost excess due to entitlement restrictions amounted to 1.56 billion € over the 20-year period, compared to regular access (Bozorgmehr & Razum 2015).

Entitlement restrictions are costly in monetary terms. However, it remains unknown whether they also have negative health consequences for refugees. There still is no systematic health data collection during the first 15 months of residence (Frank et al. 2017; Razum et al. 2016). A sentinel-type data collection system in selected facilities hosting refugees throughout Germany, which had been proposed by a group of public health researchers and which the Ministry of Health had in principle agreed to fund, may start, but only after another year of deliberations.

1.5 Contradictory normative agendas may coexist

Somewhat surprisingly, normative agendas that seem contradictory to us do coexist in practice, as the following example shows. The German government subscribes to the UN declaration of 1948, which defines the best possible health, and access to health care, as inalienable human rights (UN 1948). The WHO promotes Universal Health Coverage as a strategy for operationalising this right and for achieving equity in health. By definition, *Universal* Health Coverage is not restricted to 'developing countries' but applies everywhere (Ji & Chen 2016). Germany has explicitly subscribed to Universal Health Coverage in its 2013 Global Health Strategy (Bundesministerium für Gesundheit 2013) and in a subsequent statement by several Ministers of Health (Touraine et al. 2014). This has two implications: First, the German Global Health Strategy and the 1948 UN declaration endorsed by Germany state that health and access to health care is a human right. Therefore, this right applies to *all* population groups. Thus, it ought not be treated as if it were only a citizens' right. This means it ought to apply also to all population groups in Germany, which includes refugees. Germany's actual political emphasis on Universal Health Coverage, however, is directed at closing the gap between rich and poor countries, for example, by introducing health insurance in lower-income countries such as India (which is commendable). Universal Health Coverage is not applied to closing equity gaps *within* Germany. Viewed from Germany's Universal Health Coverage perspective, however, residence status is not a defensible criterion for restricting entitlement to health care.

The example of many other countries demonstrates that a more equal entitlement for migrants and refugees can be achieved. The International Organization for Migration (2016) produces a so-called Migrant Integration Policy Index (MIPEX), which also includes a summary score on health care for immigrants and refugees. In this international comparison, Germany scores low, attaining a rank of 22 out of 38 countries. Other EU countries such as Denmark, Italy, the Netherlands and Austria perform considerably better because they put into practice more elements of a human rights approach to immigrant and refugee health.

However, German politicians, even those who hold sympathies for refugees, rarely question the citizens' right perspective in public; in private, they say they are 'caught between the devil and the blue sea'. Members of parliament of one of the governing parties expressed off the record that they believe refugees should be granted full entitlement to health care. However, they have no intention to change the restrictive Article 4 of the Asylum Seekers' Benefit Act because they worry that they would then lose voters to populist and right-wing parties.

Second, the argument of universality suggests that we ought to extend our view of refugee health beyond the nation-state container. If one assumes a global heath perspective, then Universal Health Coverage applies not only to refugees in Germany or other EU countries, it also extends to war-torn countries and refugees on the move (Smith 2016). When taking up this normative position, public health researchers and practitioners cannot ignore that thousands of people are receiving hardly any health care in their country of origin and while fleeing from persecution and war. Interdisciplinary research on new immigration models for the EU and a global social protection mechanism, in addition to support for health care facilities that are established along the flight routes, are just a few of many possible courses of action for public health (Razum, Kaasch & Bozorgmehr 2016). In the long run, major policy changes and a new approach towards global health that takes the increasing interdependence between nations into account are necessary (Frenk, Gomez-Dantes & Moon 2014) – unfortunately not a likely scenario in an age of nationalist surge (Tollefson 2016).

1.6 Conclusion

Migration contributes to the health-related diversity, or heterogeneity, of today's societies in Europe. A life course approach helps to better understand why migrants experience health risks and develop health needs that may differ from those of the non-immigrant majority populations of their new home countries. The respective aspects of health-related heterogeneity are increasingly being acknowledged in many European societies. However, these societies and their health systems are still struggling to address health-related diversity adequately, as the empirical examples from Germany have shown.

A part of the underlying problem is that public health researchers and health care providers often work with normative agendas that are no longer appropriate for an increasingly heterogeneous society. Researchers and practitioners may not be fully aware of their normative agendas. However, even if researchers and practitioners are aware of these agendas, such agendas tend to persist for a long time, constraining research and practice. Applying the life course approach to immigrant health helps public health researchers and service providers look beyond the nation-state container and call for strategies to fight inequalities between nations and increase social protection globally. It also shows that increased political efforts are necessary to remove entitlement restrictions faced by people who carry one particular marker of diversity such as refugee status. A life course perspective, in other words, can help to avoid the trap of demoting the human right to health to a mere citizens' right.

More generally speaking, public health researchers should not simply assume that their research is neutral or inherently positive. Researchers inevitably make decisions: what aspects they research but also what aspects they *refrain* from researching. They must become more aware of such restrictions and of their consequences.

Finally, public health researchers must translate theory and research findings back into practice. They should not only reflect on *what* they are doing and how their work is constrained by their normative agendas; they must also critically reflect on what they *ought* to do to improve the health of disadvantaged population groups – especially if such groups have been overlooked for far too long.

References

Arnold, M., Razum, O., & Coebergh, J.W. 2010, 'Cancer risk diversity in non-western migrants to Europe: an overview of the literature', *European Journal of Cancer*, vol. 46, no. 14, pp. 2647–2659.

Bade, K.J. 2017, *Migration – Flucht – Integration: Kritische Politikbegleitung von der 'Gastarbeiterfrage' bis zur 'Flüchtlingskrise'. Erinnerungen und Beiträge*, p. 616, Von Loeper Literaturverlag, Karlsruhe, viewed 16 August 2017, www.imis.uni-osnabrueck.de/fileadmin/4_Publikationen/PDFs/Bade_Migration.pdf.

Ben-Shlomo, Y., & Kuh, D. 2002, 'A life course approach to chronic disease epidemiology: conceptual models, empirical challenges and interdisciplinary perspectives', *International Journal of Epidemiology*, vol. 31, no. 2, pp. 285–293.

Bermejo, I., Nicolaus, L., Kriston, L., Holzel, L., & Harter, M. 2012, 'Vergleichende Analyse psychosomatischer Beschwerden bei Personen mit spanischem, italienischem, türkischem und russischem Migrationshintergrund' [Culture sensitive analysis of psychosomatic complaints in migrants in Germany], *Psychiatrische Praxis*, vol. 39, no. 4, pp. 157–163.

Bozorgmehr, K., Mohsenpour, A., Saure, D., Stock, C., Loerbroks, A., Joos, S. et al. 2016a, 'Systematic review and evidence mapping of empirical studies on health status and medical care among refugees and asylum seekers in Germany (1990–2014)', *Bundesgesundheitsblatt – Gesundheitsforschung – Gesundheitsschutz*, vol. 59, no. 5, pp. 1–22.

Bozorgmehr, K., Noest, S., Thaiss, H.M., & Razum, O. 2016b, 'Die gesundheitliche Versorgungssituation von Asylsuchenden. Bundesweite Bestandsaufnahme über die Gesundheitsämter', *Bundesgesundheitsblatt – Gesundheitsforschung – Gesundheitsschutz*, vol. 59, no. 5, pp. 545–555.

Bozorgmehr, K., & Razum, O. 2015, 'Effect of restricting access to health care on health expenditures among asylum-seekers and refugees: a quasi-experimental study in Germany, 1994–2013', *PLoS ONE*, vol. 10, no. 10, p. e0131483.

Bozorgmehr, K., & Wahedi, K. 2016, 'Reframing solidarity in Europe: frontex, frontiers, and the fallacy of refugee quota', *The Lancet Public Health*, vol. 2, no. 1, pp. e10–e11.

Brzoska, P., Sauzet, O., Yilmaz-Aslan, Y., Widera, T., & Razum, O. 2016, 'Self-rated treatment outcomes in medical rehabilitation among German and non-German nationals residing in Germany: an exploratory cross-sectional study', *BMC Health Services Research*, vol. 16, no. 1, p. 105.

Brzoska, P., Voigtländer, S., Spallek, J., & Razum, O. 2010, 'Utilization and effectiveness of medical rehabilitation in foreign nationals residing in Germany', *European Journal of Epidemiology*, vol. 25, no. 9, pp. 651–660.

Bundesministerium für Gesundheit. 2013, *Shaping global health. Taking joint action. Embracing Responsibility. The Federal Government's Strategy Paper*, Berlin, viewed 13 July 2018, www.bundesgesundheitsministerium.de/fileadmin/Dateien/5_Publikationen/Gesundheit/Broschueren/Screen_Globale_Gesundheitspolitik_engl.pdf.

Cattacin, S., & Chimienti, M. 2007, 'From control policies to health policies as a tool for inclusion', *International Journal of Public Health*, vol. 52, no. 2, pp. 73–74.

Classen, G. 2011, Das Asylbewerberleistungsgesetz und seine Novellen auf dem Prüfstand, in B. Kasparek & M. Schodder (eds.), *Grenz- statt Menschenschutz? Asyl- und Flüchtlingspolitik in Europa*, Heinrich-Böll-Stiftung, Berlin, pp. 39–45.

David, M., Borde, T., Brenne, S., Henrich, W., Breckenkamp, J., & Razum, O. 2015, 'Caesarean section frequency among immigrants, second- and third-generation women, and non-immigrants: prospective study in Berlin/Germany', *PLoS ONE*, vol. 10, no. 5, p. e0127489.

David, M., Borde, T., Brenne, S., Ramsauer, B., Henrich, W., Breckenkamp, J. et al. 2014, 'Comparison of perinatal data of immigrant women of Turkish origin and German women - results of a prospective study in Berlin', *Geburtshilfe Frauenheilkd*, vol. 74, no. 5, pp. 441–448.

Droste, M., Kemal Gün, A., Kiefer, H., Koch, E., Naimi, I., Wächter, M. et al. 2015, *Das kultursensible Krankenhaus. Ansätze zur interkulturellen Öffnung*, Beauftragte der Bundesregierung für Migration, Flüchtlinge und Integration, Berlin, viewed 16 August 2017, www.bundesregierung.de/Content/Infomaterial/BPA/IB/Das_kultursensible_Krankenhaus_09-02-2015.pdf;jsessionid=E83D912161027EBA64EA6D0EB44103F7.s2t2?__blob=publicationFile&v=18.

Frank, L., Yesil-Jürgens, R., Razum, O., Bozorgmehr, K., Schenk, L., Gilsdorf, A. et al. 2017, 'Gesundheit und gesundheitliche Versorgung von Asylsuchenden und Flüchtlingen in Deutschland' [Health and healthcare provision to asylum seekers and refugees in Germany], *Journal of Health Monitoring*, vol. 2, no. 1, pp. 24–47.

Frenk, J., Gomez-Dantes, O., & Moon, S. 2014, 'From sovereignty to solidarity: a renewed concept of global health for an era of complex interdependence', *Lancet*, vol. 383, no. 9911, pp. 94–97.

International Organization for Migration. 2016, *Summary Report on the MIPEX Health Strand and Country Reports (Vol. 52)*, IOM Regional Office Brussels, Migration Health Division, Brussels.

International Organization for Migration. 2017, *Missing Migrants*, viewed 16 August 2017, https://missingmigrants.iom.int.

Ji, J.S., & Chen, L. 2016, 'UHC presents universal challenges', *Health Systems & Reform*, vol. 2, no. 1, pp. 11–14.

Kuh, D., Ben-Shlomo, Y., Lynch, J., Hallqvist, J., & Power, C. 2003, 'Life course epidemiology', *Journal of Epidemiology and Community Health*, vol. 57, no. 10, pp. 778–783.

Marmot, M., Allen, J., Bell, R., Bloomer, E., Goldblatt, P.; on behalf of the Consortium for the European Review of Social Determinants of Health and the Health Divide. 2012, 'WHO European review of social determinants of health and the health divide', *Lancet*, vol. 380, no. 9846, pp. 1011–1029.

Marmot, M.G., & Syme, S.L. 1976, 'Acculturation and coronary heart disease in Japanese-Americans', *American Journal of Epidemiology*, vol. 104, no. 3, pp. 225–247.

McKee, M., & Galsworthy, M.J. 2016, 'Brexit: a confused concept that threatens public health', *Journal of Public Health*, vol. 38, no. 1, pp. 3–5.

Mediendienst Integration. n.d. Viewed August 16 2017, https://mediendienst-integration.de/migration/bevoelkerung.html.

Nicolai, T., Fuchs, O., & von Mutius, E. 2015, 'Caring for the wave of refugees in Munich', *The New England Journal of Medicine*, vol. 373, no. 17, pp. 1593–1595.

Ooms, G. 2016, 'Health: a human right or a citizen's right?' *Paper presented at the 6th EUPHA European Conference on Migrant and Minority Health*, Oslo.

Pries, L. 2016, *Migration und Ankommen. Die Chancen der Flüchtlingsbewegung*, Campus, Frankfurt am Main.

Razum, O., & Bozorgmehr, K. 2016, 'Restricted entitlements and access to health care for refugees and immigrants: the example of Germany', *Global Social Policy*, vol. 16, no. 3, pp. 321–324.

Razum, O., Bunte, A., Gilsdorf, A., Ziese, T., & Bozorgmehr, K. 2016, 'Gesundheitsversorgung von Geflüchteten: Zu gesicherten Daten kommen', *Deutsches Ärzteblatt International*, vol. 113, no. 4, pp. 130–133.

Razum, O., Kaasch, A., & Bozorgmehr, K. 2016, 'Commentary: from the primacy of safe passage for refugees to a global social policy', *International Journal of Public Health*, vol. 61, no. 5, pp. 523–524.

Razum, O., Karrasch, L., & Spallek, J. 2015, 'Migration. Eine vernachlässigte Dimension gesundheitlicher Ungleichheit?' *Bundesgesundheitsblatt – Gesundheitsforschung – Gesundheitsschutz*, vol. 59, no. 2, pp. 259–265.

Razum, O., & Twardella, D. 2002, 'Time travel with Oliver Twist - towards an explanation for a paradoxically low mortality among recent immigrants', *Tropical Medicine and International Health*, vol. 7, no. 1, pp. 4–10.

Razum, O., & Wenner, J. 2016, 'Social and health epidemiology of immigrants in Germany: Past, present and future', *Public Health Reviews*, vol. 37, no. 1, pp. 1–17.

Razum, O., Wenner, J., & Bozorgmehr, K. 2016, 'Wenn Zufall über den Zugang zur Gesundheitsversorgung bestimmt: Geflüchtete in Deutschland' [When chance decides about access to health care: the case of refugees in Germany], *Gesundheitswesen*, vol. 78, no. 11, pp. 711–714.

Razum, O., Zeeb, H., Meesmann, U., Schenk, L., Bredehorst, M., Brzoska, P. et al. 2008, *Migration und Gesundheit. Schwerpunktbericht der Gesundheitsberichterstattung des Bundes*, Robert Koch-Institute, Berlin.

Smith, J.D. 2016, 'Thinking beyond borders: reconceptualising migration to better meet the needs of people in transit', *International Journal of Public Health*, vol. 61, no. 5, pp. 521–522.

Spallek, J., Zeeb, H., & Razum, O. 2011, 'What do we have to know from migrants' past exposures to understand their health status? A life course approach', *Emerging Themes in Epidemiology*, vol. 8, no. 1, p. 6.

Statistisches Bundesamt. 2015, *Bevölkerung und Erwerbstätigkeit. Bevölkerung mit Migrationshintergrund. Ergebnisse des Mikrozensus 2014*, Statistisches Bundesamt, Wiesbaden, viewed 13 July 2018, www.destatis.de/DE/Publikationen/Thematisch/Bevoelkerung/MigrationIntegration/Migrationshintergrund2010220147004.pdf?__blob=publicationFile.

Süssmuth, R. 2001, *Zuwanderung gestalten – Integration fördern. Bericht der Unabhängigen Kommission 'Zuwanderung'*, Bundesministerium des Inneren, Berlin, viewed August 16 2017, www.fluechtlingsrat.org/download/berkommzusfas.pdf.

Tollefson, J. 2016, 'Researchers baffled by nationalist surge', *Nature*, vol. 540, pp. 182–183.

Touraine, M., Gröhe, H., Coffie, R.G., Sathasivam, S., Juan, M, Louardi, EL. H. et al. 2014, 'Universal health coverage and the post-2015 agenda', *Lancet*, vol. 384, no. 9949, pp. 1161–1162.

UN. 1948, *The Universal Declaration of Human Rights, General Assembly Resolution 217 A*, UN, Paris.

Wächter-Raquet, M. 2016, *Einführung der Gesundheitskarte für Asylsuchende und Flüchtlinge. Der Umsetzungsstand im Überblick der Bundesländer*, Bertelsmann, Gütersloh, viewed 16 August 2017, www.bertelsmann-stiftung.de/fileadmin/files/BSt/Publikationen/GrauePublikationen/Studie_VV_Gesundheitskarte_Fluechtlinge_2016.pdf.

Wimmer, A., & Glick Schiller, N. 2002, 'Methodological nationalism and the study of migration', *European Journal of Sociology*, vol. 43, no. 2, pp. 217–240.

Yano, H. 2001, Anwerbung und ärztliche Untersuchung von 'Gastarbeitern' zwischen 1955 und 1965, in P. Marschalck & K.H. Wiedl (eds.), *Migration und Krankheit*, (Vol. 1), Universitätsverlag Rasch, Osnabrück, pp. 65–83.

2 The health of migrants in the UK

Evidence and implications for health care

Hiranthi Jayaweera

2.1 Introduction: framing migrant health in the UK

Many factors influence the health of migrants, before and after they migrate and during the migration process. They include migrants' demography, socio-economic circumstances and health in countries and areas of origin, reasons for migration, the nature of migration journeys, the way they are received in destinations, their circumstances and health status upon arrival and over time and their entitlement and access to health care in the receiving context. While it is more commonly perceived that migration affects health, it is also important to consider that the relationship between migration and health can be converse: health affects migration as, for instance, in relation to who chooses or is allowed to immigrate or emigrate, and in pre-migration and post-migration medical testing for infectious diseases or fitness to work (Coker 2004). Health is also a key indicator of integration, a two-way process concerning how migrants adapt to and how they are received in the society in which they come to live, and is important for other integration outcomes, such as employability or civic participation, which are dependent on good health (Spencer & Cooper 2006).

The focus of this chapter is the health of people *born abroad* who cross UK borders. Within this framework, a broad definition of 'migrant' is used, to encompass diversity among migrants. The definition includes workers, students, refugees, asylum seekers, family members and undocumented migrants. They may be recently arrived and/or temporary migrants, as well as those who have lived in the UK for many years (Blinder 2017). In relation to health care, the definition ranges from those who, according to immigration and residency regulations, have full entitlement to publicly funded health care, to those who are considered not 'lawfully resident' and are denied entitlement free of charge to some health services. The chapter predominantly focuses on adult migrants, for whom there exist the most evidence.[1]

Over the past several decades the size of the migrant population in the UK and the nature and extent of its diversity have changed considerably. The large-scale movement of people from former British colonies in South Asia and the Caribbean to work and join families in Britain over half a century ago has shifted to a vastly more varied pattern. Labour and family migration have continued but have at times become more temporary and circular. Alongside this are increasing numbers of people fleeing global political conflicts, as well as international students, and migrants from the European Union (EU), including from countries joining the EU since 2004, in accordance with 'free movement' regulations (Czaika 2014). In the 2011 Census, around 13% of the UK population was recorded as born outside the UK, a rise from 9% in 2001 (Krausova 2014). The size, diversity and geographical settlement patterns of the migrant population have major implications for the provision of health services alongside other public services. Significantly, there has been a geographical spread of recently arrived migrants beyond urban centres, characteristic of the early post-Second World War settlement patterns, to other urban areas as a result of dispersal policies for asylum seekers, and to rural areas because of the demand (in particular) for agricultural workers from new EU countries. These 'new immigrant gateways' have been experiencing challenges in coping with a larger population accessing public services, underpinned by a lack of knowledge of different migrant categories, their needs and how to meet those needs (Waters & Jimenez 2005). Research with health policymakers and health care providers in local areas suggests that this is a continuing test for policy, planning and service provision (Jayaweera 2016). While not the focus of this chapter, it is also important to note that migrants themselves form a substantial proportion of health professionals in the UK (e.g., around a third of doctors and a fifth of nurses) and are thus key to the provision of health care (Jayaweera & McCarthy 2015).

The aim of this chapter is to describe the current state of knowledge regarding the health of migrants in the UK and examine some of the factors that are associated with their health. While many migrants may experience good health, I argue that there are legal, social and ethical barriers for others to achieving and maintaining good health that have significant implications for the provision of health care in ways that are sensitive to the specific circumstances and needs of different migrant categories. The chapter explores the evidence on migrants' health status and access to health care, and gaps in that evidence. It ends with some recommendations for policy and practice change.

2.2 The health care system and entitlement in the UK

The UK health care system is dominated by the National Health Service (NHS), free at point of use for citizens and permanent residents and paid from general taxation. Over the past two decades there have been increasing restrictions to entitlement and access to NHS services for migrants (Johnson & Jayaweera 2017). At present, there is a distinction in regulations stipulating free access to NHS primary and community health care on the one hand, and those stipulating free access to NHS care in hospital and other secondary health settings on the other, with the latter largely dependent on the immigration status of the patient. According to a redefinition of 'ordinary residence' as part of the 2014 Immigration Act to mean only those who have permanent residence in the UK, new 'temporary' migrants from countries outside the European Economic Area (EEA) planning to remain in the UK for six months or more, including workers on the points-based system[2] and their dependants, family members joining British citizens or permanent residents and international students, are subject to paying an annual health surcharge; this allows them access to NHS hospital services free at the point of delivery. Categories exempt from charging include EEA migrants exercising their free movement rights, non-EEA migrants granted refugee status, those applying for asylum or humanitarian protection whose claims have not yet been determined, children looked after by a local authority and refused asylum-seekers with Home Office or local authority support (Department of Health 2016).

Some categories of health care remain free to all, irrespective of immigration status or nationality, largely on the grounds of international human rights obligations and the protection of public health. These include treatment given in an accident and emergency department or similar walk-in centre; diagnosis and treatment of certain communicable diseases such as tuberculosis (TB), HIV and pandemic flu; compulsory psychiatric treatment; family planning services; and treatment of a physical or mental condition caused by violence, including gender-based violence (Department of Health 2016). Rules coming into effect in April 2017 have tightened the surveillance and detection of 'chargeable' patients at the point of entry to secondary health care. Further, the government proposes to extend charging to non-exempt migrants such as undocumented migrants and refused asylum seekers accessing previously free treatment *outside* of an NHS hospital. This includes primary care and health care funded by the NHS but provided by voluntary agencies, as well as accident and emergency services, including ambulance services (Department of Health 2017).

2.3 Evidence and gaps in evidence

2.3.1 Interrogating the data

One of the main challenges to understanding health and barriers to health care among migrants in the UK is the *type* of information that is collected. Unlike in most other European countries, collection and analysis of population health data in the UK generally prioritises ethnicity, encompassing shared origins, culture, religion, language and identity, over immigration variables (Senior & Bhopal 1994). Primary care and hospital records, and chronic disease registries for cancer, heart disease and diabetes, for example, currently record mainly the ethnicity of patients and do not either have or make available country of birth information (Aspinal 2014). Coverage of ethnicity is still incomplete in routine health datasets and inconsistencies in coding remain, but valid ethnicity now exists for 90% of newly registered patients in primary care and over 75% of hospital inpatients (Mathur et al. 2014). On the other hand, country of birth, but not ethnicity, is recorded in birth and death registrations, except in Scotland where there is a voluntary option since 2012 to record ethnic group also at death registration (Johnson 2012). Registers of communicable diseases, such as TB and HIV surveillance databases, also classify people by country of birth, possibly because being a migrant is considered a risk factor for some infectious diseases (Aspinal 2014).

The divergent indicators used in different types of health datasets create challenges, for example, in understanding chronic disease incidence, prevalence and treatment compared to cause-specific mortality rates for migrants. Recently, however, there has been a greater move towards linking administrative and health records, as in the case of linking babies' hospital birth records with birth registration records which contain parents' countries of birth. This type of record linkage makes it possible, for example, to examine birth outcomes such as birthweight and preterm birth, as well as delivery outcomes for migrant mothers in comparison with mothers born in the UK (Dattani, Datta-Nemdharry & Macfarlane 2011). Population based surveys on health or with health-related questions are also increasingly including demographic questions on respondents' ethnicity, country of birth and in some cases length of residence in the UK, thus enabling analyses of health outcomes by migration variables, although the relatively small number of migrants and exclusion of categories such as 'asylum seekers' in some surveys poses a challenge to comprehensive understanding (Jayaweera & Quigley 2010). However, the government targets to reduce social inequalities in health refer to ethnic differences in outcomes and in cross-cutting social determinants of health, such as smoking and housing, and there is no specific focus on migrant groups, clearly because migrant variables are not uniformly available in routine data (Marmot et al. 2010).

As part of recent NHS reforms in the UK, the 2012 Health and Social Care Act intensified *local* evidence-based processes of strategic assessment and planning to improve the public's health and reduce inequalities. Vulnerable migrant groups, such as refugees and asylum seekers, Roma, undocumented migrants, victims of trafficking and slavery and those who are homeless and destitute, are highlighted among population groups who may have the poorest health and for whom there is least information on health needs and inadequate provision of health care services (Department of Health 2013). Despite the existence of guidance on the importance of a basic understanding of the demography of a local area, including change brought about through migration, the evidence needed to inform 'health inclusion' of migrants locally remains patchy (Jayaweera 2016; Rose et al. 2011). There is a need for a more comprehensive collection and analysis of data to understand whether and why migration factors interacting with ethnicity and socio-demographic factors may mean that needs and barriers of migrants could differ from those of minority ethnic groups born in the UK, while acknowledging the existence of common experiences as well. These data gaps and limitations need to be borne in mind when considering the current evidence on the health of migrants and their access to health care in the UK, which are discussed in the following sections.

2.3.2 Physical and mental health status

The health of migrants is likely to differ, initially at least, from that of non-migrants in *both* countries of origin and destination. But contrary to assumptions of the 'healthy migrant', there is no uniform evidence that migrants are healthier than people they leave behind or come to live among; there are too many health determinants that need to be accounted for as pointed out earlier, including biological, demographic and socio-economic factors (McKay, Macintyre & Ellaway 2003). There are also many reasons for migration (Blinder 2017), and health may not be a primary determining factor where there is a need to flee political conflict or environmental disasters or to join family members abroad. There are variations in health status in different migrant categories, and there is more evidence for some categories than for others in the UK, largely because of limitations in data collection as shown above.

Although asylum seekers and refugees tend to be mostly invisible in large scale datasets because they are not included or identified, their mental health in particular has received more attention than that of some other migrant categories in research and commentaries. Higher rates of trauma-related psychological distress, anxiety and depression have been documented among asylum seekers and refugees than among the general population, not only because of experiences in countries of origin and in transit but also because of difficult conditions they face in UK society, including isolation, loss of social status, poverty and insecure legal immigration status and the impact of detention and dispersal policies (McColl, Mckenzie & Bhui 2008). There is relatively limited information on the health status of economic and family migrants and international students. It is generally expected that workers and students are often youthful and healthy, but health issues among broader migrant groups include maternal and child health (Jayaweera & Quigley 2010). A recent literature review of the health status of migrants from Eastern Europe, who tend to be mainly economic migrants, highlights issues for a minority in some local areas such as: stress, anxiety and loneliness sometimes compounded by increased alcohol intake, especially among homeless migrants; higher-risk sexual behaviour especially among men, associated with risk of HIV and sexually transmitted diseases (STDs); and the negative health impact of poor quality housing and overcrowding, associated with private rented or employment-linked accommodation (Madden et al. 2014). Health consequences of poor working conditions and inadequate safety practices in some industries employing migrants have also been documented (McKay, Craw & Chopra 2006).

A fairly comprehensive understanding of some communicable disease outcomes for migrants nationally is possible because, as stated earlier, country of birth information is available, for instance in recording statutorily notifiable diseases such as TB and HIV. The majority of cases of TB, and HIV among heterosexuals, occurs among non-UK-born people (Wagner et al. 2014). Most recent TB data for England show that while rates are higher among non-UK-born people than among the UK-born (51.2 cases vs 3.4 cases per 100,000 population in 2015), there is a decline over time for non-UK-born rates which is likely to be associated with a reduction in the number of new migrants from high TB burden countries as well as the impact of pre-entry screening measures and improving TB control (Aldridge et al. 2016). Patterns by country of birth *and* ethnic group show wide differences both among non-UK-born and UK-born people, with highest rates among non-White ethnic groups from particular countries like India, Pakistan and Somalia, and an increase in the number of cases born in Romania (Public Health England 2016). There is evidence that, increasingly, a smaller proportion of TB cases is identified in recent migrants: 60% of non-UK-born TB cases in 2015 were diagnosed after 6 years of arrival. The issue of latent TB as well as visits by migrants to countries of origin where they may be become infected may be factors (Public Health England 2016; Wagner et al. 2014). But low income and poor living conditions in the UK, especially among some recent migrants, may also be important. TB is a disease that has historically been associated with poverty and deprivation (Abubakar et al. 2012). However, there is no robust evidence in routine surveillance systems, beyond homelessness, drug and alcohol misuse and imprisonment as social risk factors, to enable us to explore broader socio-economic factors affecting TB among migrants (Public Health England 2016).

For non-communicable diseases (NCDs) there is evidence that cause-specific standardised mortality ratios vary by country of birth and by the disease examined. High coronary heart disease (CHD) but low combined cancer mortality rates have been reported among migrants from the Indian sub-continent relative to people born in England and Wales and to those migrating from Scotland and Ireland. High stroke mortality rates among migrants of Caribbean and African origin have also been reported. Sex and country of birth differences in mortality from individual cancers, and changes across time and generations, have also been found. For example, there are higher mortality ratios for breast cancer among West African-born women than among women born in England and Wales and those born in the Indian subcontinent (Harding, Rosato & Teyhan 2008; Wild et al. 2006). Some studies report that, in general, age-standardised mortality rates among migrants rise with increasing length of residence in the receiving country and declines in death rates over time are smaller for many migrant groups in England and Wales compared to the receiving country-born population (Harding 2004; Harding, Rosato & Teyhan 2008). Reviews including the UK among other European countries suggest a more diverse pattern where cause-specific mortality is concerned (Arnold, Razum & Coebergh 2010; Razum & Twardella 2002).

Examining NCD *morbidity* patterns among migrants is more challenging because of the absence of migration variables in routine health datasets. But data linkage between cancer registrations and the Census has shown lower cancer incidence overall among men and women born in South Asia compared to all men and women in the population studied (Harding & Rosato 1999). Commensurate with mortality rates, high rates of coronary disease incidence among South Asian-origin men and women compared to other population groups have been found in Scotland although longer term survival rates among South Asians are no worse than for other groups despite higher prevalence of diabetes (Zaman & Bhopal 2013).

The above account has demonstrated variations in migrant health outcomes by disease type and ethnic and migration variables, taking into account data gaps and limitations. However, understanding why these variations exist is more complex. The following section critically examines a central explanation associated with migrant health.

2.3.3 Health behaviour and 'acculturation': a critical perspective

Associations have been found between differences in NCD outcomes in migrant groups and different patterns of health behaviour including diet, exercise, smoking and alcohol consumption, although the evidence specifically for migrants rather than ethnic minorities is limited. For instance, there is evidence that older African-Caribbeans in the UK, who are more likely to be migrants, have a higher intake of a more traditional Caribbean diet of fruits and vegetables than their younger UK-born counterparts, thus contributing to a protective effect on heart disease (Agyemang et al. 2009). However, other risk factors such as genetic predisposition, and physiological differences in metabolism and adiposity interacting with behavioural factors such as physical activity and calorie intake have also been debated, for example, with reference to the greater susceptibility of South Asian groups compared to some other migrant groups and the receiving country population to Type 2 diabetes and heart disease (Zaman & Bhopal 2013). Many studies incorporate the premise that moving to a new country is associated with vulnerability to unhealthy lifestyles such as smoking, alcohol consumption and nutritionally deficient diet. A theoretical framework, commonly used to explain changes in health behaviour of migrants as risk factors for health outcomes, is that of 'acculturation'. This framework derives from broader 20th century anthropological and sociological approaches to migrants' loss of original culture and the adoption of values, beliefs and behaviour prevalent in receiving societies (Hunt, Schneider & Comer 2004). It has largely been applied in health research as an attempt to explain the decline – over time or by other indicators – of initially positive health behaviour and risk factor profiles of migrants commonly described as 'the healthy migrant effect' (Davies, Blake & Dhavan 2011). Acculturation is often used loosely as 'a given' term with reference to changes in migrants' health after migration, even in studies that do not necessarily engage with it more theoretically.

Subjecting this concept to critical scrutiny in the face of evidence highlights several of its weaknesses where migrant health is concerned. First, there may not be a singular, uniform pattern of migrant health behaviour in receiving countries. There is evidence that smoking and alcohol consumption patterns vary according to ethnicity, country of origin including exposure prior to migration, and general population demographic determinants of such behaviour including sex and age (Agyemang et al. 2009; Bhopal et al. 2012). For example, a unique analysis of intergenerational patterns of health behaviour in the Health Survey for England (HSE) 1999–2004 reported percentages of non-smokers that varied widely across ethnic groups (Black Caribbean, Indian, Pakistani, Bangladeshi, Chinese, Irish, White) and between migrants and the UK-born within the different ethnic minority groups (Smith, Kelly & Nazroo 2009). In the same survey,

Bangladeshi men had far higher smoking rates than Whites, Pakistanis and Indians, but Bangladeshi women like other South Asian women had very low rates (Zaman & Bhopal 2013). A multivariate analysis of migrant mothers of infants in the Millennium Cohort Study (MCS) showed that while lower rates of smoking and alcohol consumption remained among many minority ethnic groups compared to white British mothers, even after adjusting for length of residence and socio-demographic circumstances, a linear trend of increasing smoking and alcohol consumption according to length of residence in the UK disappears after adjusting for ethnicity and socio-demographic variables (Jayaweera & Quigley 2010). These patterns suggest that changes in health behaviour after migration, and according to ethnicity in the UK, may not be as clear-cut or uniform as set out in the acculturation thesis.

Second, together with the assumption that the adoption of unhealthy behaviour by migrants is inevitable when they move to affluent Western societies, there is an idea inherent in some acculturation accounts of essentially one mainstream receiving country behavioural pattern that migrants are adopting. Given that there are demographic and socio-economic disparities or gradients in population health outcomes and health behaviour, as, for example, in the socio-economic gradients in smoking, obesity, lack of physical exercise and unhealthy diet in England (Marmot et al. 2010), it is far more likely that migrants, for whatever reason, manifest health behaviours that are common to specific groups, whether these are, for example, economic, ethnic or locality based. It is important to make clear who we are talking about – for example, disaggregating the category 'South Asian' often used in reporting NCD rates and patterns, by socio-economic position, sex, age, national origin, religion etc.; and understanding whose (similarly disaggregated) 'risky' health behaviours in receiving societies are taken on by migrants, if at all. 'Segmented assimilation' approaches may provide a more useful framework to comprehend these behavioural processes, emphasising the existence of different reference groups in the receiving society and varied patterns of interaction (Abraido-Lanza et al. 2006). More ethnographic research in local areas would be helpful to understand specific patterns and determinants of health behaviour among different migrant populations (see, e.g., Falge, Chapter 4, pp. 57 ff).

Third, less attention has been paid to how migrant health outcomes in receiving societies compare with outcomes of populations in countries of origin. While country of origin health evidence for migrants from lower and middle income to higher income countries is limited, research findings show the high and growing prevalence and risk of NCDs such as cardiovascular disease (CVD) and diabetes in their domestic populations, especially in urban areas. Globally, almost three quarters of NCD-related deaths and 82% of NCD deaths below the age of 70 years occur in low- and middle-income countries (World Health Organisation 2017). The global case-control Interheart study of coronary risk factors showed very similar patterns in countries of origin of South Asian migrants to those among migrant counterparts in receiving countries: for example, high rates of smoking among Bangladeshi men, low levels of smoking and alcohol consumption among women in all South Asian countries and low alcohol consumption in the predominantly Muslim countries of Pakistan and Bangladesh (Joshi et al. 2007). A comparative study of overweight and obesity among Ghanaians living in both rural and urban areas in Ghana and among Ghanaian migrants in the Netherlands found that there was an increasing gradient in overweight and obesity among migrants from rural areas to urban areas in Ghana, even when adjusted for age and education (Agyemang et al. 2008). Such findings suggest the importance of considering social determinants of health in local populations and areas, and the pre-migration health of those who are mobile, in understanding patterns of and reasons for health outcomes among migrants in receiving contexts.

While changes in health behaviour may play an important part in migrants' vulnerability to ill health over time in the receiving country, an understanding of the framework of *structural* constraints surrounding choice in health behaviour for migrants who are poor and living in deprived areas is also imperative, for example, the economics and geography of access to good quality and nutritional food in preventing obesity. The proliferation of cheap fast-food outlets catering to religious preferences has been shown, for instance, to be associated with dietary practices among adolescent children of migrant Bangladeshi parents in a deprived East London neighbourhood (Lofink 2010).

2.3.4 Access to and uptake of health care

There is relatively more evidence on access to and uptake of health care among migrants in the UK than on health status and health behaviour, but this is largely from small scale, local and qualitative studies. Often the focus in these studies is on barriers to access. The barriers identified include inadequate information, particularly for new migrants unfamiliar with health care systems in the UK; insufficient support in interpreting and translating for people with limited English fluency; limited access to reliable transport because of poverty and poor services in areas of deprivation where many recent migrants live; confusion around entitlement to some types of services, particularly among migrants with insecure immigration status; and cultural insensitivity of some front-line health care providers (Jayaweera, D'souza & Garcia 2005; Johnson 2006; Puthussery 2016). While some of these barriers have been identified in migrants who are more vulnerable, such as recent arrivals or those with limited English fluency or undocumented migrants with limited entitlement to free health care, some of the barriers appear to cut across length of residence, affecting longer established migrants as well. There is, again, limited quantitative evidence according to migration variables such as country of birth, length of residence and legal status in the receiving country. However lower uptake of cancer screening and antenatal care have been documented among non-UK-born populations compared to those who are UK-born although ethnicity and socio-demographic factors have also been identified as important (Jayaweera & Quigley 2010; Webb et al. 2004). A record linkage study of factors influencing registration with primary health care among newly arriving migrants screened for TB at airports showed that less than a third were registered with a general practitioner, despite the possibility of high health needs. Men, older migrants, students, individuals from African countries and asylum seekers were less likely to register (Stagg et al. 2012). Evidence from the 2010 National Maternity Survey showed that non-UK-born ethnic minority women (as a single group) compared with white women born in the UK reported later initial and booking contact with midwives, poorer information provision, and less likelihood of being offered antenatal education classes and of saying they were treated with respect by midwives during antenatal care (Redshaw & Heikkila 2010). From the perspective of health care implementation, recent qualitative research exploring the views of health policymakers and health care professionals in local areas on commissioning health care services for vulnerable migrant women such as asylum seekers, Roma and women with limited English fluency found a mismatch between *policy* on health inclusion locally and inclusive *practice*. It was revealed that statutory health services do not adequately address wider determinants of health, such as the implications of some migrants not having recourse to public funds, or exploitative employment conditions. There is also less evidence of service change compared to smaller projects on needs assessment and signposting for health professionals (Jayaweera 2016).

An issue relating to migrants' access to health care that is receiving important attention in research and practice in the face of changing immigration health policy, as discussed above, is the health impact of a lack of, or perceived uncertainty around, entitlement to free health care among undocumented migrants. The ever-intensifying stratification of rights to health care for migrants leads to a situation where lack of access to essential health services on the same basis as citizens or permanent residents negatively affects health care-seeking behaviour, with implications for poorer health outcomes (Kelly, Morrell & Sriskandarajah 2005). A recent Doctors of the World case study highlighted that among 35 pregnant women who attended one of their drop-in clinics, all but one woman had no general practitioner, despite an average length of residence of over four years, around a third accessed antenatal care after 20 weeks and two women lost their babies but were charged for hospital care (Doctors of the World UK 2015).

2.4 Conclusion

As in the case of the general population most migrants have good health. They make significant contributions to the UK, including as providers of health care and social care, and protecting their health is important for the society as a whole. This chapter has provided an overview of what is known about the health of adult migrants in the UK. It has also set out some of the key gaps in available data that prevent a comprehensive understanding of migrant health outcomes and needs.

Two key points highlighted in the chapter are the ever shifting migration patterns and the consequent diversity of migrant categories living in the UK that create both similarities and differences in health needs, and which change over time. Diversity includes not only country of origin and ethnic differences but also, for instance, age, gender, socio-economic and religious differences. Broadly, the evidence suggests that longer established migrant populations from the

Indian subcontinent and the Caribbean have health concerns and service needs that differ in some respects from those of the recent EU migrants coming to the UK to undertake low-skilled temporary or seasonal work. Similarly, migrants with regular immigration status are differently placed in relation to health care entitlements compared with those with irregular status. But there are also many commonalities across categories: for example, determinants of chronic illnesses and inadequate meeting of language and cultural support needs. While policy starts at national level, most health implications are at *local* level, where understanding who makes up the migrant population, and what their needs are, is imperative to providing appropriate and sometimes targeted health care. While the impact on health care demand arising both from changing numbers of EU migrants after the UK leaves the EU and from upcoming Syrian refugee settlement patterns are as yet uncertain, it is important that both national and local health policies and practice have a preparedness and responsiveness, moving forward, that also takes into account existing migrant populations and determinants of their health. For this to happen, there is an imperative need to improve collection of data on migration variables in routine health data systems. There is also a need for more robust and widespread information about health needs and barriers to access, including among harder-to-reach groups with problems in accessing mainstream health services, so that local commissioning gaps could be identified and addressed, such as in providing better and more targeted interpretation and translation services and classes in English language fluency. The role of voluntary sector organisations in providing holistic outreach approaches and wrap-around support to help migrants overcome a variety of problems that impact on health, enabling them to engage productively with the NHS and access mainstream services, is also important, and deserves more recognition and support.

Notes

1 While children may face some of the same issues as adults, their experiences warrant a separate consideration. Therefore, a comprehensive focus on studies that specifically deal with children, and those born in the country to which parents have migrated, is beyond the remit of this chapter.

2 A points-based immigration system selects migrants on the basis of possessing certain attributes that are valued, such as educational qualifications, occupational skills and language proficiency (Gower 2016).

References

Abraido-Lanza, A., Armbrister, A.F., Flórez, K.R., & Aguirre, A.N. 2006, 'Toward a theory-driven model of acculturation in public health research', *American Journal of Public Health*, vol. 96, no. 8, pp. 1342–1346.

Abubakar, I., Stagg, H., Cohen, T., Mangtani, P., Rodrigues, L.C., Pimpin, L. et al. 2012, 'Controversies and unresolved issues in tuberculosis prevention and control: a low-burden-country perspective', *The Journal of Infectious Diseases*, vol. 205, no. 2, pp. 293–300.

Agyemang, C., Addo, J., Bhopal, R., de Graft Aikins, A., & Stronks, K. 2009, 'Cardiovascular disease, diabetes and established risk factors among populations of sub-Saharan African descent in Europe: a literature review', *Globalization and Health*, vol. 5, no. 1, p. 7.

Agyemang, C., Owusu-Dabo, E., de Jonge, A., Martins, D., Ogedegbe, G., & Stronks, K. 2008, 'Overweight and obesity among Ghanaian residents in the Netherlands: how do they weigh against their urban and rural counterparts in Ghana?', *Public Health Nutrition*, vol. 12, no. 7, pp. 909–916.

Aldridge, R., Zenner, D., White, P., Williamson, E.J., Muzyamba, M.C., Dhavan, P. et al. 2016, 'Tuberculosis in migrants moving from high-incidence to low-incidence countries: a population-based cohort study of 519, 955 migrants screened before entry to England, Wales and Northern Ireland', *The Lancet*, vol. 388, no. 10059, pp. 2510–2518.

Arnold, M., Razum, O., & Coebergh, J. 2010, 'Cancer risk diversity in non-western migrants to Europe: an overview of the literature', *European Journal of Cancer*, vol. 46, no. 14, pp. 2647–2659.

Aspinal, P. 2014, *Hidden needs: identifying key vulnerable groups in data collections: vulnerable migrants, gypsies and travellers, homeless people, and sex workers*, Inclusion Health Board, London.

Bhopal, R., Bansal, N., Steiner, M., & Brewster, D.H. 2012, 'Does the "Scottish effect" apply to all ethnic groups? All-cancer, lung, colorectal, breast and prostate cancer in the Scottish Health and Ethnicity Linkage Cohort Study', *BMJ Open*, vol. 2, no. 5, p. e001957.

Blinder, S. 2017, *Immigration by category: workers, students, family members, asylum applicants*, The Migration Observatory at the University of Oxford, Oxford.

Coker, R. 2004, 'Compulsory screening of immigrants for tuberculosis and HIV: is not based on adequate evidence, and has practical and ethical problems', *British Medical Journal*, vol. 328, no. 7435, pp. 298–300.

Czaika, M. 2014, *Determinants of migration to the UK*, The Migration Observatory at the University of Oxford, Oxford.

Dattani, N., Datta-Nemdharry, P., & Macfarlane, A. 2011, 'Linking maternity data for England, 2005–6: methods and data quality', *Health Statistics Quarterly*, vol. 49, no. 1, pp. 53–79.

Davies, A., Blake, C., & Dhavan, P. 2011, 'Social determinants and risk factors for non-communicable diseases (NDCs) in South Asian migrant populations in Europe', *Asia Europe Journal*, vol. 8, no. 4, pp. 461–473.

Department of Health. 2013, *Statutory guidance on joint strategic needs assessment and joint health and wellbeing strategies*, Department of Health, London.

Department of Health. 2016, *Guidance on implementing the overseas visitor hospital charging regulations 2015*, Department of Health, London.

Department of Health. 2017, *Making a fair contribution: government response to the consultation on the extension of charging overseas visitors and migrants using the NHS in England*, Department of Health, London.

Doctors of the World UK. 2015, *Access to healthcare in the UK*, Doctors of the World UK, London.

Gower, M. 2016, *The UK's points-based system for immigration*, House of Commons Briefing Paper No. 7662, London.

Harding, S. 2004, 'Mortality of migrants from the Caribbean to England and Wales: effect of duration of residence', *International Journal of Epidemiology*, vol. 33, no. 2, pp. 382–386.

Harding, S., & Rosato, M. 1999, 'Cancer incidence among first generation Scottish, Irish, West Indian and South Asian migrants living in England and Wales', *Ethnicity & Health*, vol. 4, no. 1–2, pp. 83–92.

Harding, S., Rosato, M., & Teyhan, A. 2008, 'Trends for coronary heart disease and stroke mortality among migrants in England and Wales, 1979–2003: slow declines notable for some groups', *Heart*, vol. 94, no. 4, pp. 463–470.

Hunt, L., Schneider, S., & Comer, B. 2004, 'Should "acculturation" be a variable in health research? A critical review of research on US Hispanics', *Social Science and Medicine*, vol. 59, no. 5, pp. 973–986.

Jayaweera, H. 2016, *Commissioning health services for vulnerable migrant women in England: evidence on policies and practices*, Maternity Action and Women's Health and Equality Consortium, London.

Jayaweera, H., & McCarthy, H. 2015, *Workplace integration of migrant health workers in the UK*, International and European Forum of Migration Research, Turin.

Jayaweera, H., & Quigley, M. 2010, 'Health status, health behaviour and healthcare use among migrants in the UK: evidence from the Millennium Cohort Study', *Social Science and Medicine*, vol. 71, no. 5, pp. 1002–1010.

Jayaweera, H., D'souza, L., & Garcia, J. 2005, 'A local study of childbearing Bangladeshi women in the UK', *Midwifery*, vol. 21, no. 1, pp. 84–95.

Johnson, M. 2006, 'Integration of new migrants', in S. Spencer (ed.), *Refugees and other new migrants: a review of the evidence on successful approaches to integration*, Centre on Migration, Policy and Society, Oxford.

Johnson, M. 2012, 'Problems and barriers in the collection of ethnicity and migration related data', in D. Ingleby, A. Krasnik, V. Lorant & O. Razum (eds.), *Health inequalities and risk factors among migrants and ethnic minorities: COST series on health and diversity volume 1*, Garant, Antwerp-Apeldoorn.

Johnson, M., & Jayaweera, H. 2017, *Migrant integration policy index health strand: country report United Kingdom*, International Organisation for Migration, Brussels.

Joshi, P., Islam, S., Pais, P. et al. 2007. 'Risk factors for early myocardial infarction in South Asians compared with individuals in other countries', *Journal of the American Medical Association (JAMA)*, vol. 297, no. 3, pp. 286–294.

Kelly, R., Morrell, G., & Sriskandarajah, D. 2005, *Migration and health in the UK: IPPR factfile*, Institute for Public Policy Research, London.

Krausova, A. 2014, *Migration in Great Britain: census factsheet*, The Migration Observatory at the University of Oxford, Oxford.

Lofink, H. 2010, '"The worst of the Bangladeshi and the worst of the British': exploring eating patterns and practices among British Bangladeshi adolescents in East London', *Ethnicity & Health*, vol. 17, no. 4, pp. 385–401.

Madden, H., Harris, J., Harrison, B., & Timpson, H. 2014, *A targeted health needs assessment of the Eastern European population in Warrington*, Centre for Public Health, Liverpool John Moores University, Liverpool.

Marmot, M.G., Allen, J., Goldblatt, P., Boyce, T., McNeish, D., Grady, M. et al. 2010, *Fair society, healthy lives: strategic review of health inequalities in England post-2010*, The Marmot Review, London.

Mathur, R., Bhaskaran, K., Chaturvedi, N., Leon, D.A., vanStaa, T., Grundy, E. et al. 2014, 'Completeness and usability of ethnicity data in UK-based primary care and hospital databases', *Journal of Public Health*, vol. 36, no. 4, pp. 684–692.

McColl, H., Mckenzie, K., & Bhui, K. 2008, 'Mental healthcare of asylum-seekers and refugees', *Advances in Psychiatric Treatment*, vol. 14, no. 6, pp. 452–459.

McKay, S., Craw, M., & Chopra, D. 2006, *Migrant workers in England and Wales: an assessment of migrant worker health and safety risks*, Health and Safety Executive, London.

McKay, L., Macintyre, S., & Ellaway, A. 2003, *Migration and health: a review of the international literature*, MRC Social and Public Health Sciences Unit, Glasgow.

Mckeigue, P., & Karmi, G. 1993, 'Alcohol consumption and alcohol-related problems in Afro-Caribbeans and South Asians in the United Kingdom', *Alcohol & Alcoholism*, vol. 28, no. 1, pp. 253–258.

Puthussery, S. 2016, 'Perinatal outcomes among migrant mothers in the United Kingdom: is it a matter of biology, behaviour, policy, social determinants or access to healthcare?', *Best Practice & Research Clinical Obstetrics and Gynaecology*, vol. 32, pp. 39–49.

Raphaely, N., & O'Moore, E. 2010, *Understanding the health needs of migrants in the South East region*, Health Protection Agency and the Department of Health, London.

Razum, O., & Twardella, D. 2002, 'Time travel with Oliver Twist: towards an explanation for a paradoxically low mortality among recent migrants', *Tropical Medicine and International Health*, vol. 7, no. 1, pp. 4–10.

Redshaw, M., & Heikkila, K. 2010, *Delivered with care: a national survey of women's experience of maternity care*, National Perinatal Epidemiology Unit, University of Oxford, Oxford.

Rose, N., Stirling, S., Ricketts, A., & Chappel, D. 2011, *Including migrant populations in joint strategic needs assessment: a guide*, Health Inequalities and Local Improvement Team, Department of Health, London.

Senior, P., & Bhopal, R. 1994, 'Ethnicity as a variable in epidemiological research', *British Medical Journal*, vol. 309, no. 6950, pp. 327–330.

Smith, N., Kelly, Y., & Nazroo, J. 2009, 'Intergenerational continuities of ethnic inequalities in general health in England', *Journal of Epidemiology and Community Health*, vol. 63, no. 3, pp. 253–258.

Spencer, S., & Cooper, B. 2006, *Social integration of migrants in Europe: a review of the European literature 2000–2006*, Centre on Migration, Policy and Society, University of Oxford, Oxford.

Stagg, H., Jones, J., Bickler, G., & Abubakar, I. 2012, 'Poor uptake of primary healthcare registration among recent entrants to the UK: a retrospective cohort study', *BMJ Open*, vol. 2, no. 4, p. e001453.

Wagner, K., Lawrence, L.J., Anderson, L., Yin, Z., Delpech, V., Chiodini, P.R. et al. 2014, 'Migrant health and infectious diseases in the UK: findings from the last 10 years of surveillance', *Journal of Public Health*, vol. 36, no. 1, pp. 38–35.

Waters, M., & Jimenez, T. 2005, 'Assessing immigrant assimilation: new empirical and theoretical challenges', *Annual Review of Sociology*, vol. 31, pp. 105–125.

Webb, R., Richardson, J., Esmail, A., & Pickles, A. 2004, 'Uptake for cervical screening by ethnicity and place-or-birth: a population based cross-sectional study', *Journal of Public Health*, vol. 26, no. 3, pp. 293–296.

Wild, S., Fischbacher, C., Brock, A., Griffiths, C., & Bophal, R. 2006, 'Mortality from all cancers and lung, colorectal, breast and prostate cancer by country of birth in England and Wales, 2001–2003', *British Journal of Cancer*, vol. 94, no. 7, pp. 1079–1085.

World Health Organisation. 2017, *The determinants of health*, Health Impact Assessment, viewed 8 April 2017, www.who.int/hia/evidence/doh/en/.

Zaman, M., & Bhopal, R. 2013, 'New answers to three questions on the epidemic of coronary mortality in south Asians: incidence or case fatality? Biology or environment? Will the next generation be affected?' *Heart*, vol. 99, no. 3, pp. 154–158.

3 Bearing witness

Observations of the health of people without access to the regular health care system in Médecins du Monde's health care and advocacy programmes in London and Munich

Lucy Jones, Anna Miller, Sabine Fürst, Carolin Bader and Lea Gelfert

3.1 Introduction

This chapter looks at the health and wider social circumstances of people excluded from public health care services in Germany and the UK, with a focus on migrants. It is based on the experience of the Médecins du Monde (MdM) programmes in London and Munich, drawing on data collected in these programmes in 2014. Established in 1980, MdM is an international network of non-governmental organisations working to improve access to health care and the protection of human rights. Since conception, MdM's mission has been twofold: to provide health care to those in need and to bear witness to the life circumstances of patients. Today, MdM runs health care programmes across the world using patient testimonies and data to advocate for universal access to health care. In this chapter, we aim to compare data from clinics in London and Munich, and we reflect on the needs of the patients in these clinics. We then go on to discuss the consequences of exclusion from public health care and describe the actions that are needed to improve the situations of these patients in the long term.

3.2 Exclusion mechanisms in the health care systems of the UK and Germany

The UK and Germany have highly rated health care systems which both aspire to universal access (Schneider et al. 2017). The UK National Health Service (NHS) is a taxation-based system founded on the principle of universal access (NHS 2008; Steele & Devlin, Chapter 7, pp. 112 ff). The German health care system is a social insurance-based system that includes a general obligation for all people to be insured (Institute for Quality and Efficiency in Health Care 2018; Kaltenborn, Chapter 6, p. 101). In practice, health coverage is not universal in either country – the two MdM programmes in Munich and London provide care to people who are excluded from public health care in both health care systems.

The public health care system in the UK, the NHS, is funded through national taxation and is free at the point of service to certain groups of residents. British citizens and those granted indefinite leave to remain[1] as well as EU migrants, refugees and asylum seekers can access NHS services free of charge.[2] Non-EU migrants on a visa for 6 months or longer are required to pay a health care surcharge, giving them free access to NHS services. Undocumented migrants including people whose visas have expired and refused asylum seekers, must pay for many health care services (Immigration Act 2014, s. 39). Charges are inflated to 150% of the tariff for the service, making them economically inaccessible for most. Some services are exempt from charges, including primary care, treatment in Accident and Emergency departments, certain types of violence,[3] infectious diseases and family planning services. Recognised and suspected victims of trafficking are also exempt from charges.

Germany has a highly developed health care system. Health care is, however, expensive and most people cannot afford to pay for their health care out-of-pocket. The majority of the population is covered by statutory or private health insurance; some groups receive services through the social service department. Not being covered by one of these mechanisms means in effect no access to affordable health care. This includes also German citizens without insurance or with lapsed insurance. In Germany, health care coverage is greatly linked with employment status. Those who are unemployed or self-employed with little income can fall through the gaps of the health care system.

People from other EU countries without formal employment in Germany do not have access to health care if they cannot prove their insurance in their country of origin. A recent law, enacted in 2016,[4] excludes certain EU citizens from new EU member states (those with less than five years residency in the country, and those who are unemployed, without financial means or without acquiring their residence permit through their children) from social benefits, including all health care coverage.

The Asylbwerberleistungsgesetz (Asylum Seeker's Benefits Act) regulates health care entitlement for asylum seekers (Kaltenborn, Chapter 6, pp. 102 ff). For the first 15 months of their stay in Germany, asylum seekers' access to health care is restricted to care for acute illnesses and pain (Act on Benefits for Asylum Applicants, ABAA §4(1)) and can only be extended to other essential health care services on a case-by-case basis. This level of health care is considerably lower than the level of health care that is provided according to the catalogue of minimum services of the statutory health insurance. Undocumented migrants by law have the same restricted access to health care as asylum seekers. However, to apply for the coverage of the costs for non-emergency care involves sharing personal information with state officials, who are obliged to report the individual to the police or immigration authorities if someone cannot provide a valid residence permit (§87 residence act).

In summary of the legal regulations in both countries, the gaps in the health care systems of the UK and Germany are significant since certain groups of migrants are structurally excluded from full access to public health care. We use the term 'excluded patients', to refer to those who are or feel unable to access public health care services. Excluded patients are marginalised and often living in life circumstances that make them vulnerable. They are unlikely to be able to afford private health care. By providing health care to these individuals, the MdM programmes act as an essential safety net and also play a role in protecting public health by providing health care for patients with communicable diseases, linking them into public screening programmes and antenatal care.

3.3 MdM programmes in London and Munich

The MdM programme in London is a clinic that provides short-term medical care and an advocacy service supporting patients to access NHS health care services as well as housing, immigration and debt advice, and migrant and community support networks. A specialist women and childrens' clinic provides enhanced reproductive, child and mental health services, psychosocial support and monthly outreach clinics are hosted by migrant and community support groups. The clinics are staffed by volunteer general practitioners (GPs), nurses and support workers. Service users are offered consultations with a GP or nurse, and a consultation with a support worker who carries out a thorough social assessment.

The programme in Munich is similar, providing free basic medical care and specialist consultations for women, children, chronic and psychiatric diseases. It has established a network of doctors to refer patients to specialist care, as well as pharmacies and laboratories. Social consultations to support integration into the regular health care system and social support services are also a key part of the programme.

An important feature of the MdM clinics is that their service is anonymous and confidential. For undocumented migrants, this is particularly valued as both the UK and German health care systems share their information with the immigration enforcement department (except in emergency care in Germany, where confidentiality is also maintained). Both services provide interpreters for patients, either in person or by phone.

In addition to providing health care and social support, volunteers in both programmes collect anonymous data and testimonies from patients to support MdM's advocacy work. The data cited in the following sections were collected by the respective programmes in 2014, and were published in MdM's annual Observatory Report 'Access to Health care for People Facing Multiple Vulnerabilities in Health' (Chauvin et al. 2015).[5] In this chapter, we focus on the comparison of the data from the two clinics in Munich and London and discuss possible consequences for further action in the context of the two countries Germany and the UK.

3.4 Comparative analysis

3.4.1 Who is excluded from health care services?

In 2015, the Munich clinic carried out 1,648 medical and psycho-social consultations with 464 patients. Out of these patients, 41% did not have any health care insurance coverage and a further 50% had only partial coverage due to their legal status or because they could not afford a health care insurance with a full coverage. The London clinic carried out 1,454 social, medical or social-medical consultations with 1,395 patients, 82.7% of which were not accessing other health care services. The following patient data collected in the programmes provide a picture of who is excluded from public health care systems.

The country of origin and immigration status of patients seen in the two programmes differ significantly, reflecting the gaps in the two different health care systems. In Munich, the majority of patients were EU migrants (68%), most commonly from Bulgaria, Romania, Poland, Serbia and Bosnia, followed by German citizens (15%). All in all, 9% of all the patients were undocumented migrants. Contrastingly, in the London clinic, 94% of patients were non-European nationals, most commonly from Asia (57%) and sub-Saharan Africa (23.5%). EU migrants made up just 2.7% of patients and only 0.8% of people seen were British citizens. The majority of patients (55%) were undocumented migrants, including irregular entrants, visa overstayers and refused asylum seekers.

The MdM clinics in the UK and Germany see patients in need of health care that would have been provided by public health care services, regardless of the person's immigration status or ability to pay. For example, in Germany emergency care is given to everyone that seeks support in public hospitals, and in the UK, primary care and accident and emergency services, can be accessed free of charge by anyone regardless of their immigration status. These patients choose to approach MdM clinics because of the wide range of barriers they face when accessing public health care services. This includes lack of knowledge of entitlements or how to access public health care services, fear of health care bills, language barriers and fear of being reported to immigration authorities.

3.4.2 Reasons for exclusion

Both programmes record the reasons why service users were or felt excluded from mainstream health care services. In Munich, economic factors were the most common barrier to health care: 24% of all patients could not afford to pay for private medical consultations or medication, and 16% could not afford health insurance. Sociopolitical barriers were also present: 12% faced language barriers, 6% experienced administrative problems, such as difficulties with the insurance or the social security office, and 6% did not understand how to access the health care system. In the UK clinic, the most commonly reported barriers to access health care were sociopolitical ones: 52% of patients had not tried to access health care services, 17% did not know how to access services, 29% were blocked by administrative barriers and 14% faced language barriers.

3.4.3 Reasons for consulting MdM programmes

In Munich, patients' self-disclosed primary reason for attending the programme was for medical care (95.6%); however, 41.6% of patients also came to the clinic for assistance with administrative, legal or social issues. In the UK, this figure was even higher; 94.1% of patients came to the clinic for help with administrative, legal or social matters whilst just 34.3% presented for medical care.

The high proportion of patients accessing MdM services for non-medical reasons may seem surprising, but it provides valuable insight into the practicalities of providing health care to excluded patients. When a person approaches an MdM clinic for non-medical reasons, it does not mean they do not need medical care. Rather, it shows what a patient views as their most pressing need, and how this is often prioritised over health care. The administrative, legal and social challenges that motivated patients to make contact with MdM services include the need for immigration, housing, welfare support and advice, an inability to meet their basic needs (such as food, housing and clothing). If a patient is sleeping on the streets, or facing eviction, or unable to feed themselves or their children, or restricting their movements for fear of arrest, it is likely they will view these problems as more pressing than seeing a doctor or addressing an ongoing health problem.

Identifying the factors that motivate patients to make contact with health care services is an important consideration when designing and delivering health care services for excluded patients. Firstly, it shows the importance of having knowledge of local support services and a referral and signposting system. Secondly, it shows that in order to reach excluded patients, health care services need to be able to provide support to address the issues that the patient sees as most important. This is achieved in the MdM clinics by establishing a reputation for supporting patients with administrative, legal and social problems, and also by being physically located with other service providers. The MdM Munich programme is based in the same building as an immigration advice service, and the London clinic is housed with a migrant advice and support service.

3.4.4 Consequences of exclusion from public health care services

Excluding patients from public health care services has various consequences. For some patients, the barriers they face are so significant that they receive no health care at all; for others, it means late or reduced access to health care and treatment. For health care personnel and health care providers, understanding the impact of wider social, political and economic circumstances on health, and how to address these issues, is crucial.

The analysis of the data from both clinics indicates that service users were in poor health and were often in urgent need of health care. In the London clinic, 29.4% of patients reported their general health was bad or very bad. This percentage is considerably higher than the percentage in the general population of UK, in which 8.4% of people rate their health as bad or very bad (Eurostat 2014). In the Munich clinic, the percentage was 36.6% in comparison to the percentage of 8.1% in the German general population (Eurostat 2014). The vast majority of patients presenting at both clinics required health care urgently or fairly urgently (Germany 93%, UK 71% of patients).

Both clinics saw a high prevalence of unreviewed chronic conditions: 39.9% of patients in the London clinic had at least one chronic condition that had never been checked or monitored by a doctor before. In Munich this figure was 43%, most frequently hypertension (13%), diabetes (8%) or respiratory tract infections. In some cases, patients were unaware of their condition or had not had a diagnosis and were not taking medication. In others, patients try to manage their condition themselves, buying medication over the internet or consulting a doctor from their country of origin. Without review by a practitioner, this self-management of conditions can present other health care risks.

Another part of exclusion is a lack of access to preventative health care services. In Munich, 65% of pregnant women had their first antenatal examination after 12 weeks. A research study carried out in the London clinic showed that women frequently received antenatal care late; 62% of initial antenatal checks were after 12 weeks and 34% after 20 weeks; 50% of women had fewer than the recommended number of appointments (Shortall et al. 2015). Two women, in the cohort of 35, had early neonatal deaths, reflecting the comparatively poor maternal health outcomes observed in other cohorts of migrant mothers (Bollini et al. 2009; Jayaweera 2014).

Both of the MdM clinics see patients with mental health needs. If these needs remain unmet, higher levels of poor mental health are to be expected in these patients. Most will experience at least one, and usually many, of the following risk factors: separation from family, social isolation, poverty, unstable housing or street homelessness, lack of immigration status and poor working conditions. Some have experienced trauma having witnessed war, armed conflict, the death of family and friends, violence, sexual violence, dangerous journeys and time spent in prison or detention. The experience of being excluded from health care services and managing health conditions without a practitioner can compound mental health problems. A service user at the London clinic explains how she and her mother, who had diabetes and a history of depression, felt after they were turned away from three doctors' clinics by administrative staff:

> Then I basically gave up hope. I thought that is it. My mum is going to [go] blind, something is going to happen... I could even cry now .... I don't want my mum to feel bad. She must be feeling like nothing.
>
> (Service User, London clinic)

3.4.5 Impact on practitioners and providers

Providing care for excluded patients has consequences for health care practitioners and providers. Excluded patients often present with medical problems that are either caused or exacerbated by the socio-economic circumstances they are living in, such as poor housing, bad working conditions, lack of access to food, social isolation and stress related to immigration status. The ability to address their health care needs is often significantly reduced because of the complexity of these circumstances. As a practitioner, it is difficult to separate a patient's medical needs from their wider socio-economic and legal circumstances. An understanding of how wider social, political and economic circumstances impact on health, and an ability to identify and address these wider circumstances, is key. For this reason, MdM take a holistic approach to health care, placing great importance on social assessments which capture critical elements of a person's history, living arrangements, safety, housing, family relations, migration status, friendship connections and other social support, experience of the migration process and any other important events, such as trauma and violence. These histories are critical in understanding a patient's interconnected needs.

3.5 Bearing witness in practice

Témoignage – bearing witness to the circumstances and suffering of the patients we see – has always been an integral part of MdM's work. This stems from the understanding that advocating on behalf of a patient is part of the role of a doctor. This *témoignage* takes many forms, ranging from speaking to the media, campaigning to raise public awareness of an issue,[6] acting as advisors to policymakers at national and international level[7] and taking legal action to improve access to health care. In 2015, MdM France launched proceedings which successfully reduced the scope of the pharmaceutical company Sofosbuvir's patent claims for (and therefore the cost of) hepatitis C treatment (Kelland 2015). In the same year, a legal challenge taken by MdM France against the Lille municipal government resulted in a court order for the implementation of trash collection, installation of toilets and water points, and creation of an access route for medical emergency services in a camp in Calais (Blamont & Labbe 2015).

A crucial part of MdM's advocacy work is its annual European Observatory Report.[8] With partner NGOs across Europe, MdM programmes (including the MdM London and Munich clinics) collect data and testimonies from people excluded from public health care services. This report strengthens the evidence base of unmet health care needs in Europe and is a valuable tool for governments and health care systems wishing to reduce vulnerabilities in health care and provide truly universal health care access. It is also a valuable data set for academics.

Although advocacy is a key part of MdM's ethos and operations, it can present challenges when delivering health care to people living in vulnerable circumstances. Collecting data on patients, public advocacy and media work can be a source of concern for patients. Confidentiality is the cornerstone of the doctor-patient relationship and every effective health care service, and it takes on an additional level of importance when providing health care to those who are fearful of authorities, such as undocumented migrants, sex workers and drug users. These patients have concerns about their data being collected – even for health care purposes – and can be reluctant to share their testimony with MdM staff or speak to journalists. It is only by establishing a reputation as a confidential and reliable provider of high quality health care services – and with the guarantee that data will be fully anonymised – that MdM is able to gain the trust of patients, collect and analyse data and share their stories in order to advocate for change. All patients are given the option to opt out of data collection. However, for many, knowing that their data and testimonies may help to address the barriers to health care services so that others in the future will not face the same problems as them, is appealing and empowering.

3.6 Conclusion

As the health care systems in Germany and the UK continue to exclude people from health care services, the need for MdM's work continues to be important. People without access to health care avoid or postpone seeking help for medical conditions. The situation is especially precarious for people in high need of protection because of their vulnerability like (pregnant) women and children. Withholding health care has significant consequences for the health of individuals and also for public health. Studies have shown that the exclusion of certain groups from accessing primary health care has negative economic consequences as exclusion often leads to an increased need for emergency treatment which is more expensive than early prevention and treatment (European Union Agency for Fundamental Rights 2015).

Equally important as providing health care for excluded patients is accounting and providing a voice for them. MdM's programmes' opportunity to collect data on the health conditions of their patients represents a unique source of knowledge on groups that are rarely included in national statistics. This enables MdM to raise awareness of political decision-makers, to challenge the structural barriers in health care systems and to advocate for concrete legal reforms and their consequent implementation.

Although MdM and many other voluntary organisations play a vital role in providing health care and support to excluded patients in the UK and Germany, there will be many more who struggle to access public health care services and who cannot reach MdM services. The responsibility to provide universal access to health care does not sit with civil society and voluntary organisations; governments must fulfil their obligations to ensuring available, affordable, high-quality health care to everybody, as outlined in international human rights documents.[9]

Notes

1 To be considered 'ordinarily resident' and therefore entitled to free NHS services, British citizen and those with leave to remain also need to be 'properly settled' in the UK (Shah v Barnet London borough Council and other appeals [1983] 1 ALL ER 226).
2 Patients are charged for some NHS services, including prescription medication, dentals services and optometry services, at flat or banded rates although there is an exemption for those on a low income.
3 Torture, female genital mutilation (FGM), domestic and sexual violence.

4 Gesetz zur Regelung von Ansprüchen ausländischer Personen in der Grundsicherung für Arbeitsuchende nach dem Zweiten Buch Sozialgesetzbuch und in der Sozialhilfe nach dem Zwölften Buch Sozialgesetzbuch.

5 The data that described here was presented during an international workshop in Munich in 2016. The focus of the presentation was the comparison between data from the UK and Germany to that date, pointing to the different effects of the two different health care systems. Since then, more annual reports have been published (e.g., Aldridge et al. 2017; Simonnot et al. 2016). In comparison of the data summarised here with the later reports, it is especially interesting to analyse the effects of the so-called European refugee crises that supposedly began in 2015.

6 For example: 2013 Medicos del Mundo Spain launched '"Nadie Desechado (Nobody Denied)' to fight against the Royal Decree Law 16/2012 that restricted access to health care to pensioners, immigrants or low-income families (see Medicos del Mundo n.d., 2017 MdM UK launched '#StopSharing' challenging an agreement which allowed the UK Home Office to access NHS patient data for immigration enforcement, (Doctors of the World 2017).

7 For example, (1) MdM acted as technical adviser in European parliament working groups on the reform of the common European asylum system (Dublin directive, Reception directive). The final proposal directives included broader access to health care that initially proposed; (2) DOTW UK is the current NGO representative on the UK Government Department of Health Steering Group on NHS Charges.

8 The annual observatory report is available through the following website: European Network to reduce vulnerabilities in health Observatory reports: https://mdmeuroblog.wordpress.com/resources/publications/, viewed 14 July 2018.

9 Article 12, United Nations International Covenant on Economic, Social and Cultural Rights 1966 and Article 24 of the United Nations Convention on the Rights of the Child 1990.

References

Aldridge, R.W., Miller, A.K., Jakubowski, B., Pereira, L., Fille, F., & Noret, I. 2017, *Falling through the cracks: the failure of universal healthcare coverage in Europe*, European Network to Reduce Vulnerabilities in Health, London.

Blamont, M., & Labbe, C. 2015, *French court orders toilets, trash collection at Calais migrant camp*, 2 November 2017, viewed 13 November 2017, http://uk.reuters.com/article/us-europe-migrants-calais/french-court-orders-toilets-trash-collection-at-calais-migrant-camp-idUKKCN0SR28M20151102.

Bollini, P., Pampallona, S., Wanner, P., & Kupelnick, B. 2009, 'Pregnancy outcome of migrant women and integration policy: a systematic review of the international literature', *Social Science and Medicine*, vol. 68, no. 3, pp. 452–461.

Chauvin, P., Simonnot, N., Vanbiervliet, F., Vicart, M., & Vuillermoz, C. 2015, *Access to healthcare for people facing multiple vulnerabilities in health*, Doctors of the World – Médecins du Monde International Network, Paris.

Doctors of the World. 2017, *Take action against the home office accessing NHS Data!* n.d., viewed 13 November 2017, www.doctorsoftheworld.org.uk/news/medics-mobilise-against-nhs-patient-data-sharing.

Eurostat. 2014, *Self-perceived health by sex, age and educational attainment level*, viewed 10 November 2017, http://ec.europa.eu/eurostat/en/web/products-datasets/-/HLTH_SILC_02.

European Network to reduce vulnerabilities in health. n.d. *Observatory reports*, viewed 9 July 2018, https://mdmeuroblog.wordpress.com/resources/publications/.

European Union Agency for Fundamental Rights. 2015, *Cost of exclusion from healthcare – the case of migrants in an irregular situation*, Publications Office of the European Union, Luxembourg.

Institute for Quality and Efficiency in Health Care, IQWiG, Germany. 2018, *Health insurance in Germany*, viewed 9 July 2018, www.informedhealth.org/health-insurance-in-germany.2698.en.html?part=versicherung-32.

Jayaweera, H. 2014, *'Health of migrants in the UK: what do we know?' Migration Observatory Briefing*, COMPAS, University of Oxford, Oxford, viewed 10 November 2017, www.migrationobservatory.ox.ac.uk/wp-content/uploads/2016/04/Briefing-Health_of_Migrants_in_the_UK.pdf.

Kelland, K. 2015, *Gilead faces challenge to European patent on pricey hep C drug*, Reuters, 10 February, viewed 13 November 2017, http://uk.reuters.com/article/us-health-gilead-hepc-idUKKBN0LE0WL20150210.

Medicos del Mundo. n.d. Lanzamos la campaña "nadie desechado" para sensiblizar a la ciucadanía sobre el impacto de los recortes en sanidad n.d., viewed 13 November 2017, www.medicosdelmundo.org/actualidad-y-publicaciones/noticias/lanzamos-la-campana-nadie-desechado-para-sensibilizar-la.

NHS. 2018, *Principles and values that guide the NHS* 2015, viewed 10 November 2017, www.nhs.uk/NHSEngland/thenhs/about/Pages/nhscoreprinciples.aspx.

Schneider, E., Sarnak, O., Squires, D., Shah, A., & Doty, M. 2017, *Mirror, mirror 2017: international comparison reflects flaws and opportunities for better U.S. health care*, The Commonwealth Fund, viewed 1 March 2018, www.commonwealthfund.org/interactives/2017/july/mirror-mirror/.

Shortall, C., McMorran, J., Taylor, K., Traianou, A., Garcia de Frutos, M., Jones, L., & Murwill, P. 2015, *Experiences of pregnant migrant women receiving ante/peri and post-natal care in the UK: a longitudinal follow-up study of doctors of the world's London drop-in clinic attendees*, viewed 10 November 2017, www.doctorsoftheworld.org.uk/Handlers/Download.ashx?IDMF=f239ee99-7695-47e6-9273-05cc4486f6c9.

Simonnot, N., Rodriguez, A., Nuernberg, M., Fille, F., Aranda-Fernández, P.E., & Chauvin, P. 2016, *Access to healthcare for people facing multiple vulnerabilities in health in 31 cities in 12 countries. Report on social and medical data gathered in 2015 in 11 European countries and Turkey*, European Network to Reduce Vulnerabilities in Health, London.

Legislation

Convention on the Rights of the Child 1990.

Gesetz zur Regelung von Ansprüchen ausländischer Personen in der Grundsicherung für Arbeitsuchende nach dem Zweiten Buch Sozialgesetzbuch und in der Sozialhilfe nach dem Zwölften Buch Sozialgesetzbuch.

Immigration Act 2014.

International Covenant on Economic, Social and Cultural Rights.

The National Health Service (Charges to Overseas Visitors) Regulations 2015.

4 Dynamics of informal exclusion

Migrants' health as experienced in the City Lab Bochum

Christiane Falge

4.1 Introduction

In regard to knowledge circulation between science, society and politics, relations between universities and society are characterized by a power asymmetry, in which academic 'hegemonic' knowledge is positioned above the knowledge of citizens, while their knowledge is often overlooked. The academic knowledge produced in the institutions of the global North is based on Western 'rationality' and 'scientificity' and is constructed by a homogenous group of academicians (Boidin, Cohen & Grosfoguel 2012; Mbembe 2016). Attempts at decolonization of this knowledge have been formulated, for instance, in the field of collaborative action or participatory research (Napier-Moore 2010; Rappaport 2008). Some researchers began to operate in cities, to apply collaborative research approaches to communities with the aim to create new forms of knowledge by collaboratively creating it with urban citizens. Niewöhner, for instance, who calls cities 'laboratories of knowledge' (Niewöhner 2014, p. 28), argues that collaboration and reflexivity develop not in the distance but in the context of intensive exchange and by being involved in the field of urban everyday life. In regard to collaborative research (Sykes & Treleaven 2009), an attempt is made to acknowledge the great heterogeneity and plurality of forms of knowledge within and outside universities. To comprehend this heterogeneity and facilitate knowledge circulation, city researchers recommend replacing conventional, time-restricted research projects with long-term research infrastructures (Niewöhner 2014; Sykes & Treleaven 2009) as spaces where universities and urban players can meet at eye level in order to grasp the complexity of 'actual people's lives as lived' (Niewöhner 2014, p. 205).

The City Lab Bochum is a long-term collaborative health promotion project that has been established to provide such a space. Here, medical anthropologists, migration researchers and citizens study peoples' health by focusing on locality. They aim to create a new relationship between the university and the city. The City Lab's research results can suggest structural transformations that create favourable conditions for people to be healthy. The results in this chapter emerge from three years of intermittent ethnographic research since 2015, a family-centred ethnographic case study and a vulnerability assessment. The insights stem from data collected specifically to find out more about migrants' pathways to health and well-being and about the role 'culture' plays in this context. Here, we use the working definition of culture as 'a process of negotiation that instead of shared values, norms and practices is a discursive field' (Schiffauer 1997).

4.2 Diversity, urban health and migration

The systemic nature of multiple massive dispossessions taking place worldwide related to global economic transformations affects people and localities in different manners (Sandbrook et al. 2007). Alongside 'everyday' migration, these dispossessions are also a major trigger of migration to the global North (Glick Schiller & Çağlar 2018). Hence, we currently observe that 'across the globe, more people, from more varied backgrounds, are coming into regular contact with one another' (Vertovec 2011, p. 7). As a result, cities are transforming, and localities are characterized by increasing urban (socio-cultural) diversity. This new diversity is often accompanied by structural inequality, such as people's specifically poor living and working conditions and lower access to health and well-being. It confronts states with emerging scientific and policy challenges to deliver welfare to these places, and requires providers to understand and meet the needs of their diverse service users (Law 2009; Vickers, Craig & Atkin 2013). Declining resources associated with the decline of the welfare state (Banting & Kymlicka 2006) and austerity, combined with the backlash against multiculturalism (Grillo 2010), make it increasingly difficult for people living in multidiverse communities to access health care. Hence, the field of diversity and urban health is challenged to develop models that provide equal access to health care for all, including these communities. So far, however, these issues have largely been overlooked in research about urban health. In Germany, they have mostly been studied through public health- and epidemiology-initiated cohort studies (Borde 2009; Razum, Karrasch & Spallek 2016; Razum & Saß 2015).

As a result of migration, the issue of urban health is highly relevant to cities. Migration research has long focused on the segregation of migrants, a phenomenon noted by, among others, researchers from the Chicago School, who described the existence of ethnic support networks in ethnically homogenous neighbourhoods (Park & Burgess 1925). The perception of ethnically diverse urban neighbourhoods as 'problematic' therefore generally dominates the discourse. The crisis of the urban, it is argued, is induced by processes of socially selective migration and impoverishment. Solidarity among local residents decreases, and the area transforms into a 'ghetto' (Häußermann 2010). Anyhow, increasingly, structural aspects are also mentioned as explanatory factors for ethnic segregation, such as the limited financial resources of migrants, which coincides with discriminatory rental practices (Farwick 2009). Hence, some migration scholars view migration as a positive asset (Glick Schiller & Çağlar

2016). As a reaction to the methodological critique of the 'ethnic lens' (Glick Schiller, Çağlar & Guldbrandsen 2006), these migration scholars realized that 'geography matters fundamentally' and migration research shifted its focus from ethnicity to locality, specifically to the urban neighbourhood. In this line of research, migration scholars have worked to counter dominant political narratives about problematic ethnic minority cultures (Vertovec & Wessendorf 2010). However, many studies then analysed migration with concepts of social relations that are primarily shaped in the context of difference (Rogaly & Qureshi 2013; Wessendorf 2013). This approach, Glick Schiller argues, might distract migration scholars from seeing and understanding '[...] that some residents build social relations in which, whatever their differences, [...] by common domains of affect [...], mutual respect and shared aspirations' (Glick Schiller & Çağlar 2016, p. 2). With this critique, the more recent concept of cosmopolitan sociability (Glick Schiller & Çağlar 2016) introduces a view of local diversity as a 'simultaneous rootedness and openness to shared human emotions, experiences and aspirations rather than to a tolerance for cultural difference' (Glick Schiller, Darieva & Gruner-Domic 2011, p. 399). It enables researchers to see how migrants in precarious contexts participate in social relationships characterized by specific localities (Glick Schiller 2015, p. 4). This perspective responds to the concepts focusing on differences (Vertovec 2007) and the 'Crisis of the Urban', similarly to the perspective of this article about the urban neighbourhood to be introduced here.

4.3 Health and migration

In regard to the field of health and migration, epidemiologists criticize the lack of health-related information about migrants because to date, migrants are not routinely taken into account in official statistics, which often only distinguish between German and foreign nationalities (Razum & Saß 2015, p. 513). This lack of differentiation is significant because first-generation migrants seem to have particularly poor health outcomes and at the same time are considered difficult to reach with conventional epidemiological research methods (Knipper & Bilgin 2009). Whereas epidemiologists call for migrant-specific data in order to detect group-related health inequalities, medical anthropologists[1] recommend that epidemiologists, in their cohort-related studies, should critically reflect on whether seemingly 'migrant-specific' themes could not be better analysed from another perspective (Knipper & Bilgin 2009). This aims to avoid a perspective about migration per se as barrier to health care because it might draw away attention from other social, medical or legal questions (Knipper & Bilgin 2009, pp. 88–89).[2] Similarly, migration scholars argue that going beyond a migrant lens would enable a differentiated view of peoples' pathways to health and well-being, as neoliberal health policies may affect people differently in distinct localities and irrespective of their origin (Napier et al. 2014).

In line with the above, the material presented here does not have an ethnic focus, however, the sample excluded non-migrants.

4.4 Introduction to the City Lab

Bochum, which is located in North Rhine Westphalia in Germany, is affected by a restructuring process that followed the collapse of the mining industry in the 1970s. In the early 21st century, major industrial enterprises were closed down, such as Opel in 2008 and Nokia in 2014. Bochum, a city with a 9% unemployment rate (Stadt Bochum 2018b) that ranked by trend and demography 27th out of 30 German cities (Nitt-Drießelmann, Wedemeier & Schüßler 2015), has undergone different phases of migration and is today characterized by a highly diverse urban structure. Among the first significant groups of migrants were Polish people, who came in the late 19th century as labour migrants. Further migrants from Southern Europe followed (1960–1970s), whereas in the 1990s, the migrant population predominantly consisted of asylum seekers. In 2015, the migrant rate reached 19%; the number of refugees rose to 4,962 and decreased to 2,588 in 2018 (Stadt Bochum 2018a).

Bochum Hustadt, where the City Lab is based, is a socio-economically marginalized part of the city. Official statistical data for Hustadt are not available but exist for Querenburg, the wider administrative district. Querenburg's population is considered as disproportionately disadvantaged, with a low average income and a high unemployment rate (8.9%) (Stadt Bochum 2017b). It belongs to the urban district with the highest index-value of health challenges (Stadt Bochum 2017a, p. 75), with 43.7% of the population being migrants and originating from at least 40 different countries. Hustadt was built in the 1960s for university employees and workers from the nearby Opel factory and experienced a major transformation when the majority of high income earners (university and Opel employees) removed from the area and people with low incomes moved in during the 1990s. Today, it is inhabited by approximately 4,000 people, with approximately 90% being migrants, and it has an estimated unemployment rate of approximately 50% (field notes Falge 2018).[3] Many people in Hustadt either depend on welfare or work two jobs with up to 18 daily working hours in mainly low-skill labour sectors facing physically challenging working conditions (see also Figgen, Evers & Van Loocke-Scholz 2012). Some have also established small businesses as mechanics, kiosk or supermarket owners. People reported various diseases resulting from their conditions of work, with disc prolapse being the most common. These conditions create a high level of physical and mental exhaustion among the mainly male residents, as explained to us by Ayse about her husband:

> My husband leaves at 8:00 and comes home at 9:00 pm. Sometimes he falls straight asleep. Though he is still young, he already is shagged out (Deutsch: 'kaputt'), suffering from backpain.
>
> (Ayse, 35 years)

Several migrants who live in Hustadt today grew up with their families under difficult conditions in nearby asylum seekers' homes before they entered the area. Nima, a young man who stayed for seven years in an asylum seekers' home before they were given a flat in Hustadt, sharing two rooms with his family of five, remembered as follows:

> The conditions in the asylum seekers' home were like in jail. Collective toilets, collective showers, bunk beds. [A]ll who were in that home turned criminals. Yes, they bred them [the criminals] there.
>
> (Nima, 27 years, male)[4]

In addition, people mentioned discrimination experiences in educational contexts, where they often received little support from teachers as well as from their parents due to their overall unfamiliarity with the German language and educational system. There are, however, also some young achievers in Hustadt, who, despite difficult conditions, are proceeding upward socially. Burhan, for instance, grew up in an asylum home but recently graduated from medical and social science school and is now working as a surgeon.

The City Lab was established in Hustadt in 2015 as a 12-year long-term health-related research location with the objective of health-related collaborative knowledge production that matters for people in Hustadt. Part of the City Lab's endeavour to create new relationships with the city was put into action by relocating university seminars to the site, which sensitizes students for their future work with local communities. Teaching occurs in a room[5] rented by the university in the neighbourhood. From within the theoretical framework established through course work, students conduct applied ethnographic fieldwork and develop health projects with residents on-site. Collaboration in the City Lab specifically refers to designing questionnaires together with community researchers, discussing research results with them and jointly following the aim to improve health conditions in Hustadt. This can take shape in the form of a project organized by students and university staff together with people from the neighbourhood. So far, the interventions have included information and counselling services for specific target groups regarding prevention and health promotion in the areas of cancer, nutrition, long-term care insurance, media consumption and exercise. The students set up or extend access facilities for families with members in need of health care and provide sport or exercise options on-site. Based on these first activities and as part of the collaborative approach, the City Lab, together with a local association with a focus on multicultural youth welfare service (Verein für multikulturelle Kinder- und Jugendhilfe – Migrationsarbeit, IFAK e. V.), applied and secured funding for a 4.5 year health-related project targeting on the design of culturally sensitive prevention offers.

4.5 Ongoing studies at the City Lab

The following section presents and synthesizes study results from three projects located in the City Lab: (1) an ongoing ethnographic case study of a recently migrated Syrian family, (2) a pilot Vulnerability Assessment for Refugees and

Migrants (RM-VA) and (3) student-led projects performed as part of academic papers. All studies were designed to identify barriers that would restrict participants' access to health care, to foster health and well-being and to identify the significance of culture in this context. In the case of the family ethnography, a specific element of collaboration was added, as the family had mandated a researcher (the author) to conduct a collaborative research project, hoping for advocacy to improve their disabled son's condition. The study results were discussed with the family and they agreed on its publication.

Here, specifically, the students' projects and the ethnographic study combined research with taking action, whereas the RM-VA served as a pilot study for future tools to improve migrants' access to health care.

4.5.1 The health ethnography of a family

The ongoing ethnographic study is based on weekly, three-day[6] field research visits to a family of five in the Hustadt that the author has been conducting since October 2016. To emphasize the methodological approach with the resultant deep immersion in the field, it is written from the first perspective. The ethnography sketched out here presents the family's attempts to gain better access to health care and therefore foster their health and well-being. The field is not limited to the family boundaries but rather includes its wider social network, the neighbourhood Hustadt as a whole, and methodically, this ethnography includes participation in the everyday private and public life of the family, such as in parental talks in kindergarten and visits to the doctor, to the authorities and to health care institutions. I immerse myself in the transnational social field of the family, take part in WhatsApp video chats with relatives in Syria, Holland and Wuppertal, spend time with the mother and other mothers watching their kids on the playground and accompany the daughter to the elementary school in the district, where I meet other mothers. At the end of the day, I write fieldnotes, which I analyse reflexively (Breidenstein et al. 2015).

The Mohammad family[7] fled to Germany from Syria in 2015. They have been recognized as entitled to asylum and are hence entitled to equal health care coverage as people who receive health benefits from the statutory health insurance agency[8] (§ 2 AsylbLG, § 48 SGB XII, § 27 ff SGB V). The parents, Lahing (35) and Leyla (35), have three children: Burhan (12), Hevidar (7) and Bilind (4). In 2011, their daughter Hamrin died from chronic renal insufficiency at the age of eight years. Bilind was also born with chronic renal insufficiency, and shortly after his arrival, he had an operation at a hospital in Hamburg in which a gastric tube (percutaneous endoscopic gastronomy [PEG]) was inserted. Since then, his medication and food have been administered via the PEG. He now has a chance to survive much longer; yet, at some point, he might need a kidney transplantation to survive.

At the beginning of my research, Bilind had no place in a kindergarten and spends eight hours every day with his smartphone or tablet or in front of the television. His motor, social and linguistic development is slightly delayed, his attention span is low, and he seemingly alternates between hyperactivity and lethargy. He often sleeps during the day and is awake through the afternoon until after midnight. Due to the time-consuming care situation, Leyla has hardly built any social relationships outside the family and does not like being in public spaces. She seems insecure when she is outside the apartment and suffers a small breakdown after a joint visit to the language café, where she becomes aware of her low language skills compared to other refugees.

The family gathers in the apartment late in the afternoon. When I get there in the evening, the father Lahing is often asleep on the sofa. Neither the television nor the children playing around him seem to disturb his seemingly comatose sleep. At first, I attribute these phases to 'depression', which could be possible consequences of a post-traumatic stress disorder. Only later, I am able to establish a connection to a combination of factors, one of which is the care for the son. This consists of seven PEG dispensations daily every five hours, three of them during the night, and an injection shortly before going to bed. Bilind receives the nightly PEG dispensations via a drip, and an alarm goes off if the tube kinks, which happens several times every hour. He has to be diapered three times at night because of the liquid he receives, which means that the parents' sleeping phases are less than two to three hours and then, interrupted by the drip alarms, diaper changes and Bilind calling for a drink of water. This care system paired with a constant worry for his son is added on top of his daily routine, such as his German class, household duties, school and kindergarten issues and most of all the humiliating and time-consuming interactions with the Job Centre and the Foreigners' Authority. As these institutions are not accessible by phone, Lahing has to go there for any minor issue, sometimes on a daily basis, which often results in long waiting hours in overcrowded, ill-equipped rooms (see also Weissköppel 2016).[9] In his opinion, he often receives contradictory information by apparently badly trained, overworked clerks whom he perceives as unfriendly and who seem unfamiliar with current refugee law and migrants' legal entitlements. This combination leads to chronic demoralization and exhaustion, especially for the father.

I found that the family lacks knowledge about important resources, legal rights and opportunities, and they lack power for constructing optimal health conditions, which indicates a lack of cultural aperture of the (local) health care system (Falge, Ruzza & Schmidtke 2012). Cultural aperture refers to structural transformations implemented by public institutions in order to account for cultural diversity.

In the process of my research, power hierarchies between me and the family were partly dismantled as my status changed from that of a stranger to a family member by being called 'sister' by the family father and 'aunt' by the children. The research did, however, also unveil hidden power hierarchies. For example, the family accepted the fact that a kindergarten refused to take Bilind because of his disability and did not apply for care benefits, although care was obviously needed. When I then first called *incognito* at a kindergarten in order to highlight the family's need for an inclusive kindergarten place, it was refused with the statement 'care for these [disabled] children would be too laborious'. Only during my second call as a university professor did I receive an appointment, and it was my professorial power which triggered a process where in the end the system provided for the child's needs. One and a half years after arriving in Germany, after appraisals had been initiated (care appraisal, presentation at the Social Paediatric Centre, Sozialpädiatrisches Zentrum [SPZ])[10] and following intensive discussions with the Job Centre, Social Services and the statutory health insurance, Bilind was given a place in an inclusive kindergarten at the recommendation of the SPZ. The health insurance's confirmation of cost coverage for outpatient dispensation (via the PEG tube insertion) by a children's care service at the kindergarten was received a further six months after application. This delay occurred because the statutory health insurance only covers nursing care benefits after two years of insurance, which the family had not yet arrived at. Another four months later, after numerous rejections from care providers who were contacted, a care provider agreed to take over Bilind's care service despite the low fee of 10,50 € per dispensation. Finally, with a ten-month delay after he was given a place in the kindergarten and 28 months after he had arrived in Germany, full advantage was taken of the time-consuming process. Bilind could stay at the kindergarten for the whole day, and Leyla could apply for a place in a German-language course. She waited a further six months for a place, and from November 2017 onwards, she learned German three times a week, three years after arriving in Germany. This was her first opportunity, after fleeing from war, to do something for her own personal development and to establish her own social network.

In addition to the abovementioned power hierarchies between me and the family, further power hierarchies came to the fore in the process of application for health care benefits (the acceptance of a care level) for which I had applied with the family. The insurance initially granted a lower care level, which included no financial support, following a 15-minute assessment in the family's home, to which we objected and that was followed by a second assessment that occurred in my presence and led to a higher care level with annual care support up to 6.192 €. Again, it was the power of a professor that improved access to health care entitlements.

After this award, the parents seemed vitalized, empowered and self-confident. All in all, the changes in circumstances stimulated the health condition of the entire family. Bilind now uses his smartphone only two hours daily, instead of eight, and his gross and fine motor skills are improving. His attention span is longer, and he is beginning to do puzzles and to speak German. Leyla is learning German with enthusiasm, is intensifying her social contacts, takes part in the weekly Women's Breakfast organized by the primary school in the district and invites a neighbour to her home. The additional financial support provided by the care benefits reduces the financial pressure on the family. In addition to his German course, Lahing is beginning to seek advice from the Job Centre about possible work and to plan his future in Germany. The two cases (care level acceptance and place in the kindergarten) illustrate existing power hierarchies between a professor and a refugee family with regard to access to health care.

4.5.2 Pilot vulnerability health assessment for refugees

Like the ethnographic study, the pilot vulnerability health assessment for refugees and migrants (RM-VA)[11] was designed to understand what factors create and contribute to existing health vulnerabilities in groups of migrants and refugees currently living in Hustadt. Understanding health vulnerabilities among those groups in a systematic fashion was meant to enable long-term strategy building that is culturally sensitive and effective. We decided to perform the health vulnerability assessments following a methodology initially developed by Napier (2014), as that approach offered a data and analysis protocol well suited to our needs in Hustadt.

Data for the pilot RM-VA were collected in Hustadt through a brief demographic survey, in-depth, semi-structured interviews conducted by trained fieldworkers, and a set of ethnographic observations recorded by the fieldworkers. Data were analysed both statistically and following the principles of thematic and content analysis, using the Nvivo software package (Nvivo Pro 11, QSR International 2016)[12] for coding and visual analyses of transcribed interview data. The RM-VA was supported by the advisory group Napier and Volkmann. It was conducted by a collaborative research team (hereafter called fieldworkers) consisting of two refugees, four students researchers and the author, who were trained by Napier and Volkmann at a two-day workshop at the Hustadt City Lab. After training, the fieldworkers spent two continuous weeks in the neighbourhood in order to access the field through participant observation. Subsequently, they spent six to eight hours weekly in the City Lab during teaching sessions relating to the RM-VA. Importantly, break times were spent outside the class room (facilitating student-resident interaction in the Hustadt campus), and lunch was taken in a local nongovernmental organization (HUKultur), where the collaborative group frequently met and exchanged information with residents. Interviews were conducted in the participants' homes during that time, that is, from October 2016 to January 2017. Fieldworkers worked alone and in teams of two: one refugee-researcher and one student-researcher each. Depending on the participant, the interviews were conducted in Kurdish, Arabic, English or German. The refugee-researcher then took the role of both fieldworker and interpreter where the interviews were in Arabic or Kurdish. A brief demographic survey questionnaire preceded the RM-VA interview. Survey questions were asked by the fieldworkers, and the responses were entered in a tick-box format on a printed paper version of the survey. The RM-VA interview was then performed in a manner that encouraged conversation around the various aspects of the RM-VA protocol. After the interview, the fieldworkers briefly noted their observations and summarized the main aspects of the interview in an executive summary. Thus, each interview produced the following for analysis: a table with the demographic data, a taped and transcribed interview, and comments and observations from the fieldworkers themselves. All interviews were translated and transcribed in German prior to analysis. Participants were recruited on-site by the fieldworkers well in advance of the data collection phase. The data were analysed by me with the support of the Advisory Group based on the principles of thematic and content analysis (TCA) (Joffe & Yardley 2004). Fieldworkers jointly developed codes from the interviews, and coding was performed by the whole collaborative team.

As can be observed from Table 4.1, 12 interviews were conducted among migrants and refugees of both genders (seven female and five male) from different countries and ethno-religious background—seven of these left their country of origin as adults, four as infants and one was born in Germany. Their average age was 37 years (17–62). Five were long-term migrants (over ten years outside the country), two were medium-term migrants (three to ten years outside the country), four were recent migrants (less than two years outside the country) and one was born in Germany. In regard to their health, out of 12 participants, 5 had significant chronic diseases and 5 an increased body mass index (BMI) with 2 being obese and 3 overweight. Seven smoked and nine did not engage in regular physical exercise. Nobody was diagnosed with high blood pressure. In the study design, we differentiated between vulnerability that interviewees described (i.e., stress) and vulnerability that we inferred (i.e., related to, e.g., lack of basic language skills, extreme financial pressure or chronic health conditions). None of the participants was diagnosed with mental health conditions; however, three described as suffering from mental health problems and six from stress. Two refugees living in refugee homes reported feeling isolated.

Although these results are not statistically significant, they are nevertheless striking in the context of this pilot study with respect to high biological and psychological vulnerability, as illustrated in Table 4.2.

Table 4.1 Results from the vulnerability assessment

Synonym	*Origin*	*Self-Identifies as*	*Age*	*Generation*	*Smoker*	*Chronical Disease DiDiseaeDidiseases*
Mahsun	Syria	Arabic/Muslim	28	1		x
Rizvan	Syria	Curdish/Muslim	38	1	x	
Berivan	Syria	Curdish/Muslim	44	2	x	x
Dilan	Germany	Curdish/Muslim	17	1		
Helin	Syria	Curdish/Muslim	56	1	x	
Pervin	Syria	Arabic/Muslim	48	1	x	
Israel	Nigeria	Igbo/Christian	33	1		
Fatma	Turkey	Curdish/Muslim	46	1	x	
Dilara	Turkey	Curdish/Muslim	42	1	x	x
Rezan	Syria	Curdish/Muslim	21	1		x
Can	Turkey	Turkish/Muslim	50	1		
Hatice	Turkey	Turkish/Muslim	62	1	x	x
Number	12	12		12	7	5

Note: The table shows absolute numbers, x means yes.

Table 4.2 Biological and physiological vulnerability

Biological vulnerability	*In numbers*	*Psychological vulnerability*	*In numbers*
Chronical diseases:	5 of 12	Diagnosed disorder	0 of 12
Increased BMI	5 of 12	Described symptoms	3 of 12
Smokers	7 of 12	Stress	6 of 12
Lack of exercise	9 of 12	Isolation	2 of 12

Note: Displayed are the absolute numbers.

From the TCA, we identified themes that revealed relevant information about peoples' access to health care. Some interviewees described health care provision in Germany as good, for example, 'if we go to the hospital they receive us in a good way and the whole situation is enjoyable' (Mahsum, male, 28 years), sometimes better than the health care provision in the country of origin. Language and communication were, however, frequently mentioned as a problem, because in the absence of free access to professional translation services in German hospitals, the responsibility to assure communication is often left to patients, and people from the community are not immediately available, as Rezan explained:

> If I feel unwell nobody just accompanies me [to the hospital], I have to pay 20 € for a translator. Only in case I die, somebody might help me. There is no Arabic doctor or translator and as much as I try with my German, I will not be able to accurately describe the pain. Nobody helps.
>
> (Rezan, male, 21 years)

Due to their unfamiliarity with the health care system, many respondents consult the hospital instead of a general practitioner (GP), as explained by Israel:

> One mainly visits the hospital. One does not know doctors and that is why one goes to the hospital. They are surprised if there is nothing huge, even if one knows nobody.
>
> (Israel, male, 33 years)

Here, migrants' unfamiliarity with the German health care system clashes with the hospitals' significant labour shortage of nurses and doctors, which affects health care personnel's empathy for migrants' coming to hospitals with 'nothing major'. This connects with the respondents' general dissatisfaction with the health care provision in Germany, as expressed by Hatice:

> Now the doctors do not care, the nurses also not ... They have no knowledge and no respect [...] You ask something, they don't answer. They never tell you anything if you don't ask [...] for instance they give you medicine, but don't tell you how to use it.
>
> (Hatice, female, 62 years)

Participants were dissatisfied with the little time allocated for verbal interaction and with the doctor-patient communication. In particular, refugees referred to the lack of information about health care benefits, and those benefits could only be accessed with struggle. Some migrants for instance lamented that doctors' health care interventions are often limited to prescribing painkillers and that examinations supplemented by (expensive) instrumental diagnostic procedures are often denied or conducted 'too late'. Dalal's mother, for instance, received Ibuprofen for severe stomach pain during monthly visits at a clinic over a period of one year until the doctor performed an ultrasonic examination. A huge gallstone discovered was immediately operated on (Dalal,[13] female, 19 years).

Similarly, Ahmad's brother was repeatedly sent home with a diagnosis of 'stomach upset' until the family changed the hospital, where instrumental diagnosis discovered a tumour:

> In the hospital in Bochum they did not recognize it first. They said that it's just nausea. He was always vomiting. They said that he had eaten something wrong... Then this got more and more frequent and he was vomiting again and again ... And then we went to another doctor... Then we went to Essen, there is a good children's clinic and they helped us there. [...] [T]hey realized that he had a tumour and then they operated [...] he has survived [...] but ... there are some damages, ... he is 'mentally disabled'....
>
> (Ahmad,[14] male, 21years)

In addition, all 12 interviewees from the RM-VA mentioned financial pressure as a barrier to health care. A cancer patient argued that he could not afford certain treatments that s/he was obliged to fund.

Confronted with a health care system that lacks intercultural aperture (Falge & Zimmermann 2014) or that excludes people with few financial resources, 10 out of 12 of our informants mentioned informal help and support from the community as a major facilitator to health care. The community would provide translation services during health consultations and in other institutions (field notes Falge 2018a). This is also underlined by Can:

> There are people here who help each other mutually. I always help by translating, if they have problems with their children at school, if they need to fill something somewhere, if a conversation needs to be held somewhere at a doctor.
>
> (Can, male, 50 years)

Interestingly, these informal help and support structures, hereafter defined as cosmopolitan sociabilities, were often cross-cutting ethnic ties, which our non-ethnic focus enabled us to see. Newcomers, for instance, would very often refer to their friends from other ethnic groups or origin countries as helping with translations. Leyla, who came from Syria in 2016, for instance, was almost fluent in German and had acquired her language skills from her Afghani neighbours.

Similar cross-ethnic cosmopolitan sociabilities were practiced by Fatma, who emphasized the following:

> I have many friends and if they don't speak German, I have to help them. [...] I need to help whether people come from Syria, Iraq or Iran – no problem, I help all of them.
>
> (Fatma, female, 46 years)

Though people would usually tolerate barriers and moments of exclusion or discrimination, some interviewees mentioned acts of resistance, such as Berivan, who cited the case of her brother's referral to a disability school against their parents' will and his readmission to a regular school upon the parents' juridical interventions (Berivan, female, 44, Syrian Kurd, first generation). Another example concerned a few Muslim women who were thrown out of a gym.

Whereas our interviewees clearly identified with Hustadt as their home and with a sense of belonging to the community on-site, our data also indicates that people share a perception of non-belonging to large parts of the German society beyond the Hustadt boundaries. Rizvan argues that ideally, Germans and migrants need to approach each other by taking a step towards one another. This however, is opposite to his experience:

> If you head one step towards a German he goes two steps backward. (laughter).
>
> (Rizvan, male, 38 years)

Hatice, when asked about her experiences of discrimination, responded as follows:

> Yes, of course. Especially as a Turk they don't accept us.
>
> (Hatice, female, 62 years)

Responding to our questions about cultural practices, most people emphasized that the Hustadt context enabled the performance of cultural practices, unlike places with smaller proportions of migrants:

> Hustadt – unlike Castrop Rauxel where I lived before - allows us to celebrate our traditional feasts.
>
> (Berivan, female, 44, Syrian Kurd, first generation)

Public celebrations such as the annual Nerwroz (Kurdish New Year) festival and the Sugar Feast (ending of Ramadan) create great joy and euphoria among the Hustadt community. During the sugar feast, children walk from house to house to receive sweets from people, and people invite each other to break the fast. These practices strengthen social cohesion and promote health and well-being across different ethnic and religious groups.

Beyond the different means of celebrating feasts or preparing food, cultural differences were not perceived by interviewees to play a major role in terms of barriers between them and the receiving society. Rather, the interviewees emphasized that as a result of migration, they felt alienated from their previous homeland culture:

> I don't know what I actually do differently, but I see myself to act differently as compared to my siblings in Syria.
>
> (Berivan, female, 44 years)

Older migrants from the first generation lamented the demise of cultural practices through rapid change, arguing that '80% of the people in Hustadt would not live according to the traditions' (Can, male, 50 years). In contrast, younger migrants of the second generation emphasized continuity with regard to their obligation to care for their parents.

These results show that some barriers to health care are migrant-specific such as the absence of professional translation services, the unfamiliarity with the health care system and certain informal dynamics of exclusion (see also Falge & Bradby 2018). It should be noted that, there are barriers that might equally apply to non-migrants such as the lack of information about health care benefits, the limitation of interventions to prescribing painkillers, the late conduct of expensive instrumental diagnostic procedures and financial pressure.

4.6 Summary of study results and beyond

The combined results from three years of intermittent ethnographic research by members of the City Lab Hustadt along with the family ethnography and the RM-VA indicate that culture is not perceived by research participants as a barrier to health care. Rather, the opposite is the case, as cosmopolitan sociability turns out to be an important resource by connecting people with the health care system. Hence, in a condition in which public funds are cut as a result of the demise of the welfare state, the community partially fills the gaps where service provision misses out. Whereas people emphasize the significance of sociabilities for health and well-being, financial pressure was mentioned most frequently as a constraint. Moreover, the overall results, and specifically the family ethnography, showed that the culture of the receiving institutions may negatively affect the health and well-being of migrants due to deficits in intercultural aperture. The culture of the German health care system and most of the other public institutions connected to it seem to face a deficiency in terms of a lack of outreach structures. This culture leads to an informal exclusion of all those people who are neither used to actively ask for their rights nor even know for which rights to ask. As a result they lack information about their basic entitlements to resources such as care insurance, child care rights and sometimes about family doctors. Many of the institutions our study participants tried to access seemed to be rather designed for a well-educated, financially secured middle-class milieu and its habit to actively consult health care. People with weaker financial and educational resources and less system familiarity may fall off the grid or need support through, for example, social workers or volunteers. As mentioned by our study participants, certain entitlements to health care may not be perceived as a right by them, but rather as a privilege that is either completely unknown or can only be accessed through struggle. However, this might be related to the specific locality we studied and might differ in other localities. In the City Lab, these issues and the barriers created by missing outreach structures and a lack of translation services featured prominently.

It was part of the collaborative research design to jointly work against inequalities. Hence, City Lab researchers contributed to the community's health literacy by offering them knowledge about legal entitlements and communication skills to claim health-related resources. In addition to the negative experiences during health care provisions with regard to discriminatory practices and denial of instrumental diagnostics, respondents reported about humiliating, time-consuming and islamophobic tendencies in the local institutional landscape. As previous studies have shown, such forms of open or hidden discrimination also negatively affect peoples' health and well-being (Krieger et al. 2011).

4.7 Conclusion

Through collaborative research projects, the City Lab Bochum has created a space for the establishment of new relationships between the university and the city. As actors within the City Lab we learnt that time and intensive exchanges and involvements in the field are necessary to create encounters at eye level. This approach made us aware of existing power hierarchies but sometimes those hierarchies also changed and hence enabled us to better listen to and better understand each other. By involving refugee and migrant researchers, we gained access to the community easily and understood certain local practices better. The concept of cosmopolitan sociability helped us to understand local diversity as a domain of shared humanity, which made us notice how people responded to inequality in health care by supporting each other as translators and by contributing to each other's well-being in the absence of formal support structures.

Moreover, this research enabled us to detect that health-related interventions for people living in precarious contexts should not be limited to the health care system but rather address a wider institutional landscape. Current discriminatory practices in the Job Centre and the foreign authorities should be addressed in health-related policymaking, as they directly affect peoples' health and well-being.

Changes induced in the context of the City Lab so far are limited to minor transformations and could only fill some gaps of a health care system that seems to informally exclude large parts of the society from full access to health care.

This work should not end here; rather, as indicated by our research results, it should proceed to enforce the following major structural transformations:

- Expanding the intercultural aperture of the German health care system through multilingual outreach services while increasing the number of migrants in public institutions;
- Granting all residents immediate access to full health care coverage;
- Developing tools for the inclusion of new migrants into health care services;
- Establishing a cooperative network between policy makers, health care and related social institutions to improve access to health care;
- Establishing new relations between universities and cities and engaging residents in health-related research and interventions.

Although migrant communities provide resources to increase the access to health care to foster health and well-being of each other, these resources have their own limitations and do not replace absent knowledge about entitlements, free access to professional translation or access to expensive diagnostic examinations. In further consequence, families are informally excluded from health care as the system does not provide appropriate means to inform people and support them in gaining access to their entitlements. Therefore, we need to pose the question: Are we dealing with a system that is apparently set up to deliberately exclude people? Whatever the answer may be, what we learned from this study is that equity in this health care system is not assured which leads us to the conclusion that the culture of this health care system as well as the culture of local health care provision needs to change.

Acknowledgements

I would like to express my warm thanks to Napier and Volkmann for their voluntary engagement in the RM-VA and for the interesting and cheerful exchanges we had in the City Lab and at their home. Again, I would also like to express my gratitude to Mahur Hesamiashrafi and Sophia Sümmermann for allowing me to use data from their Academic Works about the Hustadt community.

Notes

1 Similar claims are forwarded by anthropologists of migration who argue in favour of "de-migrantising" migration studies by no longer studying migrants "at the margins" but rather as part of society (Labor Migration 2014).
2 For an alternative approach, see, for instance, Dreissig's hospital ethnography (2015), which depicts the inherent power hierarchies inscribed in hospital hierarchies between nurses and medical doctors as barriers to health care.
3 As mentioned above, the statistical authorities of Bochum do not provide figures for this small-scale area. Therefore, we can only refer to fieldnotes here.
4 This interview was not part of the RM-VA, but held in the context of the academic paper of Mahur Hesamiashrafi. The interviewee belongs to the first generation of Iranian migrants.

5 This room, the so-called HULab was set up for all the universities in the region (Hustadt e. V. 2016).
6 The time I actually spend in the family is limited to evenings, nights and mornings as I am doing this after work at the university.
7 Anonymization procedures were followed by attaching all names used in this article with fictive synonyms.
8 Problems can arise when they want to access benefits of the long-term care insurances.
9 According to several lawyers contacted during the course of this study who regularly visit the Job Centre, 50% of the Job Centre decisions are incorrect (fieldnotes Falge 2018).
10 German: Sozialpädiatrisches Zentrum, SPZ.
11 The design of the RM-VA assessment was based on a longstanding assessment tool designed by Napier for vulnerable populations (VA) and by Volkmann and Napier for non-communicable disease vulnerability (RM-VA).
12 See QSR International (2018).
13 This interview was not part of the RM-VA, but held in the context of the author's ethnographic research.
14 This interview was not part of the RM-VA, but held in the context of the academic paper of S. Sümmermann. The interviewee belongs to the second generation of Iraqi migrants.

References

Banting, K., & Kymlicka, W. 2006, *Multiculturalism and the welfare state: recognition and redistribution in contemporary democracies*, Oxford University Press, Oxford.

Boidin, C., Cohen, J., & Grosfoguel, R. 2012, 'Introduction: from university to pluriversity: a decolonial approach to the present crisis of western universities', *Human Architecture*, vol. 10, no. 1, p. 2.

Borde, T. 2009, 'Migration und Gesundheitsförderung – Hard to reach? Neue Zugangswege für "schwer erreichbare" Gruppen erschließen', in Bundeszentrale für gesundheitliche Aufklärung (BZgA) (ed.), *Gesundheitsförderung konkret*, 12, Jahrgang, pp. 18–31.

Breidenstein, G., Hirschauer, S., Kalthoff, H., & Nieswand, B. (eds.) 2015, *Ethnografie: Die Praxis der Feldforschung*, UVK Verlagsgesellschaft, Konstanz.

Falge, C. (2018): Unpublished Fieldnotes.

Falge, C., & Zimmermann, G. 2014, 'Die Interkulturelle Öffnung im Gesundheitssystem: Ein kritischer Überblick', in E. Vanderheiden & C.H. Mayer (eds.), *Toolbox! Interkulturelle Öffnungsprozesse in Organisationen gestalten*, Vandenhoeck & Ruprecht, Göttingen, pp. 325–332.

Falge, C., & Bradby, H. 2018. *The power of a professor: Health Care Provision for deserving refugees in Germany*, Jul 25 2018, viewed October 4, 2018,
www.cost-ofliving.net/the-power-of-a-professor-health-care-provision-for-deserving-refugees-in-germany.

Farwick, A. 2009, *Segregation und Eingliederung: Zum Einfluss der räumlichen Konzentration von Zuwanderern auf den Eingliederungsprozess*, Verlag für Sozialwissenschaften, Wiesbaden.

Figgen, M., Evers, G., & Van Loocke-Scholz, A. 2012, *Belastung – Auswirkung – Bewältigung. Arbeitsbedingungen in NRW aus Sicht türkeistämmiger Beschäftigter. transfer 1,* Landesinstitut für Arbeitsschutz Nordrhein-Westfalen, Düsseldorf.

Glick Schiller, N., & Çağlar, A. 2016, 'Displacement, emplacement and migrant newcomers: rethinking urban sociabilities within multiscalar power', *Identities*, vol. 23, no. 1, pp. 17–34.

Glick Schiller, N., Çaglar, A., & Guldbrandsen, T.C. 2006, 'Beyond the ethnic lens: locality, globality, and born-again incorporation', *American Ethnologist*, vol. 33, no. 4, pp. 612–633.

Glick Schiller, N., Darieva, T., & Gruner-Domic, S. 2011, 'Defining cosmopolitan sociability in a transnational age: an introduction', *Ethnic and Racial Studies*, vol. 34, no. 3, pp. 399–418.

Grillo, R. 2010, 'British and others: from "race" to "faith"', in S. Vertovec & S. Wessendorf (eds.), *The multiculturalism backlash*, Routledge, London, pp. 60–81.

Hustadt, e.V. 2016, *Hulabor startet in der Bochumer Hustadt*, 19 October, viewed 14 July 2018, www.huisthu.de/hulabor-startet-in-der-bochumer-hustadt/.

Joffe, H., & Yardley, L. 2004, 'Content and thematic analysis', in D.F. Marks & L. Yardley (eds.), *Research methods for clinical and health psychology*, Sage, London, pp. 56–68.

Knipper, M., & Bilgin, Y. 2009, *Migration und Gesundheit*, Konrad-Adenauer-Stiftung e.V., Sankt Augustin/Berlin.

Krieger, N., Waterman, P.D., Kosheleva, A., Chen, J.T., Carney, D.R., Smith, K.W. et al. 2011, 'Exposing racial discrimination: implicit and explicit measures: the my body, my story study of 1005 US-born black and white community health center members', *PloS One*, vol. 6, no. 11, p. e27636.

Law, I. 2009, 'Racism, ethnicity, migration and social security', in J. Millar (ed.), *Understanding social security*, Policy Press, Bristol, p. 75.

Mbembe, J.A. 2016, 'Decolonizing the university: new directions', *Arts and Humanities in Higher Education*, vol. 15, no. 1, pp. 29–45.

Napier, D.A, Ancarno, C., Butler, B., Calabrese, J., Chater, A., Chatterjee, H. et al. 2014, 'Culture and health', *The Lancet*, vol. 384, no. 9954, pp. 1607–1639.

Napier-Moore, R. 2010, 'Research into action', *Alliance News. Principle and Practice, GAATW-IS Reflections on Feminist Participatory Action Research*, no. 34, pp. 26–29.

Niewöhner, J. 2014, 'Ökologien der Stadt: Zur Ethnografie bio-und geopolitischer Praxis' [Ecologies of the City: Ethnographies of Bio-and Geopolitical Practice], *Zeitschrift für Volkskunde*, vol. 110, no. 2, p. 185.

Nitt-Drießelmann, D., Wedemeier, J., & Schüßler, J. 2015, *HWWI/Berenberg-Städteranking 2015: Die 30 größten Städte Deutschlands im Vergleich*, Hamburgisches Welt-Wirtschafts-Institut, Berenberg Private Bankiers, Hamburg.

Park, E.R., & Burgess, E.W. 1925, 'The city: suggestions for investigation of human behavior in the urban environment', *American Journal of Sociology*, vol. 20, no. 5, pp. 577–612.

QSR International. 2018, *Helping you discover the rich insights from humanized data*, viewed 14 July 2018, www.qsrinternational.com/.

Rappaport, J. 2008, 'Beyond participant observation: collaborative ethnography as theoretical innovation', *Collaborative Anthropologies*, vol. 1, no. 1, pp. 1–31.

Razum, O., Karrasch, L., & Spallek, J. 2016, 'Migration', *Bundesgesundheitsblatt – Gesundheitsforschung – Gesundheitsschutz*, vol. 59, no. 2, pp. 259–265.

Razum, O., & Saß, A.C. 2015, *Migration und Gesundheit: Interkulturelle Öffnung bleibt eine Herausforderung*, Springer, Berlin.

Rogaly, B., & Qureshi, K. 2013, 'Diversity, urban space and the right to the provincial city', *Identities*, vol. 20, no. 4, pp. 423–437.

Sandbrook, R., Edelman, M., Heller, P., & Teichman, J. 2007, *Social democracy in the global periphery: origins, challenges, prospects*, Cambridge University Press, Cambridge.

Schiffauer, W. 1997, *Fremde in der Stadt*, Suhrkamp, Frankfurt.

Stadt Bochum. 2017a, *Basisgesundheitsbericht Bochum. Dezernat für Soziales, Jugend und Gesundheit,* Stadt Bochum, Bochum.

Stadt Bochum. 2017b, *Kleinräumiger Arbeitslosenquotient 2017 in den Bezirken in Bochum*, Statistik der Bundesagentur für Arbeit und Einwohnerstatistikdatei der Stadt Bochum, viewed 6 June 2018, www.bochum.de/C125708500379A31/vwContent ByKey/.

Stadt Bochum. 2018a, *Menschen. Flüchtlinge in Bochum. Aktuelle Zahlen. Stand: 4. Juni 2018*, viewed 13 April 2018, www.bochum.de/C125708500379A31/vwContent ByKey/W2A5A9RK432BOCMDE.

Stadt Bochum. 2018b, *Arbeitslose im Städte- und Regionenvergleich*, viewed 4 June 2018, www.bochum.de/C125708500379A31/vwContentByKey/W27CMHX3113BOLDDE.

Vertovec S. 2007, 'Super-diversity and its implications', *Ethnic and Racial Studies*, vol. 29, no. 6, pp. 1024–1054.

Vertovec, S. 2011, 'Migration and new diversities in global cities: comparatively conceiving, observing and visualizing diversification in urban public spaces', *MMG Working Paper* 11–08, Göttingen.

Vertovec, S., & Wessendorf, S. 2010, 'Introduction', in S. Vertovec & S. Wessendorf (eds.), *The multicultural backlash: European discourses, policies and practices*, Routledge, London, pp. 1–31.

Vickers, T., Craig, G., & Atkin, K. 2013, 'Addressing ethnicity in social care research', *Social Policy & Administration*, vol. 47, no. 3, pp. 310–326.

Wessendorf, S. 2013, 'Commonplace diversity and the "ethos of mixing": perceptions of difference in a London neighbourhood', *Identities. Global Studies in Culture and Power*, vol. 20, no. 4, pp. 407–422.

Part II

Migrants' access to health care

5 Migrants' right to health in international and European human rights law

Can it still unfold its integrative dynamic in an era of restrictive immigration policies?

Amrei Müller

5.1 Introduction

The protection of migrants' human rights, including migrants' human right to health, reveals the tension between human rights and citizens' rights. This tension is a fundamental feature of the current international legal order, including the human rights regime, and, as will be sketched out below, a feature so essential that it cannot and should not be abolished hastily. Rather, this tension should be made to work as a 'fruitful tension' (Besson 2012, p. 353) that gradually increases the rights of migrants[1] within their host countries, eventually offering them the possibility to obtain the whole range of citizens' rights including franchise, reflecting their integration into the social, economic, cultural and political life of the host community through permanent residency or even naturalisation. As shall be shown, the workings of this 'fruitful tension' can be observed in the interaction between international and domestic human rights law, including between domestic legislation, regional and international treaty provisions and jurisprudence relating to the right to health of migrants. On the other hand, migration policies adopted by (populist) politicians in recent years in many European countries – including Germany, the United Kingdom and at European Union (EU) level – threaten to undermine this productive tension. This leads to both the *de facto* barring of distinct categories of migrants from entering European states and the setting up of additional hurdles to the gradual integration of migrants who already are in the territories of European states into their host communities. The latter happens *inter alia* through policies that restrict migrants' access to health care and other essential public services.

This contribution will analyse how these tensions and processes play out in the protection of migrants' right to health in Europe, primarily in international and European human rights law,[2] but also occasionally in its interaction with domestic human rights law. To this end, first, further observations are added about the tension between citizens' rights and human rights, highlighting the underlying reasons for this tension that is firmly built into the international legal order, including international and European human rights law (Section 5.2).

In Section 5.3, the discussion moves to the more concrete questions about migrants' health rights that evolve within this tension. It examines the role that the right to health plays concerning the two main questions that are particularly important for the situation in which migrants find themselves: it inquires how the right to health influences migrants' possibilities to enter their host country (e.g. their right to seek asylum), and their protection against expulsion once they have entered their host country (Section 5.3.1). It then discusses migrants' health rights once they find themselves in their (European) host country (Section 5.3.2). Section 5.4 ends with brief concluding remarks.

5.2 The origins of the tension between citizens' rights and migrants' rights

In the contemporary legal order, 'securing'[3] human rights remains first and foremost a duty that states owe to individual rights-holders under their jurisdiction.[4] This bounded nature of human rights protection is explained by the fundamental interconnection between human rights, equality and democracy (political community) that permeates every regional and international human rights treaty,[5] and which is also protected by the public international law principle of political self-determination.[6] These interconnections indicate that human rights protection needs political communities whose members agree to guarantee each other's rights on the basis of equality; equality in political participation in turn being consolidated through human rights. This also implies that human rights shall be protected through democratic institutions. Only such institutions have the capacity to specify, consolidate and balance the obligations arising from the human rights of all members of a political community, and allocate them to executive and administrative, legislative or judicial authorities within the community to be discharged effectively (Besson 2015, pp. 251–253). Provisions in regional and international human rights treaties that require states to 'determine by law'[7] any limitations to, but also any proactive measures[8] required to implement abstract human rights norms in a particular domestic context, further confirm this. Domestic laws concretising, limiting and/or balancing human rights need to be adopted through domestic democratic processes, as has been reiterated by the European Court of Human Rights (ECtHR or the Court)[9] and can be implied from statements of the UN Committee on Economic, Social and Cultural Rights (CESCR or the Committee).[10]

Leaving aside the special case of the EU, so far, political communities and their democratic institutions remain national, and with it the primary protection of human rights. This, together with the open questions about the practical feasibility and normative desirability of human rights protection through *global* institutions, means that states will retain their rights to determine who is permitted to enter their territories, and who will become a member of their political community and benefit from the full protection of human rights as specified in domestic law (usually referred to as citizens' or sometimes residents' rights). This is further cemented by public international law principles of state sovereignty and territorial integrity;[11] as well as some provisions in regional and international human rights treaties which oblige state parties to secure certain rights for citizens only (in particular political rights and rights concerning residency)[12] and/or give more limited rights to non-citizen migrants than to citizens.[13] The latter also confirms that international and regional human rights law is not built on the assumption of full legal equality between citizens and non-citizens (Rubio-Marin 2014b, p. 6), recognising that citizens have 'a special relationship'[14] to their countries (political communities) which grants them a higher level of human rights protection within them.

This reality is challenged by the very phenomenon of migration and provisions in regional and international human rights treaties that test states' rights to control who enters[15] and remains[16] within their territories, by provisions that protect the human rights of 'everyone'[17] or 'all individuals'[18] under the jurisdiction of a particular state, regardless of citizenship, as well as by provisions and principles that arguably require states to adopt specific measures to protect the human rights of migrants.[19] These international and regional provisions reflect the universal vocation of human rights, which is equally enshrined in these treaties. It constantly pushes states to decrease the gap between citizens' rights and non-citizens' rights, by either providing extensive temporary protection for those who cannot avail themselves of the protection of their home political communities and state institutions,[20] and/or by demanding to gradually include more individuals into the political community through affording them permanent residency or naturalisation, the latter allowing full enjoyment also of political rights set out in Article 25 of the International Covenant on Civil and Political Rights (ICCPR).

It is against the background of these tensions[21] between the requirement to protect human rights (often concretised as citizens' or residents' rights in domestic law) on the basis of political equality through membership in political communities and thus through domestic democratic institutions within national borders on the one hand, and the universalist call of many regional and international human rights treaties on states to 'secure' the human rights of everyone on the other hand, that migrants' human rights to health are examined in the following. As will be shown, this necessary tension leads to a situation in which the scope of migrants' health rights can depend on the degree to which they are integrated into their host political community; and, relatedly, on the extent to which states can invoke the public interest to control immigration to limit migrants' health rights, including by expelling them to their home or third countries with less developed health systems. This situation is constantly challenged by the universalist vocation of particularly Article 12 of the International Covenant on Economic, Social and Cultural Rights (ICESCR), setting out everyone's right to the highest attainable standard of physical and mental health (the right to health).

5.3 Migrants' right to health in European and international human rights law

There are two main areas where the right to health of migrants set out in European and international human rights law plays an important role: first, in limiting the rights of states to decide which non-citizens enter and remain in their territories (or rather, are not expelled), and second in pushing states to grant non-citizens who find themselves under the jurisdiction of a particular state the same access to health facilities, goods and services as citizens. Both areas will be analysed in more detail in the following.

5.3.1 *Migrants' rights to enter and remain in their host countries and the right to health*

Due to the above-explained fundamental interconnection between human rights, democracy (political community) and equality that permeates international and regional human rights treaties, these treaties do not contain a human right to freedom of movement across national borders. Only nationals have rights to enter the territory of the state of which they are nationals and are protected against expulsion.[22] This leaves states with a broad discretion to decide on the admission of migrants and their expulsion. However, European and international human rights law as well as refugee law puts certain restrictions on this broad discretion. Some of these restrictions emerge from health rights, concerning both admission and expulsion.

Regarding admission, the right to health limits the admissibility of health grounds, based on which certain categories of migrants are excluded from entering a particular country, both migrants who wish to invoke their right to seek asylum[23] and migrants who wish to enter a state for other reasons. For example, the UN Special Rapporteur on the Right to Health (SRH) has criticised states' immigration policies that require migrants to undergo compulsory medical testing for conditions such as HIV, tuberculosis and pregnancy.[24] He noted that such restrictions, in particular concerning people living with HIV/AIDS, serve no useful public health purpose as they lead to stigmatisation and discrimination against these people, deterring them from utilising prevention and care facilities.[25] This is in violation of non-discrimination provisions[26] and the right to equal protection of the law as set out in Article 26 ICCPR. The latter, as an independent non-discrimination clause,[27] prohibits 'discrimination in law or in fact in *any* field regulated and protected by public authorities',[28] including immigration control. In addition, compulsory testing is inconsistent with the principle of informed consent, which is an important aspect of the right to health.[29]

The right to health also influences the protection against expulsion of migrants once they find themselves on the territory and under the jurisdiction of their host state, primarily by shaping the interpretation of the *non-refoulement* principle. Under this principle, deriving originally from Article 33 of the 1951 UN Refugee Convention, states are prohibited to expel or return a refugee 'to the frontiers or territories where his life or freedom would be threatened on account of his race, religion, nationality, membership of a particular social group or political opinion'.[30] Human rights law has expanded this principle to all categories of migrants, including those who reside in their host country illegally, obliging states to abstain from deporting or extraditing non-nationals facing a risk of serious violation of their human rights in the destination country.[31] In the European context, the ECtHR has developed the list of rights protected by the principle of *non-refoulement* consistently,[32] and has included some aspects of the right to health, albeit only 'very exceptional'[33] cases. In a 2016 Grand Chamber judgment on the question of whether health care needs can shield migrants from expulsion, the Court confirmed that this is the case only exceptionally where the removal of a migrant involves a risk of 'a serious, rapid and irreversible decline' in health 'resulting in intense suffering or to a significant reduction in life expectancy',[34] and therefore amounts to inhuman and degrading treatment contravening Article 3 ECHR.[35] Though somewhat lower than in earlier ECtHR judgments,[36] this still very high threshold means in practice that only seriously ill migrants are protected from expulsion under the ECHR.[37] The cautious approach[38] of the ECtHR is partly explained by the fact that the ECHR does not contain an explicit provision on the right to health, leaving it to rely on the prohibition of torture and ill-treatment to adjudicate health-related expulsion cases. To come within the scope of Article 3, any ill-treatment must 'attain a minimum level of severity'.[39] Moreover, domestic restrictive immigration policies, often combined with counter-terrorism rhetoric, constantly challenge any cautious expansion of the ECtHR's and UN human rights treaty bodies' jurisprudence on the non-*refoulement* principle. An example is the reaction to the ECtHR judgment *Othman (Abu Qatada) v. the United Kingdom*,[40] which led the United Kingdom government to threaten to leave the ECHR and the Council of Europe (Bates 2015, p. 3) – a threat that is only sporadically suspended because of the United Kingdom government's preoccupation with Brexit. However, though it has not decided on such a case so far,[41] the CESCR could potentially go further than the ECtHR when adjudicating a migrant's individual complaint about the risk of being subjected to violations of the right to health due to removal from her host state, and with it from access to adequate health care since the CESCR could directly rely on Article 12 ICESCR.[42] Still, for many migrants in European host states this avenue is closed because few European states have ratified the Optional Protocol to the ICESCR (OP-ICESCR) so far.[43]

The right to health has played a role in two additional areas relating to the expulsion or deportation of migrants. First, it has put limits to states' refusals to grant resident permits to migrants due to medical concerns, thereby contributing to providing migrants with increased residential stability. In *Kiyutin v. Russia*, the ECtHR decided that the refusal of the Russian government to grant a residence permit to an Uzbek national married to a Russian national on the grounds that he had tested positive for HIV amounted to discrimination on account of his health status, in breach of Article 14 ECHR, read in conjunction with Article 8 ECHR.[44] Second, to migrants who find themselves in detention awaiting deportation,[45] states must provide access to adequate physical and mental health care,[46] in a way similar as to all other detainees.[47] Moreover, the ECtHR, the HRC and the SRH have called on states to consider less restrictive, non-custodial alternatives to detention, in particular of migrants suffering ill health.[48]

5.3.2 *Migrants' health rights in their host country*

The foregoing section revealed that once migrants find themselves under the jurisdiction of a European state, they are not fully protected against expulsion by international and European human rights law, including the health rights contained therein. However, as will be shown in the following, the right to health, in particular the right to health set out in Article 12 ICESCR, pushes states to grant access to health care for all migrants that is equal to that of citizens as long as these migrants are under the jurisdiction of the state. This push for equal access can, in turn, promote migrants' social integration into their host communities, something that can also offer them greater residential stability and protection from expulsion in the long-term.[49] In addition, European and international human rights law urges states to adopt measures specifically aimed to ensure that migrants have access to adequate health care.

Based on the assumption of their temporary stay in their host country and their limited integration into the political community, there are human rights treaties which limit migrants' rights to access health care in their host countries. For example, Article 28 of the Convention on the Protection of the Rights of All Migrant Workers and Members of their Families (ICRMW)[50] contains only a limited right to health for this category of migrants.[51] It reads:

> Migrant workers and members of their families shall have the right to receive any medical care that is urgently required for the preservation of their life or the avoidance of irreparable harm to their health on the basis of equality of treatment with nationals of the State concerned. Such emergency medical care shall not be refused them by reason of any irregularity with regard to stay or employment.

Other treaties relevant to the European context, such as the European Social Charter (ESC)[52] and its revised version, the Revised European Social Charter (ESCRev)[53] limit their personal scope of application to nationals of contracting parties who are 'lawfully resident or working regularly'[54] within the territory of a contracting party. This limited personal scope of application pertains also to the health-related provisions in Articles 3, 11 and 13 of both the ESC and the ESCRev. Similarly, the health-related rights in the European Convention on the Legal Status of Migrant Workers[55] apply only on the basis of reciprocity, that is, only to lawfully resident migrant workers who are nationals of other contracting parties.[56] On a more general level, the International Convention on the Elimination of All Forms of Racial Discrimination (ICERD) also indicates that it does not apply to any 'distinctions, exclusions, restrictions or preferences made by a State Party ... between citizens and non-citizens'.[57] Though not containing an explicit provision on health rights, the UN Refugee Convention likewise grants the particular category of migrants it protects – refugees[58] – socio-economic rights[59] in a gradual manner: the scope of their rights depends on the 'level of attachment' with their host state (Hathaway 2005, pp. 154 ff.; Hathaway 2012, p. 191).

This narrow approach is challenged by international and regional treaties which, with the aforementioned few exceptions concerning political rights and the right to residential stability, proclaim that they set out the human rights of *everyone* who finds him- or herself under the jurisdiction of a state that has ratified the respective treaty.[60] Everyone includes nationals and non-nationals, and thus *all* migrants, no matter whether they are regular or irregular migrants.[61] These treaties thus constantly push states to grant migrants human rights that are equal to those of citizens, including those in regard to the enjoyment of the right to health. As shall be shown in the following, this push has constantly been reinforced by UN treaty bodies, UN Special Rapporteurs, the ECtHR and the European Committee on Social Rights (ECSR) interpreting and applying their respective international and regional human rights treaties in their interaction with national authorities.

On a general level, treaties and the bodies supervising their implementation emphasise that human rights law requires equal treatment of nationals and non-nationals. The ICCPR, ICESCR and ECHR prohibit discrimination on grounds of nationality or legal status.[62] In its General Comment 15 on the position of aliens under the ICCPR, the HRC stresses that 'each one of the rights of the Covenant must be guaranteed without discrimination between citizens and aliens',[63] and has issued several *Views* that confirm that Articles 2(1) and 26 ICCPR prohibit discrimination on the grounds of nationality.[64] The CESCR adds that socio-economic rights apply to everyone 'including non-nationals, such as refugees, asylum-seekers, stateless persons, migrant workers and victims of international trafficking, regardless of legal status and documentation',[65] and has noted in particular in regard to the right to health that states shall not deny or limit 'equal access for all persons, including … asylum seekers and illegal immigrants, to preventive, curative and palliative health services'.[66] The ECtHR has issued a number of judgments that reiterate the protection from discrimination on the grounds of nationality, including in the field of social security and access to health care.[67] Even the bodies supervising the implementation of the aforementioned treaties that limit their scope of application to non-nationals on the basis of reciprocity and/or to lawfully present non-nationals or offer non-nationals a considerably lower level of protection of the right to health, have adopted an expansive interpretation of their respective treaties. For example, the ECSR has held in complaints against the Netherlands, France and Belgium[68] that non-nationals in an irregular situation should be granted effective access to health care and housing to protect their 'most basic rights enshrined in the Charter'[69] despite the restriction on the personal scope of application found in the Appendixes to the ESC and the ESCRev. The UN Committee on Racial Discrimination (CERD) has noted that Article 2(1) ICERD allows states to draw only such distinctions between nationals and non-nationals that do not result in the limitation of non-nationals' rights set out in other human rights treaties, such as the ICCPR and the ICESCR, thus including the right to health in Article 12 ICESCR.[70] Similarly, the UN Committee on the Rights of Migrant Workers (CMW) stated, concerning the very restricted scope of the right to health in Article 28 ICRMW, that this provision should be interpreted in line with Article 12 ICESCR, creating broader obligations for states.[71] Interpreting their respective instruments in light of other international and regional human rights instruments,[72] these Committees thus work towards restricting states' possibilities for limiting the rights of non-nationals, including those in the area of health care. Nevertheless, neither is the prohibition of discrimination in European and international human rights law absolute, nor is the scope of the right to health under Article 12 ICESCR unlimited which states have to secure to everyone under their jurisdiction. Further light shall be shed on these limitations, taking account also of some aspects of European immigration policies in the area of health care.

The CESCR has pointed out that differential treatment on the basis of nationality (or other prohibited ground) can only be justified if the criteria for such treatment are 'reasonable and objective', that is if their aim is legitimate under the ICESCR and if there is a 'clear and reasonable relationship of proportionality between the aim sought to be realised and the [differentiating] measures or omissions and their effects'.[73] With this, the CESCR largely echoes the doctrine of the HRC[74] and the ECtHR.[75] In line with Article 4 ICESCR, a legitimate aim under the ICESCR is 'the promotion of general welfare in a democratic society'.[76]

Under these Article 4 criteria, excluding non-nationals or certain categories of non-nationals from any access to health care, or granting them access to emergency care only, seems, if at all, very difficult to justify.[77] For example, European states have argued that limiting non-nationals' access to health care is necessary to protect limited public resources (e.g. Trummer & Krasnik 2017, p. 590), and thus arguably 'promotes general welfare'. The CESCR has, however, clearly expressed that differential treatment 'on the basis of a lack of available resources is not an objective and reasonable justification' *per se*,[78] a statement strengthened by the Committee's constant reiteration that the obligation of non-discrimination under the ICESCR is an immediate duty[79] that is not subject to 'progressive realisation' utilising 'maximum available resources'.[80] The Committee's pronouncements also indicate that when allocating limited resources and setting priorities in health care, states should pay particular attention to the needs of 'marginalised and vulnerable groups'.[81] Migrants often count as such.[82] Moreover, it is highly questionable whether limiting certain migrants' right to health to emergency care protects public resources and thus 'general welfare'. A study by the EU Fundamental Rights Agency (FRA) indicates that the costs of urgent interventions can be much higher than giving all migrants access to preventive and curative health services.[83] 'General welfare' can also be undermined by the increasing public health risks for the population at large that excluding migrants from health services can bring about.[84]

Some European states restrict migrants' access to health care with the aim to deter migrants travelling to Europe in the first place and to create an unpleasant (in the case of the UK even 'hostile'[85]) environment for irregular migrants who are already present in European states that 'incentivises them to "self-deport"'.[86] They regularly seek to justify this with reference to their rights to control immigration.[87] Even if one is ready to accept the doubtful assumption that such policies of differential treatment actually deter migrants and thus could promote 'general welfare',[88] they would hardly pass the proportionality test: it is highly questionable whether the severe effects that granting migrants access solely to emergency health care is likely to have on these migrants' well-being[89] as well as the wider effects of such policies[90] can be described as proportionate to the immigration control aims sought by these measures. Against this background, the policies of numerous European countries that curtail migrants' health-related rights[91] can hardly be described as being in line with the non-discrimination and equality provisions of European and international human rights treaties (Biswas et al. 2012, p. 56; Flegar, Dalli & Toebes 2016, p. 18), something that has also been confirmed by the CESCR in its concluding observations on the United Kingdom and German state reports of 2016 and 2011 respectively.[92]

Beyond the issue of non-discrimination, questions can be asked about the *actual scope* of health care facilities, goods and services to which migrants who find themselves under the jurisdiction of a state party to the ICESCR should have access to on an equal basis with nationals under Article 12 ICESCR, and whether state parties shall take specific measures that facilitate migrants' access to health care. As indicated, the rights set out in the ICESCR are subject to 'progressive realisation' in accordance with 'maximum available resources'.[93] This implies that the scope of the right to health that individuals under the jurisdiction of a particular state can enjoy will vary in light of the resources this state has at its command, as will the scope of corresponding state obligations. To avert the danger of states depriving the obligation to progressively realise socio-economic rights of 'all meaningful content'[94] by continually pointing to the alleged lack of resources and to give the notion of 'progressive realisation' a clearer direction, the Committee adopted the minimum core approach (Müller 2017). Under this approach, the CESCR defines 'minimum essential levels of each of the rights'[95] set out in ICESCR that states must ensure as a matter of highest priority.[96] In relation to the right to health, the CESCR's definition of its minimum core content has been criticised for its vagueness and impracticability (Forman et al. 2016; Tobin 2012, pp. 243–251), and questions remain concerning the most appropriate underlying axioms – be they values, needs or interests – on which to base the minimum core content of socio-economic rights (e.g. Young 2008). However, recognising the potential of the approach to bring a certain degree of clarity to the concept of 'progressive realisation' if the internationally (abstract) minimum core is duly concretised and operationalised at the domestic level, including as a 'springboard for further action' (van Bueren 1999, p. 95) to implement non-core rights; and distilling an emerging consensus from pronouncements of the Committee, other international instruments and national law and jurisprudence, it can be argued that the right to access essential health goods and services (that is, access to primary health care) forms the minimum core content of the right to health.[97] Leaving aside the so-called 'underlying determinants of health',[98] the following health goods and services make up the internationally defined minimum core content of the right to health:

- Access to reproductive, maternal and child health care;
- Access to immunisation against the major infectious diseases occurring in the community;
- Access to services for the prevention, treatment and control of most prevalent epidemic and endemic diseases;
- Access to essential drugs, as from time to time defined under the WHO Action Programme on Essential Drugs; and
- Access to education and information concerning the main health problems in the community, including methods of preventing and controlling them (Müller 2017, p. 70).

All states are obliged to implement the minimum core right to health and other minimum core socio-economic rights immediately,[99] reflecting first and foremost the underlying urgent human interest to survive (Bilchitz 2007, pp. 222 ff.). This sits with the assumption that the minimum core right to health and other minimum core rights constitute absolute minimum thresholds of rights, ensuring that no limitations are placed on rights that extinguish them entirely (Müller 2017, pp. 72–75). This also implies that the implementation of the minimum core right to health is affordable for every country, if need be with the international assistance.[100] Thus, at the very least, migrants should have access to essential health goods and services in their host states, on an equal basis with nationals.

Beyond their immediate obligations to implement the minimum core right to health, states have non-core obligations to take 'deliberate, concrete and targeted steps'[101] to progressively secure more far-reaching (non-core) aspects of the right to health, utilising maximum available resources. This implies developing a national health policy for the building of a comprehensive health system that gives everyone physical and economic[102] access to scientifically and medically appropriate preventive, curative and palliative health services of good quality.[103] The exact priorities, shape and scope of these health policies and national law directing it depend on the circumstances within a particular country, including the varying environmental, cultural and socio-economic factors that influence the health of the population. Given the relative wealth of European states like the United Kingdom and Germany, health goods and services that are to be made available to the population will go considerably beyond what is required by the minimum core right to health. Migrants should benefit from health policies and access good and services on an equal footing with nationals.

In addition, and as mentioned above, when it comes to adopting all 'appropriate legislative, administrative, budgetary, judicial, promotional and other measures' towards the full realisation of core and non-core aspects of the right to health, the CESCR has repeatedly emphasised that states shall pay particular attention to the health needs of vulnerable and marginalised members of society,[104] among them migrants. This, together with states' obligations to 'attenuate or suppress conditions that perpetuate discrimination'[105] against certain groups, indicates that states shall adopt *special measures* to ensure that migrants do indeed gain equal access to health care in their host states. The Committee has, for example, observed that migrants often face specific obstacles in accessing health care, among them lack of documentation required as well as language and cultural barriers.[106] Irregular migrants in particular are frequently hindered by their fear of being detained for deportation, a fear that increases significantly in states that link access to health care with immigration control by obliging some or all health care providers to report irregular migrants to immigration authorities.[107] Among the latter states are Germany[108] and the United Kingdom.[109] States need to address these challenges by adopting appropriate measures, for example, by providing linguistically appropriate health services, including through interpreters and health information and education in languages commonly understood by migrants;[110] and by erecting a 'strict wall ... between health-care personnel and law [immigration] enforcement authorities'.[111]

Moreover, migrants may have particular health needs, either due to the reasons for their migration or flight, or due to the work they frequently engage in in their host states. Migration in general, and flight from persecution, armed conflict or other situations of violence in particular, are stressful experiences that can have an impact on the mental health of migrants. The right to health includes a right to non-discriminatory access to quality psychosocial and mental health services[112] through which states should provide services tailored to the specific mental health needs of migrants.[113] Concerning occupational health rights of migrant workers, the SRH has emphasised that states should 'ensure that occupational health laws and policies address the unique vulnerabilities of migrant workers in dirty, dangerous and degrading (3D) industries and are implemented, monitored and enforced'.[114] This includes the areas of construction, agricultural, domestic and sex work,[115] and the CESCR has called in particular on United Kingdom authorities to reinforce their efforts to protect migrant workers from abuse and exploitation at work.[116] Cases decided by the ECtHR show that non-implementation of these duties can also lead to findings of violations of Article 4 ECHR – the prohibition of slavery, servitude and forced or compulsory labour.[117]

Last but not least, the discussion shall return to the 'fruitful tension' between international and European human rights law's universal vocation and citizens' rights, a tension that pushes for the gradual integration of migrants into their host societies, and that can eventually lead to them obtaining residential stability through permanent residency and/or citizenship through naturalisation. The latter will offer full equality in the enjoyment of human rights, including political participation rights. Granting migrants full access to health facilities, goods and services as required under Articles 12 and 2(2) ICESCR can contribute to this gradual integration. Enjoying the right to health and other socio-economic rights that give access to education, work, housing and private and family life have been described as '*preconditions* for, or *vessels* of, the integration of migrants' into their host communities (Rubio-Marin 2014a, p. 90, emphasis in original; Kälin 2003, p. 279). Indeed, the ECtHR's jurisprudence on expulsion reveals that the 'solidity of *social, cultural and family* ties'[118] that non-nationals have developed with their host country over a longer period of time can, together with other factors,[119] shield them from deportation.[120] This reinforces the push of international and European human rights law to gradually integrate everyone into the political community by whose decisions they are affected, and on the making of which they should consequently have an influence on the basis of political equality, granted through political participation rights. Denying or severely restricting migrants' access to socio-economic rights including the right to health as is promoted by current national and some EU-wide immigration policies will hinder this integration process and can therefore amount to disintegrative 'integration' policies detached from citizenship or permanent residency policies, undermining migrants' prospects to gradually gain full membership in their new political communities (Rubio-Marin 2014, p. 75).

5.4 Concluding remarks

This chapter examined the scope and content of migrants' right to health in European and international human rights law, a scope and content that shall be equal to that of the right to health of citizens. Equal access is, however, widely undermined by restrictive immigration policies that many European countries, including the United Kingdom and Germany, have adopted in recent years. This leads not only to deteriorating health situations of the affected migrants – something that can have devastating consequences for individual migrants – but can also entrench origin-based divisions running through European societies. In conclusion, this chapter joins other studies on the human right to health of migrants in calling on European states to extend access to quality preventive, curative and palliative health care to all migrants regardless of their status. This will allow European and international human rights law and its universalist calling to deploy its integrative dynamic on domestic human rights law, ensuring the continued functioning of inclusive democratic societies in Europe in an era where migration flows are only to increase.

Notes

1 Note that this piece covers the right to health of all regular and irregular migrants, among them refugees, asylum seekers, migrant workers and victims of trafficking.
2 This focus is explained by the European focus of this book. Regional developments in the Inter-American and African human rights protection systems will not be analysed.
3 Art.1 ECHR.
4 Almost all human rights treaties contain jurisdiction clauses, e.g. Art.1 ECHR and Art.2(1) ICCPR. The CESCR has confirmed that the rights set out in the ICESCR also arise out of jurisdictional links between individual rights-holders and states,

see e.g. CESCR, General Comment 4 – The Right to Adequate Housing, (1991) contained in UN Doc HRI/GEN/1/Rev.1, 29 July 1994, pp. 53–59, para.13; and General Comment 19 – The Right to Social Security, UN Doc E/C.12/GC/19, 4 February 2008, para.75. This has been confirmed and codified in Art.2 of the Optional Protocol to the ICESCR (OP-ICESCR).

5 See provisions on democracy/democratic societies in European and international human rights treaties: Arts.8(2)-11(2) ECHR; Arts.14(1), 21 and 22(2) ICCPR; Arts.4(1) and 8(1)(a) and (c) ICESCR; and on non-discrimination/equality: Art.14 ECHR, Arts.2(1) and 26 ICCPR; Art.2(2) ICESCR.

6 Art.1(2) UN Charter, Art.1 ICCPR and Art.1 ICESCR.

7 Among them Arts.2(1), 5(1), 8(2)-11(2) ECHR; Arts.2(2), 6(1), 9(1), 11(3), 14(1) and 17(2) ICCPR; Arts.4 and 8(1)(a), (c) and (d) ICESCR.

8 See e.g. ECtHR, *K.U. v. Finland*, Judgment (Chamber), Appl.No.2872/02, 2 December 2008, para.49; and *Storck v. Germany*, Judgment (Chamber), Appl. No.61603/00, 16 June 2005, para.101, with further references.

9 See e.g. *Barthold v. Germany*, Judgment (Chamber), Appl.No.8734/97, 25 March 1985, para.46; and *Coëme and Others v. Belgium*, Judgment (Chamber), Appl. Nos.32492/96 et al., 22 June 2000, paras.98–99 and Frowein and Peukert (2009, p. 279).

10 CESCR, General Comment 3 – The Nature of State's Obligations (1990), contained in UN Doc HRI/GEN/1/Rev.1, pp. 48–52, para.8; CESCR, General Comment 19, n.4, para.63.

11 Arts.2(1) and 2(4) UN Charter.

12 Art.3 P-I ECHR (referring to 'the people', implying citizens) and Art.25 ICCPR (political participation rights); Art.3 P-4 ECHR and Art.12(4) ICCPR (rights to enter and not be expelled). See also Weissbrodt and Divine (2012, p. 157) and, concerning relevant ECtHR jurisprudence on the right to vote, Harris et al. (2014, p. 926).

13 E.g. Art.28 ICRMW.

14 See e.g. HRC, General Comment 27 – Freedom of Movement, UN Doc CCPR/C/21/Rev.1/Add.9, 1 November 1999, para.19; and Da Lomba (2014, 345), observing that international human rights law assumes that individuals enjoy 'some degree of membership in the nation-state'.

15 E.g. the right to seek asylum (Art.14(2) UDHR).

16 E.g. the right to non-*refoulement* (see nn.31 and 32); prohibition of collective expulsion of aliens (Art.4 P-4 to the ECHR).

17 See e.g. Art.1 ECHR; Arts.6, 7, 8(1)(a), 9, 11(1) and (2) and 12(1) ICESCR; Art.9(1) and 14 and ICCPR.

18 See e.g. Art.2(1) ICCPR.

19 See pp. 88–89 below.

20 The UN Refugee Convention of 1951 provides such surrogate (though selective) protection to refugees who are excluded from their home political communities that fail to recognise their political equality by denying them the most basic human rights. (See also Chetail 2014, pp. 23–25).

21 This tension has also been described by Benhabib (2004, p. 19).

22 See e.g. Art.3 P-4 ECHR; Art.12(4) ICCPR; Art.13 UDHR.

23 Art.14 UDHR.

24 Report of the UN Special Rapporteur on the Right of Everyone to the Enjoyment of the Highest Attainable Standard of Physical and Mental Health, Anand Grover, UN Doc A/HRC/23/41, 15 May 2013, paras.29–33 (with further references on the details of these immigration policies); and Perruchoud (2012, p. 132).

25 Report of the SRH, n.24, para.30. See also CESCR, General Comment 20 – Non-discrimination in Economic, Social and Cultural Rights, UN Doc E/C.12/

GC/20, 2 July 2009, para.33; and OHCHR/UNAIDS, "International Guidelines on HIV/AIDS and Human Rights, 2006 Consolidated Version", 2006, paras.126–127 and 131 (available at: http://data.unaids.org/Publications/IRC-pub07/JC1252-InternGuidelines_en.pdf).

26 Art.2(1) ICESCR; Art.2(1) ICCPR; Art.14 ECHR; Art.E ESCRev. More on non-discrimination below in Section 5.3.2.

27 Unlike Art.2(1) ICCPR, Art.2(2) ICESCR and Art.14 ECHR, Art.26 ICCPR is a general non-discrimination clause that can be invoked independently of any other substantive guarantee in the ICCPR. See also HRC, General Comment 18 – Non-discrimination (1989) contained in UN Doc HRI/GEN/1/Rev.1, 29 July 1994, pp. 26–28, para.12; and the analysis by de Schutter (2010, pp. 562–571).

28 HRC, General Comment 18, ibid., para.12 (emphasis added).

29 Report of the SRH, n.24, para.31; and Report of the SRH on the Right to Health and Informed Consent, UN Doc A/64/272, 10 August 2009.

30 Art.33 UN Refugee Convention, 1951.

31 See e.g. Art.3 of the Convention against Torture (CAT) and Art.16 of the UN Convention for the Protection of All Persons from Enforced Disappearances. The ECHR and ICCPR have been construed by the ECtHR and HRC to prohibit *refoulement*, see e.g. ECtHR, *Soering v. UK*, Judgment (Plenary), Appl.No.14038/88, 7 July 1989, paras.87–88; HRC, General Comment 20 – Prohibition of Torture (1992), contained in UN Doc HRI/GEN/1/Rev.1, 29 July 1994, pp. 30–33, para.9, and General Comment 31 – The Nature of the General Legal Obligation Imposed on States Parties to the Covenant, UN Doc CCPR/C/21/Rev.1/Add.13, 26 May 2004, para.12.

32 The ECtHR has applied the non-*refoulement* principle to numerous situations involving the risk of torture and inhuman or degrading treatment or punishment, violations of the right to life (death penalty), flagrant violations of the right to a fair trial, arbitrary detention and violations of the right to private and family life and freedom of religion. For details see Ktistakis (2013, pp. 79–96); den Heijer (2008).

33 *N. v. UK*, Judgment (Grand Chamber), Appl.No.26565, 27 May 2008, para.42.

34 *Paposhvili v. Belgium*, Judgment (Grand Chamber), Appl.No.41738/10, 13 December 2016, para.183.

35 For similar findings, see *D. v. UK*, Judgment (Chamber), Appl.No.30240/96, 2 May 1997, paras.52–54; and *Aswat v. UK*, Judgment (Chamber), Appl.No.17299/12, 16 April 2013, para.57.

36 In these cases, the Court put the threshold so high that only migrants who were very close to death were protected from expulsion on health reasons, see e.g. *N. v. UK*, n.33, para.42; *Bensaid v. UK*, Judgment (Chamber), Appl.No.44599/98, 6 February 2001, para.40; and *AS v. Switzerland*, Judgment (Chamber), Appl. No.39350/13, 30 June 2015, paras.31 and 37.

37 For a detailed analysis of *Paposhvili v. Belgium,* see Stoyanova (2017).

38 For a critical analysis, see e.g. Greenman (2015), Mantouvalou (2009). Note, however, that these pieces do not yet take account of the judgment *Paposhvili v. Belgium,* in which the ECtHR finally rejected to balance the physical integrity of the migrant against the economic interests of the expelling state. This takes account of the fact that the prohibition of torture and inhuman or degrading treatment in Art.3 ECHR is absolute.

39 See e.g. ECtHR, *Saadi v. Italy*, Judgment (Grand Chamber), Appl.No.37201/06, 28 February 2008, para.134.

40 ECtHR, *Othman (Abu Qatada) v. United Kingdom*, Judgment (Chamber), Appl. No.8139/09, 17 January 2009.

41 The CESCR can receive individual complaints under the OP-ICESCR since May 2013.

42 However, in such cases, it is likely that the CESCR would still balance a migrant's right to health against the host state's public interest to control immigration in line with Art.4 ICESCR, a balancing exercise similar to those that the ECtHR performs in expulsion cases involving Art.8 ECHR (e.g. *Boultif v. Switzerland*, Judgment (Chamber), Appl.No.54273/00, 2 August 2001, para.48).
43 As of May 2018, of the European states, only Belgium, Finland, France, Italy, Luxembourg, Portugal, Slovakia and Spain have ratified the OP-ICESCR (see: http://indicators.ohchr.org, accessed 27 May 2018).
44 *Kiyutin v. Russia*, Judgment (Chamber), Appl.No.2700/10, 10 March 2011, para.74.
45 Art.5(1)(f) ECHR and Art.9 ICCPR allow for such detention. Concerning the interpretation of Art.9 ICCPR in that regard, see HRC, General Comment 35 – Liberty and Security of Person, UN Doc CCPR/C/GC/35, 15 December 2014, para.18.
46 HRC, *Shafiq v. Australia*, Communication No 1324/2004, UN Doc CCPR/C/88/D/1324/2004, 31 October 2006, para.7.3; *C. v. Australia*, Communication No 900/1999, UN Doc CCPR/C/76/D/900/1999, 28 October 2002, paras.8.2 and 8.4; ECtHR, *A. A. v Greece*, Judgment (Chamber), Appl.No.12186/08, 22 July 2010, para.65; and Report of the SRH, n.24, paras.34–36 with further references.
47 See CESCR, General Comment 14 – The Right to Health, UN Doc E/C.12/2000/4, 11 August 2000, para.34; and numerous judgments of the ECtHR, e.g. *Holomiov v. Moldova*, Judgment (Chamber), Appl.No.30649/05, 7 November 2006, paras.121–122 (violation of Art.3); and *Tarariyeva v. Russia*, Judgment (Chamber), Appl.No.4353/03, 14 December 2006, paras.88–89, 111 and 117 (violations of Arts.2 and 3).
48 See *Yok-Ekale Mwanje v. Belgium*, Judgment (Chamber), Appl.No.10486/10, 20 December 2011, paras.124–125 (finding a violation of Art.5(1)(f) ECHR because the authorities had not considered a less drastic measure to detention of the seriously ill applicant).
49 See in this regard the developments in ECtHR jurisprudence concerning Art.8 rights of settled migrants analysed by Thym (2014).
50 Convention on the Protection of the Rights of All Migrant Workers and Members of their Families (ICRMW), 1990.
51 Art.2(1) ICRMW defines 'migrant workers' as any 'person who is to be engaged, is engaged or has been engaged in a remunerated activity in a state of which he or she is not a national'. The rights listed in part III of the ICRMW apply to all migrant workers, including undocumented/irregular migrants; whereas the rights listed in part IV apply only to migrants in a regular situation.
52 European Social Charter (ESC), opened for signature 18 October 1961, CETS No 35 (entered into force 26 February 1965).
53 Revised European Social Charter (ESCRev), opened for signature 3 May 1996, CETS No 163 (entered into force 1 July 1999).
54 Paragraph 1 of the Appendix to the ESC; and paragraph 1 of the Appendix to the ESCRev. The Appendixes form an integral part of the ESC and the ESCRev respectively.
55 European Convention on the Legal Status of Migrant Workers, opened for signature 24 November 1977, ETS No 93, entered into force 1 May 1983. Arts.19 and 20 of the Convention contain health-related rights (rights to social and medical assistance and rights concerning the prevention of industrial accidents and occupational diseases).
56 Art.1(1) European Convention on the Legal Status of Migrant Workers, ETS No 93, entered into force 1 May 1983.
57 Art.1(2) ICERD.

58 Refugee status is defined in Art.1(A)(2) of the 1951 Refugee Convention, read in conjunction with the 1967 Protocol relating to the Status of Refugees.
59 However, the Refugee Convention is not a human rights treaty and the entitlements of refugees are not generally formulated as refugee rights. Rather, the Convention spells out state obligations in some detail. See also Chetail (2014, pp. 39–40).
60 See nn.17 and 18.
61 CESCR, Statement on Duties of States towards Refugees and Migrants under the International Covenant on Economic, Social and Cultural Rights, UN Doc E/C.12/2017/1, 13 March 2017, para.6. An exception is Art.12 ICCPR granting the right to liberty of movement and freedom to choose one's residence only to those aliens who are 'lawfully within the territory of a State'.
62 Whilst Art.2(1) and 26 ICCPR, Art.2(2) ICESCR and Art.14 ECHR do not explicitly include the nationality or legal status of people as prohibited grounds for discrimination, this gap has been closed by the HRC's, CESCR's and ECtHR's interpretation of the phrase 'other status' in Art.2(1) ICCPR, Art.2(2) ICESCR and Art.14 ECHR respectively. See nn.64, 65 and 67.
63 HRC, General Comment 15 – The Position of Aliens under the Covenant (1986), contained in UN Doc HRI/GEN/1/Rev.1, 29 July 1994, pp. 18–21, para.2.
64 E.g. HRC, *Ibrahim Gueye et al. v. France*, Communication No.196/1985, UN Doc CCPR/C/35/D/196/1985, 3 April 1989, paras.9.4 and 9.4; and *Karakurt v. Austria*, Communication No.965/2000, UN Doc CCPR/C/74/D/965/2000, 4 April 2002, paras.8.4–9.
65 CESCR, General Comment 20, n.25, para.30; and CESCR, Statement on Refugees and Migrants, n.61, para.11.
66 CESCR, General Comment 14, n.47, para.34; and CESCR, Statement on Refugees and Migrants, n.61, para.12.
67 See e.g. *Gaygusuz v. Austria*, Judgment (Chamber), Appl.No.17371/90, 16 September 1996, paras.46–51; *Koua Poirrez v. France*, Judgment (Chamber), Appl. No.40892/98, 30 September 2003, para.46; *Andrejeva v. Latvia*, Judgment (Grand Chamber), Appl.No.55707/00, 18 February 2009, paras.91–92.
68 E.g. *International Federation of Human Rights Leagues (FIDH) v. France*, Complaint No.14/2003, decision on the merits of 8 September 2004; *Defence of Children International (DCI) v. the Netherlands*, Complaint No.47/2008, decision on the merits of 20 October 2009; *Defence for Children International (DCI) v. Belgium*, Complaint No.69/2012, decision on the merits of 23 October 2012; and *European Federation of National Organisations working with the Homeless (FEANTSA) v. the Netherlands*, Complaint No.86/2012, decision on the merits of 2 July 2014.
69 *FEANTSA v. the Netherlands*, n.68, para.58.
70 CERD, General Recommendation 30 – Discrimination against Non-citizens, UN Doc CERD/C/64/Misc.11/rev.3, 1 October 2004, paras.2–3.
71 CMW, General Comment 2 – Rights of Migrant Workers in an Irregular Situation and Members of their Families, UN Doc CMW/C/GC/2, 28 August 2013, para.72. Note also that very few European states have ratified the ICRMW, indicating that they are clearly bound by the higher standard in Art.12 ICESCR.
72 See e.g. ECSR, *DCI v. the Netherlands*, n.68, para.35; CERD, General Recommendation 30, n.70, paras.2–3; CMW, General Comment 2, n.71, para.72.
73 CESCR, General Comment 20, n.25, para.13.
74 HRC, General Comment 18, n.27, para.13; and the HRC's *Views* cited n.64.
75 E.g. ECtHR, *Gaygusuz v. Austria*, n.67, para.42. And Harris et al. (2014, pp. 792–795).
76 Art.4 ICESCR.
77 Note, however, that the CESCR rarely applies these criteria directly in its concluding observations when it criticises European or other states for their questionable immigration policies. See: Angeleri (2017, pp. 178, 179).

78 CESCR, General Comment 20, n.25, para.13.
79 This interpretation is *inter alia* based on the wording of Art.2(2) ICESCR, stating that states '*undertake to guarantee* that the rights enunciated in the ... Covenant are exercised without discrimination.' See also concerning access to health care: CESCR, General Comment 14, n.47, para.43 a); and more generally, General Comment 3, n.10, para.1; and Report of the SRH, n.24, para.38.
80 As set out in Art.2(1) ICESCR.
81 CESCR, General Comment 14, n.47, paras. 37, 40 and 43(a) and (f).
82 See e.g. CESCR, Guidelines on Treaty-specific Documents to be Submitted by States Parties under Articles 1 and 17 of the International Covenant on Economic, Social and Cultural Rights, UN Doc E/C./12/2008/2, 18 November 2008, paras.42 and 43(a)–(b); and General Comment 21 – Right of Everyone to Take Part in Cultural Life, UN Doc E/C.12/GC/21, 21 December 2009, paras.34–35. Note that the terminology used by the CESCR is not uniform. It also refers to 'persons and communities requiring special protection' or the 'disadvantaged and marginalised'. For an analysis, see: Chapman and Carbonetti (2011).
83 FRA, The Cost of Exclusion from Healthcare: The Case of Migrants in an Irregular Situation, Vienna, 2015, at 35; Trummer and Krasnik (2017, p. 590).
84 Report of the SRH, n.24, para.40; and Parliamentary Assembly of the Council of Europe, Resolution 1946 (2013), on Equal Access to Health Care, para.3.
85 The UK 'hostile environment' policy was developed from 2010 by the then home secretary Theresa May. In a 2012 interview with *The Telegraph* she declared the aim of the government's immigration policy as 'to create here in Britain a really hostile environment for illegal migration' (Theresa May interview: "We're going to give illegal migrants a really hostile reception", *The Telegraph*, 25 May 2012).
86 Concerning UK immigration policy, see 'Theresa May's 'Hostile Environment' at Heart of Windrush Scandal', *The Guardian*, 17 April 2018; concerning also other European countries, see HUMA Network, 'Access to Health Care and Living Conditions of Asylum Seekers and Undocumented Migrants in Cyprus, Malta, Poland and Romania', 2011; Ryan and Mantouvalou (2014, p. 177).
87 See e.g. the Netherland's reaction to the ECSR decision *(FEANTSA) v. the Netherlands*, n.68, in the Address by the Representative of the Netherlands at the GR-SOC meeting of 16 September 2014, *European Federation of National Organisations working with the Homeless (FEANTSA) v. the Netherlands*, Complaint No 86/2012, Appendix to Resolution CM/ResChS(2015)4, adopted by the Council of Europe Committee of Ministers on 15 April 2015. See also FRA, 'Fundamental Rights of Migrants in an Irregular Situation in the European Union', Vienna, 2011, at 39–46.
88 See e.g. HUMA Network, n.86, at 190, dispelling the myth of access to health care as a 'pull factor' for migration to Europe.
89 These effects of excluding migrants from access to health care are described in FRA, 'Migrants in an Irregular Situation: Access to Health Care in 10 European Union Member States', Vienna, 2011, at 37–39.
90 On some of the wider effects of the UK 'hostile environment' policy, see: 'End of Mission Statement of the Special Rapporteur on Contemporary Forms of Racism, Racial Discrimination, Xenophobia and Related Intolerance at the Conclusion of Her Mission to the United Kingdom of Great Britain and Northern Ireland', 11 May 2018, available at: www.ohchr.org/EN/NewsEvents/Pages/DisplayNews.aspx?NewsID=23073&LangID=E.
91 For an overview of these policies covering EU member states, see FRA, Rights of Migrants in an Irregular Situation, n.87, at 71–83.
92 CESCR, Concluding Observations on the Sixth Periodic Report of the United Kingdom of Great Britain and Northern Ireland, UN Doc E/C.12/GBR/CO/6, 16 July 2016, paras.55–56; and Concluding Observations – Germany, UN Doc E/C.12/DEU/CO/5, 11 July 2011, para.13.

93 Art.2(1) ICESCR.
94 CESCR, General Comment 3, n.10, para.9.
95 Ibid., para.10.
96 Ibid.; and General Comment 14, n.47, para.47; General Comment 12 – The Right to Food, UN Doc E/C.12/1999/5, 12 May 1999, para.17.
97 For a detailed analysis, based *inter alia* on comparative elements and discussing various practical and normative difficulties concerning the minimum core approach, see: Müller (2017, pp. 70–75).
98 Note that the CESCR in its General Comment 14 suggests that the 'underlying determinants of health' form part of the minimum core content of the right to health. The present author thinks that these 'underlying determinants' are protected by the minimum core content of other socio-economic rights and therefore do not to form part of the minimum core content of the right to health.
99 Most recently reiterated by the CESCR in its Statement on Refugees and Migrants, n.61, paras.9–10.
100 See e.g. CESCR, General Comment 14, n.47, paras.45; General Comment 3, n.10, para.10; and Statement on Poverty and the International Covenant on Economic, Social and Cultural Rights, UN Doc E/C.12/2001/10, 10 May 2001, para.17.
101 CESCR, General Comment 14, n.47, para.30; and General Comment 13 – The Right to Education, UN Doc E/C.12/1999/10, 8 December 1999, para.43.
102 'Economic access' implies affordable access. This does, however, not mean that states have an obligation to provide all health services free of charge for migrants and citizens. Rather, under their obligation to *fulfil* the right to health, states have to set up 'a public, private or mixed health insurance system which is affordable for all', including for indigent migrants (see CESCR, General Comment 14, n.47, para.36).
103 CESCR, General Comment 14, n.47, paras.12, 30 and 36.
104 See nn.81 and 82.
105 CESCR, General Comment 20, n.25, para.9; and General Comment 15 – The Right to Water, UN Doc E/C.12/2002/11, 20 January 2003, para. 16(f).
106 CESCR, Statement on Refugees and Migrants, n.61, para.12; Report of the SRH, n.24, paras.42–43.
107 Ibid., para.12.
108 FRA, Rights of Migrants in an Irregular Situation, n.87, at 82.
109 See Chapter 7 by Steele and Devlin in this volume.
110 Report of the SRH, n.24, para.43.
111 CESCR, Statement on Refugees and Migrants, n.61, para.12; FRA, Rights of Migrants in an Irregular Situation, n.87, at 45–46 and 83.
112 SRH, Report on the Right to Mental Health, UN Doc A/HRC/35/21, 28 March 2017.
113 Report of the SRH, n.24, para.67–69.
114 Ibid., para.46.
115 Ibid., paras.47–61.
116 CESCR, Concluding Observations – United Kingdom, 2016, n.92, paras.34–35.
117 E.g. ECtHR, *Siliadin v. France*, Judgment (Chamber), Appl. No. 73316/01, 26 July 2005; *Rantsev v. Cyprus and Russia*, Judgment (Chamber), Appl.No.25965/04, 7 January 2010; and *Chowdury and Others v. Greece*, Judgment (Chamber), Appl. No.21884/15, 30 March 2017.
118 E.g. ECtHR, *Üner v. the Netherlands,* Judgment (Grand Chamber), Appl.No.464 10/99, 18 October 2006, para.58 (emphasis added).
119 These have been set out by the ECtHR in its judgment *Boultif v. Switzerland*, n.42, para.48.
120 For a detailed analysis, see Thym, n.49.

References

Angeleri, S. 2017, 'The impact of the economic crisis on the right to health of irregular migrants, as reflected in the jurisprudence of the UN Committee on Economic, Social and Cultural Rights', *European Journal of Migration and Law*, vol. 19, no. 2, pp. 165–190.

Bates, E. 2015, 'The UK and Strasbourg: a strained relationship – the long view', *University of Leicester School of Law Research Paper No. 15-05.*

Benhabib, S. 2004, *The rights of others: aliens, residents, citizens*, Cambridge University Press, Cambridge.

Besson, S. 2012, 'The right to have rights: from human rights to citizens' rights and back', in M. Goldoni & C. McCorkindale (eds.), *Hannah Arendt and the Law*, Hart Publishing, Oxford, pp. 335–355.

Besson, S. 2015, 'The bearers of human rights duties and responsibilities for human rights: a quiet (r)evolution?', *Social Philosophy and Policy*, vol. 32, no. 1, pp. 244–268.

Bilchitz, D. 2007, *Poverty and fundamental rights: the justification and enforcement of socio-economic rights*, Oxford University Press, Oxford.

Biswas, D., Toebes, B., Hjern, A., Ascher, H., & Norredam, M. 2012, 'Access to health care for undocumented migrants from a human rights perspective: a comparative study of Denmark, Sweden and the Netherlands', *Health and Human Rights*, vol. 14, no. 2, pp. 49–60.

van Bueren, G. 1999, 'Alleviating poverty through the constitutional court', *South African Journal of Human Rights*, vol. 15, no. 1, pp. 52–74.

Chapman, A., & Carbonetti, B. 2011, 'Human rights protection of vulnerable and disadvantaged groups: the contributions of the UN Committee on Economic, Social and Cultural Rights', *Human Rights Quarterly*, vol. 33, pp. 682–732.

Chetail, V. 2014, 'Are refugee rights human rights? An unorthodox questioning of the relations between refugee law and human rights law', in R. Rubio-Marin (ed.), *Human rights and immigration*, Oxford University Press, Oxford.

Da Lomba, S. 2014, 'Vulnerability, irregular migrants' health-related rights and the European Court of Human Rights', *European Journal of Health Law*, vol. 21, no. 4, pp. 339–364.

den Heijer, M. 2008, 'Whose rights and which rights? The continuing story of non-*refoulement* under the European Convention on Human Rights', *European Journal of Migration and Law*, vol. 10, no. 3, pp. 277–314.

de Schutter, O. 2010, *International human rights law*, Cambridge University Press, Cambridge.

Flegar, V., Dalli, M., & Toebes, B. 2016, 'Access to preventive health care for undocumented migrants: a comparative study of Germany, the Netherlands and Spain from a human rights perspective', *Laws*, vol. 5, no. 1, p. 9.

Forman, L., Caraoshi, L., Chapman, A.R., & Lamprea, E. 2016, 'Conceptualising minimum core obligations under the right to health: how should we define and implement the 'morality of the depths'?' *International Journal of Human Rights*, vol. 20, no. 4, pp. 531–548.

Frowein, J., & Peukert, W. 2009, *Europäische Menschenrechtskonvention*, N.P. Engel Verlag, Kehl am Rhein.

Greenman, K. 2015, 'A castle built on sand? Article 3 ECHR and the source of risk in *non-refoulement* obligations in international law', *International Journal of Refugee Law*, vol. 27, no. 2, pp. 264–296.

Harris, D., O'Boyle, M., Bates, E., & Buckley, C. (eds.) 2014, *Law of the European Convention on Human Rights*, Oxford University Press, Oxford.

Hathaway, J. 2005, *The rights of refugees under international law*, Cambridge University Press, Cambridge.

Hathaway, J. 2012, 'Refugees and asylum', in B. Opeskin, R. Perruchoud & J. Redpath-Cross (eds.), *Foundations of international migration law*, Cambridge University Press, Cambridge, pp. 177–204.

Kälin, W. 2003, 'Human rights and the integration of migrants', in A. Aleinikoff & V. Chetail (eds.), *Migrants and international legal norms*, TMC Asser Press, The Hague.

Ktistakis, Y. 2013, *Protecting migrants under the European Convention on Human Rights and the European Social Charter*, Council of Europe Publishing, Strasbourg.

Mantouvalou, V. 2009, '*N v UK*: no duty to rescue the nearby needy?' *The Modern Law Review*, vol. 71, no. 5, pp. 815–828.

Müller, A. 2017, 'The minimum core approach to the right to health', in S. Klotz, M. Schmidhuber, A. Frewer & H. Bielefeldt (eds.), *Healthcare as a human rights issue*, transcript Verlag, Bielefeld, pp. 55–93.

Perruchoud, R. 2012, 'State sovereignty and freedom of movement', in B. Opeskin, R. Perruchoud & J. Redpath-Cross (eds.), *Foundations of international migration law*, Cambridge University Press, Cambridge, pp. 123–151.

Rubio-Marin, R. 2014a, 'Integration in immigrant Europe: human rights at a crossroads', in R. Rubio-Marin (ed.), *Human rights and immigration*, Oxford University Press, Oxford, pp. 73–105.

Rubio-Marin, R. 2014b, 'Introduction', in R. Rubio-Marin (ed.), *Human rights and immigration*, Oxford University Press, Oxford, pp. 1–18.

Ryan, B., & Mantouvalou, V. 2014, 'The labour and social rights of migrants in international law', in R. Rubio-Marin (ed.), *Human rights and immigration*, Oxford University Press, Oxford, pp. 177–211.

Stoyanova, V. 2017, 'How exceptional must 'very exceptional' be? Non-*refoulement*, socio-economic deprivation, and *Paposhvili v Belgium*', *International Journal of Refugee Law*, vol. 29, no. 4, pp. 580–616.

Thym, D. 2014, 'Residence as de facto citizenship? Protection of long-term residence under article 8 ECHR', in R. Rubio-Marin (ed.), *Human rights and immigration*, Cambridge University Press, Cambridge, pp. 106–144.

Tobin, J. 2012, *The right to health in international law*, Oxford University Press, Oxford.

Trummer, U., & Krasnik, A. 2017, 'Viewpoints – migrant health: the economic argument', *The European Journal of Public Health*, vol. 27, no. 4, pp. 590–591.

Weissbrodt, D., & Divine, M. 2012, 'International human rights of migrants', in B. Opeskin, R. Perruchoud & J. Redpath-Cross (eds.), *Foundations of international migration law*, Cambridge University Press, Cambridge, pp. 152–176.

Young, K. 2008, 'The minimum core of economic, social and cultural rights: a concept in search of content', *Yale Journal of International Law*, vol. 33, p. 113.

International instruments

Convention against Torture (CAT).

European Convention on Human Rights (ECHR).

European Convention on the Legal Status of Migrant Workers.

European Social Charter (ESC).

International Covenant on Economic, Social and Cultural Rights (ICESCR).
International Covenant on Civil and Political Rights (ICCPR).
International Convention on the Elimination of All Forms of Racial Discrimination (ICERD).
International Convention on the Protection of the Rights of All Migrant Workers and Members of Their Families (ICRMW).
Optional Protocol to the International Covenant on Economic, Social and Cultural Rights (OP-ICESCR).
Revised European Social Charter (ESCRev).
UN Charter.
UN Convention for the Protection of All Persons from Enforced Disappearances.
UN Protocol relating to the Status of Refugees.
UN Refugee Convention.
Universal Declaration of Human Rights (UDHR).

6 Entitlements to social health benefits for asylum seekers and refugees in Germany

Markus Kaltenborn

6.1 Introduction

In recent years, public attention has increasingly focused on the issue of medical care for foreigners in Germany.[1] This focus stems from both the extent to which refugees require medical care and the recurring discussion of the social assistance granted to nationals of other EU Member States. There are complicated legal questions behind these rather political debates. Frequently, the question arises as to who is responsible for the costs of medical treatment, but a prior question is whether a foreigner is in fact given access to medical services at all.

For unambiguous emergency treatment, the latter question is answered in the affirmative, and there are criminal legal consequences if physicians and other service providers refuse assistance (§ 323c *Penal Code* [*Strafgesetzbuch*, StGB]). In addition, in most cases, professional codes of conduct – wherever necessary – are likely to exert sufficient pressure on service providers.[2] However, it should not be overlooked that funding the emergency services provided often raises serious difficulties for service providers (Makoski 2014; Schwarz 2009).[3] Furthermore, there are medical services that financially solvent foreigners in Germany find difficult to obtain. The focus is often on organ transplants, which apart from the financial constraints is primarily dependent on the availability of a suitable organ. In particular, whether and under what conditions foreigners may or should be entitled to be added to the list of potential recipients from a donor body is legally controversial (Huster & Ströttchen 2016).

Between these two extremes, the legal situation becomes quite confusing. Generally, the German health care system is based on the concept of social insurance as embodied in the principle of social solidarity. This system also includes foreigners. A differentiation, however, must be made between E U citizens, other foreigners and persons entitled to benefits under the *Act on Benefits for Asylum Applicants* (*Asylbewerberleistungsgesetz*, AsylbLG).

6.2 Different entitlements for different citizens

For citizens of the European Union, detailed coordination provisions are laid down in the *Regulation on the Coordination of Social Security Systems*[4] and the corresponding *Implementing Regulation.*[5] At this point, a large number of case variants are conceivable due to the principle of free movement. Nevertheless, the following basic principles can be formulated:

- Every citizen of the European Union who is habitually resident in Germany and who is employed is subject to German social law and thus, as a rule, to compulsory insurance according to § 5 para. 1 no. 1 *Social Code Book V* (SGB V).[6]
- For civil servants employed by a German authority, German law applies.[7]
- For employees who are self-employed in Germany, German law, thus, § 193 (3) *Insurance Contract Act* (*Versicherungsvertragsgesetz*, VVG) or compulsory insurance pursuant to § 5 para. 1 no. 13 SGB V, applies.

For voluntary insurance, cross-border commuters, students, retirees and other special constellations, the EU regulations provide for special arrangements and compensation mechanisms between the social insurance institutions in the Member States (cf. Devetzi 2016).

For temporary stays in another Member State, insured persons in their home country are allowed to use the European Health Insurance Card (EHIC). In this way, they receive the necessary supplies for the temporary period. In turn, compensation occurs between the social security agencies.[8]

As a result, it can be said that for the majority of conceivable cases, the standards of German statutory health insurance apply equally to German citizens and EU citizens. This may not be the case if the person concerned is not employed in Germany. It is necessary to differentiate between those who have never been employed and those who have been but are now unemployed. Persons who receive an unemployment benefit (Arbeitslosengeld I or II) are compulsorily insured under the statutory health insurance pursuant to § 5 para. 1 no. 2 und no. 2a SGB V. It is only possible for foreigners to receive unemployment benefit II under the strict conditions of § 7 para. 1 SGB II. If, however, the citizen was once compulsorily insured under the statutory health insurance scheme, for example, as a result of employment pursuant to § 5 para. 1 no. 1 SGB V, insurance protection for him and his dependents (through family insurance) remains applicable according to § 188 para. 4 SGB V.

Unless citizens of the European Union are not compulsorily insured according to these principles of the statutory health insurance, they are granted claims under §§ 23, 48 SGB XII, 264 SGB V, which, in response to the jurisprudence of the Federal Social Security Court,[9] have been curtailed in December 2016.[10] The aim is to ensure that even citizens of the European Union can only receive regular social benefits if they have already worked in Germany – then § 2 para. 3 *Freedom of Movement Law* (*Freizügigkeitsgesetz/EU*), and thus the exception according to § 7 para. 1 s. 2 no. 1 SGB II or § 23 para. 3 s. 1 no. 1 SGB XII, applies – or if they have not been required to leave the country in accordance with § 7 para. 1 s. 4 SGB II or § 23 para. 3 s. 7 SGB XII and have stayed in Germany for at least five years.[11] Otherwise, – or if they have only entered the country to receive social assistance – the persons concerned receive only the so-called bridging services pursuant to § 23 para. 3 s. 5 SGB XII. These services include any medical and dental treatment necessary for the treatment of acute diseases and painful conditions, including the supply of pharmaceutical products and surgical materials and other services necessary for recovery or for the improvement or alleviation of disease. These benefits are limited to one month in accordance with § 23 para. 3 s. 3 SGB XII.[12]

For all other foreigners, there is no comparable system of coordination available and German law applies. As long as they cannot or do not want to pay themselves, their entitlement to medical services depends on their residence status. As soon as they have a secure residence status, a work permit and employment that triggers the insurance obligation pursuant to § 5 SGB V, they are insured (and their dependents through family health insurance) regardless of their nationality. In the case of an omission of compulsory insurance, they are also subject to continued insurance under § 188 para. 4 SGB V.

Unemployed persons are dependent on benefits under SGB II or SGB XII in the event of a need for assistance. The restrictions already presented regarding EU citizens also apply here; in both security systems, the entitlement to benefits depends on a right of residence: people are not allowed to enter the country just to obtain social assistance. If the benefit entitlement pursuant to section § 23 para. 3 SGB XII is excluded, the abovementioned bridging benefits are also only available for one month. Therefore, there is only temporary protection for acute health problems.

A special case is the foreigner who is entitled to benefits under the AsylbLG. Their entitlement to health care is at the centre of this article. In the following, first the legal basis for the health care of this group of persons will be illustrated (III.). Subsequently, the question as to whether the legislature has adequately observed constitutional and international law when designing these benefits will be answered (IV.).[13]

6.3 Health services under the act on benefits for asylum applicants (AsylbLG)

According to § 7 para. 1 s. 2 no. 3 SGB II or according to § 23 para. 2 SGB XII, refugees who fall within the scope of the AsylbLG – regardless of whether they have a residence permit or whether they (such as rejected asylum seekers and so-called "undocumented migrants") are obliged to leave the host country[14] – must content themselves with the benefits under the AsylbLG during the first 15 months of their stay in Germany. This means that compared to other groups of persons – at least for this period of their residence in Germany – the legislator grants asylum seekers only a reduced range of medical services; moreover, these are often rendered to them only after a considerable time delay due to bureaucratic obstacles.[15] Asylum seekers are not included in the system of statutory health insurance (unlike social welfare recipients according to §§ 48, 52 SGB

XII) but are subject to the special regulations of §§ 4 and 6 AsylbLG. Only after the expiry of a 15-month stay in Germany do the benefit provisions of SGB V apply to them.[16]

The regulation of § 4 para. 1 AsylbLG provides that necessary medical and dental treatment, including the supply of medicines, surgical materials and other services necessary for the recovery, improvement or alleviation of illnesses, are to be granted only for the treatment of acute illnesses and painful conditions. The claim also includes protective vaccinations and medically necessary preventative examinations; the supply of dental prosthesis is restricted to those cases in which such supply cannot be postponed for medical reasons. In addition, § 6 allows more extensive benefits to be granted, in particular if they are indispensable in individual cases to safeguard subsistence or health, to meet the special needs of children, or to fulfil an administrative obligation to co-operate.

An "acute illness" within the meaning of § 4 AsylbLG can only be presumed in those cases in which an unexpected occurrence of rapid and violent irregular condition or state of mind requires medical or dental treatment (LSG Nordrhein-Westfalen, 6.5.2013 - L 20AY145/11 - juris para. 52; Frerichs 2014, § 4, para. 38; Wahrendorf 2018, § 4, para. 26). Thus, the treatment of chronic disease is excluded from the scope of the standard, unless the disease is associated with (acute or chronic) painful conditions (Frerichs 2014, § 4, para. 43) or accompanied by an acute disease state (e.g., a lung infection for an HIV-infected person).[17] The wording in § 4 para. 1 s. 2 AsylbLG (benefit provision only in "cases which cannot be postponed for medical reasons") clearly shows that dental prosthesis can only be granted in very limited cases.[18] In summary, it can be said that the care claim of § 4 AsylbLG is primarily directed at the treatment of disease symptoms, rather than at long-term therapy (Eichenhofer 2013, p. 170). § 6 AsylbLG cannot completely compensate for these deficits either, since only those health services that are absolutely necessary from a medical point of view and for which an equally suitable and possibly more cost-effective alternative is not available are considered "indispensable" within the meaning of this regulation (Wahrendorf 2018, § 6, para. 18).

Indeed some authors call for a constitutionally compliant interpretation of the provision in the sense that the level of health services nearly meets the standard of the statutory health insurance – at least this should apply to cases where the actual stay of the asylum seeker in Germany already exceeds the margin of a short stay.[19] However, § 6 AsylbLG will continue to be interpreted in a restrictive manner[20] in order to preserve the legal gap between the level of service provision defined by the lawmaker compared to the entitlements according to SGB XII or SGB II. All in all, it can be seen that (even in a very broad interpretation) the standard of care according to §§ 4, 6 AsylbLG falls short of the standard provided for other persons who are entitled to social security; in this respect, it appears to be justified to speak only of "medical emergency treatment" (see also Janda 2013; ProAsyl 2014) being available to asylum seekers in Germany.

6.4 Is §§ 4, 6 AsylbLG in line with human right to health?

In July 2012, the Federal Constitutional Court had to decide on two law suits regarding the AsylbLG initiated by the Superior State Social Court of North Rhine-Westphalia. The Court decided that the cash amounts and the basic payments according to § 3 AsylbLG must be regarded as unconstitutional because they breach the basic right to an ensured decent minimum for subsistence (Art. 1 para. 1 *Grundgesetz* [GG] in conjunction with Art. 20 para. 1 GG).[21] The judges of Karlsruhe also criticized the four-year waiting period regulated in § 2 AsylbLG, which asylum seekers must observe to claim social welfare benefits. These and several other provisions of the AsylbLG have since been amended by several legislative amendments.[22] Despite the criticisms expressed regarding the legal changes in recent hearings,[23] however, the legislator has hitherto adhered to the medical emergency treatment ordered in § 4 AsylbLG.

Apparently, the parliamentary parties supporting the government were not able to recognize a constitutional obligation to adjust the provision, presumably not least because the Federal Constitutional Court did not investigate the compatibility of the health regulations of this law with the constitution in its ruling on the AsylbLG. However, even if the Court had considered §§ 4, 6 AsylbLG in its decision, it is not certain that this would have necessitated a change, which is compelling for constitutional reasons. To the legislature, the Court admits a very wide margin of assessment in clarifying the obligations for protection that arise from the fundamental right to physical integrity (Art. 2 para. 2 GG). The derivation of specific health-related benefit claims from the constitution has hitherto been recognized only for rare cases (treatment of a life-threatening illness outside the generally accepted care standard[24]). Apart from that, the legislature is given substantial scope to elaborate its "obligation to protect" and the corresponding regulations (Di Fabio 2016, Art. 2 para. 2, para 94).

The assessment of §§ 4, 6 AsylbLG might possibly be different if not only Art. 2 para. 2 GG but also the general principle of equality (Art. 3 para. 1 GG) were used as the standard of review. From the viewpoint of equality, it is difficult to understand why, on the one hand, people eligible for social assistance are granted medical care on nearly the same level as patients with statutory health insurance (Flint 2018, para 34 et seq.), but on the other hand, access to health care services according to §§ 4, 6 AsylbLG is limited to emergency care. A justification of this unequal treatment is likely to be difficult, since the risk of disease and the need for medical treatment are, of course, not dependent on the residence status of the persons concerned (Janda & Wilksch 2010, p. 571; Zentrale Ethikkommission bei der Bundesärztekammer 2013, p. 901). Nevertheless, it is conceivable that the Federal Constitutional Court would (still) accept the health regulations of the AsylbLG as being justified under constitutional law. With regard to those benefits that secure the livelihood of asylum seekers, constitutional judges have made it clear that the legislature is not allowed to differentiate on the basis of residence status.[25] However, again, the Court has given the legislature a wide margin of assessment.

The fact that medical emergency care according to the AsylbLG is open to criticism becomes especially clear when international law is included in the assessment of the law.[26] Germany is bound to the requirements of the *International Covenant on Economic, Social and Cultural Rights (ICESCR).*[27] The rights guaranteed in this international treaty include "the right of everyone to the enjoyment of the highest attainable standard of physical and mental health" (Article 12 (1) ICESCR; cf. Ssenyonjo 2016, p. 507 et seq.; Tobin 2012, p. 75 et seq). The content of the human right to health was clearly defined in a *General Comment* written by the Committee on Economic, Social and Cultural Rights (CESCR) in 2000 (CESCR 2000); this document has become the relevant reference document for the global political and legal debate on health-related human rights protection. In Section 19, the authors of the *General Comment No. 14* stress the need for equal access to health care:

> States have a special obligation to provide those who do not have sufficient means with the necessary health insurance and health-care facilities, and to prevent any discrimination on internationally prohibited grounds in the provision of health care and health services [...].

One of the core obligations to be observed by all Contracting States in any situation is, among other things, "to ensure the right of access to health facilities, goods and services on a non-discriminatory basis, especially for vulnerable or marginalized groups" (CESCR 2000, para. 43a).

In *General Comment No. 19*, which serves to clarify the right to social security (Art. 9 ICESCR), this requirement is again raised in a similar form (CESCR 2008, para. 38). In addition, according to the CESCR, it is important that

> the Covenant rights apply to everyone including non-nationals, such as refugees, asylum-seekers, stateless persons, migrant workers and victims of international trafficking, regardless of legal status and documentation.
>
> (CESCR 2009, para. 30)

Compliance with ICESCR is regularly reviewed by the CESCR based on state reports. During the recent reporting procedure for Germany in 2011, the Committee expressed concern, *inter alia*, about the social situation of asylum seekers and in this context criticized Germany for providing only emergency care to this group of people (CESCR 2011, no. 13[28]). For the years 2017/2018, the review procedure is now under way. The state report presented by the Federal Government offers the following statement on this subject:

> In addition [...] health care for asylum seekers was improved. After 15 months, they receive, in principle, the same level of health services as provided by statutory health insurance, and they receive services from the health insurance funds in the same way as recipients of social assistance. With the First Asylum Package of 20 October 2015, the Federal Government has also improved asylum seekers' access to vaccinations under the

> ABAA.[29] Further changes expand the possibilities of providing benefits in kind to asylum seekers in initial reception centres and collective accommodation. Asylum seekers also receive appropriate health care before the end of the 15-month period under the existing rules. And this is not restricted solely to emergency care. Although in principle the entitlement only covers services relating to the treatment of acute illnesses or pain (Section 4 (1) of the ABAA), it is also supplemented by "other services" if these are essential to safeguard health or required to meet children's particular needs (Section 6 (1) of the ABAA). This enables the competent authority to meet special needs in individual cases.[30]

Whether this view will be shared by the CESCR remains to be seen. Despite recent legislative changes that have led to a slight improvement in the health care provided to refugees, the legal and political framework conditions are still being criticized by both the German medical association (Bundesärztekammer 2015, p. 267 et seq.) and human rights organizations (e.g., German Institute for Human Rights 2016, p. 66 et seq.[31]). There is substantial evidence that from the perspective of international law, the current design of health regulations in the AsylbLG continues to constitute unjustified discrimination against the persons covered (Rixen 2015, p. 1643; Kanalan/Krajewski 2017, p. 424; Forum Menschenrechte 2017, p. 16 et seq.; a different conclusion is reached by Frerichs 2014, § 4, para. 29; cf. also Kluth 2018, at footnote 18; Weilert 2018, p. 61).

6.5 Conclusions

In summary, it must be noted that in Germany, asylum seekers and refugees are entitled to nearly all basic health services. However, in direct comparison to other groups in German society, they have a weaker legal status, as their health care benefits are restricted in several ways. One might wonder whether, from the perspective of migration policy, these restrictions are really necessary. Regardless, from a legal viewpoint, such difference in treatment is not consistent with one of the core human rights demands, the principle of non-discrimination, which is an inherent component of all social rights including the right to health.

Acknowledgements

For many helpful comments on this article, I would like to thank my assistants *Zülal Can* and *Jonathan Ströttchen*.

Notes

1 Cf. Zeit-Online, 12.10.2016: "Bundesregierung schränkt Leistungen für EU-Ausländer ein", www.zeit.de/politik/deutschland/2016-10/sozialhilfe-eu-auslaender-andrea-nahles-bundesregierung (viewed 9 October 2018); Spiegel-Online, 22.03.2016: "So werden Flüchtlinge medizinisch versorgt", www.spiegel.de/gesundheit/diagnose/fluechtlinge-so-laeuft-die-medizinische-versorgung-a-1081702.html (viewed 9 October 2018).

2 Cf. § 7 para. 2 *Model Professional Code of* Conduct (Musterberufsordnung) for doctors – MBO-Ä 1997.
3 See also the new § 6a AsylbLG.
4 Regulation (EC) 883/04.
5 Regulation (EC) 987/09. A detailed discussion of the topic complexities can be found in the dissertation of Ascher 2017; see also Greiner & Kock 2017.
6 See Art. 11 para. 3 a) Regulation (EC) 883/04.
7 See Art. 11 para. 3 b) Regulation (EC) 883/04.
8 As to problems to receive the EHIC, cf. Farahat 2014, p. 274 et seq.
9 BSG, 03.12.2015 – B 4 AS 44/15 R, BSGE 120, 149.
10 *Law for the Determination of Standard Needs* (Regelbedarf) *as well as for the Amendment of Social Code Book II and XII* of 22.12.2016, BGBl I 2016, 3159.
11 On the question of whether the unequal treatment of nationals and non-nationals by other Member States with regard to non-contributory social assistance is in line with European law, cf. EuGH, 15.9.2015 – C-67/14, NZS 2015, p. 1517; BVerfG, 04.10.2016 – 1 BvR 2778/13; Kingreen 2015, p. 1505.
12 See the critical comments of Janda 2016.
13 The following remarks are based on Kaltenborn 2015; on the amendments to the AsylbLG by the *Act on the Acceleration of Asylum Procedures* of 20.10.2015, BGBl. 2015 I p. 1722 (in particular regarding the consequences of the restriction of entitlements pursuant to § 1 a AsylbLG for health care), see Rixen 2015, p. 1642 et seq.
14 § 1 AsylbLG refers to foreigners who are resident in the federal territory and who, for example, have a residence permit under the *Asylum Act* (*Asylgesetz*) or a residence permit due to war in their home country or for other humanitarian reasons tolerated pursuant to § 60a *Residence Act* (*Aufenthaltsgesetz*) even if the threat of deportation is not yet enforceable; spouses, life partners or minor children of these persons are also covered by the Act. Moreover, the provision also applies to foreigners who are bound to leave the country (§ 1 para. 1 no. 5 AsylbLG), which means that "undocumented migrants" (people living in a state of illegality in terms of their residence permit status) likewise fall within the scope of the AsylbLG. These people – although possessing a legal entitlement to basic health services – face severe practical problems because the fear of discovery of their status leads them to make little (or even no) use of the health rights provided by the AsylbLG; on this issue, see Bundesarbeitsgruppe Gesundheit/Illegalität 2017; German Institute for Human Rights 2007; see also Sandforth 2014; Kuehne, Huschke & Bullinger 2015.
15 On efforts to eliminate these bureaucratic problems by introducing a "health card for asylum seekers" (§ 264, para. 1 SGB V), see Kaltenborn 2015, p. 165; cf. also www.aerzteblatt.de/nachrichten/70285/Gesundheitskarte-fuer-Fluechtlinge-kaum-verbreitet (viewed 9 October 2018); www.sueddeutsche.de/news/politik/migration-gesundheitskarte-fuer-fluechtlinge-kommt-nur-schleppend-voran-dpa.urn-newsml-dpa-com-20090101-160515-99-949563 (viewed 9 October 2018).
16 See § 2 AsylbLG and § 264 para. 2, 4 SGB V.
17 For references from the jurisdiction cf. Fasselt 2009, § 4, para. 4.
18 See also BT-Drs. 12/4451, p. 9.
19 This is assumed for a residence period of two years; see, e.g., Frerichs 2014, § 6, para. 61; cf. also ibid., § 4, para. 24 (with further references).
20 Cf. the references at Frerichs 2014, § 6, para. 37; see also Ossege & Köhler 2016, p. 278. In a recent judgement, however, the Landessozialgericht Hessen (L 4 AY 9/18 B ER, 11.7.2018) made clear that § 6 AsylbLG should be interpreted in strict conformity with the Constitution. Consequently, at least for persons who are not only temporarily in the Federal Republic of Germany, it is necessary to provide medical care with all services according to the SGB V. It will be interesting to see whether other courts also agree with this decision.
21 BVerfG, 1 BvL 10/10 of 18.07.2012, NVwZ 2012, p. 1024; see also Janda 2013.
22 BGBl. 2014 I, p. 2187; BGBl. 2014 I, p. 2439.

23 Compilation of written opinions on the expert consultations of 03.11.2014 on the draft law amending the *Act on Benefits for Asylum Applicants* and the *Social Court Act* – BT-Drs. 18/2592, 18(11)220, p. 8 f., 29 ff., 84 f., 89, 98.; cf. also previously German Institute for Human Rights 2014, p. 13 et seq.; Janda & Wilksch 2010, pp. 571, 573.

24 BVerfGE 115, 25; on this decision see Huster 2006.

25 BVerfG, NVwZ 2012, p. 1024 (1027).

26 Regarding the European standards, which are not addressed in this article, see Kaltenborn 2015, p. 163.

27 ICESCR, entered into force on 3.1.1976, UNTS Bd.993, p. 3.

28 Regarding the care situation of minor asylum seekers, the committee responsible for monitoring the Convention on the Rights of the Child has come to similar conclusions; see *Committee on the Rights of the Child* 2014, no. 56 b.

29 *Act on Benefits for Asylum Applicants (AsylbLG).*

30 Sixth periodic report submitted by the Federal Republic of Germany under Articles 16 and 17 of the International Covenant on Economic, Social and Cultural Rights 2016, S. 10; www.institut-fuer-menschenrechte.de/fileadmin/user_upload/PDF-Dateien/Pakte_Konventionen/ICESCR/icescr_state_report_germany_6_2016_en.pdf (viewed 9 October 2018).

31 Cf. also www.aerzteblatt.de/nachrichten/68081/Experten-fordern-mehr-medizinische-Versorgung-fuer-Asylbewerber (viewed 9 October 2018).

References

Ascher, A. 2017, *Sozialleistungen für Unionsbürger*, Nomos-Verlag, Baden-Baden.

Bundesarbeitsgruppe Gesundheit/Illegalität. 2017, 'Gesundheitsversorgung für Menschen ohne Papiere. Aktuelle Herausforderungen und Lösungsansätze', viewed 9 October 2018, www.diakonie.de/fileadmin/user_upload/BAG_Gesundheit_Illegalitaet_Arbeitspapier_Gesundheitsversorgung_fu__r_Menschen_ohne_Papiere_April_2017_Web.pdf.

Bundesärztekammer, Deutscher Ärztetag. 2015, 'Decision Minutes, 12–15 May 2015', viewed 9 October 2018, https://www.bundesaerztekammer.de/fileadmin/user_upload/downloads/pdf-Ordner/118._DAET/118DAETBeschlussprotokoll20150515.pdf.

Committee on Economic, Social and Cultural Rights (CESCR). 2000, *General Comment No. 14, The right to the highest attainable standard of health (Article 12 of the International Covenant on Economic, Social and Cultural Rights)*, 11.8.2000, E/C.12/2000/4.

Committee on Economic, Social and Cultural Rights (CESCR). 2008, *General Comment No. 19, The right to social security (Art. 9 of the International Covenant on Economic, Social and Cultural Rights)*, 4.2.2008, E/C.12/GC/19.

Committee on Economic, Social and Cultural Rights (CESCR). 2009, *General Comment No. 20, Non-discrimination in economic, social and cultural rights (Art. 2, para. 2, of the International Covenant on Economic, Social and Cultural Rights)*, 2.7.2009, E/C.12/GC/20.

Committee on Economic, Social and Cultural Rights (CESCR). 2011, *Consideration of reports submitted by States parties under articles 16 and 17 of the Covenant, Concluding observations – Germany*, 12.7.2011, E/C.12/DEU/CO/5.

Committee on the Rights of the Child. 2014, *Concluding observations on the combined 3rd and 4th periodic reports of Germany*, 25.2.2014, CRC/C/DEU/CO/3-4.

Devetzi, St. 2016, 'Krankheit und Mutterschaft im Koordinierungssozialrecht', in M. Schlachter & H.M. Heinig (eds.), *Europäisches Arbeits- und Sozialrecht, Enzyklopädie Europarecht*, vol. 7, Nomos-Verlag, Baden-Baden, § 23.

Di Fabio, U. 2016, 'Comment to Art. 2 para. 2 Grundgesetz', in Th. Maunz & G. Dürig (eds.), *Grundgesetz-Kommentar*, Beck-Verlag, Munich.

Eichenhofer, E. 2013, 'Gesundheitsleistungen für Flüchtlinge', *Zeitschrift für Ausländerrecht und Ausländerpolitik* (ZAR), vol. 33, no. 5–6, pp. 169–175.

Farahat, A. 2014, 'Rechtsunsicherheiten beim Zugang zur Gesundheitsversorgung von Migranten', *Zeitschrift für europäisches Sozial- und Arbeitsrecht* (ZESAR), vol. 13, no. 7, pp. 269–278.

Fasselt, U. 2009, 'Comment to § 4 AsylbLG', in O. Fichtner & G. Wenzel (eds.), *Kommentar zum SGB XII – Sozialhilfe, AsylbLG*, 4th ed., Franz Vahlen, Munich.

Flint, T.H. 2018, 'Comment to § 48 SGB XII', in Ch. Grube & V. Wahrendorf (eds.), *SGB XII, § 48 SGB XII*, 6th ed., Beck-Verlag, Munich.

Forum Menschenrechte. 2017, 'Germany – list of issues – territorial obligations – submitted in response to the 6th Periodic Report of the Federal German Government on the implementation of the International Covenant on Economic, Social and Cultural Rights (ICESCR)', viewed at 9 October 2018, https://www.forum-menschenrechte.de/wp-content/uploads/2017/10/List-of-Issues-FMR-GERMANY_TERRITORIAL_FINAL.pdf.

Frerichs, K. 2014, 'Comment to §§ 4, 6 AsylbLG', in R. Schlegel & Th. Voelzke (eds.), *jurisPK-SGB XII*, 2nd ed., juris, Saarbrücken.

German Institute for Human Rights. 2007, 'Undocumented Migrants in Germany – Their Right to Health: Report of the National Working Group on Health and Illegality', executive summary, viewed 9 October 2018, https://www.institut-fuer-menschenrechte.de/fileadmin/user_upload/PDF-Dateien/Ergebnispapiere_Zusammenfassungen_Hintergrundpapiere/executive_summary_undocumented_migrants_in_germany.pdf.

German Institute for Human Rights. 2014, 'Statement on the ministerial draft bill of the Federal Ministry of Labor and Social Affairs', viewed 9 October 2018, www.institut-fuer-menschenrechte.de/publikationen/show/stellungnahme-des-instituts-zum-referentenentwurf-des-bundesministeriums-fuer-arbeit-und-soziales-en/.

German Institute for Human Rights. 2016, 'Development of the human rights situation in Germany January 2015 – June 2016. Report to the German Bundestag in accordance with § 2 para. 5 DIMRG', viewed 9 October 2018, www.institut-fuer-menschenrechte.de/fileadmin/user_upload/Publikationen/Menschenrechtsbericht_2016/Human_Rights_Report_2016_Short_version.pdf.

Greiner, St., & Kock, M.-C. 2017, 'Sozialleistungsansprüche für Unionsbürger im Spannungsfeld von Missbrauchsprävention und Arbeitnehmerfreizügigkeit', *Neue Zeitschrift für Sozialrecht* (NZS), vol. 26, pp. 201–207.

Huster, St. 2006, 'Verfassungsunmittelbarer Leistungsanspruch gegen die gesetzliche Krankenversicherung?', *Juristenzeitung* (JZ), vol. 61, no. 9, pp. 466–468.

Huster, St., & Ströttchen, J. 2016, 'Die Aufnahme von Flüchtlingen auf die Warteliste zur Organtransplantation', *Medizinrecht* (MedR), vol. 34, no. 6, pp. 415–417.

Janda, C. 2013, 'Quo vadis, AsylbLG? Möglichkeiten und Grenzen der Neuregelung existenzsichernder Leistungen für Personen mit vorübergehendem Inlandsaufenthalt nach dem Urteil des BverfG', *Zeitschrift für Ausländerrecht und Ausländerpolitik* (ZAR), vol. 33, no. 5–6, pp. 175–182.

Janda, C. 2016, 'Bundesregierung will Anspruch von EU-Bürgern auf "Hartz IV" drastisch einschränken', Legal Tribune Online, 03.11.2016, viewed 9 October 2018, www.lto.de/recht/hintergruende/h/entwurf-sgb-ii-sozialhilfe-grundsicherung-anspruch-aulaender-einschraenken-abschrekung-existenzsicherung-bundessozialgericht/.

Janda, C., & Wilksch, F. 2010, 'Das Asylbewerberleistungsgesetz nach dem "Regelsatz-Urteil" des BverfG', *Sozialgerichtsbarkeit* (SGb), vol. 57, no. 10, pp. 565–574.

Kaltenborn, M. 2015, 'Die Neufassung des Asylbewerberleistungsgesetzes und das Recht auf Gesundheit', *Neue Zeitschrift für Sozialrecht* (NZS), vol. 24, no. 5, pp. 161–166.

Kanalan, I., & Krajewski, M. 2017, 'Medizinische Versorgung irregulärer Migranten aus menschenrechtlicher Sicht', *Zeitschrift für europäisches Sozial- und Arbeitsrecht (ZESAR)*, vol. 16, pp. 418–426.

Kingreen, Th. 2015, 'In love with the single market? Die EuGH-Entscheidung Alimanovic zum Ausschluss von Unionsbürgern von sozialen Grundsicherungsleistungen', *Neue Zeitschrift für Verwaltungsrecht (NVwZ)*, vol. 34, no. 21, pp. 1503–1506.

Kluth, W. 2018, 'Gesundheitsdienstleistungen nach dem Asylbewerberleistungsgesetz', *Soziale Sicherheit*, vol. 67, no. 1, pp. 32–38.

Kuehne, A., Huschke, S., & Bullinger, M. 2015, 'Subjective health of undocumented migrants in Germany – a mixed methods approach', *BMC Public Health*, vol. 15, p. 926.

Makoski, K. 2014, 'Kostenerstattung für eine stationäre Krankenhausbehandlung für Personen, die dem AsylbLG unterfallen, Anmerkung zu BSG 7. Senat, Urteil vom 30.10.2013 - B 7 AY 2/12 R', *jurisPR-MedizinR* 4/2014.

Ossege, M., & Köhler, A. 2016, 'Medizinische Versorgung von Flüchtlingen nach dem Asylbewerberleistungsgesetz', *Gesundheitsrecht* (GesR), vol. 15, no. 5, pp. 276–280.

ProAsyl. 2014, 'Opinion on the draft law amending the Act on Benefits for Asylum Applicants and the Social Court Act', July 2014, viewed 9 October 2018, www.proasyl.de/fileadmin/fm-dam/o_Rechtspolitik/PRO_ASYL_Stellungahme_zum_Entwurf_AsylbLG_11__Juli_2014.pdf.

Rixen, St. 2015, 'Zwischen Hilfe, Abschreckung und Pragmatismus: Gesundheitsrecht der Flüchtlingskrise', *Neue Zeitschrift für Verwaltungsrecht* (NVwZ), vol. 34, no. 23, pp. 1640–1644.

Sandforth, R. 2014, 'Allgemeines Menschenrecht auf Gesundheit. Mangelhafte medizinische Versorgung von Menschen ohne Papiere', *ForumRecht*, vol. 8, no. 4, pp. 113–115.

Schwarz, K. 2009, 'Erstattung von Behandlungskosten nach der Eilfallregelung des § 25 SGB XII', *das Krankenhaus* (KH), vol. 101, no. 11, pp. 1022–1026.

Ssenyonjo, M. 2016, *Economic, social and cultural rights in international law*, Bloomsbury, London.

Tobin, J. 2012, *The right to health in international law*, Oxford University Press, Oxford.

Wahrendorf, V. 2018, 'Comment to §§ 4, 6 AsylbLG', in Ch. Grube & V. Wahrendorf (eds.), *SGB XII*, 6th ed., Beck-Verlag, Munich.

Weilert, A.K. 2018, 'Das völkerrechtliche Menschenrecht auf Gesundheit und seine Umsetzung in Deutschland', *Gesundheits- und Sozialpolitik*, vol. 72, no. 2, pp. 55–61.

Zentrale Ethikkommission bei der Bundesärztekammer. 2013, 'Stellungnahme der Zentralen Kommission zur Wahrung ethischer Grundsätze in der Medizin und ihren Grenzgebieten (Zentrale Ethikkommission) bei der Bundesärztekammer, Versorgung von nicht regulär krankenversicherten Patienten mit Migrationshintergrund", *Deutsches Ärzteblatt* (DÄBl), vol. 110, no. 18, pp. A899–A906.

Legislation and international instruments

Act on Benefits for Asylum Applicants (Asylbewerberleistungsgesetz, AsylbLG).
Freedom of Movement Law (Freizügigkeitsgesetz/EU).
Implementing Regulation on the Regulation on the Coordination of Social Security Systems, Regulation (EC) 987/09.
Insurance Contract Act (Versicherungsvertragsgesetz, VVG).
International Covenant on Economic, Social and Cultural Rights (ICESCR).
Regulation on the Coordination of Social Security Systems, Regulation (EC) 883/04.

7 Access and entitlements for migrants and visitors to the UK in the English National Health Service

Sarah Steele and Cormac Devlin

7.1 Introduction

The National Health Service (NHS) is England's state health provider, offering primary and secondary care services to all requiring treatment.[1] Established in 1948, the roles and functions of all NHS organisations are now set out in both the NHS Act 2006 and the 2012 NHS Constitution for England, which provide a set of rights for patients, public and staff, while creating responsibilities for those in and using the NHS, as well as for government. Critically, the NHS Constitution in Principle 1 commits the NHS to providing 'a comprehensive service, available to all', while Principle 2 sets out that 'access to NHS services is based on clinical need, not an individual's ability to pay' (Department of Health and Social Care 2015). Therefore, not everyone present in England is entitled to free-at-the-point-of-use health care. While everyone has a right under the NHS Constitution to access services, they do not have the right to receive treatment for free. Migrants and visitors, therefore, all have access to NHS services but may be charged for any care they receive.

The practicalities of this regime notably meant that historically, while services were chargeable, few NHS bodies sought to recoup monies owed. As Aneurin Bevan, the so-called father of the NHS, noted in 1952:

> How do we distinguish a visitor from anybody else? Are British citizens to carry means of identification everywhere to prove that they are not visitors? What began as an attempt to keep the Health Service for ourselves would end by being a nuisance to everybody. The whole agitation has a nasty taste. Instead of rejoicing at the opportunity to practice a civilized principle, Conservatives have tried to exploit the most disreputable emotions in this among many other attempts to discredit socialized medicine.
>
> (Bevan 1952)

Critically, the practical difficulties that Bevan highlighted over half a century ago still plague the NHS today, however political will in the UK has meant that across the last decade charging has been implemented and consistently expanded. Charging for migrant and visitor use of NHS services is now a hot political issue and therefore a government priority (Department of Health and Social Care 2017a).

Across the last decade, successive governments have made clear that, while all people are entitled to access health care via the NHS while in the UK, NHS treatment in England is only to be free to people classed as 'ordinarily resident', although this is subject to a broad range of exemptions, which may be due to the nature of treatment or belonging to a special class of persons who are exempt. In this chapter, we explore the increasingly complex legislation and regulations that govern charging for NHS care in England; a legal framework that is constantly changing in the face of increasing political desires to appear a 'hostile environment for migrants' (part of the Government's promise to reduce net migration significantly) (Kirkup & Winnett 2012), while negotiating an exit from the European Union (henceforth referred to as 'Brexit') (HM Government 2017).

7.2 Those ordinarily resident

As noted, those who are deemed ordinarily resident are eligible for many NHS services free of charge (see discussion of chargeable services below). Ordinary residence is not based on nationality, payment of UK taxes, National Insurance contributions, being registered with a GP, having an NHS Number, or owning property in the UK. Instead, to be considered ordinarily resident, a person must be living lawfully in the UK voluntarily and for settled purposes as part of the regular order of their life for the time being (Department of Health and Social Care 2017b).

The effect of this statement varies by national status. For example, British citizens, who have an automatic right of abode in the UK, must be settled and living in the UK to pass this test. This means that where a British citizen is living abroad or is migrating to the UK for the first time, they will only pass the test upon taking up settled residence, but otherwise will not meet the test and will be required to pay for their care. British citizens living abroad and visiting England are responsible for paying for their care, unless they are receiving an exempt category of care (see categories of exemption below).

For European Economic Area (EEA) nationals living in the UK, at least until May 2019, automatic status as ordinarily resident is assumed. However, their non-EEA family members are regarded as ordinarily resident only where the EEA family member fulfils the requirements of the right to reside, in accordance with Directive 2004/38/EC (the Free Movement Directive).[2] Currently, an EEA (or Swiss) national has the right to reside if employed, self-employed, registered as a job-seeker, economically self-sufficient or a student. EEA nationals who have resided legally in the UK for a continuous period of five years acquire a permanent right of residence (Government of the UK 2017a,b). The government has published a policy paper detailing their offer for EEA citizens in the UK following Brexit, which envisages the creation of a new 'settled status' for EU nationals and their families who have been permanently resident in the UK for a period of five years (HM Government 2017, pp. 7–8).

At present, all other non-EEA nationals must have indefinite leave to remain in the UK to fulfil the residence criteria.[3] Importantly, many non-EEA migrants to the UK have a 'no recourse to public funds' condition imposed on them during their stay in the UK.[4] NHS treatment is not a public fund for immigration purposes. As such, the endorsement is not grounds for refusing treatment. All migrants and visitors have access to services, but it is critical, therefore, to ask whether the person is exempt from charging based on either paying the health surcharge or on belonging to a category of exemption. We consider each of these in the sections that follow.

7.3 Those who have paid the health care surcharge

Since April 2015, non-EEA nationals when applying for a visa to stay in the UK for over six months are required to pay a health care surcharge unless they are exempt (The Immigration (Health Charge) Order 2015, s. 3). Those exempt include persons

- seeking asylum or applying for humanitarian protection (and their dependants);
- identified as a victim of modern slavery, including human trafficking (and their dependants);
- applying for indefinite leave to remain;
- to whom the Home Office's domestic violence concession applies (and their dependants);
- whose being made to leave the UK would be a violation of their rights under Article 3 of the European Convention of Human Rights (and their dependants) (The Immigration (Health Charge) Order 2015, Schedule 2).

We discuss these categories in more detail below. At present, the surcharge is £150 per year for students and £200 per year for all other visa and immigration applications and is paid upfront when applying for clearance to enter or to remain (The Immigration (Health Charge) Order 2015, Schedule 1). Dependants usually have to pay the same amount.

Until the 21st of August 2017, those who paid the surcharge could use the NHS on the same basis as an ordinarily resident person, however since this date those who paid the surcharge are no longer eligible for free conception services (The National Health Service (Changes to Overseas Visitors) (Amendment) Regulations 2017, Regulation 11). Patients who have paid the surcharge also must pay for prescriptions, as well as optical and dental treatment, in the same way as other non-exempt residents, as considered below. For those not ordinarily resident or required to pay the surcharge, other categories of exemption may mean that care is provided free of charge.

7.4 Those receiving certain types of care exempt from charging

Some types of care in England are deemed exempt from charging, and patients will not be charged for care of this type but may be charged for care that is not exempt that is secondary to the type of care. Examples include persons who are seen in Primary Care initially but then referred to a specialist service or outpatient clinic in a hospital, those who are seen in the Emergency Department but then moved for further care to a ward or outpatient service, and those who have a secondary condition that is not exempt even if its treatment is necessary to effectively treat an exempt condition. In sum, patients may receive only part of their treatment for free and will also be liable for any prescriptions or medical devices in line with the relevant provisions on exemption and prepayment.[5] We consider each of the exempt forms in brief in the sections that follow.

7.4.1 Primary care

Primary Care is generally the first point of contact for patients, and includes services delivered by general practitioner (GP) practices, walk-in centres, after-hours centres and minor injuries units. NHS England is the body responsible for the direct commissioning of primary care services (National Health Service Commissioning 2017), meaning that it allocates resources from its portion of the NHS budget to the aforementioned primary care services. GPs hold the discretion to accept any person as a registered NHS patient to receive care and may also register a person as a temporary patient if the person is in the practice's area between 24 hours and three months (National Health Service England 2017). There is no minimum time an individual must have been resident in the UK in order to register with a GP, and GPs must deliver emergency and immediately necessary care free of charge and two weeks cover further to this even if the patient is not registered (ibid). There is no requirement to prove identity, address, or immigration status, and therefore the failure to provide national documents or residence confirmation is not grounds for refusal to register a patient (ibid).

Indeed, GPs can only refuse registration where

1 The patient lives outside the practice's catchment area;
2 The NHS Commissioner has agreed to close the practice's list;
3 The practice has other reasonable grounds, which *cannot* pertain to race, gender, age, class, religion, sexual orientation, disability, medical condition or appearance.[6]

Practices may ask patients to complete a GMS1 form as part of their registration with the practice.[7]

Where an injury or illness is not a serious, life-threatening condition, individuals are often directed to attend a walk-in centre, after-hours centre or minor injuries unit. NHS walk-in centres offer access to a range of services and are normally managed by a nurse, although some centres offer access to doctors. GP's practices can choose whether to provide an out-of-hours service or to transfer responsibility for out-of-hours services to NHS England, so out-of-hours services vary across different areas (National Health Service Choices 2017a). Minor injuries units exist to divert patient flow from A&E to allow A&E staff to concentrate on serious, life-threatening conditions (ibid). The services provided at these units are free at the point of use for all patients and overseas patients are exempted from charges under the 2017 regulations (Department of Health and Social Care 2017b).

Notably, patients receiving free primary care may be required to pay for their prescriptions and medical devices, although again there are exemptions. There are exemptions for those over 60 years of age, under 16 years of age, 16–18 years of age but in full-time education, pregnant or have had a baby in the previous 12 months holding a valid maternity exemption certificate and those who hold a medical certificate because of a specified medical condition.[8] Patients who are not exempt from prescription charges currently pay £8.60 per item, or can apply for a prescription prepayment certificate, which is a cheaper way of paying for multiple prescriptions over a period of three months or a year (National Health Service Choices 2017b). If a person goes to a GP for treatment whilst visiting the UK and is treated as a private patient then any prescription would also be private and would have to be paid for privately (e.g. Fylde and Wyre Clinical Commissioning Group 2016).

7.4.2 Emergency care

While an increasing array of NHS services delivered to migrants in the secondary care context are chargeable, emergency medical care remains exempt at the present time (The National Health Service (Charges to Overseas Visitors) (Amendment) Regulations 2017). While the Secretary of State for Health has suggested that charging for this care is being considered, as of 2017 such changes have not been implemented, largely as a consequence of extensive pushback by the health care professions and public at large.

It remains, however, that on arrival at hospital, NHS acute trusts have been under a legal obligation since 2015 to establish whether patients are overseas visitors to whom charging applies or exempt from charging (The National Health Services (Charges to Overseas Visitors) Regulations 2015, Regulation 3). This is presently achieved both through a series of flags placed on patient files by the Home Office—the government body in charge of immigration—and through a series of residence questions posed to all individuals capable of answering questions on entry into the health care system.

Notably, where the patient is admitted from an Emergency Department into further care, or where other non-urgent treatment follows, this may not exempt him or her from charging, and therefore acute trusts have to seek prepayment or to recover charges from the person liable to pay for these NHS services. Where the treatment is non-urgent or elective, acute trusts are supposed to obtain full payment in advance of providing treatment (The National Health Service (Charges to Overseas Visitors) (Amendment) Regulations 2017). From 23 October 2017, services provided by mental health and community trusts will also be chargeable, and therefore much of the care outside Emergency

Departments and Primary Care will be chargeable unless the individual or their condition is exempt from charging (ibid).

7.4.3 Treatment for certain infectious diseases

Some treatments are exempted from charging on the basis they are deemed necessary to protect the wider public health. The exemption for treatment of certain infectious diseases acknowledges that overseas patients must be treated, regardless of their ability to pay, in order to prevent the transmission of the condition to other members of the public. The range of conditions covered by this exemption is set out in the regulations and includes acute encephalitis, acute poliomyelitis, anthrax, botulism, brucellosis, cholera, diphtheria, enteric fever (typhoid and paratyphoid fever), food poisoning, haemolytic uraemic syndrome (HUS), human immunodeficiency virus (HIV), infectious bloody diarrhoea, invasive group A streptococcal disease and scarlet fever, invasive meningococcal disease (meningococcal meningitis, meningococcal septicaemia and other forms of invasive disease), Legionnaires' Disease, leprosy, leptospirosis, malaria, measles, mumps, pandemic influenza (defined as the 'Pandemic Phase') or influenza that might become pandemic (defined as the 'Alert Phase') in the World Health Organization's Pandemic Influenza Risk Management Interim Guidance, plague, rabies, rubella, severe acute respiratory syndrome (SARS), smallpox, tetanus, tuberculosis, typhus, viral haemorrhagic fever (which includes Ebola), viral hepatitis, whooping cough, yellow fever, Middle Eastern Respiratory Syndrome (MERS) and the diagnosis and treatment of sexually transmitted infections (The National Health Service (Charges to Overseas Visitors) Regulations 2015, Schedule 1). The exemption applies both to the cost of diagnosis (even if the diagnosis results in a negative result), and the cost of treating the condition. Interestingly, the exemption does not apply to the treatment of secondary illnesses that may be present even where treatment of the secondary illness is necessary in order to successfully treat the exempt condition, unless that condition is considered as emergency care, which is exempted.

7.4.4 Family planning services

Certain family planning services are exempt from charging (The National Health Service (Charges to Overseas Visitors) Regulations 2015, Regulation 9(c)). This includes services that supply contraceptive products and devices to prevent pregnancy, including oral contraceptives, condoms, the morning-after pill, pregnancy tests and the fitting and checking of caps, diaphragms and intrauterine devices (National Health Service Choices 2017c). This exemption does not extend to termination of pregnancy, which is charged upfront for overseas patients. The exemption also does not cover infertility treatments for overseas patients, and since 21 August 2017, NHS-funded infertility treatments are no longer free for patients paying the health surcharge (The National Health Service (Charges to Overseas Visitors) (Amendment) Regulations 2017, Regulations 11, 12).

7.5 Persons in categories exempt from charging

Individuals within certain certified categories are entitled to receive care free of charge. Critically, those in these categories must receive the certification to be exempt, and therefore it has become critical that health care staff are trained in identifying potential cases where safeguarding is needed, which may also mean an individual not already certified is able to apply to be entitled to free care, amongst other services. We consider these categories in the sections that follow.

7.5.1 Refugees (those granted asylum, humanitarian protection or temporary protection by the UK)

Where an individual is found to be a refugee under the 1951 United Nations Convention Relating to the Status of Refugees, they are exempted from charging (The National Health Services (Charges to Overseas Visitors) Regulations 2015, Regulation 15(a)). Individuals who do not qualify for refugee status will be exempted if they qualify for Humanitarian Protection (granted for 5 years) or Discretionary Leave to Remain (granted for up to 3 years) (ibid). A person who has leave to enter or remain in the UK as the dependant of a refugee is also exempt from charges (The National Health Services (Charges to Overseas Visitors) Regulations 2015, Regulation 25).

When health care staff are determining whether a patient is exempt from charging under this category, they may view the patient's record through the Summary Care Record application. A 'Green: Paid or exempt from the health surcharge' banner on the patient's record will be taken as evidence of refugee status, as will confirmation of refugee status by the Home Office in the form of a Biometric Residence Permit or an Immigration Status Document.

7.5.2 Asylum seekers (those applying for asylum, humanitarian protection or temporary protection whose claims, including appeals, have not yet been determined)

An asylum seeker is a person who has applied for refugee status under the 1951 Refugee Convention and is waiting for a decision on their asylum claim (Department of Health and Social Care 2017b). Asylum seekers are exempted from patient charging pending the determination of their claim (The National Health Services (Charges to Overseas Visitors) Regulations 2015, Regulation 15(b)). Persons who have made other claims for humanitarian protection from serious harm under Article 3 of the European Convention on Human Rights also qualify for this exemption. The guidance published by the Department of Health and Social Care which accompanies the 2017 charging regulations states that NHS bodies should 'seek their own legal advice' if it is not clear on what basis a patient has made a claim.

In order to prove exemption under this category, a patient can provide an Application Registration Card issued by the Home Office. Alternatively, health care staff can seek any other form of confirmation from the Home Office that a person has made an application that is under consideration, which can include that the patient has the 'Green: Paid or exempt from the health surcharge'.

7.5.3 Individuals receiving support under section 95 of the Immigration and Asylum Act 1999 (the 1999 Act) from the Home Office

Immigration legislation makes provision for asylum-seekers who are homeless or cannot meet their other essential living needs. Under section 95 of the Immigration and Asylum Act 1999, the Secretary of State has the discretion to provide support for asylum-seekers or their dependants who appear to be destitute or likely to become destitute. It is possible for failed asylum-seekers to also receive this support where they have a child under the age of 18 years. Patients receiving this financial support under this provision or other provisions of the 1999 Act are exempt from charges.

7.5.4 Those whose application for asylum was rejected, but they are supported by government bodies

Registration with primary care in England, Wales and Scotland applies to refused asylum seekers as for any other patient regardless of immigration status. In Scotland and Wales, asylum seekers and refused asylum seekers are entitled to free secondary health care on the same terms as any other ordinary resident. In England, only those refused asylum seekers who receive section 4(2) from the Home Office, in accordance with the Immigration and Asylum Act 1999, or section 21 support from a local authority, in accordance with the National Assistance Act 1948, are entitled to free secondary health care. However, all refused asylum seekers can continue, free of charge, with any course of treatment already underway before their application was refused.[9]

7.5.5 Children looked after by a local authority

Children who are looked after by a local authority under s22(1) of the Children Act 1989 are exempt from charges (The National Health Services (Charges to Overseas Visitors) Regulations 2015, Regulation 15(e)). This includes

- Children in the care of a local authority by virtue of a care order;
- Children who are unaccompanied by a parent or guardian in the UK or abandoned or for whom there is no one with parental responsibility;
- Children who are voluntarily accommodated by a local authority.

7.5.6 Victims, and suspected victims of modern slavery or human trafficking, and their dependants

A person who is thought to be a modern slave, as determined by the UK Human Trafficking Centre or the Home Office, plus their spouse or civil partner, and any children under 18 years of age provided they are lawfully present in the UK, are exempted from charges (The National Health Services (Charges to Overseas Visitors) Regulations 2015, Regulation 16). If the UK Human Trafficking Centre or the Home Office considers that there are reasonable grounds to consider the person to be such a person, they will issue a 'reasonable grounds' decision, which will exempt the patient from charges pending a final determination. The 2017 guidance acknowledges that a patient may be provided with treatment prior to their being referred to the competent authority. Charges incurred prior to referral must be refunded or cancelled, if not already paid, when the competent authority provides a reasonable grounds decision. However, if the competent authority does not provide a reasonable grounds decision, the charges will not be refunded or cancelled.

A letter from either the UK Human Trafficking Centre or the Home Office will serve as evidence to prove an exemption under this category. Alternatively, when viewed through the Summary Care Record, a person who has made an immigration application for leave to remain as a victim of modern slavery will have a 'green' banner on their record.

When NHS staff who come into contact with a patient they suspect to be a modern slave are 'strongly encouraged' by the Anti-Slavery Commissioner to notify the Home Office using an MS1 form, although they are not required by law to make this notification in the same way that other specified public authorities are. Where the patient wishes to be referred for assistance and services, the National Referral Mechanism is to be used and proper safeguarding protocol followed by the NHS. Both pathways allow the Home Office to collect data on modern slavery, with the core difference being the identification of the modern slave.

7.5.7 Those receiving compulsory treatment under a court order, or who are detained in an NHS hospital or deprived of their liberty, including prisoners and immigration detainees

This exemption applies to patients who are

- liable to be detained under the Mental Health Act 1983;
- received into guardianship under the 1983 Act or subject to a community treatment order under that Act;
- deprived of their liberty under the Mental Capacity Act 2005;
- required to submit to treatment under a court order;
- in prison;
- in an immigration detention facility.

A court order, or evidence that detention is authorised, can be provided as evidence, and all those in prison or detention are automatically exempt from charges.

7.5.8 Humanitarian reasons

There may also be exceptional humanitarian reasons where the Secretary of State can determine that treatment should be provided to someone. This exemption also applies to their child, companion, or an individual's child who is authorised to travel with them, for whom the exemption is limited to treatment that cannot await their return home.

7.6 What happens if you can't pay?

From 23 October 2017, NHS bodies required to charge overseas patients must do so upfront for all non-urgent health care services, provided that the patient does not fall within one of the exemptions discussed above and the service provided is not exempted (The National Health Service (Charges to Overseas Visitors) (Amendment) Regulations 2017, Regulation 4). The fact that the treatment is immediately necessary or urgently required does not itself make it free of charge, although 'emergency care' is exempt, but rather means that payment must be recovered after the treatment is provided. In the event that payment cannot be recovered from a patient, an NHS debt is recorded which must now be shared with the Home Office and NHS bodies are supposed to make patients aware of the immigration consequences of not paying off debts for which they are liable (Department of Health and Social Care 2017b).

Where a patient with a recorded debt makes an immigration application to enter or remain in the UK at a future date, the Home Office can deny the application where the person has an outstanding or cumulative health care debt of

- £1,000 or more incurred on or after 1 November 2011, or
- £500 or more incurred on or after 6 April 2016 (Home Office 2017).

Where a person with leave to remain is denied further immigration authorisation as a consequence of the debt, they will be required to leave the country or may be subject to immigration detention (Immigration Act 1971, s. 3(5)).

7.7 Conclusions

England has evolved a complex system for charging and exemptions for NHS services across the last decade. For some, these arrangements are critical to sustaining the NHS in the longer term, while others view the reforms as part of the Government's 'hostile environment' policies targeting immigrants and those who cannot establish residency. Recently, denial of treatment to long-term residents and members of the so-called 'Windrush Generation' (a generation of migrants to the UK from the Caribbean area up to the 1970s), including rather notably the denial of oncology treatments to a man who could not provide proof of citizenship despite being in the UK for 44 years, received national and international press (Gentleman 2018). The framework remains hotly debated and is subject to government review (Government of the UK 2018).

This review falls against a backdrop of health care staff refusing to implement some provisions around charging, or failing to recover amounts, which they justify on the basis that they hold concerns about patient confidentiality and also about staff being asked to act as quasi-border police, distracting from their role to deliver safe and excellent care (National Audit Office 2016). To motivate implementation, the Government made changes to charging in August and October 2017 with a view to inducing health care staff to engage in charging and improve the amounts recouped (Department of Health and Social Care 2017a). However, the financial feasibility of the current regime remains in question, as many NHS bodies report it costing more to administer than they are recovering (National Audit Office 2016). At the present time, however, it appears that increases in the number of chargeable services are likely, with the Primary Care and Emergency Care exemptions being considered (Department of Health and Social Care 2017a), and regularly making the national press (Donnelly 2018). In light of the review and proposals, it is likely that the regime will further change in the coming half decade.

Notes

1 Different laws apply to health care in Wales, Scotland and Northern Ireland. In this chapter we cover only the laws as they pertain to England, and where indicated Wales or the broader UK. For information on migrant access to health care in Wales see www.wales.nhs.uk/nhswalesaboutus/budgetcharges/overseasvisitors, and in Scotland see www.gov.scot/Topics/Health/Services/Overseas-visitors, and for Northern Ireland see www.health-ni.gov.uk/articles/european-union-and-overseas-policy and related links.

2 The rights that EEA nationals and their family members hold under European law, that are referenced here, continue to apply and may only change after the UK finally withdraws from the EU. This process may take up to two years from the date that the UK formally notified the EU of its intention to leave (29 March 2017), or possibly even longer.

3 The criteria for obtaining indefinite leave to remain are set out at: www.visabureau.com/uk/indefinite-leave-to-remain.aspx (accessed: 29 August 2017).

4 Section 115 Immigration and Asylum Act 1999 states that a person will have this endorsement if they are 'subject to immigration control'.

5 See further details at www.nhsbsa.nhs.uk/exemption-certificates/medical-exemption-certificates (accessed: 5th September 2017).

6 See www.england.nhs.uk/commissioning/wp-content/uploads/sites/12/2015/11/pat-reg-sop-pmc-gp.pdf (Accessed: 1 September 2017).

7 This can be found at: www.nhs.uk/choiceintheNHS/Yourchoices/GPchoice/Documents/GMS1%5b1%5d.pdf (accessed 18 August 2017).

8 See further details at National Health Service (n.d.).

9 For more information, see Refugee Council leaflet on access to health care for asylum seekers in several languages (at www.refugeecouncil.org.uk/latest/blogs/3662_asylum_seekers_access_to_healthcare_-_download_our_new_leaflet, accessed 19 May 2018); The Royal College of General Practitioners position statement on access to primary care for failed asylum seekers and vulnerable migrants (at www.rcgp.org.uk/policy/rcgp-policy-areas/asylum-seekers-and-vulnerable-migrants.aspx, accessed 19 May 2018).

References

Bevan, A. 1952, *In Place of Fear*, William Heineman, London.

Department of Health and Social Care. 2015, *NHS Constitution for England*, Department of Health and Social Care, viewed 9 July 2018, www.gov.uk/government/publications/the-nhs-constitution-for-england.

Department of Health and Social Care. 2017a, *Making a fair contribution: government response to the consultation on the extension of charging overseas visitors and migrants using the NHS in England*, viewed 1 September 2017, www.gov.uk/government/uploads/system/uploads/attachment_data/file/590027/Cons_Response_cost_recovery.pdf.

Department of Health and Social Care. 2017b, *Guidance on implementing the overseas visitor charging regulations*, viewed 5 September 2017, www.gov.uk/government/uploads/system/uploads/attachment_data/file/639277/GuidGuid_to_Charging_Regulations_post_21_August_final__Master_version_pdf.

Donnelly, L. 2018, 'Doctors call for charges for overseas patients using A&E units', *The Telegraph*, 13 January, viewed 9 July 2018, www.telegraph.co.uk/news/2018/01/13/doctors-call-charges-overseas-patients-using-ae-units/.

Fylde and Wyre Clinical Commissioning Group. 2016, *Private versus NHS Prescriptions*, viewed 5 September 2017, www.fyldeandwyreccg.nhs.uk/download/medicines_optimisation/fact_sheets/Private-versus-NHS-Prescriptionsv2June16.pdf.

Gentleman, A. 2018, 'Theresa May refuses to intervene over man's £54,000 NHS cancer bill', *The Guardian*, 22 May, viewed 9 July 2018, www.theguardian.com/uk-news/2018/mar/22/theresa-may-refuses-to-intervene-over-mans-54000-nhs-cancer-bill-albert-thompson.

Government of the UK. 2017a, *UK residence for EU citizens: permanent residence after 5 years*, viewed 29 August 2017, www.gov.uk/eea-registration-certificate/permanent-residence.

Government of the UK. 2017b, *Safeguarding the position of EU citizens living in the UK and UK nationals living in the EU*, www.gov.uk/government/publications/safeguarding-the-position-of-eu-citizens-in-the-uk-and-uk-nationals-in-the-eu.

Government of the UK. 2018, *Review into NHS overseas visitor charges: call for submissions*, viewed 30 May 2018, www.gov.uk/government/news/review-into-nhs-overseas-visitor-charges-call-for-submissions.

Government of the UK, Home Office. 2017, *General grounds for refusal*, viewed 5 September 2017, www.gov.uk/government/uploads/system/uploads/attachment_data/file/607623/GGFG-Section-2-v28.pdf.

Kirkup, J., & Winnett, R. 2012, 'Theresa May interview: 'We're going to give illegal migrants a really hostile reception'', *The Telegraph*, 25 May, viewed 29 August 2017, www.telegraph.co.uk/news/uknews/immigration/9291483/Theresa-May-interview-Were-going-to-give-illegal-migrants-a-really-hostile-reception.html.

National Audit Office. 2016, *Recovering the cost of NHS treatment for overseas visitors*, 28 October, www.nao.org.uk/report/recovering-the-cost-of-nhs-treatment-for-overseas-patients/.

National Health Service. n.d. *Medical exemption certificates*, viewed 5 September 2017, www.nhsbsa.nhs.uk/exemption-certificates/medical-exemption-certificates.

National Health Service Choices. 2017a, *NHS out-of-hours-service*, viewed 5 September 2017, www.nhs.uk/using-the-nhs/nhs-services/urgent-and-emergency-care/nhs-out-of-hours-services.

National Health Service Choices. 2017b, *NHS in England: help with health costs*, viewed 5 September 2017, www.nhs.uk/NHSEngland/Healthcosts/Pages/PPC.aspx.

National Health Service Choices. 2017c, *What services do contraception clinics offer?* viewed 5 September 2017, www.nhs.uk/Conditions/contraception-guide/Pages/contraception-clinic-services.aspx.

National Health Service Commissioning. 2017, *Primary care commissioning England*, viewed 5 September 2017, www.england.nhs.uk/commissioning/primary-care/primary-care-comm/.

National Health Service England. 2015, *Patient registration: standard operating principles for primary medical care (general practice)*, viewed 5 September 2017, www.england.nhs.uk/commissioning/wp-content/uploads/sites/12/2015/11/pat-reg-sop-pmc-gp.pdf.

Legislation

Children Act 1989.

Immigration and Asylum Act 1999.

Mental Capacity Act 2005.

Mental Health Act 1983.

National Assistance Act 1948.

The Immigration (Health Charge) Order 2015.

The National Health Service (Charges to Overseas Visitors) (Amendment) Regulations 2017.

The National Health Service (Charges to Overseas Visitors) Regulations 2015.

8 The right to health for all? Debates surrounding access to health care for asylum seekers in Germany

Sabine Klotz

8.1 Introduction

Forced migration can cause a vulnerable situation,[1] which affects the right to health. Asylum seekers[2] are confronted with various health risks, such as traumatic experiences and inadequate access to health care, during transit and even in the receiving countries (Norredam, Mygind & Krasnik 2005, p. 285). Furthermore, asylum seekers face numerous obstacles (such as cultural, legal, administrative, and financial barriers) to health care and health-related services in comparison with citizens (Razum & Bozorgmehr 2016; Schneider, Joos & Bozorgmehr 2015). This is also the subject of concern in several country reports by the *UN Committee on Economic, Social and Cultural Rights* (CESCR). In the case of Germany, the UN Committee

> notes with deep concern the situation of asylum-seekers who [...] have access only to emergency health care' and 'urges the State party to ensure, in line with international standards, that asylum-seekers enjoy equal treatment in access to [...] health care.
>
> (CESCR 2011, para. 13)

In Germany, access to health care is regulated in §§ 4 and 6 Asylbewerberleistungsgesetz (AsybLG). The regulation implies only limited access to health care for asylum seekers focused on medical treatment for acute diseases and to those in pain. Following the decision of the *Federal Constitutional Court* (BVerfG 2012) in July 2012, the debate surrounding health care for asylum seekers has flared up in Germany. The court had decided that funds for asylum seekers must be adjusted as per the level of social welfare. Civil society organisations hoped that health care policies would also improve following this decision. Since 2015, the issue has been swept up in the political agenda as a result of the debate over an electronic health insurance card for asylum seekers (called *Gesundheitskarte*) and has led to the introduction of the *Gesundheitskarte* (adopted 29 September 2015, came into force 1 January 2016).

Therefore, this chapter analyses the debates surrounding health care access[3] for asylum seekers in Germany prior to the introduction of the *Gesundheitskarte*. First, it asks: What does the realisation of the right to health for asylum seekers encompass, and how is this right realised in Germany? (question 1). Second, it asks: Which of the discourses exist during this debate, and is there any policy change? (question 2).

8.2 Method

8.2.1 Investigation period, case selection, data material

The first question addresses the right to health for asylum seekers. It is worth mentioning that this chapter is written from a human rights perspective based on human rights law, which is codified in international treaties as well as in regional and national law. For this purpose, I only use documents of international, regional and national human rights law, law commentaries and specialised articles to clarify what the realisation of the right to health for asylum seekers encompasses.

The investigation period begins in June 2012 because the debate around health care for asylum seekers has flared up since the decision of the BVerfG (BVerfG 2012). The period ends with the introduction of the *Gesundheitskarte* on 1 January 2016.

The case selection includes the following actors: the political groups that are part of the German parliament (CDU/CSU, SPD, Die Grünen/Bündnis 90 and Die Linke) and a few civil society organisations, along with the position of the *Bundesländer*. The data material comprises documents and statements from the abovementioned actors, such as press releases, interviews in newspapers and debates in German parliament (Deutscher Bundestag).

8.2.2 Argumentative discourse analysis

The argumentative discourse analysis (ADA) investigates argumentative structures in documents or other written and oral statements, as well as a set of practices in which the statement is produced and reproduced. However, this approach is more than mere textual analysis – it is an examination of discursive mechanisms where particular (political) realities are produced between actors (Hajer 2008, p. 212). In addition, ADA is used to examine policy changes, explain how a policy comes up and why a discourse is dominant (Hajer & Versteeg 2005, p. 187).

Hajer developed several conceptual tools for analysis, such as the argumentative triangle: discourse, meaning and practices. The inherent logic of the triangle becomes apparent in the definition of discourse. Discourse is an 'ensemble of ideas, concepts and categories through which meaning is given to social and physical phenomena, and which is produced and reproduced through an identifiable set of practices' (Hajer 2006, p. 67). A discourse coalition, which refers to a group of actors that uses a particular set of storylines[4] over a specific time, is another tool (ibid., p. 70). The meaning of discourse coalition assumes that actors with different backgrounds form a coalition based on a common storyline.

Therefore, the storyline as a kind of discourse construction enables one to understand the dynamic character of discourses – this means that a constructed phenomenon or problem could change during a period of time (Hajer 2008, pp. 217–218).

One central aspect of ADA involves examining a policy change by means of discourse dominance. A discourse is dominant only if it fulfils two conditions: (1) discourse structuration – if a discourse dominates the discursive space – and (2) discourse institutionalisation – if a discourse is reflected in the institutional practices of that political domain (Hayer 1993, p. 48).

8.2.3 Qualitative content analysis

The data material is evaluated by means of qualitative content analysis oriented to an inductive category development approach (Mayring 2015). In this approach, the aspects of interpretation and the main categories would be developed as near as possible to the data material. The analysis process follows the analysis steps of inductive category development: determination of category definition, formulation of inductive categories, revision of categories to check reliability and interpretation of results (Mayring 2000).

First, I analysed 50% of the data material to develop categories and to check their determination. The data material was codified and analysed under the following aspects:

- Type of document: press release, speech, etc.
- Actor: Who is speaking? Who is the author of these documents?
- Argument: Which argument is used to construct the phenomenon or problem? Is there any noticeable storyline?
- Policy change: Is there any interest, intention or will to change aspects of policy and polity?
- Object or subject of responsibility: Who is identified as responsible for the problem or situation? Which are the causes mentioned to construct the problem or situation?
- Linguistic devices (such as metaphor) and language selection

Next, I analysed the complete data material by means of the abovementioned aspects – with a strong focus on 'argument' and 'policy change', which enables one to identify and determine different discourses as main categories. In addition, I examined the actors to detect discourse coalitions.

8.3 The right to health for asylum seekers in Germany

8.3.1 The right to health: the legal basis

The right to health[5] is anchored in several UN documents as well as in essential EU documents. The 'right of everyone to the enjoyment of the highest attainable standard of physical and mental health'[6] is legally binding for all State parties under Article 12 of the International Covenant on Economic, Social and Cultural Rights (ICESCR). This right is also recognised in several UN documents, such as the Convention on the Elimination of all Forms of Discrimination Against Women, and embedded in the preamble to the Constitution of the WHO.[7] In addition, this right is strengthened by the Convention relating to the Status of Refugees (1951) under Article 24, which calls for 'the same treatment as is accorded to nationals in respect of [...] social security (legal provisions in [...] sickness [...])'.

The right to health cannot be interpreted as a right to be healthy. No State can definitely guarantee such a right because health or health status depends on a number of variables, for example, genetic disposition or health-related behaviour, which States are unable to control (Krennerich 2016a, p. 65). However, health also depends – apart from personal or individual variables – on political action, which could also affect the individual or societal health or health status (Kälin & Künzli 2013, pp. 358–359).

Therefore, in 2011, the General Comment on the Right to Health of the Committee on Economic, Social and Cultural Rights (CESCR) elaborated on the right to health in detail and clarified the State's obligations. According to the General Comment, the right to health does not mean the right to be healthy but rather deals with conditions such that every human being is able to enjoy the 'highest attainable standard of physical and mental health' to live a life of dignity. In addition, the right to health contains freedoms (for example right to control one's health and body) and entitlements (for example the right to a system of health protection). This shows that the right to health is interrelated with other human rights (for example the right to life) and, thus, the realisation of the right to health is indispensable for, closely related to and dependent upon the exercise of other human rights (CESCR 2000, para. 8; Krennerich 2015, pp. 14–16). Accordingly, the right to health is not limited to health care or access to health care but extends to the underlying determinants of health, such as nutrition and access to health-related education (CESCR 2000 paras. 1, 3 and 4). Again, access to health care includes preventive and curative health care; this means, for example, facilities, goods and services for the diagnosis, treatment, care and prevention of diseases (Ssenyonjo 2016, p. 519). To sum up, the right to health includes both components: health care or access to health care and their underlying determinants.

Like other human rights, the CESCR emphasises that the following four interrelated and essential elements must be recognised: *availability*, *accessibility*, *acceptability* and *quality*. The functioning public health care facilities, goods and services as well as programmes are *available* in sufficient quantity within the State for the entire population. Moreover, health facilities, goods, and services must be *accessible* to everyone, especially the most vulnerable or marginalised segments of the population, without discrimination. This element has four overlapping dimensions: physical, informational and economic accessibility as well as accessibility without discrimination. Last but not least, health facilities, goods and services must respect medical ethics and be culturally appropriate (*acceptability*) as well as medically appropriate and of good *quality* (CESCR 2000, para. 12; Krennerich 2015, pp. 16–17; Krennerich 2016a, pp. 67–68; OHCHR 2008, p. 4).

Like all human rights, economic, social and cultural rights are binding on States, which ratify treaties. Therefore, States have specific legal obligations to respect, to protect and to fulfil the right to health.[8] The obligation to respect, for example, stipulates that States are 'refraining from denying or limiting equal access for all persons' (CESCR 2000, para. 34). The obligation to protect includes, for example, that states are obligated to 'adopt legislation or take other measures ensuring equal access to health care' (ibid., para. 35). One part of the obligation to fulfil is to ensure at least the so-called 'minimum core obligations'[9] (Kälin & Künzli 2013, p. 364). In comparison with civil and political rights, the economic, social and cultural rights are subject to progressive realisation. Thus, a State is obligated to 'take steps [...] to the maximum of its available resources, with a view to achieving progressively the full realization of the rights [...]' (ICESCR, Article 2(1)).

In terms of regional instruments, the right to health is also recognised in the Revised European Social Charter (ESCRev) under Article 11, as well as in the Charter of Fundamental Rights of the European Union (CFR) under Article 35. According to the Common European Asylum System,[10] health care for asylum seekers is regulated by the Reception Conditions Directive that must be implemented by the Member States (including Germany). Article 19 of this directive outlines only that asylum seekers receive the necessary health care on basic (at least) emergency health care and essential treatment of illnesses and of serious mental disorders (2013/33/EU, Article 12). However, the Reception Conditions Directive is recognised in specific situations with respect to 'vulnerable persons' (for example pregnant women and persons with mental disorders) and includes relevant provisions for 'vulnerable' asylum seekers (ibid., Articles 21–25), including protection of physical and mental health (ibid., Article 17(1)).

What is it that is especially relevant to the case of asylum seekers? The CESCR emphasises that the States must ensure that 'health facilities, goods and services are accessible to *all*, [...] in law and in fact, without discrimination on any of the prohibited grounds' (CESCR 2000, para. 12(b), emphasised by S.K.). In addition, the CESCR concretises this under the State's obligation to respect individuals 'by refraining from denying or limiting equal access [...] for all persons, including [...] asylum-seekers [...], to preventive, curative and rehabilitative health services' (ibid., para 34).

What do these abovementioned concrete terms mean regarding the right to health for asylum seekers? To return to the understanding of non-discrimination, non-discrimination and equality are two fundamental elements of human rights law and essential to enjoying the economic, social and cultural rights. Discrimination means any distinction, exclusion, restriction, preference or differential treatment that is directly or indirectly based on prohibited grounds and which intends or effects to impair or nullify the recognition, enjoyment or exercise of human rights and fundamental freedoms (CESCR 2009, paras. 2 & 7). The prohibited grounds include, for example, race, sex and language as well as national or social origin.[11] Not all distinctions between persons or groups is discrimination. However, differential treatment is discriminatory unless this could be justified as 'reasonable' and 'objective.' This means that any distinction or differential treatment must be in a reasonable relationship of proportionality and must pursue a legitimate aim. In addition, any kind of distinction must be legitimate and compatible with the nature of the Covenant rights (ibid., paras. 7, 9 & 13). For example, women have access to gender-specific health care services and protective measures – for example, maternity – due to biological differences from men. In this case, this different treatment of women is logical, not discriminatory (Otto 2014, pp. 324–325).

The CESCR emphasises that a lack of available resources does not fall within these criteria (CESCR 2009, para. 13; Interights 2011; Weiwei 2004). Moreover, many measures to eliminate health-related discrimination could be pursued with minimum resource implications, and even in times of resource constraints, vulnerable persons must be protected by the adoption of relatively low-cost targeted programmes, according to the Committee (CESCR 2000, para. 18). Despite the reference to a wide margin, according to progressive realisation, there is a certain commitment of States to guarantee the right to health without any kind of discrimination (Toebes 2017, p. 134).

8.3.2 Statutory regulation in Germany

The AsylbLG regulates in § 4 that medical treatment for asylum seekers[12] is limited to acute diseases and to individuals in pain, along with health services during childbirth and pregnancy. However, the treatment of chronic diseases is not usually granted (Grube et al. 2014, Rn. 1–34). Normally, psychotherapy and dental prostheses[13] fall under these restrictions and thus are rarely approved. However, § 6 contains permission for additional medical services not mentioned in § 4, but this paragraph can be interpreted in a restrictive way, according to legal commentaries (ibid., Rn. 1–34). Thus, § 6 would probably not guarantee an optimal level of medical treatment such as that received by patients insured under statutory health insurance (Eichenhofer 2013, p. 170).

If one examines case law related to health care for asylum seekers, it is evident that there is no coherent interpretation or application of the law. For example, a chronic patient was approved for orthopaedic shoes to ease pain by a decision of the administrative court in Baden-Württemberg. In another case, the patient was granted only painkillers instead of an artificial hip joint (Classen 2015, pp. 190–191). Additionally, courts justify a limited scope to health care with the following argument: asylum seekers are only temporally resident in Germany and long-term medical therapy is not possible (Eichenhofer 2013, p. 170).

To sum up, the AsylbLG contains only limited access to health care for asylum seekers. Because of the restrictive interpretation of § 6, asylum seekers do not enjoy an equivalent access to health care, such as that received by patients insured under statutory health insurance (Eichenhofer 2013, p. 170; Kaltenborn 2015, pp. 161–165). Furthermore, case law shows a leeway in the application and interpretation of the statutory regulation. This could be a consequence of the fact that a coherent legal claim to medical services is either not comprehensible or does not exist.

8.3.3 Implementation of law

In Germany, the federal provinces (*Bundesländer*) and municipalities are responsible for the implementation of health care for asylum seekers. The legal framework is regulated at the federal level (*Bundesebene*), where, for example, the AsylbLG can be amended (Schammann 2015, pp. 26–27; Schamman & Kühn 2016, pp. 6–7).

Generally, the social welfare office is responsible for health care issues in municipalities. If asylum seekers fall ill, they must go to the social welfare office to obtain a specific permission (*Krankenschein*). They can only go to a doctor once they have this permission. In such cases, the administrative staff decides if a medical consultation is necessary or not. It is possible that a public health officer (*Amtsarzt*) may be consulted in decisions regarding visits to a specialist, but it is the social welfare office that finally decides on the matter (Lindner 2015). This practice takes place in many municipalities in various ways.[14] Thus, a few municipalities and *Bundesländer* use an alternative model based on the *Bremer Modell*. This model implies a broad health programme for asylum seekers that aims to improve access to health care as well as housing and living facilities in the *Bundesland* Bremen. Furthermore, this *Bundesland* has an agreement with the *Allgemeine Ortskrankenkasse* (AOK) Bremerhaven, which receives a fixed sum for medical services for asylum seekers provided they procure an electronic health insurance card from the AOK. While medical services are limited to the AsylbLG, asylum seekers can directly visit a doctor through this card. Furthermore, the *Bremer Modell* tries to be respectful and culturally appropriate. For example, the reception centres for asylum seekers are manned by doctors who have a background in immigration issues and who are specially sensitised to be culturally appropriate (Gesundheitsamt Bremen 2011).

Since 2015, the federal state has enabled the introduction of the *Gesundheitskarte*. Currently, the *Bundesländer* could undertake health insurance by signing a contract which includes health care provisions for asylum seekers limited to §§ 4 and 6 AsylbLG. While it was also possible earlier to obtain this card, now health insurance providers could be obligated to sign a contract with a municipality. This improves the municipality's position with regard to negotiations with health insurance providers. Meanwhile, some *Bundesländer*[15] implement the *Gesundheitskarte* and others have introduced this card very slowly or even refused it at the provincial level, such as Bavaria (Augsburger Allgemeine 2015).

To sum up, there exist various practices in the health care of asylum seekers in *Bundesländern*. There is some room for manoeuvring in the practice and for the implementation of health care for asylum seekers as well. Thus, the access and scope of health care provisions depend on the respective *Bundesland* and municipalities, or even on the respective social welfare offices (Schammann 2015; Schamman & Kühn 2016). Therefore, there is no inherent interpretation and application of the law by courts and political actors, which could lead to different and unequal access in health care, depending on one's place of residence as well as in comparison to German citizens. In addition, the *Gesundheitskarte* does not immediately result in a common regulation or practice in all *Bundesländer* as well as an inherent interpretation and application of the law.

8.4 Debates surrounding health care for asylum seekers

8.4.1 Discourse

Through the analysis, I found three discourses in the current debate around health care for asylum seekers: the status quo discourse, the cost-benefit consideration discourse and the human rights discourse. The status quo discourse, as the name implies, addresses the lack of political will to change existing policy and/or polity. In contrast, the other discourses argue that a change is necessary because of economic arguments (cost-benefit discourse) and human rights (human rights discourse).

8.4.1.1 Status quo discourse

Generally, the health care issue is discussed in the context of the high number of asylum-seekers. Immigration is understood to be a challenge for the social security system and society (Deutscher Bundestag 2015a; Heike Schmelzle (CDU/CSU), p. 11084). Furthermore, existing health care facilities for asylum seekers are considered to be adequate medical care. Therefore, any change or improvement is not absolutely necessary because the criteria of the AsylbLG are obviously clear and fixed (ibid., Dr. Roy Kühne (CDU/CSU), p. 11091; BT.-Drs. 2014, p. 5).

One of the storylines is that the social security system should not offer incentives for migration (Deutscher Bundestag 2014b, Jutta Eckenbach (CDU/CSU), p. 5875). It assumes a relationship between the social welfare services on offer and the decision to immigrate into a country. In my opinion, this could be called the *pull-effect argument* – high standards of social welfare services for migrants (including asylum-seekers) would lead to a dramatic rise in immigration (Deutscher Bundestag 2015a, Andrea Lindholz (CDU/CSU), p. 11080; Spiegel Online 2015). Therefore, measures such as the *Gesundheitskarte* work against efforts to reduce immigration (Deutscher Bundestag 2015a, Heiko Schmelzle (CDU/CSU), p. 11085).

The other storyline is as follows: the introduction of the *Gesundheitskarte* could lead to its abuse. It argues that doctors could approve medical services that are not truly necessary and that social welfare offices would be unable to check this (Thelen 2015; Woratschka 2015). As a result, the cost for hosting asylum seekers could increase (Bewarder, Greive & Kade 2015; Deutscher Bundestag 2015a, Andrea Lindholz (CDU/CSU), p. 11081).

The discourse is reproduced through concerns and warnings, such as about what could happen if there were to be a political change in relation to the health issue. One example of such a warning is that an unlimited access to health care for asylum seekers will result in excessive demands on the German social welfare system (Deutscher Bundestag 2015a, Heiko Schmelzle (CDU/CSU), p. 11085). Moreover, it refers to rationality as well as responsibility towards a community's solidarity and its limits (Deutscher Bundestag 2015a, Heike Schmelzle (CDU/CSU), p. 11085). For example, it would be difficult to justify expanded medical services to the taxpayer (ibid., Andrea Lindholz (CDU/CSU), p. 11081). The discourse is strengthened by its reference to compatibility with the ICESCR and the decision of the BVerfG (Deutscher Bundestag 2014a, Matthhäus Strebl (CDU/CSU), p. 5307; Deutscher Bundestag 2015b, p. 4). In addition, all complaints from the human right discourse would be denied as individual cases, which are caused by the legal regulation (Deutscher Bundestag 2015a, Heike Schmelzle (CDU/CSU), p. 11085). Language tools and images – such as the 'flood of immigrants' (ibid., Dr. Roy Kühne (CDU/CSU), p. 11092) – are used to convey a certain association in this discourse.

8.4.1.2 Cost–benefit discourse

The health care issue here is discussed in the context of a high number of asylum seekers (Deutscher Bundesrat 2014, p. 4). In contrast to the status quo discourse, there is considerable emphasis on the challenges involved for municipalities (ibid., p. 4).

First, there is the following storyline: health care for asylum seekers should be improved and simplified. Therefore, the procedure should get simpler, especially in terms of eliminating bureaucratic hurdles (Deutscher Bundesrat 2015, Tarek Al-Wazir (Bündnis 90/Die Grünen), p. 387; SPD 2015). It also considers that health care for asylum seekers can generally be improved (Deutscher Bundestag 2014b, Daniela Kolbe (SPD), p. 5873; SPD 2014, p. 4).

The other storyline is that the *Bundesländer* and municipalities should relieve themselves of increasing costs that can be a burden on the administration (Deutscher Bundesrat 2014, p. 4; SPD 2014, p. 4). It assumes that this is possible given easier procedures, such as the *Gesundheitskarte*, since it, for example, works at reducing staff and therefore reducing costs (Deutscher Bundestag 2014c, p. 4). It would also argue that a common *Gesundheitskarte* also establishes a uniform and binding regulation at the federal level (Deutscher Bundesrat 2014, p. 3.). The *Bremer Modell* shows decreasing costs and faster access to health care, as per this discourse (Deutscher Bundestag 2015a, Hilde Mattheis (SPD), p. 11084).

The discourse is reproduced through economic ideas, such as cost-benefit consideration, and uses phrases such as 'efficiency'; it especially emphasises the benefits of the *Gesundheitskarte* and the necessity for its introduction (Deutscher Bundesrat 2014, p. 3). The reproduction of discourse would be strengthened by the argument that, on the basis of experience, it is proven that the Bremer Modell leads to decreasing costs and disapproves the assumption of abuse (see the status quo discourse) (Flüchtlingsrat Berlin 2015; Pro Asyl 2015; SPD 2015).

8.4.1.3 Human rights discourse

In contrast to the status quo discourse, there is a significant intention to change the existing policy that regulates health care for asylum seekers (Bündnis 90/Die Grünen 2014b; Deutscher Bundestag 2014e; Pro Asyl 2015). It is also discussed in the context of migration, including the challenges faced by asylum seekers (BAGFW 2014; Deutscher Bundestag 2015a, Harald Weinberg (Die Linke), p. 11078). Furthermore, it would be assumed – in contrast to the status quo discourse – that the AsylbLG cannot regulate immigration (Deutscher Bundestag 2014b, Kerstin Griese (Grüne), p. 5879). Therefore, it would be assumed that individuals are forced to migrate because of war or persecution – the so-called push-argument – and this requires adequate health care for asylum seekers (Deutscher Bundestag 2015a, Harald Weinberg (Die Linke), p. 11078).

The first storyline is that the existing regulation regarding health care for asylum seekers is dangerous (Flüchtlingsrat Berlin 2014, p. 42; Pro Asyl 2015). It would be claimed that there is a relevant legal uncertainty about which medical services are to be approved. This could affect all involved persons, including doctors, security staff and courts (Flüchtlingsrat Berlin 2014, p. 41). Moreover, it could result in long procedures for approving medical treatments and could lead to untreated diseases or to more serious consequences,[16] even death (Deutscher Bundestag 2014a, Ulla Jelpke (Die Linke), p. 5303; Deutscher Bundestag 2015c, p. 1; Deutscher Bundestag 2014d, p. 2; Flüchtlingsrat Berlin 2014, pp. 40–45). A layperson – not a doctor – would then be authorised to grant approvals, and this would not be acceptable in this discourse (Bundesärztekammer 2014, p. 278; Deutscher Bundesrat 2015, Tarek Al-Wazir (Bündnis 90/Die Grünen), p. 387; Deutscher Bundesrat 2015, Winfried Kretschmann (Bündnis 90/Die Grünen), p. 376). Therefore, it would be argued that it is necessary for asylum seekers to have health care equivalent to the standards of domestic health insurance, which would be possible with the implementation of a law at the federal level (such as an appropriate *Gesundheitskarte)* or through the abolition of the AsylbLG by authorities at the federal level (BT.-Drs. 18/5370; Bündnis 90/Die Grünen 2014a; Bündnis 90/Die Grünen 2015; Pro Asyl 2014b).[17]

The other storyline is that the health care provisions violate existing law, such as the right to health and the principle of equality, and also violate human dignity (Deutscher Bundestag 2014e, p. 1). It would be argued that such limited health care is compatible neither with international law nor with German constitutional law (*Grundgesetz, GG*) – especially with regard to the basic right to human dignity according to Article 1 GG – nor with the decision of the BVerfG (BAGFW 2014; Berliner Flüchtlingsrat 2014).

This discourse is reproduced from a human rights perspective because it would be argued by reference to international human rights law and national law, as well as by using expressions such as 'inhumane' or 'violation of human dignity' (Deutscher Bundestag 2014e, p. 1; Pro Asyl 2015).

8.4.2 Discourse coalition

A discourse coalition is recognised when actors share and use a set of storylines. However, it would be possible that actors were producing different discourses or sharing storylines of different discourses (Hajer 1993, p. 47). Thus, the actors of *human rights discourse* even use the argument of *cost-benefit discourse* – the introduction of the *Gesundheitskarte* will lead to a decline in costs – to argue for an improved access to health care or health care for asylum-seekers.

Let me give an overview of the existing discourse coalition in my discourse analysis: The *status quo discourse* is mainly produced by the political party CSU, and by some politicians from the CDU, as well as the position of the federal government. These actors are part of a discourse coalition that shares the abovementioned assumptions and storylines. The *cost-benefit discourse* includes the political party SPD, the Federal Council (*Bundesrat*), and politicians from the CDU, such as health minister Hermann Gröhe (CDU), who introduced the *Gesundheitskarte* on the initiative of chancellor Angela Merkel (CDU). In contrast, the human rights discourse contains the political parties *Die Linke* and *Die Grünen* as well as civil society organisations.

8.4.3 Discourse dominance

The ADA shows that there are different definitions, perceptions and evaluations of health care or access to health care for asylum seekers in Germany: the *status quo discourse* assumes that there is no problem to solve, whereas the *human rights discourse* argues for significant improvement in international and national law. The *cost-benefit discourse* also insists on policy change; however, this discourse argues for lower costs in comparison to the *human rights discourse*. Furthermore, according to the *human rights discourse*, the introduction of the *Gesundheitskarte* lowers the barriers to health care but is not enough to grant asylum seekers unrestricted access to health care, as medical services are limited to the AsylbLG (Medibüro, Medico International & Verein demokratischer Ärztinnen und Ärzte 2015).

These different definitions, perceptions and evaluations demonstrate that there are differences in the will to change the policy or improve health care or access to health care for asylum-seekers. The ADA enables us to identify a policy change by increasing our understanding of discourse dominance. It becomes clear that the *cost-benefit discourse* dominates the discursive space (discourse structuration). One indication could be the high approval from the population; according to a representative survey of the *Bertelsmann Stiftung*, two of three Germans are in favour of the *Gesundheitskarte* (Bertelsmann Stiftung 2016). In addition, the *cost-benefit discourse* reflects the institutional practices of that political domain (discourse institutionalization); the *Gesundheitskarte* is introduced by German law (Asylverfahrensbeschleunigungsgesetz), which reflects such institutional practices. In this legislative proposal, it is emphasised that medical services will be limited to §§ 4 and 6 AsylbLG, and this card will enable simplified billing relating to health care for asylum seekers (Bundesministerium des Innern 2015). These limited medical services and the argument of an easier procedure indicate that there is also a dominance of ***cost-benefit discourse*** in institutional practices in comparison with the other discourses.

The actual policy change is surprising because any change or improvement was not foreseeable. At the beginning of September 2015, the health minister Herman Gröhe generally favoured the idea of a *Gesundheitskarte* (Migazin 2015). However, the CDU/CSU – part of the federal government – expressed significant concerns that the card would provide incentives for individuals to migrate to Germany, and this prevented the introduction of the card (CDU/CSU 2015, p. 5). Given these concerns, therefore, the introduction of the *Gesundheitskarte* seems surprising. It is an example of policy change at the federal level.

8.5 Discussion

The ADA revealed a policy change in the health care for asylum seekers through the introduction of the *Gesundheitskarte.* Despite this policy change, the health card does not lead to a unified regulation in all ***Bundesländern***. Therefore, regulation at the federal level at least enables the introduction of the *Gesundheitskarte* for (willing) ***Bundesländer***. On the basis of the discourse analysis in this chapter, it is not possible to explain why the policy is changing. This could perhaps be a question for further research.

From a human rights perspective, the introduction of the *Gesundheitskarte* is definitely an improvement: it ensures that only doctors can decide what constitutes a medical necessity, which can also contribute towards non-discriminatory access to medical services and eliminate forms of exclusion. However, a limitation of the access to health care for asylum seekers still exists because health care is also limited in terms of provisions, according to the AsylbLG. This minimal health care for asylum seekers would be very problematic from a human rights perspective. According to the non-discrimination principle, it would hardly be possible to justify any limitation or restriction of equal access to health care of asylum seekers and citizens as 'reasonable' and 'objective' as well as legitimate and compatible with the Covenant rights (Krennerich 2016b).

It is questionable whether German regulations are compatible with European law. Although the Member States of the European Union must guarantee only necessary health care on basic (at least) emergency health care, the States are obligated to recognise (medical) needs of 'vulnerable' persons (Birk 2015, p. 53). For example, there is a lack of psychotherapeutic treatment for asylum seekers (Baron & Flory 2016; Deutscher Bundestag 2016, p. 1). In addition, Germany still has insufficiently implemented Article 12 of the Reception Conditions Directive,[18] because early systematic screening and identification of especially vulnerable persons have been dramatically neglected (Joksimovic et al. 2017, p. 294).

According to the decision of BVerfG (BVerfG 2012), any limitation in access to health care could only be justified if asylum seekers required less medical care or had lower health-related needs as a collective group. This assumption must be empirically proven (Eichendörfer 2013, p. 174). On the one hand, it would be difficult to classify asylum seekers as a homogeneous group with unified medical needs. In contrast, asylum seekers are a very heterogeneous group, which includes subgroups such as female refugees who need gender-sensitive sexual and reproductive health care services and persons with mental disorders who require psychotherapeutic treatment and psychosocial care. Furthermore, there is no empirical evidence pointing to a lower medical need (Eichendörfer 2013, p. 174; Kaltenborn 2015, p. 165). In contrast, studies document a high prevalence of post-traumatic disorder and depression among (recently arrived) asylum seekers (Alpak et al. 2015; Gäbel et al. 2006; Niklewski, Richter & Lehfeld 2012).

From a human rights perspective, the *Gesundheitskarte* reduced bureaucracy rather than asylum-seekers' exclusion from health care, including exclusion due to linguistic barriers. There is still a dearth of translators specialised in the health care sector, including in the translation of medical vocabulary (Sabra 2015). Additionally, the costs for translators are not covered for a complex and ongoing medical treatment such as psychotherapy (Baron & Flory 2016). Language barriers must be overcome to guarantee informed consent and guarantee participation in health-related decision-making, which is also founded in the right to health (CESCR 2000, paras. 11 & 23). One approach to improving basic communication in everyday conversations is the development of a translation app called 'universal doctor'[19] and pictograms,[20] through which health-related personnel could inform asylum seekers of health issues – including explanations of the side effects of medication (Scholz 2016, pp. 195–196). However, this approach should not be viewed uncritically, because a dialogue between doctors and asylum seekers is only possible on a low, basic level; therefore, it make sense that people use these only for their everyday interactions. Certainly, there are further challenges that could lead to exclusion from health care, such as cultural barriers. To reduce these barriers, it would be necessary to implement an approach in health programmes and health care services which recognises the right to the health element 'acceptability'. Some ideas or concepts, such as inter-culturalism and exemplary best-practice projects such as *Mit Migranten für Migranten*,[21] *Bremer Modell* and *Düsseldorfer Modell*,[22] face these challenges, but a holistic approach has still not been implemented (Peters et al. 2014).

8.6 Conclusion

The *Gesundheitskarte* improves access to health care for asylum-seekers. However, the card does not immediately result in more medical services in practice. Furthermore, we can expect that the *Gesundheitskarte* will not be implemented in all German *Bundesländer*. Hence, access to health care for asylum seekers depends on their place of residence. To fulfil, respect and protect the right to health for all humans, including asylum seekers in Germany, rather courageous holistic approaches are needed to face challenges such as linguistic and cultural barriers, as well as formal barriers, to obtain full access to health care.

Notes

1 For an overview of the concept of vulnerability and different approaches, see, for example, Wrigley & Dawson 2016.
2 The term is used for persons seeking asylum and those with *Duldung*. In Germany, *Duldung* is not legally recognised as a residence permit.
3 At this point, it should be mentioned that the right to health does not only deal with equal access but rather also includes the so-called underlying determinants (see Chapter 8.3). I focus on health care for asylum seekers in this chapter. It would be too wide ranging to also delineate the underlying determinants.
4 A storyline is a statement that sums up a narrative. It could be understood as a short version of the actors' discussion. Furthermore, it is an instrument used by actors to compete with other actors for a specific definition of a phenomenon and a specific view of reality (Hajer 2004, p. 279).
5 For a detailed overview, see Tobin 2012.
6 The article is using the short equivalent 'the right to health,' which means the anchored right under Article 12 ICESCR.
7 Although the WHO definition is not legally binding, this definition of health is commonly used in human rights discourse. This definition was a turning point to understanding health beyond a limited biomedical understanding to a social dimension within the context of individual well-being. According to the WHO, health not only includes the absence of disease and infirmity but also recognises the state of complete physical, mental, and social well-being (Krennerich 2016a; Mann et al. 2013).
8 For a general view of the State's obligation relating to the right to health, see Krennerich 2013, 2015 & 2016a.
9 For a detailed overview of minimum core obligations, see, for example Forman 2015.
10 For more information about European asylum policy, see for example, Bendel 2016; Klotz 2017.
11 For all prohibited grounds, see the anchored principle of non-discrimination under Article 2(2) ICESCR or CESCR 2009. The list of prohibited grounds is not exhaustive. In addition, the CFR includes similar prohibited grounds under Article 21(1) CFR.
12 According to §§ 2 AsylbLG, asylum-seekers have access to the German health insurance system after a stay of 15 months. During the first 15 months – and for persons with Duldung – health care for asylum-seekers is regulated by the AsylbLG.
13 Civil society organisations document that if an asylum-seeker suffers from a toothache, there is no medically sustainable treatment but for the tooth to be extracted (Pro Asyl 2015).
14 The Robert Bosch foundation shows that there are differences in this process between municipalities in the south and north of Germany, which could lead to different outcomes. For example, children and teenagers can get up to five psychotherapy sessions without any examination by a public health officer (*Amtsarzt*) in the municipalities investigated in the north of Germany (Robert Bosch Stiftung 2014).
15 For an overview of the *Bundesländer*, which introduced the *Gesundheitskart*e, see Wächter-Raquet 2016, pp. 16–25.
16 One example could be the 'case of Leonardo' in Zirndorf. The 15-month-old baby, Leonardo, suffered from meningococcal infections. The guards at the reception centre in Zirndorf refused to call an ambulance, though his parents asked for one. The guards were condemned by the court for neglecting to help a person in danger (Pro Asyl 2014a).

17 There was also a campaign by a civil organisation to abolish the AsylbLG; see www.stopasylblg.de.

18 The Reception Conditions Directive contains common standards of reception conditions throughout the European Union; that asylum applicants have, for example, access to housing, food, health care, education for minors and access to employment under certain conditions.

19 This app is available in 17 languages at www.universaldoctor.com/.

20 One example is the pictograms of the International Pharmaceutical Federation; see www.fip.org/pictograms.

21 In this project, integrated migrants will educate intercultural guides to inform other migrants about the German health system as well as health-related issues (Scholz 2016, p. 196). For more information, see www.ethno-medizinisches-zentrum.de/index.php?option=com_content&view=article&id=28.

22 This model is based on diversity competence and is used for psychosomatic treatment in hospitals (Joksimovic et al. 2017, pp. 298–300).

References

Alpak, G., Unal, A., Bulbul, F., Sagaltici, E., Bez, Y., Altindag, A., Dalkilic, A., & Savas, H.A. 2015, 'Post-traumatic stress disorder among Syrian refugees in Turkey: a cross-sectional study', *International Journal of Psychiatry in Clinical Practice*, vol. 19, no. 1, pp. 45–50.

Augsburger Allgemeine. 2015, 'Aigner sagt Nein zur Gesundheitskarte für Flüchtlinge', *Augsburger Allgemeine*, 21 September, www.augsburger-allgemeine.de/bayern/Aigner-sagt-Nein-zur-Gesundheitskarte-fuer-Fluechtlinge-id35557337.html.

BAGFW (Bundesarbeitsgemeinschaft der Freien Wohlfahrtspflege). 2014, *BAGFW-Stellungnahme zum Referentenentwurf des Bundesministeriums für Arbeit und Soziales vom 04.06.2014 zur Änderung des Asylbewerberleistungsgesetzes und des Sozialgerichtgesetzes*, BT-Drs. 18/2592, Berlin.

Baron, J., & Flory, J. 2016, *Versorgungsbericht zur psychosozialen Versorgung von Flüchtlingen und Folteropfern in Deutschland*, BAfF e.V., Berlin.

Bendel, P. 2016, *Refugee policy in the European Union – protect Human Rights!, WISO-Diskurs 03/2016*, Friedrich-Ebert-Stiftung, Bonn.

Bertelsmann Stiftung. 2016, *Gesundheitskarte für Flüchtlinge droht zu scheitern*, viewed 4 July 2018, www.bertelsmann-stiftung.de/de/unsere-projekte/integrierte-krankenver sicherung/projekt nachrichten/gesundheitskarte-fuer-fluechtlinge/.

Bewarder, M., Greive, M., & Kade, C. 2015, 'Union streitet über Gesundheitskarte für Flüchtlinge', *WeltN24*, 16 September, Axel Springer, Berlin.

Birk, U.A. 2015, 'Das neue Asylbewerberleistungsgesetz', *Info Also*, vol. 2, pp. 51–53.

Bundesärztekammer. 2014, *Beschlussprotokoll des 117. Deutschen Ärztetages in Düsseldorf vom 27.05. bis 30.05.2014*, viewed 4 July 2018, www.bundesaerztekammer.de/aerztetag/aerztetage-ab-2006/117-deutscher-aerztetag-2014-in-duesseldorf/beschlussprotokoll.

Bundesministerium des Innern. 2015, *Entwurf eines Asylverfahrensbeschleunigungsgesetzes. Gesetzesentwurf der Bundesregierung*, viewed 4 July 2018, http://dip21.bundestag.de/dip21/btd/18/061/1806185.pdf.

Bündnis 90/Die Grünen. 2014a, *Asylgesetze: Grüne erstreiten Verbesserungen für Flüchtlinge und Kommunen im Bundesrat*, viewed 4 July 2018, www.gruene.de/themen/buergerrechte-demokratie/asylgesetze-gruene-erstreiten-verbesserungen-fuer-fluech tlinge-und-kommunen-im-bundesrat.html.

Bündnis 90/Die Grünen. 2014b, *Menschenwürde ist migrationspolitisch nicht relativierbar*, viewed 4 July 2018, www.gruene-bundestag.de/integration-fluechtlingspolitik/menschenwuerde-ist-migrationspolitisch-nicht-relativierbar-18-07-2014.html.

Bündnis 90/Die Grünen. 2015, *Traumabehandlung für Flüchtlinge und Asylsuchende*, viewed 4 July 2018, www.gruene-bundestag.de/gesundheit/traumabehandlung-fuer-fluechtlinge-und-asylsuchende-01-10-2015.html.

BVerfG. 2012, *Urteil des Ersten Senats vom 18. Juli 2012 – 1 BvL 10/10 – Rn. (1–140)*, viewed 4 July 2018, www.bverfg.de/e/ls20120718_1bvl001010.html.

CDU/CSU. 2015, *Mit gemeinsamer Kraftanstrengung verfolgte Flüchtlinge schützen. Asylmissbrauch bekämpfen*, Beschluss Fraktionsvorstand, 2 September, viewed 4 July 2018, www.cducsu.de /sites/default/files/asyl_fluechtlinge_endfassung.pdf.

CESCR. 2000, *General comment no. 14. The right to the highest attainable standard of health, article 12 of the International Covenant on Economic, Social and Cultural Rights*, 8 November, E/C.12/2000/4.

CESCR. 2009, *General comment no. 20. Non-discrimination in economic, social and cultural rights (art. 2, para. 2, of the International Covenant on Economic, Social and Cultural Rights)*, 2 July, E/C.12/GC/20.

CESCR. 2011, *Considerations of reports submitted by states parties under articles 16 und 17 of the convention. Concluding observations – Germany*, 12 July 2011, E/C.12/DEU/CO/5.

Classen G. 2015, *Rechtsprechungsübersicht zum Flüchtlingssozialrecht*, Berlin, 8 November, viewed 4 July 2018, www.fluechtlingsinfo-berlin.de/fr/gesetzgebung/Urteile2.pdf.

Deutscher Bundesrat. 2014, *Entwurf eines Gesetzes zur Änderung des Asylbewerberleistungsgesetzes und des Sozialgerichtsgesetzes. Antrag der der Freien und Hansestadt Hamburg*, 10 October, BR. Drs. 392/2/14.

Deutscher Bundesrat. 2015, *Stenografischer Bericht zur 937. Sitzung*, Berlin, 16 October, Plenarprotokoll 937.

Deutscher Bundestag. 2014a, *Stenografischer Bericht zur 57. Sitzung*, Berlin, 9 October, Plenarprotokoll 18/57.

Deutscher Bundestag. 2014b, *Stenografischer Bericht zur 63. Sitzung*, Berlin, 6 November, Plenarprotokoll 18/63.

Deutscher Bundestag. 2014c, *Entwurf eines Gesetzes zur Änderung des Asylbewerberleistungsgesetzes und des Sozialgerichtsgesetzes – Drucksache 18/2592 – Stellungnahme des Bundesrates und Gegenäußerung der Bundesregierung*, 29 October, Drucksache 18/3000.

Deutscher Bundestag. 2014d, *Gesundheitliche Versorgung nach dem Asylbewerberleistungsgesetz*, 22 July, Drucksache 18/2184.

Deutscher Bundestag. 2014e, *Sozialrechtliche Diskriminierung beenden – Asylbewerberlei stungsgesetz aufheben. Antrag der Partei Die Linke*, 14 October, Drucksache 18/2871.

Deutscher Bundestag. 2015a, *Stenografischer Bericht zur 115. Sitzung*, Berlin, 2 July, Plenarprotokoll 18/115.

Deutscher Bundestag. 2015b, *Verbesserung der gesundheitlichen Versorgung von Asylbewerberinnen und Asylbewerbern. Antwort der Bundesregierung*, 27 April, Drucksache 18/4758.

Deutscher Bundestag. 2015c, *Medizinische Versorgung für Asylsuchende und Geduldete diskriminierungsfrei sichern. Antrag der Fraktion Die Linke*, 30 June, Drucksache 18/5370.

Deutscher Bundestag. 2016, *Verbesserungen der gesundheitlichen und psychosozialen Versorgung von Geflüchteten zur Umsetzung der EU-Aufnahmerichtlinie. Antwort der Bundesregierung*, 4 July, Drucksache 18/9009.

Eichenhofer E. 2013, 'Gesundheitsleistungen für Flüchtlinge', *Zeitschrift für Ausländerrecht (ZAR)*, vol. 5–6, no. 33, pp. 169–174.

Forman L. 2015, 'Can core obligations under the right to health achieve their ambitions?' *Zeitschrift für Menschenrechte*, vol. 9, no. 2, pp. 36–48.

Flüchtlingsrat Berlin. 2014, *Stellungnahme zum Gesetzentwurf der Bundesregierung: Entwurf eines Gesetzes zur Änderung des Asylbewerberleistungsgesetzes und des Sozialgerichtsgesetzes, 17. Oktober – BT-Drs. 18/2592 vom 22.09.2014*, Berlin.

Flüchtlingsrat Berlin. 2015, *Krankenversichertenkarten nach §§ 4 und 6 AsylbLG für Berlin! Forderungen Flüchtlingsrat Berlin*, viewed 4 July 2018, www.fluechtlingsrat-berlin.de/gesetzgebung.php#Med.

Gäbel, U., Ruf, M., Schauer, M., Odenwald, M., & Neuner, F. 2006, 'Prävalenz der posttraumatischen Belastungsstörung (PTSD) und Möglichkeiten der Ermittlung in der Asylverfahrenspraxis', *Zeitschrift für Klinische Psychologie und Psychotherapie*, vol. 35, no. 12, pp. 12–20.

Gesundheitsamt Bremen. 2011, *Das Bremer Modell Gesundheitsversorgung Asylsuchender*, viewed 4 July 2018, www.gesundheitsamt.bremen.de/.../3_GBE_Gesundheitsver sorgung_Asylsuchender.pdf.

Grube, C., Wahrendorf, V., Bieback, K., Flint, T., & Streichsbier, K. 2014, *SGB XII Sozialhilfe mit Asylbewerberleistungsgesetz*, Beck, München.

Hajer, M. 1993, 'Discourse coalitions and the institutionalization of practice: the case of acid rain in Britain', in F. Fischer & J. Forester (eds.), *The argumentative turn in policy analysis and planning*, Duke University Press, Durham & London, pp. 43–76.

Hajer, M. 2004, 'Argumentative Diskursanalyse. Auf der Suche nach Koalitionen, Praktiken und Bedeutung', in R. Keller, A. Hirseland, W. Schneider & W. Viehöver (eds.), *Handbuch sozialwissenschaftliche Diskursanalyse*, Springer, Wiesbaden, pp. 271–298.

Hajer, M. 2006, 'Doing discourse analysis: coalitions, practices, meaning', in M. van den Brink & T. Metze (eds.), *Words matter in policy and planning. Discourse theory and method in social science*, Koninklijk Nederlands Aardrijkskundig Genootschap, Utrecht, pp. 65–74.

Hajer, M. 2008, 'Diskursanalyse in der Praxis: Koalitionen, Praktiken und Bedeutung', in F. Janning & K. Toens (eds.), *Die Zukunft der Policy-Forschung. Theorien, Methoden, Anwendung*, Springer, Wiesbaden, pp. 211–222.

Hajer, M., & Versteeg, W. 2005, 'A decade of discourse analysis of environmental politics: achievements, challenges, perspective', *Journal of Environmental Policy and Planning*, vol. 7, no. 3, pp. 175–184, viewed 5 April 2017.

Interights. 2011, *Non-discrimination in international law. A handbook for practitioners*, Interights, London.

Joksimovic, L., Karger, A., Kunzke, D., & Schröder, M. 2017, 'Flüchtlinge als Patienten. Über die Notwendigkeit einer ganzheitlichen Versorgung', in C. Ghaderi & T. Eppenstein (eds.), *Flüchtlinge. Multiperspektivische Zugänge*, Springer, Wiesbaden, pp. 291–304.

Kaltenborn, M. 2015, 'Die Neufassung des Asylbewerberleistungsgesetzes und das Recht auf Gesundheit', *Neue Zeitschrift für Sozialrecht*, vol. 24, no. 5, pp. 161–165.

Kälin, W., & Künzli, J. 2013, *Universeller Menschenrechtsschutz. Der Schutz des Individuums auf globaler und regionaler Ebene*, Helbing Lichtenhahn, Basel.

Klotz, S. 2018, 'Einwanderungspolitik und Integrationspolitik im internationalen Vergleich', in I. Gogolin, V. Georgi, M. Krüger- Potratz, D. Lengyel & U. Sandfuchs (eds.), *Handbuch der Interkulturellen Pädagogik*, UTB, Stuttgart, pp. 267–274.

Krennerich, M. 2013, *Soziale Menschenrechte*, Wochenschau Verlag, Schwalbach am Taunus.

Krennerich, M. 2015, 'Menschenrechte und Gesundheit', *Zeitschrift für Menschenrechte*, vol. 9, no. 2, pp. 8–35.

Krennerich, M. 2016a, 'Das Menschenrecht auf Gesundheit. Grundzüge eines komplexen Rechts', in A. Frewer & H. Bielefeldt (eds.), *Das Menschenrecht auf Gesundheit. Normative Grundlagen und aktuelle Diskurse*, transcript Verlag, Bielefeld, pp. 57–92.

Krennerich, M. 2016b, 'Internationale soziale Menschenrechte als Maßstab für den Umgang mit Asylsuchenden', *Zeitschrift für Politikwissenschaft*, vol. 26, no. 1, pp. 95–103.

Lindner, K. 2015, 'Die gesundheitliche Versorgung von Asylsuchende in Deutschland. Aktuelle politische Entwicklungen', *Migration und Soziale Arbeit*, vol. 1, pp. 81–88.

Mann, J., Gostin, L., Gruskin, S., Brennan, T., Lazzarini, Z., & Fineberg, H. 2013, 'Health and human rights', in M. Grodin, D. Tarantola, G.A. George & S. Gruskin (eds.), *Health and human rights in a changing world*, Routledge, London & New York, pp. 16–27.

Mayring, P. 2000, 'Qualitative content analysis', *Forum: Qualitative Social Research*, vol. 1, no. 2., pp. 1–10, viewed 4 July 2018, http://www.qualitative-research.net/index.php/fqs/article/view/1089/2383

Mayring, P. 2015, *Qualitative Inhaltsanalyse. Grundlagen und Techniken*, Beltz, Weinheim.

Medibüro, Medico International & Verein demokratischer Ärztinnen und Ärzte. 2015, *Gesundheitskarte zweiter Klasse? – Medizinische Minderversorgung von Asylsuchenden beenden!* press release from 22 September, viewed 4 July 2018, http://stopasylblg.de/wp-content/uploads/2015/09/PM_Medizinische-Minderversorgung-von-Asylsuchenden _beenden_15–09–22.pdf.

Migazin. 2015, 'Union gegen Gesundheitskarte für Flüchtlinge. CDU-Bundesminister dafür. Migazin', *Migazin*, viewed 4 July 2018, www.migazin.de/2015/09/04/abstimmungsprobleme-union-gesundheitskarte-fluechtlinge-cdu/.

Niklewski, G., Richter, K., & Lehfeld, H. 2012, *Abschlussbericht im Verfahren Az.: Z2/0272.01-1/14 für "Gutachterstelle zur Erkennung von psychischen Störungen bei Asylbewerberinnen und Asylbewerbern-Zirndorf"*, Klinikum Nürnberg, Nürnberg.

Norredam, M., Mygind, A., & Krasnik, A. 2005, 'Access to health care for asylum seekers in the European Union – a comparative study of country policies', *European Journal of Public Health*, vol. 16, no. 3, pp. 285–289.

OHCHR. 2008, *The right to health. Factsheet No. 31*, viewed 4 July 2018, www.refworld.org/docid/48625a742.html.

Otto D. 2014: 'Women's right', in D. Moeckli, S. Shah, S. Sivakumaran & D. Harris (eds.), *International human rights law*, University Press Oxford, Oxford, pp. 316–332.

Peters, T., Grützmann, T., Bruchhausen, W., Coors, M., Jacobs, F., Kaelin, L. et al. 2014, 'Grundsätze zum Umgang mit Interkulturalität in Einrichtungen des Gesundheitswesens. Positionspapier der Arbeitsgruppe Interkulturalität in der medizinischen Praxis in der Akademie für Ethik in der Medizin', *Ethik in der Medizin*, vol. 26, no. 1, pp. 65–75.

Pro Asyl. 2014a, *Fall Leonardo: Mitarbeiter von Asylbewerberunterkunft zu Geldstrafen verurteilt*, press release from 14 April, viewed 4 July 2018, www.proasyl.de/pressemitteilung/fall-leonardo-mitarbeiter-von-asylbewerberunterkunft-zu-geldstrafen-verurteilt/.

Pro Asyl. 2014b, *AsylbLG. Millarden-Deal auf Kosten der Gesundheit von Flüchtlingen*, press release from 28 November, viewed 4 July 2018, www.proasyl.de/pressemitteilung/asylblg-milliarden-deal-auf-kosten-der-gesundheit-von-fluechtlingen/.

Pro Asyl. 2015, *Gesetzlich verordnete Lebensgefahr – Das deutsche Asylbewerberleistungsgesetz*, press release from 22 May, viewed 4 July 2018, www.proasyl.de/de/news/detail/news/gesetzlich_verordnete_lebensgefahr_das_deutsche_asylbewerberleistungsgesetz/.

Razum, O., & Bozorgmehr, K. 2016, 'Restricted entitlements and access to health care for refugees and immigrants: the example of Germany', *Global Social Policy*, vol. 16, no. 3, pp. 321–324.

Robert Bosch Stiftung. 2014, *Lebenslagen von Asylbewerbern. Vorschläge zur Verwaltungs- und Verfahrensvereinfachung*, Robert Bosch Stiftung, Stuttgart.

Sabra, M. 2015, 'Gesundheitsverorgung von Flüchtlingen. Zwischen Kosten- und Menschenrechtsfragen', *Deutschlandfunk*, 18 June, viewed 11 September 2017.

Schamman, H. 2015, 'Rette sich, wer kann? Flüchtlingspolitik im Föderalismus', *Aus Politik und Zeitgeschichte (APuZ)*, vol. 65, no. 25, pp. 26–31.

Schamman, H., & Kühn, B. 2016, *Kommunale Flüchtlingspolitik in Deutschland*, Friedrich-Ebert-Stiftung, Bonn.

Schneider, C., Joos, S., & Bozorgmehr, K. 2015, 'Disparities in health and access to healthcare between asylum seekers and residents in Germany: a population-based cross-sectional feasibility study', *BMJ Open*, vol. 5, no. 11, pp. 1–10.

Scholz, J. 2016, 'Rahmenbedingungen der Gesundheitsversorgung von Flüchtlingen. Das Menschenrecht auf Gesundheit', in P. Bendel (ed.), *Was Flüchtlinge brauchen – ein Win-Win-Projekt. Ergebnisse einer Befragung in Erlangen*, FAU University Press, Erlangen, pp. 183–202.

Ssenyonjo, M. 2016, *Economic, social and cultural rights in international law*, Hart, Oxford & Portland.

SPD. 2014, *Aktionsprogramm zur Flüchtlingspolitik – Maßnahmen zur Unterstützung der Kommunen und der Flüchtlinge*, 24 November, viewed 1 February 2017, www3.spd.de/scalableImageBlob/125582/data/20141124_spd_aktuell_fluechtlingshilfe-data.pdfn.

SPD. 2015, *Flüchtlinge schneller versorgen mit Gesundheitskarte*, Pressemitteilung vom 23. September, viewed 4 July 2018, www.spdfraktion.de/presse/pressemitteilungen/fluechtlinge-schneller-ver sorgen-gesundheitskarte.

Spiegel Online. 2015, 'Kretschmann besteht auf Gesundheitskarte', *Spiegel Online*, 4 September, viewed 4 July 2018, www.spiegel.de/politik/deutschland/fluechtlinge-kretschmann-besteht-auf-gesundheitskarte-a-1051335.html.

Thelen P. 2015, 'CSU warnt vor Gesundheitskarte für Asylbewerber', *Handelsblatt*, 14. September, viewed 4 July 2018, www.handelsblatt.com/politik/deutschland/fluech tlingskrise-csu-warnt-vor-gesundheitskarte-fuer-asylbewerber/12317308.html.

Tobin, J. 2012, *The right to health in international law*, Oxford University Press, Oxford.

Toebes, B. 2017, 'The right to health and the global rise of non-communicable diseases', in S. Klotz, H. Bielefeldt, M. Schmidhuber & A. Frewer (eds.), *Healthcare as a human rights issue. Normative profile, conflicts and implementation*, transcript Verlag, Bielefeld, pp. 123–143.

Wächter-Raquet, M. 2016, *Gesundheitsversorgung von Asylsuchenden. Gesundheitskarte und psychotherapeutische Versorgung: ein Sachstandsbericht*, Bertelsmann Stiftung, Gütersloh.

Wiewei, L. 2004, E*quality and non-discrimination under international human rights law*, Research Notes 03/2004, Norwegian Centre for Human Rights, Oslo.

Woratschka, R. 2015, 'Gesundheitskarte für Flüchtlinge. CSU fordert "Schadensbegrenzung"', *Der Tagespiegel*, 25 September, viewed 4 July 2018, www.tagesspiegel.de/wirtschaft/gesundheitskarte-fuer-fluechtlinge-csu-fordert-schadensbegrenzung/12370372.html.

Wrigley, A., & Dawson, A. 2016: 'Vulnerability and marginalized populations', in D.H. Barrett, L. Ortmann & A. Dawson (eds.), *Public health ethics: cases spanning the globe*, Public health ethics analysis 3, Springer Verlag, Wiesbaden, pp. 203–240.

Legislation and international instruments

Asylbewerberleistungsgesetz (AsybLG).
Asylverfahrensbeschleunigungsgesetz.
Convention on the Elimination of all Forms of Discrimination Against Women.
Convention relating to the Status of Refugees (1951).
Revised European Social Charter (ESCRev).
International Covenant on Economic, Social and Cultural Rights (ICESCR).
Reception Conditions Directive.

Part III

(Re)constructing migrants in health research

9 Questioning categorisation practices

'Migrants' and 'ethnic groups' in public health classification(s)

Penelope Scott and Hella von Unger

9.1 Introduction

In public health, ethnicity and migration-related classification systems (or classifications) and their constituent categories are integral to the collection of ethnic and migrant-related data. Classifications that involve categorising groups and populations according to their ethnic background or migration status are useful to governments, for example, in epidemiological studies assessing mortality and morbidity related to infectious diseases such as HIV/AIDS as well as identifying the health-specific needs of diverse groups. Literature in the field has focused on the utility of data generated by ethnicity classifications to public health research, the validity of ethnicity categories and the conceptual and methodological challenges of measuring 'race' and ethnicity (Aspinall 2011; Ford & Harawa 2010; Mays et al. 2003).[1] We argue, however, that a critical perspective on ethnicity and migration-related classifications as a discursive practice of the state facilitates an interrogation of these information systems and reveals the sociality of scientific knowledge. More specifically, these classifications and their inherent categories constitute a lens through which the social and historical factors that shape the construction of migrants and infectious disease can be examined. This perspective brings into focus the biopolitical function of classification in public health and the tensions surrounding the use of ethnicity and migration-related categories in disease surveillance and control.

In developing this argument, the chapter first provides an overview of the use of the terms 'migrant' and 'ethnicity' in European public health reporting and presents examples of ethnicity and migration-related categories used in HIV/AIDS health reporting classification systems in the UK and Germany. It reviews classical sociology of knowledge studies focussing on classification and the social construction of medical knowledge as well as recent theoretical and methodological developments in the sociology of knowledge to show why a sociological perspective on the categories used in public health classifications is a productive line of enquiry. The chapter critically examines the theoretical and methodological principles underpinning the construction of ethnicity and migration-related categories in public health and discusses their biopolitical function. A final section of the chapter considers how a recent theoretical and methodological research programme, the *Sociology of Knowledge Approach to Discourse Analysis* (SKAD), can be employed to deconstruct ethnicity and migration-related categories to empirically show the socio-historical processes involved in their creation.

9.2 How are 'migrants' and 'ethnic minorities' classified in European public health?

While in the United States the use of the term 'race' and racial classifications are important practices in public health (Goodman 2000; Harawa & Ford 2009; Kaufman 1999; Krieger et al. 1993; Williams 1997; Williams & Collins 1995), within Europe the use of such terminology and classifications has been avoided since World War II. In many EU countries, the preferred method in health care contexts for collecting data on groups considered ethnically different to the majority population is according to migrant status (Johnson 2008), and/or in some countries such as the UK, ethnicity. The terms 'migrant' and 'ethnicity' have implications for the classifying principle(s) selected for categorisation (i.e., developing categories). In order to study HIV in relation to mobility, for example, the principle(s) guiding categorisation must draw on accurate and comparable data on migration, health and diseases to establish links between these data sets (European Centre for Disease Prevention and Control 2011b). However, the social constructedness of the respective terms raises certain epistemological issues that render classification for the purposes of epidemiological research and health reporting complex and imprecise. A principal conceptual problem regarding the term 'migrant' concerns the lack of a consensus in defining who constitutes a migrant. Various glossaries (European Union 2009; International Organisation for Migration 2004; United Nations Educational, Scientific and Cultural Organisation 2008) provide definitions and classifications of forms of migration, but the ascribed meaning of the term migrant is not consistent across countries. Instead, its bureaucratic definition is informed by the idiosyncrasies of national immigration legislation, reflecting the 'partial' perspectives of policy makers (Polzer 2008). Its sociopolitical meaning, however, is constructed through discursive practices grounded in the ideologies and superstructures of migration and diversity in each nation state.

Regarding bureaucratic designations, the most frequently used categorisations of migrants and ethnic minorities in EU countries, other than the UK, are 'country of birth', 'country of origin', 'country of nationality' and 'country of citizenship' (European Centre for Disease Prevention and Control 2011b, p. 11).[2] Each of these definitions of migrant status possesses limitations (Rechel, Mladovsky & Devillé 2012). The category definitions are inherently static as they are not indicative of mobility or migration trajectory. Therefore, the boundedness and immutability of the category migrant cannot indicate when groups are no longer defined as 'migrants' but become socially (re)constructed as 'minorities' that are differentiated from the majority population according to ethnicity or other identity markers. These definitions of migrant status further conflate different subgroups of migrants such as economic migrants, trafficking victims, asylum seekers and refugees, all of whom may experience differing levels of vulnerability to infectious diseases such as HIV/AIDS as well as differing access to health services. The conflation of these groups not only homogenises the category's members but also makes invisible other migrants such as the undocumented, who constitute a group that is methodologically and ethically difficult to reach because of denunciation laws in some countries.

In addition to 'migrant' categories, some countries (including the UK but not Germany) collect data on 'ethnicity'. The UK is exceptional with regard to its policy of ethnic monitoring in health care services; the Department of Health started ethnicity data collection in 1995, subsequent to the inclusion of a question on ethnicity in the 1991 census (Psoinos et al. 2011). Aside from the data protection issues surrounding the collection of ethnicity data (Krizsán & Zimmermann 2001; Simon 2007) the complexity of the term 'ethnicity' as a theoretical concept and social construct makes it difficult to operationalise in research and classification work. Drawing on Weber's classical sociological treatise *Economy and Society*, Bulmer (1996) defines an ethnic group as:

> [...] a collectivity with a larger population having a real or putative common ancestry, memories of a shared past, and a cultural focus upon one or more symbolic elements which the group's identity, such as kinship, religion, language shared territory, nationality or physical appearance.
>
> (p. 35)

Group ethnic identity is sometimes viewed as pre-social and constructed through *primordialist* claims to common origins, no matter how tenuous these claims may appear in the practice of everyday life and social organisation. It may also be seen as *situational*, invoked by members of a specific group as a means of self-identification in situations where such identification is useful or necessary. Ethnic identity may have an *instrumentalist* function and may be used to mobilise a specific group to gain advantages in the market place or more resources from the state (Cornell & Hartmann 1998; Jenkins 1997). These shifting meanings and functions of ethnicity as a social construct form the slippery theoretical foundation of ethnicity classification work. The categories developed aim to capture identities constituted through the unique historical and social processes of a country, such as colonialism, types of immigration experienced and forms of racist practice, all of which shape ethnic relations (Aspinall 2012). The confluence of these forces, in specific socio-historic contexts, influences the construction of ethnic identities and the various discourses on ethnic diversity that develop.

9.3 Epidemiological discourses on 'migrants' and 'ethnic groups' in the UK and Germany

In the Foucauldian tradition, discourses can be understood as communicative events that stabilise, at least temporarily, meaning attributions and interpretations that institutionalise an order of knowledge (Keller 2013). Central to the

Foucauldian notion of discourses is their performative function in constituting reality and the self-reinforcing relationship between power and knowledge (Danaher, Schirato & Webb 2000; Deleuze 2006; Dreyfus & Rabinow 1983). For Foucault (1980), knowledge and power are intertwined: power is constituted through accepted forms of knowledge, scientific understanding and claims to 'truth'. As such, the classification of migrant and ethnically diverse populations in epidemiology and public health reporting can be viewed as a discursive practice in the production of knowledge. These classifications organise knowledge about specific groups into its constituent categories. This knowledge and, by extension, the categories are invested with the power to generate further knowledge and define the boundaries of what can be said about these groups. The result of the deployment of these categories is a range of both intended and unforeseeable effects, including the construction of social identities and opportunities for the articulation of identity politics (Epstein 2007). Crucial to how public health discourses – and discursive practices such as categories – operate are the terms that are used, and the meanings ascribed to them, which may change in different social and historical contexts.

In English-speaking discourses, particularly in the UK, the term 'ethnicity' has been gradually replacing 'race' in epidemiological research (Afshari & Bhopal 2002; Bhopal 2014; Chaturvedi 2001). The use of the term 'ethnicity' to design classifications of migrant and ethnic minority populations necessarily requires, however, an assumption that ethnic groups exist and that it is acceptable and possible to collect ethnicity-related data. In the UK for example, one of the categories used in recent HIV/AIDS health reporting is 'black African heterosexual', which makes explicit reference to ethnicity and a phenotypical identity marker (skin colour)[3] combined with sexuality (Public Health England 2013). In TB reporting, the category 'black African' is used (Scott, von Unger & Odukoya 2017). Whereas the UK records ethnicity in censuses and health care utilisation registries, in Germany, 'ethnic' data are not collected. Instead, migration-related categories have been developed, such as *Migranten* (migrants) and *Menschen mit Migrationshintergrund* (people with a migrant background), to collect data on first- and second-generation immigrants (RKI 2008; Statistisches Bundesamt 2006). Regarding HIV/AIDS health reporting, migration-related data were not collected until 2001, except for one category *Hochprävalenzländer* (high prevalence countries), which was used in the classification of HIV transmission risks until 2011.[4] With respect to TB, nationality and country of birth have been used (von Unger, Odukoya & Scott 2016). Why was this the case? Some authors note that the lack of ethnicity classifications in Germany is due to specific concerns: first, such practices may stir national memories of the categories developed under National Socialism, and second, the data may be misused to incite racism and discrimination (Simon 2007). The different discourses on migration-related and ethnicity classifications, as well as the different epidemiological categories used, exemplify how classification practices are embedded in specific socio-historical contexts. This underscores the need to subject classification systems to critical sociological analysis. Country comparisons are a useful analytic strategy to identify and interrogate what are regarded as accepted practices in different contexts.[5]

9.4 A sociology of knowledge approach to classification and medical knowledge

Theorising the nature and scope of knowledge, particularly medical knowledge, is a key concern of sociological enquiry. One of sociology's defining assumptions is that biomedical knowledge of health and disease is created in a political, social and cultural environment (White 2002). Similarly, questions relating to the genesis, role and implications of classifications have been a long-standing preoccupation of social theorists. Durkheim's classical studies (Durkheim 1915; Durkheim & Mauss 1963) focused on classificatory processes and developed one of the central tenets of the sociology of knowledge: 'the classification of things (...) reproduces [the] classification of men' (Durkheim & Mauss 1963, p. 11). Durkheim attempted to explain all fundamental categories of human thought, such as time, space, weight, force and mass, although he did not establish their social origins. He argued that these concepts that we use to think with do not reflect nature but instead, reflect the social organisation of society. Ludwik Fleck (1935 [1979]) applied this insight to the study of scientific and medical ideas. His seminal work on syphilis (1935 [1979]) and anatomical drawings (1935 [1981]) showed how medical knowledge and its main categories were created and that they too were a product of the social. His notion of 'thought collectives' theorised medical knowledge revealing it to be the outcome of historically located interactions between different individuals and groups with differing views of reality. This view radically reformulated scientific facts as fundamentally social in origin. Fleck's study on syphilis further historicised medical knowledge by demonstrating that knowledge does not progress in a linear trajectory but is contingent on changes in thought styles.

The constructed nature of medical knowledge and its impact on social organisation and experience have been explored by numerous influential scholars. In the anthropological study *Natural Symbols,* Mary Douglas (1973) demonstrated that medicine is similar to other areas of human thought that are essentially cosmological: it has a particular worldview that conjoins diverse experiences and invests them with meaning. As such, medicine comprises a set of categories that serves to filter and construct experiences. Douglas (1986) also explored the connections between classifications and social institutions stressing the meanings of these classifications for social groups. In contrast to the classic studies of Durkheim and Douglas, which sought to explain the origins of classification through their social functions, more recent theoretical developments in the sociology of knowledge seek to understand classifications from the perspective of their social construction (Bowker & Star 2000).

A related approach has stemmed from an interest in the genesis, implementation and implications of classification systems as part of discourses and particular orders of knowledge (Keller 2011). A productive outcome of this interest has been the development of the *Sociology of Knowledge Approach to Discourse Analysis* (SKAD) (Keller 2011). In SKAD, classifications are a useful lens to analyse discourses (von Unger, Scott & Odukoya 2018). SKAD's methodological tools can be used to empirically address questions concerning the origins, trajectories and effects of discursive practices such as ethnicity and migrant classifications and their constituent categories used in public health reporting. Integral theoretical elements of this research approach are not only Foucault's notion of the socio-historical contingency of knowledge but also the coercive aspect of knowledge, which he theorised with his concept of knowledge/power. This raises questions of how categories as discursive practices in public health achieve power effects.

9.5 Public health, classification and biopower

Public health has emerged as one of the technologies of *biopower*, a form of regulatory power that works primarily through the state (Foucault 1990). *Biopower* is responsible for the administering of life through techniques such as the collection of statistical data as well as surveillance and control, which are dependent upon the classification of groups. The field of epidemiology has a defining role in public health projects and intensifies its biopolitical functions due to its focus on the documenting of patterns of disease in populations and across groups. As one consequence, public health has served to identify and construct migrants and ethnic minorities as 'high-risk groups' for certain communicable infectious diseases such as tuberculosis and HIV/AIDS, leading to the biosecuritisation of the migrant body through diverse interventionist practices (Del Amo et al. 2004; European Centre for Disease Prevention and Control 2011a; Ho 2004; Kehr 2009; Warren 2013).

Knowledge about migrants' risk status has achieved materiality in the development of epidemiological categories used for monitoring and controlling the health of various migrant and ethnic groups.[6] In these categories, 'race and cultural differences are codified in defining what it means to be at risk of acquiring or transmitting an infectious disease' (Reitmanova & Gustafson 2012, p. 912). As discursive practices, the categorisation of migrant groups and ethnic minorities contributes to the constitution of power/knowledge complexes, which justify enhanced interventionism and surveillance (Kehr 2012) and achieve power effects through a raft of laws, regulations and other socio-political practices.

Yet as a technology of *biopower*, public health also exhibits tensions regarding categorisation as both a technique of control and a tool for redressing health inequalities and inequities. In the latter respect, the intersections between public health and human rights are visible in the core function of public health to ensure accessibility of services on a non-discriminatory basis (Mann et al. 1999; UNCESCR 2000). The successful fulfilment of this mandate requires the categorisation of potentially vulnerable groups, which in turn proves to be an enabling mechanism for health and human rights activism. Thus, the exclusionary/inclusionary paradox in public health's institutional function finds expression in the deployment of categories both as a means of surveillance and as a marker of the vulnerable groups most needy of protection. This translates into migrants' and ethnic minorities' dual construction as being 'a risk' and 'at risk'. The 'order of knowledge' established and disseminated by these epidemiological categories thus becomes an accepted part of social life silencing questions about the categories' origin. In reality, following the trail between these categories and their knowledge sources is fraught with intellectual challenges thus revealing the complexity inherent in their construction and in the design of classification systems more generally.

9.6 Classification, identification and categorisation: clarifying the terms

The conceptual difficulties of ethnicity and migration-related classifications in public health are related first, to trends in contemporary migration, mobility and politics contextualising classification projects, and second, to the complexity of classification work. With respect to migration trends, an important development is the emergence of new forms of mobility and transnational practices as globalisation facilitates the transcendence of spatial and cultural boundaries. These phenomena have given rise to postmodernist claims concerning the destabilisation and fragmentation of identities as individuals are no longer confined to developing identities embedded in a singular geographic location (Hall 1996). The use of hyphenated identities to reconcile multiple ethno-national identity categories (Verkuyten 2005) and the construction of 'new ethnicities' representing the fusion of different cultural identities (Harris 2006) have come to underscore the fluidity and varied inflections of ethnic identity in immigration societies. It is in this shifting terrain of mobility and identity (re)making that the work of ethnicity classification is located.

Devising classifications of ethnic groups is, however, not just practical work. As Jenkins (2000) notes, identification, which entails the specification of differences and similarities, is integral to classification. How individuals identify themselves and others along the axes of similarity and difference is central to social identification. It is a productive and ongoing enterprise, and, as Jenkins (2000, p. 8) notes, 'there are thus two-ideal typical modes of identification: *self-* or *group* identification (internally oriented) and *categorisation* of others (externally oriented). All actors are subject to both'. The social constitution of *group identities* and *categories* is, therefore, based on interdependent processes of *internal group identification* and *external social categorization*, respectively (Jenkins 1996). The theoretical distinction between *group identities* and *categories* has practical consequences in everyday life. Whereas groups are known as such by their members, categories, which may be initially unrecognised by their constituents, are made recognisable by forms of power/knowledge such as social policy, medicine and epidemiology (Jenkins 2000).

The internal–external dialectic of collective identification precludes, however, the reification of group identities and social categories. Instead, these constructs are constantly subject to renegotiation through the continual processes of *group identification* and *social categorisation* (Jenkins 2000). This (re)negotiation of group and category boundaries is at times rooted in identity politics and underlines the centrality of power to processes of social identification. Significantly, it highlights the asymmetrical power relationship between *groups*, which exercise the privilege of self-determination and the constituents of *categories*, which are treated as objects of definition.

The processes of *group identification* and *social categorisation* constitute the theoretical groundwork for the classification of ethnic groups. The resulting classification system is, as Bowker and Star (2000, p. 10) write in relation to classification systems generally, 'a set of boxes [...] into which things can be put to then do some kind of work – bureaucratic or knowledge production'. The classification system should possess a number of properties, including consistent and unique classificatory principles, mutually exclusive categories and complete coverage of 'the world it describes' (ibid.). As the authors note, these are ideal characteristics, and it is improbable that any classification system can fully meet these requirements.

The epistemological challenges of designing a classification system are thus quite weighty, even more so when persons, as opposed to material objects or animals, are the subjects of the categories to be developed. Pierik (2004, p. 527) defines the former type of category as 'a set of individuals that are considered equivalent on a specific attribute'. This attribute is a feature regarded as uniform among the individuals in the category. The attribute can be invariable, such as eye colour, or variable, such as weight. It may also be the result of choice, such as membership in a political party, or it may not, such as place of birth. The reductionism inherent in categorising individuals according to select characteristics facilitates an understanding of categories' inferred or observable relationships (Sokal 1974) and fulfills 'a basic human need for cognitive parsimony' (Hogg & Abrams 1988, p. 72). Significantly, the work of developing categories involves choices, 'and each category valorises some point of view and silences another' (Bowker & Star 2000, p. 5). This inevitably makes some people invisible and engenders consequences that cannot always be foreseen. As Bowker and Star (2000, p. 4) aptly comment, classifications are 'artefacts embodying moral and aesthetic choices that in turn craft people's identities, aspirations and dignity'.

The constructedness of categories and the classification systems they comprise is their defining characteristic. This constructedness necessitates their interrogation to understand how classifications are developed and used in achieving the ends for which they are designed. At the same time, questioning them seeks to reveal how they structure social processes and silence certain points of view. In this regard, Polzer (2008) writes that a series of elements in categorisation need to be considered. These include *partiality*, which means that all categories must be analysed through the particular perspective of the actor or actors who constructed them. *Functionality* refers to the functions or uses for which categories are developed which define their characteristics. *Conflation* is an aspect of how the characteristics of the category are implemented, which homogenises members of the category. *Immutability* refers to the relationship the category has with change over time; categories are rarely mindful of members' previous identities and do not allow for future identity trajectories. *Self-confirmation* is achieved in the Foucauldian (1972) tradition by the creation of 'knowledge', data and an archive of the group using the categories' defined characteristics. This is a self-reinforcing process that further affirms the impression of the categories' immutability. *Negotiability* refers to the way in which interactions between different groups – those being defined and those creating the categories – are implicated in categorisation. As Polzer (2008, p. 480) further notes, these theoretical elements of categorisation can be distilled into a series of questions that serve to examine categories. These include the following:

a Who is defining the category and from which perspective? (*partiality*)
b What is the purpose of defining the category at a particular point in time? (*functionality* and *immutability*)
c What characteristics of the category are emphasised over others? (*conflation*)
d What sources of information are used or created to confirm the existence of the category? (*self-confirmation*)
e What reasons and opportunities are there for the individuals who are targeted for categorisation to remain invisible? (*negotiability*)

The associated conceptual and methodological challenges of designing classifications of ethnic minority and migrant populations in epidemiological research illustrate the tensions between assigning individuals to categories that must fulfil scientific criteria for validity as well as capture salient attributes of a population identified as different to the majority population. Within European Union countries, these processes of social identification are rooted in their respective immigration histories, administrative structures and political attitudes towards immigration, diversity and the protection of migrants' rights. Tracing these processes and unravelling the mix of factors implicit in the creation of ethnic minority and migrant-related classifications essentially constitute an empirical enterprise. Such a project is also sociological because it seeks to understand how the interactions of professional/lay interests, of power and of ethnicity and class enter into the formation of knowledge about migrants, ethnic minorities and communicable infectious diseases. This raises further questions about which methodological approaches are appropriate to the task.

9.7 A sociology of knowledge approach to the classification of 'migrants' and 'ethnic minorities'

The Sociology of Knowledge Approach to Discourse Analysis (Keller 2011; 2013) is a comprehensive research programme grounded in Foucauldian discourse theory, that offers methodological tools that can address the question(s) raised above. SKAD is concerned with reconstructing processes and practices associated with meaning and knowledge production in various institutional fields, such as the sciences, as well as with their consequences. These outcomes are both effects of discourses and 'pre'-conditions for new discourses. This approach sees discourses as not only actualised in linguistic practices, but also stabilised by *dispositifs*, which are institutionalised infrastructures and measures such as classifications, statistics, laws, technologies and areas of responsibility (Keller 2013). Crucially, these *dispositifs* not only serve to (re)produce a discourse but also generate specific forms of social reality and achieve 'power effects'. The public health reports referred to in this chapter can be framed as a constitutive element of the *dispositif* under-girding epidemiological discourses on infectious diseases, migrants and ethnic minorities. Although SKAD locates discourse research in the area of the sociology of knowledge, it allows for the development and use of qualitative research methods to pursue its analytical and empirical aims. A particularly good fit is grounded theory and its post-modern version 'Situational Analysis' (Clarke 2005; Clarke, Friese & Washburn 2015). Because discourses are considered socio-historically situated practices that constitute objects rather than representing them, this implies that data such as oral and written texts and other representations including images and visual data are crucial sources when analysing how discourses are structured and how they produce knowledge claims (Keller 2012).

Given the primacy of the 'socio-historical' in SKAD, a number of thematic questions emerge in endeavours to reconstruct the processes, contexts and practices associated with the production of categories in German and UK health reporting discussed in this chapter. Inscribed onto these categories are the longer-term historical practices related to inter-ethnic relations and political ideologies on managing diversity. Both Germany and the UK were colonial powers, a historical fact that generates questions such as how far attitudes and approaches of actors doing categorisation work are influenced by colonial histories and discourses? Do historical memories and conceptualisations of nationhood feature in the process? A second related theme concerns the issue of language, and more specifically, languages of diversity in both the UK and Germany. This raises questions such as how contemporary notions of ethnic and 'racial' differences are encoded and communicated, and in what ways this has been influenced by each nation's past? Where and what are the silences regarding diversity – what cannot be spoken about? A third thematic line of enquiry relates to the possible influence of contemporary scientific interest in genetics and 'race' on epidemiology. Genetic research and the emergence of 'race'-specific or ethnicity-specific medicines appear to be reviving the notion of race as having a biological base – at least in the Anglo-American discourse (Darity, Royal & Whitfiel 2010; Fujimura, Duster & Rajagopalan 2008; Graves 2010; Jorde & Woodland 2004). How far do these ideas penetrate epidemiological thinking and the process of categorisation of migrant and ethnic minority groups in the UK and in Germany? A fourth theme concerns health activism and migrant community organisations which interact and negotiate with the powerful institutional state actors behind categorisations. What is the role of these civil society groups in the framing of ethnic difference and the development of migrant /ethnic minority categories? In what ways do they articulate resistance in power/knowledge complexes and in the process, create new forms of knowledge and (re)make identities? As Epstein (1996) shows in the US context, civil society actors have strongly influenced medical knowledge production and HIV discourses in general. A similar influence has been exerted by HIV activists in Europe. Why have similar discursive formations of actors and speaker positions for tuberculosis not emerged? These questions are by no means exhaustive but represent a starting point for examining the processes of knowledge production and discursive practices pertaining to the categories used in epidemiological discourses.

9.8 Conclusion

This chapter has discussed how the practical work of developing ethnicity and migrant classification systems for health reporting purposes is embedded in theoretical issues of identity ascriptions, the power of definition exercised by state actors and discourses on migrants and communicable diseases. As constructs that both organise and create forms of knowledge, these classification systems and the categories comprising them are discursive practices that have consequences and display power effects in different domains, such as communicable disease prevention. The 'order of knowledge' institutionalised by these classifications is neither fixed nor stable. Their inherent categories evolve and develop through country specific social and historical processes. This raises the larger question of how these processes can be investigated empirically to understand the statements, speaker positions and actor formations implicit in the discursive constructions of these categories. *The Sociology of Knowledge Approach to Discourse Analysis* is presented as a methodological programme facilitating answers to this question.

Notes

1 For critical sociological perspectives on classification practices in medicine and epidemiology, see, for example, Epstein (2007) and Shim (2002).
2 At the time of the study (2012–2015), the UK was still part of the European Union.
3 Although racial classification is officially avoided, the label 'black' is also a racialized identity marker.
4 In 2011, the category HPL was omitted from health reporting and the cases previously ascribed to this category have since been subsumed into the category 'heterosexual transmission' (RKI 2012). The majority of people included in this category originated in sub-Sahara Africa and south-east Asia. At the same time, new categories have been introduced relating to country of origin and country of infection.
5 Every methodological choice comes with strengths and limitations. Country comparisons run the risk of reproducing 'methodological nationalism' (Wimmer & Glick-Schimmer 2003).
6 Epidemiological research exploring the health of migrant groups not only finds higher risks amongst certain migrant groups for certain diseases (such as HIV and TB), but also finds the opposite: lower risks for other diseases (such as heart disease), a phenomenon also described as the 'healthy migrant effect' (Razum 2008).

References

Afshari, R., & Bhopal, R. 2002, 'Changing pattern of use of 'ethnicity' and 'race' in scientific literature', *International Journal of Epidemiology*, vol. 31, no. 5, pp. 1074.

Aspinall, P. 2011, 'The utility and validity for public health of ethnicity categorization in the 1991, 2001 and 2011 British censuses', *Public Health*, vol. 125, no. 10, pp. 680–687.

Aspinall, P. 2012, 'Answer formats in British census and survey ethnicity questions: does open response better capture 'superdiversity'?', *Sociology*, vol. 46, no. 2, pp. 354–364.

Bhopal, R. 2014, *Migration, ethnicity, race and health in multicultural societies. Second Edition*, Oxford University Press, Oxford.

Bowker, G., & Star, S. 2000, *Sorting things out: classification and its consequences*, MIT Press, Cambridge, MA.

Bulmer, M. 1996, 'The ethnic group question in the 1991 census of population', in D. Coleman, & J. Salt (eds.), *Ethnicity in the 1991 census of population*, HMSO, London.

Chaturvedi, N. 2001, 'Ethnicity as an epidemiological determinant – crudely racist or crucially important?', *International Journal of Epidemiology*, vol. 30, no. 5, pp. 925–927.

Clarke, A. 2005, *Situational analysis, grounded theory after the postmodern turn*, Sage, Thousand Oaks, CA.

Clarke, A., Friese, C., & Washburn, J. (eds.) 2015, *Situational analysis in practice: mapping research with grounded theory*, Left Coast Press Inc., Walnut Creek, CA.

Cornell, S., & Hartmann, S. 1998, *Ethnicity and race: making identities in a changing world*, Pine Forge Press, Thousand Oaks, CA.

Danaher, G., Schirato, T., & Webb, J. 2000. *Understanding Foucault*, Sage, London.

Darity, Jr., W., Royal, C., & Whitfield, K. 2010, 'Race, genetics and health: an introduction', *The Review of Black Political Economy*, vol. 37, no. 1, pp. 1–6.

Del Amo, J., Bröring, G., Hamers, F., Infuso, A., & Fenton, K. 2004, 'Monitoring HIV/AIDS in Europe's migrant communities and ethnic minorities', *AIDS*, vol. 18, no. 14, pp. 1867–1873.

Deleuze, G. 2006, *Foucault*, Continuum Books, New York & London.

Douglas, M. 1973, *Natural symbols*, Penguin, Harmondsworth.

Douglas, M. 1986, *How institutions think. First Edition*, Syracuse University Press, Syracuse, NY.

Dreyfus, H., & Rabinow, P. 1983, *Michel Foucault: beyond structuralism and hermeneutics. Second Edition*, University of Chicago Press, Chicago, IL.

Durkheim, E. 1915, *The elementary forms of the religious life*, The Free Press, New York.

Durkheim, E., & Mauss, M. 1963, *Primitive classification*, University of Chicago Press, Chicago, IL.

Epstein, S. 1996, *Impure science: aids, activism and the politics of knowledge*, University of California Press, Berkley.

Epstein, S. 2007, *Inclusion: the politics of difference in medical research*, University of Chicago Press, Chicago, IL.

European Centre for Disease Prevention and Control. 2011a, *Migrant health: HIV testing and counselling in migrant populations and ethnic minorities in EU/EEA/EFTA member states*, ECDC, Stockholm.

European Centre for Disease Prevention and Control. 2011b, *Migrant health: improving HIV data comparability in migrant populations and ethnic minorities in EU/EEA/EFTA countries: findings from a literature review and expert panel*, ECDC, Stockholm.

European Union. 2009, *Asylum and migration glossary: a tool for better comparability*, European Union, Brussels.

Fleck, L. 1935 [1979], *The genesis and development of a scientific fact*, University of Chicago Press, Chicago, IL.

Fleck, L. 1935 [1981], 'On the question of the foundations of medical knowledge', *Journal of Medicine and Philosophy*, vol. 6, pp. 237–256.

Ford, C., & Harawa, N. 2010, 'A new conceptualization of ethnicity for social epidemiologic and health equity research', *Social Science and Medicine*, vol. 71, no. 2, pp. 251–258.

Foucault, M. 1972, *The archaeology of knowledge*, Tavistock, London.

Foucault, M. 1980, 'Truth and power', in C. Gordon (ed.), *Power/knowledge: selected interviews and other writing 1972–1977*, Pantheon Books, New York.

Foucault, M. 1990, *The history of sexuality volume 1: an introduction*, Pantheon Books, New York.

Fujimura, J., Duster, T., & Rajagopalan, R. 2008, 'Race, genetics, and disease: questions of evidence, matters of consequence', *Social Studies of Science*, vol. 38, no. 5, pp. 643–656.

Goodman, A. 2000, 'Why genes don't count (for racial differences in health)', *American Journal of Public Health*, vol. 90, no. 11, pp. 1699–1702.

Graves, Jr., J. 2010, 'Biological vs. social definitions of race: implications for modern biomedical research', *The Review of Black Political Economy*, vol. 37, no. 1, pp. 43–60.

Hall, S. 1996, 'The question of cultural identity', in S. Hall, D. Held, D. Hubert & K. Thompson (eds.), *Modernity: an introduction to modern societies*, Blackwell, Massachusetts & Oxford, pp. 596–634.

Harawa, N., & Ford, C. 2009, 'The foundation of modern racial categories and implications for research on black/white disparities in health', *Ethnicity & Disease*, vol. 19, no. 2, pp. 209–217.

Harris, R. 2006, New ethnicities and language use, Palgrave MacMillan, Basingstoke.

Ho, M. 2004, 'Sociocultural aspects of tuberculosis: a literature review and a case study of immigrant tuberculosis', *Social Science & Medicine*, vol. 59, no. 4, pp. 753–762.

Hogg, M., & Abrams, D. 1988, *Social identifications: a social psychology of intergroup relations and group processes*, Routledge, London.

International Organization for Migration. 2004, *Glossary on migration*, IOM, Geneva.

Jenkins, R. 1996, *Social identity*, Routledge, London.

Jenkins, R. 1997, *Rethinking ethnicity*, Sage, London.

Jenkins, R. 2000, 'Categorization: identity, social process and epistemology', *Current Sociology*, vol. 48, no. 3, pp. 7–25.

Johnson, M. 2008, 'Making difference count: ethnic monitoring in health (and social care)', *Radical Statistics*, vol. 96, pp. 38–45.

Jorde, L., & Woodland, P. 2004, 'Genetic variation, classification and 'race'', *Nature Genetics Supplement*, vol. 36, no. 11, pp. 28–33.

Kaufman, J. 1999, 'How inconsistencies in racial classification demystify the race construct in public health statistics', *Epidemiology*, vol. 10, no. 2, pp. 101–103.

Kehr, J. 2009, 'The politics and poetics of migrant tuberculosis: modelling a 'social disease' in French public health', in V. Kalitzkus & P. Twohig (eds.), *The tapestry of health, illness and disease*. Rodopi, Amsterdam, pp. 99–124.

Kehr, J. 2012, 'Blind spots and adverse conditions of care: screening migrants for tuberculosis in France and Germany', *Sociology of Health & Illness*, vol. 34, no. 2, pp. 251–265.

Keller, R. 2011, 'The sociology of knowledge approach to discourse analysis (SKAD)', *Human Studies*, vol. 34, no. 1, pp. 43–65.

Keller, R. 2012, 'Entering discourses: a new agenda for qualitative research and sociology of knowledge', *Qualitative Sociology Review*, vol. 8, no. 2, pp. 46–75.

Keller, R. 2013, *Doing discourse research: an introduction for social scientists*, Sage, London.

Krieger, N., Rowley, D., Herman, A., Avery, B., & Phillips, M. 1993, 'Racism, sexism, and social class: implications for studies of health, disease, and well-being', *American Journal of Preventative Medicine*, vol. 9, no. 6, pp. 82–122.

Krizsán, A., & Zimmermann, M. 2001, *Ethnic monitoring and data protection: the European context*, Central European University Press, Budapest.

Mann, J., Lawrence, G., Gruskin, S., Brennan, T., Lazzarini, Z., & Fineberg, H. 1999, 'Health and human rights', in J. Mann, S. Gruskin, M. Grodin & G. Annas (eds.), *Health and human rights: a reader*. Routledge, New York & London, pp. 7–20.

Mays, V., Ponce, N., Washington, D., & Cochran, S. 2003, 'Classification of race and ethnicity: implications for public health', *Annual Review of Public Health*, vol. 24, pp. 83–110.

Pierik, R. 2004, 'Conceptualizing cultural groups and cultural difference: the social mechanism approach', *Ethnicities*, vol. 4, no. 4, pp. 523–544.

Polzer, T. 2008, 'Invisible integration: how bureaucratic, academic and social categories obscure integrated refugees', *Journal of Refugee Studies*, vol. 21, no. 4, pp. 476–497.

Psoinos, M., Hatzidimitriadou, E., Butler, C., & Barn, R. 2011, *Ethnic monitoring in healthcare services in the UK as a mechanism to address health disparities: a narrative review*, Swan IPI, London.

Public Health England. 2013, 'New HIV diagnoses and the number of people accessing HIV care in the United Kingdom. HIV and AIDS Reporting Section, Centre for Infectious Disease Control and Surveillance', UK, London, viewed 1 December 2014, http://webarchive.nationalarchives.gov.uk/20140714084352; www.hpa.org.uk/web/HPAweb&HPAwebStandard/Page/1201094588844.

Razum, O. 2008, 'Migrant mortality, healthy migrant effect', in E. Kirch & R. Wilhelm (eds.), *Encyclopedia of public health*, Springer, Netherlands, pp. 932–935.

Rechel, B., Mladovsky, P., & Devillé, W. 2012, 'Monitoring migrant health in Europe: a narrative review of data collection practices', *Health Policy*, vol. 105, no. 1, pp. 10–16.

Reitmanova, S., & Gustafson, D. 2012, 'Exploring the mutual constitution of racializing and medicalizing discourses of immigrant tuberculosis in the Canadian press', *Qualitative Health Research*, vol. 22, no. 7, pp. 911–920.

Robert Koch Institute. 2008, *Migration und Gesundheit. Schwerpunktbericht der Gesundheitsberichterstattung des Bundes*, RKI, Berlin.

Robert Koch Institute. 2012, 'HIV bei Migranten in Deutschland', *Epidemiologisches Bulletin*, vol. 3, pp. 19–26.

Scott, P., von Unger, H., & Odukoya, D. 2017, 'A tale of two diseases: discourses on TB, HIV/AIDS and im/migrants and ethnic minorities in the United Kingdom', *Social Theory and Health*, pp. 1–24.

Shim, J. 2002, 'Understanding the routinized inclusion of race, socioeconomic status and sex in epidemiology: the utility of concepts from technoscience studies', *Sociology of Health and Illness*, vol. 24, no. 2, pp. 129–150.

Simon, P. 2007, *'Ethnic statistics' and data protection in the council of Europe countries*. Study Report, Council of Europe, Strasbourg.

Sokal, R. 1974, 'Classification: purpose, principles, progress, prospects', *Science*, vol. 185, no. 4157, pp. 1115–1123.

Statistisches Bundesamt. 2006, *Leben in Deutschland: Haushalte, Familien und Gesundheit – Ergebnisse des Mikrozensus 2005*, Statistisches Bundesamt, Wiesbaden.

United Nations Committee on Economic, Social and Cultural Rights (UNCESCR). 2000, *General comment no. 14: the right to the highest attainable standard of health (Art. 12 of the Covenant)*, viewed 28 June 2017, www.refworld.org/docid/4538838d0.html.

United Nations Educational, Scientific and Cultural Organisation. 2008, *People on the move: handbook of selected terms and concepts* (version 1.0), United Nations, New York & Geneva.

Verkuyten, M. 2005, *The social psychology of ethnic identity*, Psychology Press, Hove.

von Unger, H., Scott, P., & Odukoya, D. 2018, 'Using SKAD to analyze classification practices in public health: methodological reflections on the research process', in R. Keller, A.K Hornidge & W. Schünemann (eds.), *The sociology of knowledge approach to discourse: Investigating the politics of knowledge and meaning-making*, Routledge, London, pp. 169–185.

von Unger, H., Odukoya, D., & Scott, P. 2016, 'Kategorisierung als diskursive Praktik: Die Erfindung der "Ausländer-Tuberkulose"', in S. Bosancic & R. Keller (eds.), *Perspektiven Wissenssoziologischer Diskursforschung*, Springer, Wiesbaden, pp. 157–176.

Warren, A. 2013, '(Re)locating the border: pre-entry tuberculosis (TB) screening of migrants to the UK', *Geoforum*, vol. 48, pp. 156–164.

White, K. 2002, *An introduction to the sociology of health and illness*, Sage, London.

Williams, D. 1997, 'Race and health: basic questions, emerging directions', *Annals of Epidemiology*, vol. 7, no. 5, pp. 322–333.

Williams, D., & Collins, C. 1995, 'Socioeconomic and racial differences in health: patterns and explanations', *Annual Review of Sociology*, vol. 21, pp. 349–386.

Wimmer, A., & Glick-Schiller, N. 2003, 'Methodological nationalism, the social sciences, and the study of migration: an essay in historical epistemology', *International Migration Review*, vol. 37, no. 3, pp. 576–609.

10 Culturally sensitive palliative care research

What should we do with 'those people', or what should we do with ourselves?

Piret Paal

10.1 Introduction

According to the World Health Organization, 'palliative care is an important component of integrated treatment for young and old throughout the life course' (WHO 2014). The main goal of palliative care is to enable people to live a comfortable and satisfying life despite their illness-related burdens and concerns. At the core of palliative care is patient- and family-centred complex symptom management and care (Carduff et al. 2018; Munday, Johnson & Griffiths 2003; Pask et al. 2018). To relieve the physical, social, psychological, and spiritual sorrows, an interdisciplinary and multi-professional attempt is made to take care of patients in their social context, seeing family and friends as an important part of patients' support systems. Whether in institutional settings, such as a hospital, hospice, nursing home, or day care centre, or in outpatient care, professional caregivers accessing patients' bodily, mental, social, and spiritual realms need to have competencies that extend beyond guideline-driven formal assessment and care models.

Applying a palliative care philosophy (Randall & Downie 2006) in Western medicine requires a great deal of human maturity. Possessing such maturity means accepting that even the most skilled expert equipped with the world's best technologies cannot control everything. Palliative care admits that death is a natural part of life that need not be postponed 'no matter what'. Unlike other medical disciplines, palliative care aims to care and comfort by managing symptoms. The palliative care approach respects patients' wishes and needs, putting patient autonomy and dignity first; it also acknowledges that these wishes and needs are subject to change. Therefore, the main role of the professional caregiver is to build a relationship with the patient, reflect on what is said or indicated, ask questions, and assure that the patient is not left alone, even if treatments to relieve symptoms fail. Despite a growing need for palliation (WHO 2015), palliative care is still a marginalized aspect of health care that is too often ignored and/or rejected by health care providers and patients alike. The reason for this is rooted deep in human nature – universally, people live their lives rejecting the idea of dying. In everyday life, this means not talking about it. Acknowledging and accepting the defeat that death represents to health professionals makes communication with patients and their caregivers difficult. In this regard, the ethicist Jayne M. Waterworth has written that 'those who can afford the luxury of thinking about dying and death abstractly (their own and that of others) are unlikely actually to be dying or facing death themselves' (Waterworth 2004). Accordingly, researchers dealing with death and dying have a unique role in advancing palliative care as part of health care.

Given that death is ultimately inevitable despite all efforts, communication about palliative care takes competencies that go far beyond 'delivering the bad news' (Paal et al. 2017). Person-centred and autobiography-oriented approaches have proven to be the most effective strategy for palliative care assessment that correspondingly improves patients' quality of life (Cain et al. 2018). Absent or poor-quality communication, on the other hand, results in confusion, reduced satisfaction, poor quality of life, and inadequate symptom relief for both patients and their families (Brighton et al. 2017). Health care professionals report being ill-prepared for such difficult conversations, and thus far, the effect of communication skills training remains unclear (Selman et al. 2017).

To improve access to palliative care services, four major barriers have been defined: (1) poor public awareness of how palliative care can help; (2) cultural and social barriers, such as beliefs about pain and dying; (3) insufficient skills and capacities of health care workers; and (4) overly restrictive regulations for opioid pain relief (WHO 2015). Remaining conscious of the cultural beliefs in this statement, removing these barriers, as defined by the WHO, is important for developing palliative care services all over the world. Nevertheless, the question of culture and cultural competencies emerges frequently in palliative care-related discussions (Crawley 2005; Galanti 2000; Gysels et al. 2012; Jovanovic 2012; Koffman 2014), but the evidence on culturally specific needs in palliative care is extremely limited (Soom-Amman & Gross-Salis 2014; Cain et al. 2018). The main question is to what extent does culture matter in pluralistic societies where many cultures are emerging and interacting? Given the lack of evidence, how should researchers explore and examine culturally specific needs without stigmatizing and creating stereotypes? In terms of educational needs, should palliative care professionals be educated in cultural sensitivity, or should more effort be put into communication training that incorporates identifying and addressing patient-centred needs? Last but not least, should cultural barriers within palliative care be assessed before looking for barriers elsewhere?

The following chapter offers a critical appraisal of the current challenges in palliative care research seeking to improve access to palliative care services for people with a history of migration in contemporary German society. This chapter begins with some relevant definitions to understand the meaning of culture, migration, and altered identity in the context of migration. It then provides information on cultural competencies in palliative care and reflects on recent research developments in this field, including commenting on the prevailing standpoint epistemology. It calls for listening to patients, utilizing a participatory approach to conduct research into palliative care, and expanding collaboration, networking, and diversity management within palliative care.

10.2 Reflecting on one's own perspective

In order to be able to relate with their patients' concerns, palliative care experts must be able to reflect on their own perspectives. To provide a reflection within the reflection, my formal training has been in linguistics and medical anthropology. As a young scholar, I was interested in death-related customs, rituals, and illness narratives. Later, being affected by the groundbreaking works of Arthur Kleinman, Oliver Sacks, Arthur W. Frank, Cheryl Mattingly and Rita Charon, I concentrated on exploring cancer patients' illness experiences and meaning-making within the textual data. Approximately ten years ago, I began working in an interdisciplinary centre for palliative care. Since then, I have been involved in several research projects to explore patients' and caregivers' resources and needs in palliative care, as well as investigating professional caregivers' and volunteers' educational needs in the palliative and end-of-life care context. I have worked as a researcher in a palliative care ward, in a hospice, in outpatient care, and in nursing home settings. Since entering the field of palliative care, I have been continuously confronted with the question of culturally sensitive palliative care. In discussions with my colleagues, I was frequently asked – as an expert in cultural issues – the following question: 'What should we do with "those people"?' By 'those people', they generally meant ethnic or religious minorities. My answer would always be, 'What should we do with ourselves?' (Paal 2012). From early on, I have argued for patient-centeredness, which is, listening to the patient's story, in health care. I strongly agree that our cultural beliefs and values, influenced by language and sociocultural context, affect how we perceive particular hazardous life events. However, when people migrate, their identities are altered in many ways. I have moved from Estonia to Finland, then to Germany, and am currently working in Austria. I speak five languages well and understand few more, allowing me to participate in communication in many settings. From my 20 years of experience as an expatriate, combined with other expertise described above, I have come to believe that when talking about culture-based needs in palliative care, service providers, educators, and researchers must be profoundly challenged to reflect on the short history of palliative and end-of-life care culture in Western medicine.

10.3 Culture, identity alteration, and migration

Culture is a highly context-dependent concept explained as 'a patterned behavioural response that develops over time as a result of imprinting the mind through social and religious structures and intellectual and artistic manifestations' (Helman 2000). This imprinting of the mind is affected by language as well as by repeating the behavioural patterns of our surroundings. When stepping into new social realms, people are expected to review and adapt their perceptions of the world.

Changes in personal lives, as well as in sociocultural contexts, force people to learn and adopt new communication styles, rethink their understanding of time and space, and accept altered forms of societal organization. It is imperative to understand that the various forms of identity alteration (i.e., assimilation, integration, separation, or marginalization) are merely situationally triggered patterns of behaviour, seldom permanent conditions. A person who can manage well in the workplace may nevertheless feel isolated inside his or her religious group or be otherwise marginalized as a representative of a certain cultural identity in another setting. People are able to adopt different context-dependent identities, making it challenging to predict how any one individual will be affected by the imprinting of the mind and what the outcomes will be in terms of behavioural patterns. This uncertainty is especially evident when people experience a radical change in their personal lives, such as a life-threatening illness, or in their sociocultural surroundings, for example, migrating to an entirely different location.

Migration represents a temporary or permanent removal from known behavioural patterns and familiar surroundings. Migration is typically a change in the usual place of residence. A decision to migrate may be a personal choice (such as for studies, work or family) or a response to a safety issue (as with asylum seekers) or a crisis situation (as with refugees). Many different forms of migration exist, including in-migration, out-migration, immigration and emigration. The latter two refer to when international boundaries are crossed. Any movement of a person or a group of persons from one geographical unit to another, for temporary or permanent settlement, is called migration. For example, the settlers may remain in their home country or a host country; transit migrants (like circular migrants or seasonal workers) come temporarily and then move on to another country or move back and forth between countries (WHO 2016). There is no universally accepted definition of the term 'migrant'. Instead, who counts as migrant is a political definition and concern related to population monitoring, planning and decision-making.

10.4 Vulnerability in migrants?

Recent immigration legislation (2005) and the expansion of health insurance coverage of palliative care at home in Germany (2007) have raised public awareness of health care-related issues in a migrant population now coming of age (Paal & Bükki 2017). Hence, the past five years have witnessed a burst of interest in studies concerning migrants' needs in palliative and end-of-life care.

Migrants in the German context are often referred to as persons with an immigrant background (*Menschen mit Migrationshintegrund*). Until recently, according to the definition of the German Office of Statistics,

> persons with an immigrant background are all those who have immigrated to the current territory of the Federal Republic of Germany since 1949, as well as all foreigners born in Germany and all persons born in Germany as Germans with at least one parent who had immigrated to Germany after 1949 or was born there as a foreigner.

This definition was revised in 2017, when that of the year 1949 was replaced with 1955 (*Statistisches Bundesamt* 2017). It is assumed that this change stemmed from a decision, affected by the latest refugee crisis, to keep the number of migrants in Germany stable.

Reports emerging from German-speaking contexts frequently refer to 'the migrant issue' (*das Migrantenproblem, das Migrationsproblem*) in palliative and end-of-life care. For example, a Swiss concept for palliative care argues that, 'typically, the migration issue applies across all care disciplines and professions, which is why the relevant competencies should be taught right from the training stage' (Federal Office of Public Health FOPH et al. 2014). Several German guidelines make suggestions about dealing with people with a migration background, referring both to demographic changes and the challenges of globalization (Jansky & Nauck 2015; Stähli 2013). Another Swiss report on palliative care and migration reports on numerous difficulties and barriers while acknowledging that knowledge on this subject is very limited (Soom-Amman & Gross-Salis, 2014).

Does this interest in migrants indicate that the group is perceived as especially vulnerable? The idea that migration history makes patients a 'vulnerable population' has not been established in health care settings. A recent literature review demonstrated that ethnic minorities (without migration history), migrants' elderly parents, and young children may be a subject to certain 'vulnerability' (Pollack & Kronebusch 2009). However, severe health concerns and limited care options are always made up of sociocultural components, such as lack of education and health literacy, limited access to services, poverty, long-term chronic conditions, and long-term unemployment. Hence, migration history *per se* does not make patients vulnerable.

Palliative care patients tend to prefer health care structures and systems that make them feel safe and well-served (Paal & Bükki 2017). However, when patients do not trust the decisions made by health care providers in one country, they might seek help elsewhere (Jansky, Owuso-Boakye & Nauck 2017a). Thus, in some situations, people with a migration history may be more resourceful than the general population, making use of health care systems in multiple countries simultaneously. Hence, at a time when a growing number of people need palliative care services, raising 'the migrant issue' leaves the impression that palliative care professionals (or politicians) are merely expressing their own fears by building cultural barriers where none exist.

10.5 Standpoint epistemology, othering, and the need for participatory research

In Germany, the greatest culprit preventing the development of culturally sensitive palliative care services seems to be the persistence of the existing standpoint epistemology. Standpoint epistemology, to paraphrase feminist researchers, refers to the absence of diversity or the marginalization of ethnically, racially, or religiously diverse groups. These gaps in palliative care leadership and service provision (Fricker 2009), and the related lack of competencies and self-reflection among providers, result in patients with migrant backgrounds being stereotyped and subject to 'othering' (Milberg, Torres & Ågard 2016). This calls for action among researchers working in diverse populations to challenge culture-based presumptions in order to deliver high-quality care to all patients (Gunaratnam 2014; Paal 2012).

The following list of studies is not exhaustive; however, it demonstrates current tendencies in culture-related palliative care research in Germany. In Gottingen, a questionnaire was sent out to palliative care specialists to ask about their experience with patients of Turkish or Arabic descent. The same research group interviewed health care experts (from both palliative care and adjacent fields) who had specialized in caring for people with a migration background (Jansky, Owuso-Boakye & Nauck 2017b). In Munich, hospice coordinators were interviewed regarding their preparedness to meet the needs of culturally diverse patients (Wasner & Kurz 2016). In Berlin, an 'ASiA-Studie' was initiated to monitor the usage of advance directives among migrant patients (Henke et al. 2015). The same research group also conducted an epidemiological appraisal of migrants' end-of-life care needs (Henke et al. 2017). The initiative informed volunteer health mediators about palliative care services and produced information leaflets on palliative care services in multiple languages (Ethno-Medizinisches Zentrum 2018). One study was conducted among Russian-speaking migrants in Berlin (Migala, Sokolova & Flick 2017). Another study focused on migrant and non-migrant patients admitted to palliative care services; it found that all interviewees, regardless of their background, had a limited understanding of palliative care and avoided talking about the end-of-life care, as this was associated with suffering and loss of autonomy. This study also pointed out the significance of complex individual migration histories and the difficulty of differentiating migrants from non-migrants in multicultural settings (Paal & Bükki 2017). Most of these studies were funded by local Ministries of Health. I vividly recall how difficult it was to convince officials to support a two-arm exploratory study involving migrant and non-migrant patients to avoid potiential 'othering' from the beginning.

To fight what feminists call an injustice done by knowers, projects and studies on migrants should not be conducted from the standpoint of 'us (the knowledge-possessed)' studying 'those people'. The problem is that current discussions concentrate very much on deficits and negative aspects. Intercultural dialogues and building networks are perceived to consume too much time and work (Jansky, Owuso-Boakye & Nauck 2017a). To make sustainable change, migrants must be invited to participate in advancing palliative care by, for example, commenting on research results and making suggestions for further action (von Unger 2014). Research initiatives in other fields even go further and let community researchers participate in the design, data collection and analysis of research findings (see, e.g., Falge, Chapter 4, pp. 57 ff. and the following pages or Lindenmeyer, Chapter 11, pp. 175 ff.). Mutual effort is required to make the health care system more oriented to linguistic, cultural and medical diversity (Henke et al. 2017). In Germany, in particular, newer concepts of cultural competency are needed that move beyond classifying cultures and groups.

This means focusing on communication styles, social issues, and health beliefs that may be present across different cultures (Epner & Baile 2012). Otherwise, we perpetuate practices that are ethically, sociopolitically and economically questionable and perhaps even oppressive. For example, initiatives that develop special health care facilities for 'migrants' immediately raise questions about patient safety, equity and social justice.

10.6 Cultural competence

In 2012, an international PRISMA workshop was organized, with support from the European Commission, to compile a research agenda for cultural issues in end-of-life research. It sought to assess the challenges and implications of integrating the concept of culture in different contexts. Thirty experts from various fields participated in the workshop. They identified the following priorities for cross-cultural research: first, clarifying the concepts of culture and cultural competence, and second, defining the end of life in sociocultural context (Gysels et al. 2012). According to current knowledge, cultural competence goes beyond the somewhat rigid categories of knowledge, skills and attitudes (Florea 2014). Cultural competence is the continuous critical refinement and fostering of a critical consciousness – a type of thinking and knowing – of self, others and the world (Kumagai & Lypson 2009) that informs the interpretation of behaviours, symbols, rituals, and other cultural practices. Cultural competence reaches beyond definitions of race, ethnicity, gender or religion, as well as cultural, ethnic or religious checklists (Gunaratnam 2003), recognizing that such guidelines run a risk of encouraging generalizations about individual and groups, ultimately leading to the development of stereotypes, prejudices and gross misunderstandings (Koffman 2014).

Cultural competence in end-of-life care emphasizes making an effort 'to work in partnerships with patients, their family members, and communities to identify and negotiate culturally meaningful care and promote quality of life' (Cain et al. 2018) at each stage of a life-limiting illness. In contemporary pluralistic societies, health care professionals should expect that patients differ in their beliefs and preferred approaches to end-of-life care. They should therefore endeavour to discover when patients are making choices to please others, rather than following their own wishes. This means being humble (Tervalon & Murray-García 1998), asking questions, listening, and heeding the answers (Thomas et al. 2008).

10.7 Going beyond the 'migrant issue'

What actually happens when we ask questions, listen, and heed the answers? In my experience, a polite, authentic, and honest approach works best. There is no need to appear to know something that you actually do not know. It is always better to let patients teach and explain about their customs, beliefs, and traditions. Honesty also works best when responding to patients' questions. It is also always essential to be clear about the purpose of your visit. Honest reflection about research design and questions may also be informative.

In some situations, health care providers may find it difficult to position themselves. Sometimes being alone with a patient in his/her apartment might feel unsafe or uncomfortable. In some houses, air full of smoke or a noisy TV distract from the conversation. Family members or friends visiting and calling may be additional disturbances. Sometimes, the ideas that people have about life are difficult to accept. In such cases it may be difficult to find the correct reaction. However, appreciation and respect are essential, as is remembering that it is not the provider's place to argue or be judgemental.

When leaving, I always tell the patients that I will think and ask about them, which I honestly do. Some stories and emotions stay with me even after the patients are gone. In this sense, difficult conversations truly are difficult because patients' life stories and experiences personally matter to me.

I have selected four examples to include, based on field notes from my research diary, to provide more detail on the experience of having end of life discussions with patients receiving palliative care.

> Patient S. is 53 years old. She has three children. One of them lives abroad. The other two live with their mother. Patient S. is divorced, and her ex-husband has no contact with the children. Patient S. is religious and would like to visit Mecca. When she was working, she did not have time to practice religion; now, she has time and would like to discuss religious issues with someone. She would also like to go outside, but it is currently too cold. She was 7 years old when she came with her parents to Germany. She wishes her family had never left Turkey. She believes that the mobile care team can assist her, but she is not satisfied with their services. She tells me she is not afraid of death, but she is worried about passing away. She hopes that she will end in Paradise together with her parents, where she can live as a healthy person eternally. I have to ask many questions. The interview is very emotional. We cry. I need to borrow some tissues.
>
> Patient T. is 54 years old. She makes me pancakes, prepares tea, and explains that many people from the former Yugoslavia live in her house. She also tells me many things about her life and illness. 'My entire life story would take a couple of days,' she explains, laughing. She came to Germany in 1992 before the war began and had to go back to get her son. She tells me that she never got to enjoy life, as she was responsible for other people: her son, her sister, and her mother. Her illness is getting worse, and she is tired of chemotherapy – her body is tired. She has attempted to talk about her death and burial arrangements with her son, but he is not ready to discuss it. She would like to be back in Sarajevo, but she has no money for such arrangements. She hopes that she dies suddenly, so that other people do not have to take care of her. She has no care plan or will written down. She is really thankful to be in Germany. She knows from her experience how difficult it would be to get help in Serbia. This increases her satisfaction with the care she receives from the hospice.
>
> Patient J. is 86 years old. He does not speak German, but he is learning English on the iPad. He lives with his adult son, who offered to translate the interview. I notice that the translation is different from what the father says,

so I ask the father to tell his story in Ukrainian. He was a math teacher, and he likes doing Sudoku and playing chess online. His birthplace has defined his life course: without moving, he has lived under seven different regimes. He is very active, vital, clever, and philosophical. He is not religious. When I ask about death, he answers with I. Newton's question: why does an apple fall from a tree? He is interested in what is happening in the moment and says that if he could do something new, maybe he would play online games and become a millionaire. We laugh. When I leave, he gives me his favourite cookies to go. The son tells me that they did not know anything about palliative care until recently. He wished they had palliative care for his mother, who got chemotherapy until the very end and suffered a lot.

Patient E. is 70 years old. She sits in her wheelchair. I sit on the sofa; in front of me is the ironing board, which blocks my view. Patient E. tells me that she was born in White Russia. Her mother was Russian, and her father was Jewish. She studied English and was a teacher at the applied university until she moved to Germany in 1989. Jews were in danger after Perestroika, and her father wanted to leave. She did not. It was difficult for her to give up her profession and social position. She tells me that she has never felt like a migrant in Germany. However, when I ask her where she feels at home, she takes a tissue. The grave of her mother is in Minsk, and she visits it at least once a year. When in Minsk, she does not recognize the people and their desires anymore; it is all about money, not education and immaterial values. In Germany, times are also changing, and she does not feel safe anymore. I ask her if she is religious. She tells me that she was not raised in a faith but believes that the saints are protecting her. She has icons at home and she prays. During one operation, she had an experience that made her believe that there is some kind of afterlife. Hospice has a bad sound to her, but she likes to see it as an extra support. When she tells her friends about getting palliative care, they all fall silent. However, in Russia, she would not be alive anymore. Her self-expression in German was good, but she felt truly free when she could express herself in Russian.

Current knowledge emphasizes the need to personalize care and avoid stereotyping beliefs and practices while considering individuals' circumstances and life histories (Cain et al. 2018). As someone who genuinely believes in the power of making our lives meaningful via storytelling (Paal 2013), I argue that we could easily put 'these people' into the wrong groups – such as people with migration history (albeit never migrated), Jews (albeit half-Russian and orthodox), Russian speakers (albeit also speaks Ukrainian), Muslims (albeit not practising), or 'untypical Turks' (whatever that means). By doing so, we risk missing all the beautiful, sometimes tragic and devastating, nuances about the lives of these individuals. On the other hand, patients with excellent language skills, familiar looks, and local-sounding names can still be migrants and have migration-specific needs at the end of life (Paal & Bükki 2017). Passport, nationality, name, language, or skin colour do not indicate whether or not a patient belongs in a pluralistic society. Therefore, it is imperative to reflect critically on how to address the assumption that migrants need special care in regard to palliative care services. In palliative care, when we do not determine what patients are dealing with, we may miss those individual needs that actually matter in terms of patient autonomy and dignity at the end of life.

10.8 Frictions in palliative care culture

The WHO states that palliative care is an important component of integrated health care for young and old throughout the life course (WHO 2014). Both illness trajectories and demographics are shifting in this setting. The typical palliative care patient is no longer a late-stage cancer patient but could be anyone with a life-limiting disease that cannot be cured, who would temporarily benefit from more symptom control or a holistic approach. These changes mean that palliative care professionals will more frequently meet patients who have different and sometimes obstinate perceptions, hopes and beliefs regarding their expectations and convictions about what might help them.

The current situation in palliative care is an example of what has been described as friction in ethnology: a situation where cultures and traditions meet in a global setting. In this type of situation, different approaches become evident, disagreements are negotiated, and new agreements (traditions) are born. Anna Tsing called it a 'zone of awkward engagement' (Tsing 2015). Tackling the 'migrant issue' in palliative care appears to be one such engagement, as traditional palliative care expands to conquer new territory. However, the traditional standpoint epistemology is hindering this process; addressing this requires self-reflection, renegotiation and pushing one's own boundaries (Schrank et al. 2017).

To meet the needs of multicultural patients, future palliative care teams should become more heterogeneous, including health care personnel with different personal and professional backgrounds. This will require concentrating on diversity management within multicultural service organizations and facilities (including building teams, fostering mutual acceptance and respect, and providing space for discussion, reflection and growth). Structures for individual learning, advancement, and mentoring are also necessary. Existing training in cultural competence and communication have not yet resulted in the required improvements. Structural changes at the organizational level can support and help professional caregivers to break down the barriers that current practices put up.

10.9 Conclusions

This article aimed to provide an overview of the current challenges in palliative care research regarding cultural sensitivity about what, in the German context, is termed the 'migrant issue'. The article suggests that current attempts to systematically assess and understand migrants' needs are epistemically charged; most are based on palliative care providers' perspectives and put people with migration history in awkward or even negative positions. Whatever the reported outcomes, the ways problems and research questions are posed and discussed sometimes harm more than they shed light. Some contemporary approaches fail to foster either sociocultural openness or patient-centredness. However, the latter is essential in palliative care. Thus, palliative care, similarly to other health care facilities, needs to strengthen its teams and organizational structures by asking, 'What should we do with ourselves?' This will lead to more effective ways of dealing with cultural sensitivity, which requires the skill of being human to other humans in extremely vulnerable situations.

References

Brighton, L.J., Koffman, J., Hawkins, A., McDonald, A., McDonald, C., O'Brien, S. et al. 2017, 'A systematic review of end-of-life care communication skills training for generalist palliative care providers: research quality and reporting guidance', *Journal of Pain and Symptom Management*, vol. 54, no. 3, pp. 417–425.

Cain, C., Surbone, A., Elk, R., & Kagawa-Singer, M. 2018, 'Culture and palliative care: preferences, communication, meaning, and mutual decision-making', *Journal of Pain and Symptom Management*, vol. 55, no. 5, pp. 1408–1419.

Carduff, E., Johnston, S., Winstanley, C., Morrish, J., Murray, S.A., Spiller, J. et al. 2018, 'What does 'complex' mean in palliative care? Triangulating qualitative findings from 3 settings', *BMC Palliative Care*, vol. 17, no. 1, p. 12.

Crawley, L.M. 2005, 'Racial, cultural, and ethnic factors influencing end-of-life care', *Journal of Palliative Medicine*, vol. 8, Suppl. 1, pp. 58–96.

Epner, D.E., & Baile, W.F. 2012, 'Patient-centered care: the key to cultural competence', *Annals of Oncology*, vol. 23, Suppl. 3, pp. 33–42.

Ethno-medizinisches Zentrum. 2018, *MiMi Bayern – Mit Migranten, für Migranten*, viewed 4 July 2018, www.ethno-medizinisches-zentrum.de/index.php?option=com_content&view=article&id=28&Itemid=4.

Federal Office of Public Health (FOPH), Swiss Conference of the Cantonal Ministers of Public Health (CMH) and palliative CH. 2014, *Framework concept for palliative care in Switzerland: a basis for defining palliative care for the implementation of the 'National Strategy for Palliative Care'*, viewed 4 July 2018, www.palliative.ch/fileadmin/user_upload/palliative/publikum/2_PalliativeCarP/Framework_Concept_for_Palliative_Care_in_Switzerland.pdf.

Florea, M. 2014, 'Cross-cultural issues in academic palliative medicine', in E. Chang & A. Johnson (eds.), *Contemporary and innovative practice in palliative care*, InTech, Rijeka, pp. 3–18.

Fricker, M. 2009, *Epistemic injustice: power and the ethics of knowing*, Oxford University Press, New York.

Galanti, G.A. 2000, 'An introduction to cultural differences', *The Western Journal of Medicine*, vol. 172, no. 5, pp. 335–336.

Gunaratnam, Y. 2003, 'Culture is not enough', in D. Field, J. Hockey & N. Small (eds.), *Death, gender and ethnicity*, Routledge, London, pp. 166–186.

Gunaratnam, Y. 2014, 'Morbid mixtures: hybridity, pain and transnational dying', *Subjectivity*, vol. 7, no. 1, pp. 74–91.

Gysels, M., Evans, N., Meñaca, A., Andrew, E.V.W., Bausewein, C., Gastmans, C. et al. 2012, 'Culture is a priority for research in end-of-life care in Europe: a research agenda', *Journal of Pain and Symptom Management*, vol. 44, no. 2, pp. 285–294.

Helman, C.G. 2000, *Culture, health and illness*, Oxford University Press, London & New York.

Henke, O., Behzadi, A., Mauter, D., & Jenke, A. 2015, *Utilization of advanced directives among migrants in Berlin*, Paula Kubitscheck-Vogel-Stiftung, viewed 4 July 2018, www.pkv-stiftung.de/projekte/forschung-und-wissenschaft.html.

Henke, A., Thuss-Patience, P., Behzadi, A., & Henke, O. 2017, End-of-life care for immigrants in Germany: an epidemiological appraisal of Berlin, *PloS One*, viewed 4 July 2018, doi:10.1371/journal.pone.0182033.

Jansky, M., & Nauck, F. 2015, *Palliativ- und Hospizversorgung von Menschen mit Migrationshintergrund. Aktueller Stand und Handlungsempfehlungen für Hospiz- und Palliativversorger*, Klinik für Palliativmedizin, Universität Göttingen, Niedersächsisches Landesamt für Soziales, Jugend und Familie, Hannover.

Jansky, M., Owuso-Boakye, S., & Nauck, F. 2017a, *More knowledge, more action*, The Blog of the European Association for Palliative Care, viewed 4 July 2018, https://eapcnet.wordpress.com/2017/02/06/more-knowledge-more-action-palliative-care-for-people-with-a-migration-background/.

Jansky, M., Owuso-Boakye, S., & Nauck, F. 2017b, 'Palliative care for patients with Turkish or Arabic migration background in Lower Saxony: a survey from palliative care professionals' perspective', *Bundesgesundheitsblatt – Gesundheitsforschung – Gesundheitsschutz*, vol. 60, no. 1, pp. 45–54.

Jovanovic, M.M. 2012, 'Cultural competency and diversity among hospice palliative care volunteers', *The American Journal of Hospice and Palliative Care*, vol. 29, no. 3, pp. 165–170.

Koffman, J. 2014, 'Servicing multi-cultural needs at the end of life', *Journal of Renal Care*, vol. 40, Suppl. 1, pp. 6–15.

Kumagai, A.K., & Lypson, M.L. 2009, 'Beyond cultural competence: critical consciousness, social justice, and multicultural education', *Academic Medicine*, vol. 84, no. 6, pp. 782–787.

Migala, S., Sokolova, O., & Flick, U. 2017, *Palliative Lebensqualität - Inanspruchnahme von Versorgungsangeboten durch russischsprachige Migrantinnen und Migranten*, Freie Universität Berlin, viewed 4 July 2018, www.ewi-psy.fu-berlin.de/palqualsum.

Milberg, A., Torres, S., & Ågard, P. 2016, 'Health care professionals' understandings of cross-cultural interaction in end-of-life care: a focus group study', *PLoS One*, vol. 11, no. 11, e0165452.

Munday, D.F., Johnson, S.A., & Griffiths, F.E. 2003, 'Complexity theory and palliative care', *Palliative Medicine*, vol. 17, no. 4, pp. 308–309.

Paal, P. 2012, 'Ist "Kultur" in Palliative Care von Belang? Überlegungen aus anthropologischer Sicht', *Zeitschrift für Palliativmedizin*, vol. 13, no. 1, pp. 24–27.

Paal, P. 2013, 'Narrative encounters in the end of life care', in C.E. Asplund (ed.), *The therapeutic uses of storytelling*, Nordic Academic Press, Turku, pp. 159–178.

Paal, P., & Bükki, J. 2017, 'If I had stayed back home, I would not be alive any more…' – exploring end-of-life preferences in patients with migration background, *PLoS One*, vol. 12, no. 4, pp. e0175314.

Paal, P., Frick, E., Roser, T., & Jobin, G. 2017, 'Expert discussion on taking a spiritual history', *Journal of Palliative Care*, vol. 32, no. 1, pp. 19–25.

Pask, S., Pinto, C., Bristowe, K., van Vliet, K., Nicholson, C., Evans, C.J. et al. 2018, 'A framework for complexity in palliative care: a qualitative study with patients, family carers and professionals', *Palliative Medicine*, vol. 32, no. 6, pp. 1078–1090.

Pollack, H., & Kronebusch, K. 2009, 'Health insurance and vulnerable populations', in C.G. McLaughlin (ed.), *Health policy and the uninsured*, The Urban Institute Press, Washington, DC, pp. 110–134.

Randall, F., & Downie, R.S. 2006, *The philosophy of palliative care: critique and reconstruction*, Oxford University Press, London.

Schrank, B., Rumpold, T., Amering, M., Masel, E.K., Watzke, H., & Schur, S. 2017, 'Pushing boundaries. Culture-sensitive care in oncology and palliative care: a qualitative study', *Psycho-Oncology*, vol. 26, no. 6, pp. 763–769.

Selman, L.E., Brighton, L.J., Hawkins, A., McDonald, C., O'Brien, S., Robinson, V. et al. 2017, 'The effect of communication skills training for generalist palliative care providers on patient-reported outcomes and clinician behaviors: a systematic review and meta-analysis', *Journal of Pain and Symptom Management*, vol. 54, no. 3, pp. 404–416.e5.

Soom-Amman, E., & Gross-Salis, C. 2014, *Palliative Care und Migration. Literaturrecherche zum Stand der Forschung einer diversitätssensiblen Palliative Care*, Bundesamt für Gesundheit der Schweiz, viewed 4 July 2018, www.bag.admin.ch/themen/gesundheitspolitik/13764/13777/14309/index.html?download=NHzLpZeg7t,lnp6I0NTU042l2Z6ln1acy4Zn4Z2qZpnO2Yuq2Z6gpJCLeH18g2ym162epYbg2c_JjKbNoKSn6A--&lang=de.

Statistisches Bundesamt. 2017, *Bevölkerung und Erwerbstätigkeit, Bevölkerung mit Migrationshintergrund, Ergebnisse des Mikrozensus. Fachserie 1, Reihe 2.2*, viewed 4 July 2018, www.destatis.de/DE/Publikationen/Thematisch/Bevoelkerung/MigrationIntegMigrat/Migrationshintergrund2010220167004.pdf?__blob=publicationFile.

Stähli, A. 2013, *Empfehlungen zur Hospiz- und Palliativbetreuung von Menschen mit Migrationshintergrund – eine Handreichung*, DRK-Landesverband Westfalen-Lippe e.V., Münster.

Tervalon, M., & Murray-García, J. 1998, 'Cultural humility versus cultural competence: a critical distinction in defining physician training outcomes in multicultural education', *Journal of Health Care for the Poor and Underserved*, vol. 9, no. 2, pp. 117–125.

Thomas, R., Wilson, D.M., Justice, C., Birch, S., & Sheps, S. 2008, 'A literature review of preferences for end-of-life care in developed countries by individuals with different cultural affiliations and ethnicity', *Journal of Hospice & Palliative Nursing*, vol. 10, no. 3, pp. 142–161.

Tsing, A.L. 2015, *Friction. An ethnography of global connection*, Princeton University Press, Princeton.

Von Unger, H. 2014, *Partizipative Forschung. Einführung in die Forschungspraxis*, Springer-Verlag, Berlin.

Wasner, M., & Kurz, A.K. 2016, 'Schulungsbedarf von Hospizhelfern in interkultureller Kompetenz', *Palliativmedizin*, vol. 17, no. 5, pp. 1–59.

Waterworth, J.M. 2004, *Meaning in life: confronted with death. A philosophical analysis of hope*. Palgrave Macmillan UK, London.

WHO. 2014, 'Strengthening of palliative care as a component of integrated treatment throughout the life course', *Journal of Pain & Palliative Care Pharmacotherapy*, vol. 28, no. 4, pp. 130–134.

WHO. 2015, *Improving access to palliative care. Infographics on palliative care*, WHO, viewed 4 July 2018, www.who.int/ncds/management/palliative-care/Infographic_palliative_care_EN_final.pdf.

WHO. 2016, *Strategy and action plan for refugee and migrant health in the WHO European Region*, WHO Regional Office for Europe, viewed 4 July 2018, www.euro.who.int/__data/assets/pdf_file/0004/314725/66wd08e_MigrantHealMigrantHealthStrateg_160424.pdf.

11 Using superdiversity as a lens to view migrant health

Reflections on ethical and practical implications of an exploratory study involving community researchers

Antje Lindenmeyer

11.1 Introduction

This chapter focuses on experiences and findings from an exploratory study into the health histories of recent migrants to the United Kingdom (UK), guided by the concept of superdiversity. This project involved collaboration between academic researchers and a team of community researchers who were engaged in developing and conducting the research. In keeping with the overall theme of the volume, there is a strong focus on the ethical implications of this research approach. In addition to being a personal learning experience, the study incurred many challenges, including an awkward fit with formal research ethics and practical challenges linked to the diversity of researchers and migrant participants. These elements – instead of being reported briefly, as is typical for the 'methods' section of a conventional research publication – will be presented in detail and in relation to other developments in this field. Additionally, I will discuss the implications of co-constructing culturally specific health narratives and provide an overview of the study's findings.

11.2 Superdiversity and migrant health

In the UK, patterns of migration have changed radically over the last two decades from clearly recognisable, geographically distinct populations of mostly Commonwealth citizens. The accession of Central and Eastern European countries to the European Union (EU), a more globalised economy and global conflict leading to an increase in asylum seekers and refugees have resulted in larger but increasingly diversified flows of migration. The concept of superdiversity has been developed to describe this phenomenon and its many different manifestations, and to help policymakers and practitioners recognise and respond to the new conditions created by increasing global migration and population change (Meissner & Vertovec 2014). The concept of superdiversity arose from the observation of demographic and social changes in London in the early 2000s, where researchers identified an increasing diversity of countries of origin, languages and immigration statuses as well as changes in the dynamics of gender and social space and place. This social landscape (where, how and with whom people live) also encompasses social relationships and local resources. For example, large migrant communities inhabiting a particular space over time often establish community associations and places of worship as visible signs of their presence; however, newer, smaller, less organised groups tend to be less often heard and included in the public agenda (Vertovec 2007).

From these beginnings in social anthropology, the concept has been taken up and further developed in a range of academic disciplines (e.g., economics and sociolinguistics). Superdiversity stresses the importance of

> levels of socioeconomic and legal complexity distinguished by a dynamic interplay of factors such as country of origin (including variations such as ethnicity, language, religious tradition, regional and local identities), migration experience (which is often strongly related to gender, age, education, social networks and particular economic niches) and legal status.
>
> (Green et al. 2014, p. 1206)

In this way, it offers a perspective on the increased complexity described above and a focus on diverging needs driven by social and material resources and entitlements rather than, or in addition to, culture and ethnicity (Meissner & Vertovec 2014). It also recognises that many migrants live increasingly 'transnational lives', with strong links both to their country of origin and their country of migration. Over the past decades, inexpensive travel, social media and communication platforms have powerfully affected the extent to which migrants can retain strong bonds with families, traditions and organisations in their countries of origin (Vertovec 2009).

Recently, superdiversity has been described as a new and promising way to approach migrant health (Phillimore 2011; Zeeb et al. 2015). This approach helps researchers to shift the focus from potentially essentialised characteristics of ethnic or national groups that might impact health (Mladovsky 2009) towards differences within and similarities between groups. This is important because the health effects of socio-economic or immigration status, age, gender and the experience of migration itself can be felt across the life course (Nazroo 2003; see Razum & Wenner, Chapter 1). A superdiversity lens can also highlight differences between the experience of recent migrants and those who have been living in the UK for a long time. Unlike established migrants, recent migrants may be unfamiliar with health services and systems. They are also highly mobile due to frequent onward migration (within the same country or to a different country) or the state-mandated dispersal of asylum seekers. Consequently, many individuals, especially those who do not originate from Commonwealth countries, are unable to join a settled community with a sufficient critical mass to offer navigation support (Phillimore 2015). Therefore, it is essential to understand their experiences of health, illness and health services both 'back home' and in the UK and how those experiences shape their use of local health services.

11.3 Introduction to the study

To address the complexities outlined above, a team of four researchers from the Institute of Applied Health Research (IAHR) and the Institute of Research into Superdiversity (IRiS) at the University of Birmingham (see Acknowledgements) collaborated on an exploratory, qualitative study with a team of six community researchers. The main aim was to explore recent migrants' perspectives on health and illness in their home country and after coming to the UK, including their experiences with the health system in the UK. The academic research team defined 'recent migrants' as those migrants living in the UK for more than a year but less than five years as we wanted to capture the process of engagement with health services, which may be gradual and dependent on factors such as need, awareness of what is available and the degree of everyday interaction with mainstream UK society (Llacer et al. 2007; Osipovic 2013). The research was guided by a life course approach that aimed to understand diverse experiences of migration (to join a spouse, to seek asylum, to take a job) and their impact on health.

11.3.1 A pragmatic community-based approach

The project took a participatory, community-based approach. This type of design is increasingly used in health research in order to conduct research with and by local people rather than on them (Cornwall & Jewkes 1995). Goodson and Phillimore define community research as "training community members to carry out research within their own communities, often, but not always, for the benefit of those communities" (2010, p. 490). This flexible definition puts the community researcher at the heart of the research. While this approach does not give 'the community' full control over deciding what should be researched, as stipulated by some participatory methodologies (Brodie, Cowling & Nissen 2009), it allows academic researchers to tap into the unique knowledge and skills of community researchers which include the ability to challenge preconceived understandings that the academics may hold. Although data gathered by community researchers may be less rich than data collected by a qualitative researcher with many years of experience, there is also evidence that people may express their views more openly and honestly to someone with a shared background or experience. This means that communities may be defined by their members' country of origin, language or common experience (Goodson & Phillimore 2012).

For our project, a team of six community researchers played an integral part. Of these researchers, four had completed an accredited qualitative research training course at the IRiS, which introduced participants to general principles of research including the purpose of interviewing, ethics, subjectivity and researcher bias as well as turning issues faced by the community into research and interview questions. Participants subsequently conducted a short series of face-to-face interviews and analysed the data with the support of an allocated mentor (Jones &

Joseph 2012). Two community researchers were part of an earlier project involving volunteers in refugee organisations who themselves had sought refuge; one was running a small organisation for Polish migrants, and one provided spiritual support for Muslim hospital patients. The remaining two were mature social science students who had strong links with migrant communities (Chinese and Iranian); they had received qualitative research training as part of their course.

Community researchers were asked to recruit 2–4 recent migrants each with whom they shared a language using their local connections with community groups (excluding close friends and family, those in an immediate crisis situation or undocumented migrants). They were asked to aim for variation in age, gender and migration 'journey' as much as possible. This process was intended to achieve a sample with maximum variation in demographics and experiences relevant to the research (Sandelowski 1995). We aimed to capture both similarities between very different migrants and the impact of different experiences in people from similar national and ethnic groups. Identifying commonalities was especially important to provide a solid foundation for the development of policy recommendations where the provision of specialist services according to ethnic or national group may not be feasible (Phillimore, Humphris & Khan 2014).

Community researchers conducted 23 interviews (see Table 11.1) in the participants' preferred language, where possible, using an agreed-upon semi-structured interview guide that explored health and illness experiences across the life course. Questions focused on participants' understandings of health and wellbeing, what they would do when illness occurred and from whom they would seek advice (both in their country of origin and the UK). They were also asked what they saw as beneficial or detrimental to their current state of health and what happened when they were accessing health care services in the UK in comparison to their earlier experiences. Interviews were digitally recorded, transcribed into English and anonymised by the community researchers. Ideally, a sample of the interviews should have been back-translated and compared to the original recordings by a professional translator to check for quality and consistency (Bradby 2002). As we did not have the resources to incorporate this process, academic researchers fed back directly to community researchers to clarify difficult sections of the interviews and to encourage more probing and open questioning where appropriate.

There have been concerns about the ethics of involving community researchers in academic research, including control over the research, potential exploitation and adequate payment (Elliott, Watson & Harries 2002). In our case, although the research topic and overall research questions were, to a degree, academic researcher-led, community researchers were involved in formulating research questions and helping researchers interpret findings and contextualise interview data. Organising adequate payment for the community researchers proved difficult because they were neither filling an advertisable 'post' nor working as typically casual staff. Ultimately, we were able to engage them as freelance consultants with payment comparable to a junior academic researcher.

11.3.2 What links and divides community researchers and participants?

As outlined above, similarities and dissimilarities between community researchers and participants differed across the team. For some (e.g., for the Polish researcher), the 'community' was defined by both nationality and language, whereas for others, nationality and language were not synonymous. The Chinese researcher conducted interviews in both Cantonese and Mandarin, and another researcher, originally from Rwanda, interviewed participants from francophone African countries who had moved to the UK mainly to seek asylum. Another researcher, originally from Sudan, interviewed mostly African participants who were supported by a refugee organisation in which he also had a role. As interpreting services were not difficult for him to access, two of his interviews were conducted through an interpreter. The remaining two researchers recruited participants from religious communities: Muslim (focusing on migrants from India and Pakistan) and Iranian Christian.

The above paragraph makes it clear that the links between community researchers and their communities and participants were complex. All but one of the researchers shared a common language with their interviewees, which was not always their own or the researcher's first language. Other important connections were through nationality, region of origin, the experience of seeking refuge or religious beliefs. Community researchers were able to recruit a sample that was highly diverse with regard to place of origin, migration experience, gender, language and religion and that included people such as African asylum seekers, whom we believe would be very difficult for academic researchers to recruit independently. With the exception of two older participants, the sample tended to be in their twenties and early thirties, which is in keeping with recent migrants overall.

The recruitment strategies described above resulted in a complex 'positioning' of the community researchers in relation to research participants. This was to be expected as the simplistic distinction between 'insider' or 'peer' community researchers and 'outsider' academic researchers has been critiqued by those engaged in research with migrant communities. Instead, the research topic under investigation, the status, characteristics and biographical particularities of the researcher and the participant/s, and the local conditions in which the fieldwork takes place all potentially cause dynamic shifts between insider/outsider positions (Kusow 2003). Carling, Erdal and Ezzati (2014) discuss a set of 'markers' of positionality for researchers and participants derived from their own experience of ethnographic research with migrants. These markers might or might not be visible (or the researcher/participant might choose to reveal them or not). Such markers of positionality may include names (from which assumptions on nationality, ethnicity, religion and other characteristics may be made), physical appearance (from which ethnicity might or might not be inferred), professional status, age, gender, language skills, religion (including dress/accessories denoting status or religion) and experience of migration as well as other life-changing

Table 11.1 Description of the study participants

Gender	*Born in*	*Age*	*Reason for move*	*Language of interview*	*Religion*
Female	Iran	30	Seeking asylum	Farsi	Not stated
Female	Iran	40	Joining spouse	Farsi	Christian
Female	Iran	35	Seeking asylum	Farsi	Christian
Male	Iran	39	Seeking asylum	Farsi	Christian
Female	Poland	25	Study	Polish	None
Male	Poland	36	Work	Polish	None
Female	Poland	36	Work	Polish	Catholic
Female	Poland	52	Joining family	Polish	Catholic
Female	Pakistan	26	Marriage	Urdu	Muslim
Female	Pakistan	28	Marriage	Urdu	Muslim
Male	India	34	Marriage	Gujarati	Muslim
Female	India	34	Marriage	Gujarati	Muslim
Male	Iraq	37	Seeking asylum	English	Muslim
Male	Somalia	29	Joining family	Somali (interpreted)	Muslim
Female	Zimbabwe	60	Seeking asylum	Shona	Catholic
Female	Sudan	29	Seeking asylum	Zaghawa (interpreted)	Muslim
Male	Cameroon	26	Seeking asylum	French	Christian
Male	Cameroon	30	Work	French	Christian
Female	DR Congo	30	Seeking asylum	French	Muslim
Female	Uganda	26	Seeking asylum	French	Christian
Male	Ivory Coast	35	Seeking asylum	French	Christian
Female	China	38	Joining spouse	Cantonese	None
Female	China	25	Joining spouse	Mandarin	None

experiences such as parenthood (Carling, Erdal & Ezzati 2014). These considerations are widespread in qualitative health research, where researchers might stress or downplay their status (e.g., as a clinician, student, researcher or academic), leading to different dynamics in interacting with research participants (Richards & Emslie 2000). By emphasising similarity, researchers might enhance rapport and readiness to share experiences; however, participants might wish to approach a researcher with strong links to authority and possible policy influence (Kusow 2003). Likewise, researchers might take the position to not manipulate their outward appearance and behaviour. For example, a researcher whose national origin implied that she might be Muslim discussed her decision to not wear a hijab while interviewing an imam as this might be seen as a deception, whereas an ethnically Norwegian woman might have chosen to wear a hijab as a sign of respect (Carling, Erdal & Ezzati 2014). In our project, it was not possible to retrospectively decode shifts in positioning; indeed, not all of these might be consciously apparent to the researcher. In discussing their experience, community researchers mentioned topics on which connections between the interviewer and the interviewee might be important, such as the role of religion in understandings of health. In some of the interviews, there is a sense of participants implying a shared 'we' with the interviewer. These topics will be further discussed in the section on co-constructing health histories below.

11.3.3 Ethical considerations arising before and during the research

As can be inferred from the research methods outlined above, there were many ethical considerations and dilemmas that academic and community researchers had to address. Before commencing the research, a lengthy process of negotiation with the University of Birmingham's research ethics committee was necessary, focusing mainly on gaining informed consent while maintaining anonymity. It became immediately apparent that methods established for community research in the social sciences ran counter to the more formal requirements of ethics in health research, which meant that we had to shift from an informal, spoken and digitally recorded consent process to a written and signed consent form. We were eventually permitted to allow consent to proceed if participants signed with a first name only or a pseudonym if they felt uncomfortable providing their full name. Community researchers also offered participants a copy of the recording, including discussions around consent, as an alternative to formal translation of the information and consent materials into 11 different languages.

A significant, overarching ethical issue in this type of research is the balance of power. As several of the researchers were community practitioners, there was the possibility that they may be seen by participants as authority figures who might help their 'case' in the asylum process. Conversely, participants might fear that the experiences they told the researchers could negatively impact their asylum case. The risk of interviews being influenced by such assumptions could not be completely excluded. However, the consent process included reassurances that participants' narratives could not be linked back to them after the interview had been transcribed and that nothing they said would have an impact on the services they received. Community researchers were also not formally involved (e.g., as a case worker) with the people they interviewed. The migrants approached by the researchers held power in being able to agree (or not) to take part. Recruitment took much longer than anticipated; some of the community researchers described a process of trust building in which they were 'sounded out' by members of the community before they were able to conduct interviews. Academic researchers also had to relinquish some of their control over the research because they had to wait for transcribed interviews to emerge that could be discussed with the community researchers.

A few of the community researchers heard distressing narratives of migration or health experiences from participants. This possibility had been discussed during training, and the community researchers were strongly encouraged to contact the academic researchers if they wanted to discuss what had happened during an interview. There were also planned debriefing meetings to discuss interviews that had been translated and transcribed. The most distressing stories were told to researchers who had a role in refugee organisations and therefore were familiar with this possibility. They ensured that interviewees were given time to recover and offered to pause or stop the interview. However, concerns remained about a few of the participants after the interview ended. Training for community researchers had included a process to follow if they felt that participants might be in immediate danger, which is common in most qualitative health research in the UK (discussing with the interviewee where to seek help; if needed, seeking their permission to break confidentiality and, in extreme cases, going to the authorities). Community researchers also had contact details of charities supporting refugees and people in crisis to share with the interviewees. During a debriefing session, one community researcher discussed interviewing a young mother with physical and mental health issues. As the researcher had checked that the interviewee was currently supported by health care services and a charitable organisation, we agreed that there was no need for further action. However, the community researcher still felt concerned about the interviewee's ongoing health and wellbeing.

Practical ethical issues that arose throughout the research were also discussed between academic and community researchers, and solutions were sought. For example, we had ethical approval to offer participants a £20 shopping voucher for their time. Although this amounted to a nice 'thank you' for employed migrants, for asylum seekers entitled to a weekly allowance of (currently) £36.95, it was a substantial incentive. Community researchers recruiting asylum seekers told interviewees about the voucher only at the end of the interview and asked them not to tell their peers about it to avoid payment becoming the main reason for participation. Researching small, close-knit communities in which participants knew each other also posed an ethical challenge (Damianakis & Woodford 2012). When participants were from small communities and/or had passed on invitations to participate to their friends and family, the researchers were advised that they needed to be careful not to let the participant guess how other interviewees had responded.

11.3.4 Examples of 'co-constructed' health histories

Involving community researchers introduces additional complexity into research on cultural understandings of health. Ethnographers have described how illness is experienced and expressed in different cultures, such as in 'languages' of pain (Helman 1984). Narratives around health and illness can also be used to claim a positional identity, a process that can be more complicated for migrants. For example, South Americans in London who were interviewed about their medication use said they wanted to cherish traditional remedies while avoiding the negative stereotype of the poor and uneducated migrant (Ceuterick & Vandebroek 2017). Discussing health with a community researcher who is both an 'insider' and an 'outsider' may also shape the way in which participants position themselves. Guided by these insights, I returned to the interview data that the academic research team had already analysed thematically (see below), looking for content that might elucidate the dynamics between community researchers and interviewees. Although it is impossible to be completely sure, for some participants, there seemed to be a sense of a 'we' appealing to or implying the interviewer:

> With us, when we come from abroad, we would be used to antibiotics. So if we are not sometimes given antibiotics here, the illness or any ailment can take a long time to cure.
>
> (Female participant, Zimbabwe)

> ... our bodies need strong medication ... the medication here is very weak.
>
> (Female participant, Iran)

> People from Africa... when we go to see the GP, we are given very simple medication that our body does resist too much because of what we have been given back home.
>
> (Male participant, Cameroon)

The interviewees here are taking the position of the outsider with a particular need for antibiotics or strong painkillers; they say that the medicines given to them by their general practitioner (GP) do not work for them. Another example of introducing an implied 'we' is the link between health and religion:

> Illness and good health are both from God. But even though illness and good health are in God's hands, it should not be the case that we don't look after ourselves. ... We should therefore avoid things that we think make us ill.
>
> (Female participant, Pakistan)

> Sometimes people who [...] have many medical problems do get better; other people who sometimes suffer from something very small pass away from that small illness. In our religion, we are told to take care of our own health and to do what is good for our health. However, life and death are in God's hands.
>
> (Female participant, India)

Here, both the interviewee and the interviewer are Muslim. The participants are implying a collective 'we' of believers while balancing fate and God's will with the responsibility to look after one's own health. In the next excerpt, the interviewer and interviewee are female, Polish and of a similar age:

> I have a very big family, and I also remember being close with neighbours and helping each other when someone was ill. ... Everyone would try to advise, come up with home remedies or pray (laughter). Yes, my family was always very religious, so I think a lot of understanding and explanation came from religion (laughter). Some of my family members would believe that illness is God's punishment or God's trial.

Although the participant describes herself as Catholic, she distances herself from the simpler belief of the older generation. The laughter might be a defusing response to stereotypes of Polish people as superstitious (which was mentioned by the interviewer in discussions with academic researchers). However, there is also an affectionate description of old-fashioned values with families and neighbours coming together. Both of these sets of quotes suggest that research participants may be enabled to discuss complex experiences of health and illness if they can draw on common characteristics and an implied understanding between the interviewer and the interviewee.

11.3.5 Summary of study findings

Although the main focus of this chapter is the implications of involving community researchers, I would like to end with a brief summary of the overall study findings. The academic research team conducted a thematic analysis, identifying three overarching domains: what promotes good health, the phenomenon of 'medical pluralism' and understandings of justice and fairness in interaction with health services. The findings were discussed with the community researchers and then further refined.

11.3.5.1 What promotes good health?

Irrespective of their origins, the participants had quite similar understandings of what factors enable good health: a combination of a good diet, an active life, cleanliness and hygiene, social relationships and the absence of stress and worry. Healthy eating was seen as the most important contributor by a majority of the participants, followed by fresh air and regular exercise. Harmonious family relationships were included by those who lived with family; some stressed the role of the mother in ensuring good health and/or remembered their own mothers fulfilling this role. These understandings seemed deeply embedded from teachings early in life by mothers and other family members, schools (one Iranian woman mentioned a "hygiene teacher") and religious organisations.

Although some participants did not find it problematic to create these conditions after migrating, for others, migration to the UK and conditions after migration were not conducive to good health. Two asylum seekers experienced a traumatic journey that severely affected their physical and mental health. Several felt that worrying about their asylum case was very bad for their health; others found the cold weather damaging, both directly (several mentioned colds and flus, and one experienced frostbite) and by discouraging physical activity. In contrast, a Chinese participant said she appreciated the ability to take walks in green spaces. Whereas a study restricted to a single group might have focused on particular cultural understandings of health that were also mentioned (e.g., "hot" and "cold" foods), we found that overall understandings of the factors that enable good health, for example, a harmonious life and absence of stress and worry were not dissimilar from mainstream views in the UK (see Backett, Davison & Mullen 1994). However, health and wellbeing also seemed to be influenced by the migration journey and settling in the UK (e.g., the ability to live with family; having to wait for asylum claims to be decided).

11.3.5.2 Medical pluralism

Most participants engaged in some form of medical pluralism; that is, the use of more than one medical system in terms of health beliefs, behaviours or treatments (Cant & Sharma 1999). They discussed accessing different medical systems and treatments, both traditional and modern, at the same time in their country of origin and the UK. Some acquired prescription medication, including antibiotics, from family back home or migrant networks in the UK as they had presented at frontline services with what they believed to be serious problems and felt that they were sent away with paracetamol (see also Lindenmeyer et al. 2016a). More widely, however, friends and family were very important as they shared common understandings of health as well as advice and practical support. Increasing worldwide connectivity (budget flights, phone calls, Skype, the Internet) was useful to access this support.

The way that treatments were sourced differed between participants. For example, several African participants used plant-based remedies such as herbs, roots and honey that were sent by families or brought back and sold by other migrants, whereas those from Iran, India and Pakistan tended to use community-based food shops. In keeping with other researchers' findings, Chinese participants talked about using 'Western' medicine for acute illness and herbal drinks from the Chinese shop to improve general wellbeing (Green et al. 2006). Polish participants described returning to Poland for private gynaecology or dermatology services as part of regular visits to Poland to see family (see also Osipovic 2013).

11.3.5.3 Justice, fairness and access

When asked to compare health services in their home country and the UK, participants often discussed the ideal of justice and fairness in accessing health care, balancing it against the pragmatic need for fast access for an acute health problem. Free treatment was especially appreciated by people who remembered growing up with no or very basic government-funded health care. A participant from Ivory Coast commented that he was always aware that it was very difficult to have good health when living in poverty. Participants originally from rural areas recounted difficulties in reaching health centres. Instead, people sought health care locally, which could include possibly counterfeit or expired medicines sold by market traders; one participant remembered a relative dying on the way to hospital. Although those from urban areas and higher-income countries had better experiences, for most participants, the reality was a two-tier system in which specialists or more timely appointments could be accessed by making one-off payments.

Several participants who used hospital services in the UK (e.g., to give birth) were very aware of how expensive these would have been back home. However, migration could also mean losing the ability to choose health services. There seemed to be no clear pathway to specialists in the UK, even if the participant was willing to pay. Those with no experience of a GP gatekeeper system gravitated towards hospital doctors. Many were frustrated with the slow pace of UK health care systems and having to wait for appointments. Overall, participants who were familiar with 'customer pays' systems were used to deciding for themselves what kind of care they needed and whether they could afford it. Struggles over whether they or their doctor should decide which treatment was needed were apparent in their interactions with GPs recounted in the interviews.

11.4 Conclusions

Overall, involving community researchers in migrant health research allowed us to access a highly diverse sample of participants who would likely have been impossible to recruit in any other way. For both community and academic researchers, this project entailed a learning process. Although some challenges could be anticipated, others had to be discussed and resolved in an ongoing process. Dynamics between the insider and outsider positions of both community researchers and participants yielded complex discussions of health before, during and after migration. We believe that the content of these discussions, as analysed by the research team and described above, will be useful for health practitioners and policy makers with whom we are in a continuing dialogue (Lindenmeyer et al. 2016b). For example, the findings outline the need to raise awareness of different experiences and expectations linked to growing up with a very different health system or the possibility that migrants might use health services back home as well as in the UK. Further research focusing on practices of transnational health seeking, especially in relation to welfare 'bricolage' in superdiverse neighbourhoods (Phillimore et al. 2015), is currently under development.

Acknowledgements

The Research Team: Antje Lindenmeyer, Institute of Applied Health Research, University of Birmingham. Sabi Redwood, School of Social and Community Medicine, University of Bristol. Jenny Phillimore, Institute of Research into Superdiversity, University of Birmingham. Laura Griffith, Health Services Management Centre, University of Birmingham.

I would like to thank the community researchers and all the interviewees who participated. Without their time and thoughts, this project would not have been possible. The study was funded by a joint grant from the British Academy and the Leverhulme Foundation.

References

Backett, K., Davison, C., & Mullen, K. 1994, 'Lay evaluation of health and healthy lifestyles', *British Journal of General Practice*, vol. 44, no. 383, pp. 277–280.

Bradby, H. 2002, 'Translating culture and language: a research note on multilingual settings', *Sociology of Health and Illness*, vol. 24, no. 6, pp. 842–855.

Brodie, E., Cowling, E., & Nissen, N. 2009, *Understanding participation: a literature review*, INVOLVE, London.

Cant, S., & Sharma, U. 1999, *A new medical pluralism? Alternative medicine, doctors, patients, and the state*, UCL Press, London.

Carling, J., Erdal, M.B., & Ezzati, R. 2014, 'Beyond the insider-outsider divide in migration research', *Migration Studies*, vol. 2, no. 1, pp. 36–54.

Ceuterick, M., & Vandebroek, I. 2017, 'Identity in a medicine cabinet: discursive positions of Andean migrants towards their use of herbal remedies in the United Kingdom', *Social Science and Medicine*, vol. 177, no. 6 pp. 43–51.

Cornwall, A., & Jewkes, R. 1995, 'What is participatory research?', *Social Science and Medicine*, vol. 41, no. 12, pp. 1667–1676.

Damianakis, T., & Woodford, M.R. 2012, 'Qualitative research with small connected communities: generating new knowledge while upholding research ethics', *Qualitative Health Research*, vol. 22, no. 5, pp. 708–718.

Elliott, E., Watson, A.J., & Harries, U. 2002, 'Harnessing expertise: involving peer interviewers in qualitative research with hard-to-reach populations', *Health Expectations*, vol. 5, no. 2, pp. 172–178.

Goodson, L. & Phillimore, J. 2010, 'A community research methodology: working with new migrants to develop a policy related evidence base', *Social Policy and Society*, vol. 9, no. 4, pp. 489–501.

Goodson, L., & Phillimore, J. 2012, 'Community research: opportunities and challenges', in L. Goodson & J. Phillimore (eds.), *Community research for participation: from theory to method*, Policy Press, Bristol, pp. 3–20.

Green, G., Bradby, H., Chan, A., & Lee, M. 2006, '"We are not completely westernised": dual medical systems and pathways to health care among Chinese migrant women in England', *Social Science and Medicine*, vol. 62, no. 6, pp. 1498–1509.

Green, G., Davison, C., Bradby, H., Krause, K., Mejias, F.M., & Alex, G. 2014, 'Pathways to care: how superdiversity shapes the need for navigational assistance', *Sociology of Health and Illness*, vol. 36, no. 8, pp. 1205–1219.

Helman, C. 1984, *Culture, health and illness: an introduction for health professionals*, Butterworth-Heinemann, London.

Jones, P.A., & Joseph, R. 2012, 'Mentoring refugee community researchers in the UK: an empowerment tool?', in L. Goodson & J. Phillimore (eds.), *Community research for participation: from theory to method*, Policy Press, Bristol, pp. 315–330.

Kusow, A. 2003, 'Beyond indigenous authenticity: reflections on the insider/outsider debate in immigration research', *Symbolic Interaction*, vol. 26, no. 4, pp. 591–599.

Lindenmeyer, A., Redwood, S., Griffith, L., Ahmed, S., & Phillimore, J. 2016a, 'Recent migrants' perspectives on antibiotic use and prescribing: a qualitative study', *British Journal of General Practice*, vol. 66, no. 652, e802–e809.

Lindenmeyer, A., Newall, D., Redwood, S., Griffith, L., & Phillimore, J. 2016b, *Health across borders: recent migrants' experience of managing their health and wellbeing in the UK and the implications for health policy and practice*, viewed 22 August 2017, www.birmingham.ac.uk/Documents/college-social-sciences/social-policy/iris/2016/health-histories-report-final.pdf.

Llacer, A., Zunzunegui, M.V., Del Amo, J., Mazarrasa, L., & Bolumar, F. 2007, 'The contribution of a gender perspective to the understanding of migrants' health', *Journal of Epidemiology and Community Health*, vol. 61, suppl. 2, pp. ii4–ii10.

Meissner, F., & Vertovec, S. 2014, 'Comparing super-diversity', *Ethnic and Racial Studies*, vol. 38, no. 4, pp. 541–555.

Mladovsky, P. 2009, 'A framework for analysing migrant health policies in Europe', *Health Policy*, vol. 93, no. 1, pp. 55–63.

Nazroo, J.Y. 2003, 'The structuring of ethnic inequalities in health: economic position, racial discrimination, and racism', *American Journal of Public Health*, vol. 93, no. 2, pp. 277–284.

Osipovic, D. 2013, '"If I get ill, it's onto the plane, and off to Poland": use of health care services by Polish migrants in London', *Central and Eastern European Migration Review*, vol. 2, no. 2, pp. 98–114.

Phillimore, J. 2011, 'Approaches to health provision in the age of super-diversity: accessing the NHS in Britain's most diverse city', *Critical Social Policy*, vol. 31, no. 1, pp. 5–29.

Phillimore, J. 2015, 'Delivering maternity services in an era of superdiversity: the challenges of novelty and newness', *Ethnic and Racial Studies*, vol. 38, no. 4, pp. 568–582.

Phillimore, J., Bradby, H., Knecht, M., Padilla, B., Brand, T., Cheung, S.Y. et al. 2015, 'Understanding healthcare practices in superdiverse neighbourhoods and developing the concept of welfare bricolage: protocol of a cross-national mixed-methods study', *BMC International Health and Human Rights*, vol. 15, no. 1, p. 16.

Phillimore, J., Humphris, R., & Khan, K. 2014, *Migration, networks and resources: the relationship between migrants' social networks and their access to integration resources*, Initiatives and Studies on Multiethnicity Foundation, Milan.

Richards, H., & Emslie, C. 2000, 'The "doctor" or the "girl from the University"? Considering the influence of professional roles on qualitative interviewing', *Family Practice*, vol. 17, no. 1, pp. 71–75.

Sandelowski, M. 1995, 'Sample size in qualitative research', *Research in Nursing and Health*, vol. 18 no. 2, pp. 179–183.

Vertovec, S. 2007, 'Super-diversity and its implications', *Ethnic and Racial Studies*, vol. 30, no. 6, pp. 1024–1054.

Vertovec, S. 2009, *Transnationalism*, Routledge, London and New York.

Zeeb, H., Makarova, N., Brand, T., & Knecht, M. 2015, 'Superdiversity: a new concept for migrant health?', *Public Health Forum*, vol. 23, no. 2, pp. 124–125.

Part IV

Navigating pluralism in health care

12 Challenges in the provision of mental health care for refugees in Germany

A socially and culturally sensitive approach to psychological counselling and psychotherapy

Kerstin Hein and Barbara Abdallah-Steinkopff

12.1 Introduction

Refugees and asylum seekers are at high risk of suffering from mental health disorders due to forced migration, the experience of traumatic events before and during their exodus to Europe, and resettlement in unfamiliar contexts (Fazel, Wheeler & Danesh 2005; Liedl et al. 2017; Loncarevic 2007; Moser 2007; Walden 2017). The most common alterations are posttraumatic stress disorder (PTSD), depression, and generalised anxiety, but somatoform disorders are also possible (Fazel, Wheeler & Danesh 2005; Laban et al. 2004).

Mental health care professionals in Germany tend to reduce the psychological distress of refugees and asylum applicants to the consequences of traumatic events and cultural differences while neglecting the current effects of social disadvantage. While the acknowledgement of trauma and cultural background is highly important, it is also relevant to consider that post-migration factors such as an uncertain outcome of the asylum procedure, difficult living conditions in the host country, and the experience of discrimination significantly affect the psychological well-being of refugees. In this chapter, we argue that it is essential to consider the present life circumstances of refugees, as they may not only aggravate existing mental disorders but also produce new ones due to the persisting experience of helplessness and lack of control.

In addition, we focus on the challenges that arise in the context of psychosocial and psychological counselling and psychotherapy of refugees and asylum seekers in Germany. Herein, we consider psychological counselling and psychotherapy to be a special kind of intercultural encounter associated with a high risk of communicational misunderstanding. The existence of language barriers, different meanings attached to verbal and nonverbal behaviour, the somatisation of psychological distress, and disparate understandings of illness and cure may lead to incorrect diagnoses and wrong treatments.

To avoid such a situation, mental health care professionals need to develop a *socially and culturally sensitive approach* towards refugees. A socially sensitive approach avoids reducing psychological disorders to trauma and cultural differences by taking into account the current life circumstances and the effects of social inequalities on the psychological well-being of refugees. To be socially sensitive also means to be aware of the power imbalance, develop respectful relationships, and avoid paternalism and ethnocentrism.

On the other hand, mental health care professionals also need to develop a culturally sensitive approach towards their clients. In our understanding, cultural sensitivity does not imply an accumulation of knowledge about cultures or cultural stereotyping. At the heart of cultural sensitivity lies awareness of the high risk of misinterpretation associated with intercultural encounters. Culturally sensitive professionals adopt a not-knowing position, focusing their attention on the individual story of their clients and engage in a lifelong learning process of self-reflection.

In Germany, the provision of mental health care entails psychological counselling and psychotherapy. Psychotherapy is the treatment of mental disorders considered and catalogued as diseases, whereas psychological or psychosocial counselling addresses other kinds of problems such as family conflicts or life crises. In concrete professional practice, it is difficult to make a sharp distinction between psychological counselling and psychotherapy. However, there are important institutionalised differences between both alternatives. One fundamental difference is that psychotherapy is covered by health care insurance and can only be provided by certified medical or psychological psychotherapists, whereas psychological or psychosocial counselling is less regulated and can be practised by a wide range of professionals including psychologists, teachers, social workers, and other social professions. Psychological or psychosocial counselling is also not covered by health care insurances.[1] When refugees and asylum applicants need psychological assistance, they seek help at all levels of the system. Therefore, our contribution addresses the whole spectrum of mental health care professionals including psychological and psychosocial counsellors as well as medical and psychological psychotherapists.

12.2 The asylum process in Germany

The term ‘refugee’ is an internationally recognised legal classification for persons fleeing from their home country due to a well-founded fear of persecution for reasons of race, religion, nationality, membership of a specific social group, or political opinion (UNHCR 2015). Asylum seekers arriving in Germany have to report as quickly as possible to a public authority, register themselves, and submit an application for asylum. After registering, individuals receive proof of arrival and are referred to provisional accommodations in a nearby reception centre where they stay from six weeks up to six months. Afterwards, they are distributed across Germany in special communal accommodation centres. They reside in these centres during the entire asylum procedure, which currently takes between 3 and 15 months or even longer (Heinhold 2017).

When the asylum application is recognised, individuals obtain a residence permit and refugee status. Refugees are entitled to the same social benefits as German nationals and have unlimited access to the labour market. On the other hand, asylum seekers are compelled to live in the assigned accommodation centres and have a temporary residence permit and limited access to the labour market and integration courses. In other words, the living conditions and life perspectives of asylum seekers and refugees are quite different (Laban et al. 2004).

During 2016, Germany registered 745.545 asylum applications and made decisions on 695.733 requests. Protection – that is, recognition of refugee status, subsidiary protection or ban on deportation – was granted to 433.920 asylum seekers, which represented 62.4% of the cases. The majority of asylum seekers originated from Syria, followed by refugees from Afghanistan and Iraq (BAMF 2017). In the following sections we refer to all persons seeking protection and asylum as 'refugees' or as 'refugees and asylum seekers/applicants', if the subject under discussion applies to the whole group of persons seeking protection, regardless of their residence status.

12.3 Living conditions and mental health of refugees in Germany

Asylum seekers and refugees are a particularly vulnerable group. In their home countries, these individuals experienced life-threatening situations such as violence, political persecution or war, followed by a long, dangerous, and exhausting journey to Europe. The experience of these traumatic events enhances the risk of developing psychiatric disorders, particularly PTSD (Liedl et al. 2017; Moser 2007). In the host country, traumatised refugees need a secure and stable environment to be able to regain their psychological health. However, unfortunately, the living conditions of individuals during the asylum process in Germany are particularly difficult and stressful, leading to a sustained burdensome situation that jeopardises psychological well-being and aggravates already existing mental disorders (Abdallah-Steinkopff & Soyer 2013; Gravanidou 2017; Liedl et al. 2017; Liedl & Abdallah-Steinkopff 2017).

One of the most relevant factors with a negative impact on the state of mental health of asylum seekers is their *insecure residence status and the length of the asylum procedure.* After applying for asylum in Germany, individuals receive a provisional residence permit that allows them to stay in the country during the asylum process. However, there are no guarantees of a positive decision from the Federal Office for Migration and Refugees. Thus, asylum seekers remain in a state of uncertainty and fear of deportation during the entire asylum procedure and develop a sense of helplessness and lack of control (Ebert 2017; Liedl et al. 2017). The longer the procedure takes, the worse the mental conditions of asylum seekers become. In fact, international studies have shown that the rates of depressive and anxiety disorders among asylum seekers significantly increase in accordance with the duration of the asylum process (Laban et al. 2004).

Asylum seekers must further submit to *numerous restrictions and regulations.* Their mobility is highly restricted, and they have a limited access to housing, labour opportunities, and health care. In particular, adults do not understand the organisation of the public system and perceive these kinds of restrictions as incapacitating (Abdallah-Steinkopff & Soyer 2013). Moreover, many refugees have experienced traumatic events at the hand of government officials and organisations in their home countries, and therefore may see government entities as a threat (Abdallah-Steinkopff & Soyer 2013; Walden 2017).

During the asylum procedure, applicants are distributed among *special accommodation centres*. They are not able to choose the location nor allowed to move to another accommodation, city or federal state without official permission. Accommodation centres mostly encompass different forms of collective housing such as communal buildings, refurbished barracks, or a collection of containers (Heinhold 2017). The quality of accommodation centres widely varies from one federal state to another. Nevertheless, most centres have small and crowded apartments, shared hygienic facilities and kitchens, and limited possibilities for maintaining privacy. Furthermore, accommodation centres often gather together culturally and socially different groups, leading to complicated and conflicting social interactions among residents. In other words, communal accommodation centres represent a precarious form of housing that has a negative impact on the mental health of asylum seekers (Ebert 2017).

Refugees and asylum seekers have further *restricted access to the German labour market*. Although they are allowed to apply for a job three months after their arrival regardless of the status of their asylum procedure, most are considered unqualified for the German labour market. In fact, few asylum applicants and refugees have professional qualifications or university degrees, and even if they do, it is uncertain whether these certifications will be recognised in Germany. This means that most refugees in Germany are confronted with unemployment, which is experienced as a loss of status and social decline and is associated with existential fears and self-doubts (Ebert 2017; Gravanidou 2017; Loncarevic 2007; Pirmoradi 2012).

Legal restrictions and unfavourable living conditions also promote a situation of '*prescribed passivity*'. Asylum seekers find themselves in a kind of 'waiting room' without being able to establish a structured daily routine, which enhances their sense of helplessness and lack of control (Abdallah-Steinkopff & Soyer 2013; Ebert 2017; Liedl & Abdallah-Steinkopff 2017). Täubig (2009) defined this situation as the construction of everyday life under the condition of organised disorganisation and compared the life circumstances of refugees in communal accommodation centres with an existence in total institutions (Goffman 1984).[2]

In addition, many persons seeking protection suffer from *social loss and social isolation*. On the one hand, they worry about family members and relatives who remain in the home country or from whom they were separated during escape. The loss of emotionally significant persons may trigger an existential crisis and a loss of meaning in life. On the other hand, asylum seekers in particular have difficulties maintaining contact with local people, not only due to language barriers but also because government authorities tend to keep asylum seekers separated from the majority of the German population, thus reducing the opportunities for intercultural contact (Ebert 2017; Täubig 2009).

The social isolation of refugees is also reinforced by increasing levels of *discrimination and racism* among the German population towards culturally different people. Expressions of racism range from negative comments in everyday life contexts up to acts of violence against migrants and refugees. There is plenty of evidence that discrimination and racism affect the psychological well-being of affected persons and hinder their process of integration into the host society (Auernheimer 1988; Berry 1996; Hein 2013; Kilcher 2007; Loncarevic 2007).

Last but not least, refugees and other culturally diverse people are confronted with cultural differences and experience disorientation due to their exposure to an unfamiliar cultural environment. This is part of the normal process of acculturation during which affected persons learn to cope with culturally different contexts and acquire new culturally relevant social skills (Berry 1996; Ward, Bochner & Furnham 2003). At this point, it is important to emphasise that acculturation is a dynamic process of individual coping and social learning and not a persistent conflict between representatives of isolated and static cultural entities. This means that culturally diverse people do not permanently remain in a state of disorientation and cultural shock but learn to adapt to the new environment. On the other hand, the necessity of coping with diverse cultural backgrounds does not only represent a challenge for refugees and immigrants but also for professionals working with these individuals. We will deepen our understanding about this issue in the following section.

12.4 Psychosocial and psychological counselling and psychotherapy as intercultural encounter: challenging aspects of working with refugees and asylum seekers

Although refugees and asylum seekers show a high risk of developing mental health disorders and would clearly benefit from psychological assistance, only few make use of these kinds of services. One reason for this is the *limited access* of asylum seekers to the German health care system. As a matter of fact, during the asylum procedure, refugees only have access to basic health care in cases of acute illness or emergency situations (Abdallah-Steinkopff & Soyer 2013; Heinhold 2017). Although it is within the discretion of government agencies that a given psychological disorder is regarded as an acute problem that needs to be immediately addressed, usually psychosocial and psychological counselling and psychotherapy are not seen as part of the provision of basic health care and thus not accepted as an admissible treatment for asylum seekers. In addition, psychological assistance for asylum applicants is usually offered by local associations and voluntary organisations, most of which are located within urban areas. In rural areas, there are also fewer possibilities to access interpreter services. Thus, refugees and asylum seekers residing in rural areas who seek psychological assistance are in a clearly disadvantaged position. On the other hand, many affected persons do not ask for psychosocial support because of language barriers, little to no experience with these kinds of services, and prejudices surrounding mental health issues in their countries of origin (Walden 2017).

Generally, psychosocial and psychological counselling and psychotherapy for refugees and asylum seekers can be seen as a form of intercultural encounter. In principle, meetings between culturally disparate persons are no different from other social encounters. However, the probability of communicational misunderstandings increases in intercultural encounters because people with diverse cultural backgrounds also communicate differently. For instance, members of low-context cultures express information directly and rely heavily on verbal communication. On the other hand, members of high-context cultures pay more attention to situation cues and communicate in an indirect fashion.[3] Thus, persons are usually unaware of these communication patterns and tend to take them for granted. Communication patterns also exist independently from personal intention and language skills. In other words, misunderstandings in intercultural encounters may arise even if those conversing speak the same language (Maletzke 1996; Ward, Bochner & Furnham 2003).

In line with the conceptualisation of psychosocial and psychological counselling and psychotherapy as an intercultural encounter, the most salient challenges connected to therapeutic work with refugees and asylum seekers encompass language barriers, the risk of misinterpretations, and cultural stereotyping. In addition, there are challenges associated with the specific features of psychological treatment, such as differing interpretations about the purpose of the therapeutic process, misdiagnosis due to different cultural backgrounds, and disparate understandings of mental health and cure.

At the beginning of any therapeutic process with refugees, counsellors and psychotherapists first have to ensure the best possible level of communication and mutual understanding. Overcoming the *language barrier* is essential for the provision of mental health care as communication processes constitute the core of psychological treatment. Unfortunately, there are not enough native-speaking counsellors or psychotherapists in Germany to work with culturally diverse people in their mother tongues. Thus, a large part of the therapeutic work with refugees must be carried out with the support of *interpreters*.

The function of interpreters within the setting of therapeutic work does not only include a literal translation from one language to another during the session but also involves the role of a cultural mediator. Interpreters usually possess important cultural background knowledge that may assist the accurate interpretation of verbal and nonverbal contents and thus support the therapeutic process. The challenge for counsellors and psychotherapists within this constellation is to stay in charge despite the language barriers and to structure the sessions in a culturally sensitive way without handing over this task to the interpreter. To allow effective cooperation, counsellors and interpreters should prepare the therapeutic process in advance and hold short debriefing meetings after each session to exchange information and impressions. The tasks and scope of action for each professional and the definition of clear conversational rules should be discussed and defined in advance in accordance with existing guidelines (Abdallah-Steinkopff 2017).

In addition to verbal contents, particular attention has to be paid to the *nonverbal aspects of communication*. Appearance, gestures, and other forms of nonverbal behaviour provide us with information about an individual's gender, age, group membership, and emotional processes. However, nonverbal signs have no determined and universally valid significance as their meaning and relevance vary in accordance with the cultural context. Thus, individuals tend to experience their own nonverbal behaviour as self-evident and rarely question how they interpret the nonverbal expressions of others. Consequently, encounters between culturally diverse persons entail a high risk of mutual misinterpretation of nonverbal aspects. According to the literature, this holds particularly true for asymmetric power relationships, for example, between members of a cultural majority and minority (Altorfer & Käsermann 2007). In this sense, it is important for mental health care professionals to be aware of the fact that they may be misinterpreting the nonverbal signals of culturally diverse clients. The risk of developing false certainties is particularly high if clients belong to a minority culture such as refugees and asylum seekers.

Another challenging aspect of psychological work with people seeking protection concerns the definition of the therapeutic purpose. It is quite common for professionals to attribute the main problems of refugees and asylum seekers to their past experiences of traumatic events. Thereby, these professionals overlook the current living conditions of their clients and feel confused when they prefer to talk about their current life situation instead of speaking about their past. From the point of view of refugees and asylum seekers, the most urgent need is to cope with the challenges of everyday life in Germany and regaining a sense of control, self-management and self-efficacy. They also need stable living conditions to be able to develop a sense of security and make plans for the future. Some counsellors and psychotherapists react to this complex problem by taking sides and trying to solve the pragmatic issues of their clients' daily lives. However, in doing so, they act outside their area of competence and risk losing their therapeutic neutrality.[4] To avoid such a situation, it is paramount for mental health professionals to work in interdisciplinary networks including social workers and lawyers (Abdallah-Steinkopff & Soyer 2013; Ebert 2017; Gravanidou 2017; Liedl & Abdallah-Steinkopff 2017).

On the other hand, German counsellors and psychotherapists frequently complain about the fact that refugees and immigrants *express psychological distress by describing physical symptoms*. In doing so, culturally diverse clients are seen to be less aware of their psychological problems and in consequence less open to psychological change. Somatisation of psychological distress is challenging because it complicates the psychotherapeutic process and hampers the formulation of an accurate diagnosis. In fact, diagnoses of patients with migrant backgrounds are more likely to be unclear and inconclusive (Schach 1989). Culturally diverse patients also receive a psychotherapeutic indication and treatment less often than non-culturally diverse patients (Heim & Maercker 2017; Kahraman 2008).

Kahraman (2008) makes a critical remark in that she points out that people with migrant backgrounds are able to differentiate between psychological and corporal problems when they speak in their mother tongues. However, this competence is significantly reduced if they must communicate in another language. On the other hand, pain and suffering are multidimensional experiences that involve biological, psychological, and sociocultural levels. This means that the way we experience, interpret, and explain our suffering to others is not only a matter of physical or psychological alteration but also a culturally determined phenomenon (Haasen 2007; Heim & Maercker 2017). For example, in Western countries, it is common to distinguish between corporal pain and psychological suffering, whereas other cultures experience discomfort in a rather holistic way (Haasen 2007; Hüper & Kerkow-Weil 2007). This holistic approach may also explain why some culturally diverse persons use organ metaphors to describe emotional states.

Closely related to the sociocultural interpretation of suffering is the *culturally determined understanding of illness and disease.* Disease denotes a physical or psychological disorder that can be diagnosed and treated by health care professionals, whereas illness refers to the subjective experience of being ill (Zielke-Nadkarni 2007). Persons attribute subjective meaning to sickness and develop different concepts of illness.

Cultural differences regarding the conceptualisation of illness become highly relevant in the context of counselling and psychotherapy of refugees and asylum seekers. In this situation, the way of understanding psychological distress on the part of professionals gets in touch with the concept of illness of traditional cultures, where the cause of health disorders tends to be located in the social context or at supernatural level. An external attribution of the cause of illness may generate confusion among mental health care professionals coming from individual-centred societies where the origin of a disease is located within the individual or at a physical level (Abdallah-Steinkopff 2017; Domenig 2007a; Ebner 2001).

Thus, disparate concepts of illness and culture-bound descriptions of symptoms may lead to a misinterpretation of the client's condition and thus a wrong diagnosis. For instance, West African refugees describe experiences of extreme psychological burden by saying that they 'sense worms and ants crawling over their body'. The risk of German professionals misinterpreting this formulation and classifying this statement as a synesthetic delusion is high. As a matter of fact, the results of a study carried out in Canada show that the probability of misconceiving this kind of expression as a form of delusion and therefore establishing a false diagnosis is particularly high when treating ethnic minority patients or individuals with migrant backgrounds (Adeponle et al. 2012). Incorrect diagnoses constitute an inappropriate pathologisation of the subjective experience of immigrants and can lead to the wrong treatment with possible negative effects on patients' health.

An exchange of the ways in which mental health care professionals and clients understand illness and disease is crucial at the beginning of a psychological treatment. The exchange should particularly include subjective and culture-bound explanatory models about the symptoms and explore different levels of subjective meaning associated with the disease. In addition, symptoms should always be evaluated against the background of historical, social, and cultural factors.

Afterwards, a generally accepted compromise should be found. Otherwise, psychological intervention may prove to be ineffective (Heim & Maercker 2017; Mika, Abdallah-Steinkopff & Gravanidou 2015).

Another source of potential misinterpretation concerns the *use of standardised test procedures*. Despite the existence of translated versions of psychometric tests, their application in intercultural settings should still be handled with care. As a matter of fact, a literal translation of items may not express the equivalent meaning of the content or not correspond to the everyday culture of clients. In addition, certain concepts (e.g., the concept of autonomy) may have a different connotation or slightly different meanings in accordance to the cultural setting in which it is used. On the other hand, response categories (e.g., likert scales) may be unusual and confuse respondents. Finally, test results may be distorted due to items describing patterns of behaviour seen as pathological in Germany but regarded as normal in other countries. For instance, items describing situations of persecution may be interpreted as paranoia in the case of Germans or as accurate descriptions of a past experience in the case of refugees (Abdallah-Steinkopff & Soyer 2013; Stammel & Böttche 2017).

Disparate concepts of illness and different views about the purpose of psychological treatment on the part of professionals and culturally diverse clients may lead to *divergent ways of conceiving the healing process*. Persons coming from traditional cultures may expect counsellors and psychotherapists to help them to repel negative external influences (e.g., evil eye) and may become disappointed if professionals prefer to focus their attention on individual psychological change. Psychosocial and psychological counsellors and psychotherapists should be particularly aware of potential misunderstanding due to diverging healing concepts and avoid forcing psychological introspection at the beginning of a therapeutic process.

Finally, in the course of the asylum procedure, mental health care professionals may be asked to assess the mental health care status of asylum seekers and write an expert opinion to be considered during the legal proceedings at the Federal Office for Migration and Refugees or the Federal Administrative Court. The certification of recognised psychological disorders may prevent deportation and thus acquires existential meaning for asylum applicants. In 2003, the German Medical Association determined quality standards for this kind of document, based on the Istanbul Protocol (Frewer et al. 2009) and the suggestions of a special working group (Gierlichs et al. 2012). These standards are conveyed in certified training sessions for mental health care professionals, particularly medical and psychological psychotherapists. Professional assessments require several sessions to properly evaluate traumatic events. Assessors need to be able to reconstruct the details of the trauma and clear up any contradictions that may emerge during the process to ensure the credibility of their expertise. However, the exploration of trauma may constitute a scary and straining experience for the affected person as it may lead to uncontrollable stimulus satiation. Therefore, evaluators need to pay special attention to early signs of destabilisation, introduce breaks, and use stabilising measures to prevent a re-emergence of symptoms. Normally, treating psychotherapists do not perform such assessments, but delegate these procedures to uninvolved certified evaluators to avoid burdening the therapeutic relationship.

12.5 A socially and culturally sensitive approach to counselling and psychotherapy of refugees

Until now there have been no fully convincing ways of conceiving and dealing with the issue of cultural diversity. The main difficulty lies in the association of culture with essentialist concepts of nationality. In general terms, culture can be defined as the way of life of a particular social group at a particular time, including the structures of meaning and social practices. Strictly speaking, this conceptualisation is neither restricted to national cultures nor to ethnic minorities. Culture as a way of life can be applied to various kinds of social groups such as organisations or social milieus. However, since the process of nation building during the 18th and 19th centuries, culture is mainly conceived as the expression of the way of life of a nation. Thereby, national cultures are often conceived of as closed, static, and homogeneous entities leading to the assumption that the entirety of national citizens are bound to the same core values and the same way of life. National culture is also conceived of as incompatible with the cultural expression of other nationalities. From this perspective, cultural differences constitute insuperable barriers, and social inequalities tend to be interpreted in terms of cultural effects.

During recent decades, representatives of diverse social and cultural theories have questioned this approach and argued that national cultures should no longer be seen as discrete, homogeneous, and fixed entities but rather as constantly interacting and changing sets of social meaning and practices. From this point of view, persons live under the influence of various social and cultural settings and cannot be assigned to only one culture (Hein 2006).

To provide adequate mental health care services for refugees and asylum seekers, psychosocial and psychological counsellors and psychotherapists need to reflect on their understanding of culture and interculturality and develop a socially and culturally sensitive approach. Our idea of a socially and culturally sensitive approach does not offer a new and distinct theoretical understanding of the issue of cultural diversity. It rather reflects current debates surrounding culture and intercultural encounters and tries to translate these into an orientation framework for mental health care professionals attending to culturally diverse people.

In general, we think that the attitude of mental health care professionals should be *socially sensitive* by taking into account the current life situation affecting the psychological well-being of refugees and asylum seekers in Germany without reducing their problems to the experience of forced migration and traumatic events. Counsellors and psychotherapists should also avoid reducing the difficulties refugees and asylum seekers experience in Germany to cultural factors. Such approximation overlooks the fact that refugees are not only affected by acculturation stress but also have to cope with the consequences of social inequality.

On the other hand, the approach of mental health care professionals should also be *culturally sensitive* by recognising the high risk of misinterpretations associated with intercultural encounters. A culturally sensitive attitude does not mean acquiring knowledge about cultural systems as this only reinforces cultural stereotyping. Looking at clients through the lens of cultural preconceptions hinders rather than supports an accurate understanding of their subjective experience and compromises the provision of adequate mental health care.

In the following section, we propose five principles that support the development of a socially and culturally sensitive approach in the context of psychosocial and psychological counselling and psychotherapy with culturally diverse people.

12.5.1 Individual narratives instead of cultural stereotyping

Acquiring knowledge about specific cultures is an endless and mostly ineffective endeavour. It is nearly impossible to acquire in-depth knowledge about the cultural background of every client. In addition, cultural knowledge may reinforce cultural preconceptions and undermine the empathic understanding of culturally diverse people. In contrast, we propose to focus attention on individual narratives instead of considering cultural stereotypes. It is important to apprehend the individual lifeworld of each culturally diverse client. This means that our approach towards persons with migration backgrounds should be biography-centred, avoiding cultural stereotyping and the culturalisation of social inequalities. Domenig (2007b) considered this attitude to be an essential part of the development of *transcultural competences.* In line with this idea, we invite psychosocial and psychological counsellors and psychotherapists to listen to the unique stories of refugees and asylum seekers instead of guiding their behaviour in accordance to 'cultural recipes'. Narratives reflect the various cultural influences shaping the life and biography of the storyteller and allow us to understand how people with a migrant background give personal meaning to their particular experience (Anderson & Goolishian 1992; Domenig 2007b).

12.5.2 Awareness of social inequalities

Public opinion tends to attribute the problematic situation of refugees to the existence of cultural conflicts and the experience of traumatic events, without taking into account their current situation of social disadvantage. However, the uncertainty of the asylum process, the insecure status, the existence of legal restrictions, limited access to the labour market and health care system, deficient housing conditions, social isolation, and experiences of discrimination deeply affect the lives of asylum seekers in Germany. In this sense, it is essential for psychosocial and psychological counsellors and psychotherapists to know about these unfavourable living conditions and be aware of the social inequalities affecting the lives of refugees.

Professionals should also be aware of the fact that they establish asymmetric power relationships with refugees and asylum seekers. The power imbalance stems from unequal legal, social, and economic statuses. On the one side, we have refugees and asylum seekers who have few resources, little influence, and only a limited scope of action, whereas on the other side we have professionals with the prerogative of interpretation who may assume a paternalistic attitude towards their clients and unintentionally demand their cultural assimilation. Refugees and asylum seekers for their part may respond to power imbalance with suspicion, oversensitivity, retreat, helplessness, resistance, or aggression (Auernheimer 2007).

12.5.3 Interdisciplinary collaboration and networking to improve living conditions

Though the awareness of social inequalities may improve the relationship between mental health care professionals and their clients, it still does not solve the complex life circumstances of refugees in Germany. As persistent unfavourable living conditions negatively affect mental health and compromise the effectiveness of psychological treatment, it becomes imperative for psychosocial and psychological counsellors and psychotherapists to collaborate with interdisciplinary networks, particularly involving interpreters, social workers, and lawyers (Abdallah-Steinkopff & Soyer 2013).

12.5.4 The client is the expert

Cultural diversity and power imbalances in intercultural settings can be addressed through an attitude of *cultural humility*. The goal of cultural humility is to develop open and respectful relationships and to avoid paternalistic attitudes and ethnocentrism by promoting an open-minded attitude, modesty, and lack of superiority (Fisher-Bone, Montana Cain & Martin 2015; Foronda et al. 2016; Yancu & Farmer 2017; Yeager & Bauer-Wu 2013). A very similar attitude is described by the concept of the *not-knowing-position* (Anderson & Goolishian 1992). The not-knowing-position was formulated as an approach in the context of mental health care. In the not-knowing position, counsellors and therapists accept that there is no privileged standpoint of interpretation and that prior knowledge and preconceived opinions may restrain the adequate understanding of clients. Instead, they should adopt an attitude of genuine curiosity towards their dialogue partners. Professionals should view their clients as experts and engage in a process of open exploration. German counsellors and psychotherapists often perceive quick interpretations and diagnoses as a sign of professionalism. However, premature interpretations may limit a professional's ability to understand their clients' narrative (Anderson & Goolishian 1992; Gravanidou & Abdallah-Steinkopff 2008; Liedl & Abdallah-Steinkopff 2017).

12.5.5 Self-awareness, self-reflection, and self-critique

Finally, an indispensable aspect of a socially and culturally sensitive approach involves a lifelong process of self-awareness, self-reflection, and self-critique. Individuals are always prejudiced by their experience and take their lifeworld for granted. Thus, self-reflection on one's own values and practices prevents professionals from constraining the understanding of their clients and reduces the risk of misinterpretation associated with intercultural encounters (Domenig 2007b; Fisher-Bone, Montana Cain & Martin 2015; Foronda et al. 2016; Yancu & Farmer 2017; Yeager & Bauer-Wu 2013).

12.6 Conclusion

Refugees and asylum seekers are at high risk of suffering from mental health disorders. However, mental health disorders are the results not only of trauma or cultural differences but also of the detrimental living conditions that asylum seekers encounter in Germany. These circumstances may aggravate existing disorders and cause new ones.

To provide appropriate mental health care services, professionals need to develop a socially and culturally sensitive approach. To be socially sensitive means to take into account the present life circumstances of refugees and asylum seekers and to be aware of social inequalities and power imbalances. To be culturally sensitive means to be aware of the high risk of misinterpretation associated with intercultural encounters, to avoid paternalistic and ethnocentric attitudes, and to pay attention to individual stories instead of relying on cultural standards. Counsellors and therapists should further collaborate with interdisciplinary networks to address the complex situation of refugees and asylum seekers.

To develop a socially and culturally sensitive approach, mental health care professionals should regularly participate in qualified training sessions that address the intersection of legal, cultural, social, and clinical issues affecting refugees and asylum seekers. In addition to conveying legal, social, cultural, and clinical-psychological knowledge, training sessions should include practical exercises such as role playing that enable participants to switch perspectives. Changes in perspectives support professionals in developing an empathic understanding of the challenges and difficulties associated with the specific situation of refugees and asylum seekers. On the basis of this understanding, professionals will be able to orient their therapeutic work in accordance with the needs and resources of their clients.

Notes

1 Alternative or non-medical practitioners (Heilpraktiker) represent a special case within this scenario as they are allowed to provide a form of psychotherapy but are not allowed to call themselves psychotherapists. Their qualifications are less regulated, and their services are not covered by health care insurance.

2 Total institutions are establishments where individuals are cut off from the wider community for a considerable time. One central characteristic is that total institutions require an absolute adaptation of residents to the system. Thus, new members are solicited to discharge former social identities and to build new identities based on their institutional membership. Total institutions include establishments like psychiatric hospitals, prisons, or monasteries (Goffman 1984).

3 High- and low-context cultures are related to the distinction between collectivistic and individualistic cultures. Collectivist cultures place high value to interpersonal relationships and display high-context communication, whereas individualistic cultures

underline the autonomy of individuals and show low-context communication (Ward, Bochner & Furnham 2003).

4 According to Retzer (2006), therapeutic neutrality is a central therapeutic method to enable changes and the creation of new perspectives in the client system.

References

Abdallah-Steinkopff, B. 2017, 'Zusammenarbeit mit Dolmetschern', in A. Liedl, M. Böttche, B. Abdallah-Steinkopff, & C. Knaevelsrud (eds.), *Psychotherapie mit Flüchtlingen – Neue Herausforderungen, spezifische Bedürfnisse: Ein Praxisbuch für Psychotherapeuten und Ärzte*, Schattauer, Stuttgart, pp. 90–107.

Abdallah-Steinkopff, B., & Soyer, J. 2013, 'Traumatisierte Flüchtlinge: Kultursensible Psychotherapie im politischen Spannungsfeld', in R.E. Feldmann & G.H. Seidler (eds.), *Traum(a) Migration: Aktuelle Konzepte zur Therapie traumatisierter Flüchtlinge und Folteropfer*, Psychosozial Verlag, Gießen, pp. 137–166.

Adeponle, A.B., Thombs, B.D., Groleau, D., Jarvis, E., & Kirmayer, L.J. 2012, 'Using the cultural formulation to resolve uncertainty in diagnoses of psychosis among ethnoculturally diverse patients', *Psychiatric Services*, vol. 63, no. 2, pp. 147–153.

Altorfer, A., & Käsermann, M.L. 2007, 'Die Bedeutung des Nonverbalen in der Kommunikation', in D. Domenig (ed.), *Transkulturelle Kompetenz: Lehrbuch für Pflege-, Gesundheits- und Sozialberufe*, Verlag Hans Huber, Bern.

Anderson, H., & Goolishian, H.A. 1992, 'The client is the expert: a not-knowing approach to therapy', in S. McNamee & K.J. Gergen (eds.), *Social construction and the therapeutic process*, Sage, Newbury Park, pp. 25–39.

Auernheimer, G. 1988, *Der sogenannte Kulturkonflikt. Orientierungsprobleme ausländischer Jugendlicher*, Campus Verlag, F rankfurt am Main/New York.

Auernheimer, G. 2007, *Einführung in die interkulturelle Pädagogik*. Wissenschaftliche Buchgesellschaft, Darmstadt.

Berry, J. 1996, 'Acculturation and psychological adaptation', in K. Bade (ed.), *Migration – Ethnizität – Konflikt: Systemfragen und Fallstudien*, Universitätsverlag Osnabrück, Osnabrück.

Bundesamt für Migration und Flüchtlinge (BAMF). 2017, *Aktuelle Zahlen zu Asyl: Ausgabe August. Tabellen, Diagramme, Erläuterungen*, Nürnberg.

Domenig, D. 2007a, 'Behandlung und Pflege in soziozentrierten Kontexten', in D. Domenig (ed.), *Transkulturelle Kompetenz: Lehrbuch für Pflege-, Gesundheits- und Sozialberufe*, Verlag Hans Huber, Bern.

Domenig, D. 2007b, 'Das Konzept der transkulturellen Kompetenz', in D. Domenig (ed.), *Transkulturelle Kompetenz: Lehrbuch für Pflege-, Gesundheits- und Sozialberufe*, Verlag Hans Huber, Bern.

Ebert, J. 2017, 'Soziale Arbeit', in A. Liedl, M. Böttche, B. Abdallah-Steinkopff & C. Knaevelsrud (eds.), *Psychotherapie mit Flüchtlingen – Neue Herausforderungen, spezifische Bedürfnisse: Ein Praxisbuch für Psychotherapeuten und Ärzte*. Schattauer, Stuttgart, pp. 35–57.

Ebner, G. 2001, 'Grundlagen transkultureller Begutachtung', in T. Hegemann & R. Salman (eds.), *Transkulturelle Psychiatrie*, Psychiatrie Verlag, Köln, pp. 232–251.

Fazel, M., Wheeler, J., & Danesh, J. 2005, 'Prevalence of serious mental disorder in 7000 refugees resettled in western countries: a systematic review', *Lancet*, vol. 365, no. 9467, pp. 1309–1314.

Fisher-Bone, M., Montana Cain, J., & Martin, S.L. 2015, 'From mastery to accountability: cultural humility as an alternative to cultural competence', *Social Work Education*, vol. 34, no. 2, pp. 165–181.

Foronda, C., Baptiste, D.L., Reinholdt, M.M., & Ousman, K. 2016, 'Cultural humility: a concept analysis', *Journal of Transcultural Nursing*, vol. 27, no. 3, pp. 210–217.

Frewer, A., Furtmayr, H., Krása, K., & Wenzel, T. (eds.) 2009, *Istanbul-Protokoll. Untersuchung und Dokumentation von Folter und Menschenrechtsverletzungen*, V&R unipress (Medizin und Menschenrechte, 2), Göttingen.

Gierlichs, H.W. et al. 2012, *Standards zur Begutachtung psychisch reaktiver Traumafolgen in aufenthaltsrechtlichen Verfahren (SPBM)*, viewed 6 May 2018, www.bundesaerztekammer.de/fileadmin/user_upload/downloads/CurrStandardsBegutachtungTrauma2012.pdf.

Goffman, E. 1984, 'Characteristics of total institutions', in D. Kelly (ed.), *Deviant behavior: a text-reader in the sociology of deviance*, St. Martin's Press, New York, pp. 464–477.

Gravanidou, M. 2017, 'Migration', in A. Liedl, M. Böttche, B. Abdallah-Steinkopff & C. Knaevelsrud (eds.), *Psychotherapie mit Flüchtlingen – Neue Herausforderungen, spezifische Bedürfnisse: Ein Praxisbuch für Psychotherapeuten und Ärzte*, Schattauer, Stuttgart, pp. 7–17.

Gravanidou, M., & Abdallah-Steinkopff, B. 2008, 'Psychotherapeutische Arbeit mit Migranten: Alles anders oder gleich?', *Gestalttherapie*, vol. 22, no. 2, pp. 93–106.

Haasen, C. 2007, 'Psychische Störungen im Migrationskontext', in D. Domenig (ed.), *Transkulturelle Kompetenz: Lehrbuch für Pflege-, Gesundheits- und Sozialberufe*, Verlag Hans Huber, Bern.

Heim, E., & Maercker, A. 2017, 'Kulturelle Anpassung in Diagnostik und Psychotherapie', *Psychotherapeutenjournal*, vol. 16, no. 1, pp. 4–10.

Hein, K. 2006, *Hybride Identitäten: Bastelbiografien im Spannungsverhältnis zwischen Lateinamerika und Europa*, transcript Verlag, Bielefeld.

Hein, K. 2013, 'Vom Ausländer zum Jugendlichen: Interkulturelle Begegnungen, Identitätsarbeit und Handlungsfähigkeit bei jungen Migranten lateinamerikanischer Herkunft in Chile', *Forum Gemeindepsychologie*, vol. 18, no. 1, pp. 1–12.

Heinhold, H. 2017, 'Juristische Aspekte', in A. Liedl, M. Böttche, B. Abdallah-Steinkopff & C. Knaevelsrud (eds.), *Psychotherapie mit Flüchtlingen – Neue Herausforderungen, spezifische Bedürfnisse: Ein Praxisbuch für Psychotherapeuten und Ärzte*, Schattauer, Stuttgart, pp. 18–34.

Hüper, C., & Kerkow-Weil, R. 2007, 'Schmerz im Migrationskontext', in D. Domenig (ed.), *Transkulturelle Kompetenz: Lehrbuch für Pflege-, Gesundheits- und Sozialberufe*, Verlag Hans Huber, Bern.

Kahraman, B. 2008, *Die kultursensible Therapiebeziehung: Störungen und Lösungsansätze am Beispiel türkischer Klienten*, Psychosozial Verlag, Gießen.

Kilcher, A. 2007, 'Rassismus und rassistische Diskriminierung', in D. Domenig (ed.), *Transkulturelle Kompetenz: Lehrbuch für Pflege-, Gesundheits- und Sozialberufe*, Verlag Hans Huber, Bern.

Laban, C.J., Gernaat, H.B., Komproe, I.H., Schreuders, B.A., & De Jong, J.T. 2004, 'Impact of a long asylum procedure on the prevalence of psychiatric disorders in Iraqi asylum seekers in the Netherlands', *The Journal of Nervous and Mental Disease*, vol. 192, no. 12, pp. 843–851.

Liedl, A., & Abdallah-Steinkopff B. 2017, 'Psychotherapeutische Behandlung von Flüchtlingen', in A. Liedl, M. Böttche, B. Abdallah-Steinkopff & C. Knaevelsrud (eds.),

Psychotherapie mit Flüchtlingen – Neue Herausforderungen, spezifische Bedürfnisse: Ein Praxisbuch für Psychotherapeuten und Ärzte, Schattauer, Stuttgart, pp. 71–89.

Liedl, A. et al. 2017, 'Einführung', in A. Liedl, M. Böttche, B. Abdallah-Steinkopff & C. Knaevelsrud (eds.), *Psychotherapie mit Flüchtlingen – Neue Herausforderungen, spezifische Bedürfnisse: Ein Praxisbuch für Psychotherapeuten und Ärzte*, Schattauer, Stuttgart, pp. 1–6.

Loncarevic, M. 2007, 'Migration und Gesundheit', in D. Domenig (ed.), *Transkulturelle Kompetenz: Lehrbuch für Pflege-, Gesundheits- und Sozialberufe*, Verlag Hans Huber, Bern.

Maletzke, G. 1996, *Interkulturelle Kommunikation: Zur Interaktion zwischen Menschen verschiedener Kulturen*, Westdeutscher Verlag, Opladen.

Mika, J., Abdallah-Steinkopff, B., & Gravanidou, M. 2015, 'Die Exploration der Krankheitskonzepte von Flüchtlingen bezüglicher ihrer Posttraumatischen Belastungsstörung', *Psychotherapeutenjournal*, vol. 14, no. 3, pp. 134–145.

Moser, C. 2007, 'Traumatisierungen bei Migratinnen mit Folter- und Kriegserfahrungen', in D. Domenig (ed.), *Transkulturelle Kompetenz: Lehrbuch für Pflege-, Gesundheits- und Sozialberufe*, Verlag Hans Huber, Bern.

Pirmoradi, S. 2012, *Interkulturelle Familientherapie und -beratung: Eine systemische Perspektive*, Vandenhoeck & Ruprecht, Göttingen.

Retzer, A. 2006, *Passagen: Systemische Erkundungen*, Klett-Cotta, Stuttgart.

Schach, E. 1989, *Die EVasS-Studie: Eine Erhebung über ambulante medizinische Versorgung in der Bundesrepublik Deutschand: Daten und Analysen einer bundesweiten Studie des Zentralinstituts für die Kassenärztliche Versorgung*, Deutscher Ärzte-Verlag, Köln.

Stammel, N., & Böttche, M. 2017, 'Psychodiagnostik', in A. Liedl, M. Böttche, B. Abdallah-Steinkopff & C. Knaevelsrud (eds.), *Psychotherapie mit Flüchtlingen – Neue Herausforderungen, spezifische Bedürfnisse: Ein Praxisbuch für Psychotherapeuten und Ärzte*, Schattauer, Stuttgart, pp. 58–70.

Täubig, V. 2009, *Totale Institution Asyl: Empirische Befunde zu alltäglichen Lebensführungen in der organisierten Desintegration*, Juventa Verlag, Weinheim.

The UN Refugee Agency (UNHCR). 2015, *Abkommen über die Rechtsstellung der Flüchtlinge vom 28. Juli 1951: Protokoll über die Rechtsstellung der Flüchtlinge vom 31. Januar 1967*, Berlin.

Walden, J. 2017, 'Refugee mental health: a primary care approach', *American Family Physician*, vol. 96, no. 2, pp. 83–84.

Ward, C., Bochner, S., & Furnham, A. 2003, *The psychology of culture shock*, Routledge, London.

Yancu, C.N., & Farmer, D.F. 2017, 'Product or process: cultural competence or cultural humility?', *Journal of Palliative Care and Medicine*, vol. 3, no. 1, pp. e1–e4.

Yeager, K.A., & Bauer-Wu, S. 2013, 'Cultural humility: essential foundation for clinical researchers', *Applied Nursing Research*, vol. 26, no. 4, pp. 251–256.

Zielke-Nadkarni, A. 2007, 'Gesundheits- und Krankheitskonzepte', in D. Domenig (ed.), *Transkulturelle Kompetenz: Lehrbuch für Pflege-, Gesundheits- und Sozialberufe*, Verlag Hans Huber, Bern.

13 Female genital alteration in the UK

A failure of pluralism and intersectionality

Arianne Shahvisi

13.1 Introduction

In August 2016, a woman was made to remove her swimwear on a beach in Nice, France, as two police officers towered over her seated figure, overseeing her disrobing amid a throng of beach-goers whose exposed flesh was deemed more anodyne. Earlier that month, the particular swimsuit variety she was wearing – a 'burkini' (portmanteau of burqa and bikini)[1] – had been outlawed by various French seaside resorts, as the clothing was deemed to be a 'provocation' (Rubin 2016) which flew in the face of 'good morals' (Quinn 2016), and was considered to be symbolic of Islamic extremism (Breedan & Blaise 2016) in the aftermath of a Muslim man having massacred holidaymakers in Cannes earlier that summer. The burkini ban was by no means a marginal political move; it was supported by almost two-thirds of the French population (Pech 2016). Where justifications were ventured, the dominant rhetoric was one of alleged concern for the well-being of burkini-clad women. Commentators claimed to regard the swimwear as a visible manifestation of the patriarchal subjugation of Muslim women, who were deemed to have the right, or perhaps the obligation, to engage in similar levels of nakedness to other women on the beach.

Accepting this interpretation at face value is unduly charitable; there is no compelling reason to believe that resistance to the burkini stemmed from concern about the welfare of Muslim women. For one, the immediate effect was to produce an atmosphere of fear and exclusion, within which Muslim women's bodies became a criminalised spectacle, leaving them unsurprisingly and understandably more likely to avoid beaches than to embrace a newfound affinity for the bikini. Rather, the concern about the burkini was a sign of the cracked mask of multiculturalism, a product of rising Islamophobia within French society and across Europe (Ogan et al. 2014).

We should be concerned about responses to female genital alteration (FGA) within the UK for similar reasons. Again, the primary stated reason for opposition to the practice is that it enacts patriarchal control against female bodies and is framed as child abuse and violence against women and girls (HM Government 2016, p. 4). Draconian legislation around FGA appears to be designed to respond to a growing public appetite for punitive measures towards incursions against 'British values' (Dustin & Phillips 2008), regardless of the effect on the women it claims to protect. Of course, this analogy is not perfect. The burkini ban was never legally enshrined (unlike the passing of the 'Act prohibiting concealment of the face in public space' in France just six years before) and was the result of long-standing resentments brought to a head by a particular incident, while FGA legislation in the UK is the result of a protracted political debate over many decades. However, the similarities are significant. Both are concerned with choices women make, or are perhaps compelled to make, about their bodies in the realm of the intimate and sexual: that of swimwear and genitals. In neither case are women believed to be capable of making that decision for themselves, and in both cases the choice of 'Western' women is deemed to be automatically superior. The burkini debacle may have been short-lived, but by the light of its momentary flare, a good deal could be learned about anxieties regarding the threat of the 'Other,' the sense of cultural superiority that continues to characterise modern Europe, and the way in which these factors shape the debate around FGA.

In this article, I wish to show that legislation around FGA bears some important parallels to policy around the burkini. Neither is properly understood as motivated by serving the best interests of the women in question. Rather, both are motivated by, at best, an overly simplistic and poorly informed desire for gender equality which ignores intersectionality, or, at worst, deeply ingrained cultures of racism and sexism. Both have gained traction in public discourse because their racism is easily concealed within ostensible concern about the well-being of women of colour. Both fail to engage meaningfully with cultural pluralism, resulting in inconsistencies which point towards ethnocentrism.

The rise of nationalism and the increasing hubris of racist public discourses across Europe and the US makes this discussion particularly urgent. Penalising the practices of marginalised people is as unlikely to result in social cohesion as it is to promote abandonment of those practices, and renders marginalised people simultaneously more visible—in the sense of becoming criminalised—and more *invisible*, in the indirect sense of being less likely to have their perspectives heard, and in the direct sense of having good reason to take measures to avoid state surveillance.

Within this chapter, I endeavour to refer to the practice in question as 'female genital *alteration*' (FGA), rather than the more common 'female genital *mutilation*' (FGM). No community practising FGA describes the act as mutilation, and the word signals a strong negative value which prescribes a particular moral tone prior to any ethical analysis. Further, the breadth of its usage seems to reflect the unexamined racism and ethnocentrism which are commonly noted within these discourses (c.f. Ahmadu 2016). To make the complexities vivid, one might reasonably argue that genital alterations are best understood as mutilation when performed on the healthy tissue of *children*, who necessarily cannot consent, but that another term would be more apt when speaking of adults. By corollary, male circumcision in infants would then be better described as male genital mutilation. In order to avoid foreshadowing these complex discussions at the outset, I refer to FGA in place of FGM, and speak of female cosmetic genital surgeries (FCGS) and male circumcision.

My discussion of FGA will centre on the practice as requested by and performed upon *adult* women. One cannot focus on the practice as applied to legal minors without inevitably being drawn into a discussion about the ethics of male circumcision, which would divert my attention here. I refer the reader to other work within which I clarify my sex-neutral position on genital alterations for minors (Shahvisi 2016a). That said, it *is* important to acknowledge that the fact that FGA is in many cultures performed on minors who cannot consent is core to the widespread resistance to the practice and is therefore important context to bear in mind when reading what follows. Current legislation in the UK was intended primarily to protect children, and the child protection framing is undeniably a determinative backdrop to the emotive public discourse around FGA which has been key in motivating the legislation. However, were child protection straightforwardly the sole or primary factor influencing discourse, we would expect similar outrage around male circumcision and concomitant legislation. I bracket this debate in this chapter and instead focus on adult women, and the discursive framework that surrounds their access to, and relationship to, FGA, as this makes space to focus on social discourses other than the comparatively uncontroversial child protection agenda.[2]

The chapter is structured as follows. In Section 13.2, I introduce the legislation around FGA in the UK, and examine its inconsistencies within the broader social and political context. In Section 13.3, I interrogate the terms 'ritual' and 'custom' as included within the legislation and describe the way in which discourses and legislation around FGA (and the burkini) fail to take into account cultural relativism. In Section 13.4, I introduce intersectionality, describe the positionality of the women affected by FGA legislation, and argue that if taken seriously, the claim that banning FGA and the burkini is helpful amounts to a failure of intersectionality. Section 13.5 concludes this chapter.

13.2 Female genital alteration in the UK

Many varieties of non-medical genital alteration are practised in the UK. Female cosmetic genital surgeries are used to reshape, and reduce the size of, the clitoris and labia; female and male genitals are pierced; the foreskin of the penis is removed in infant males in order to adhere to religious requirements within Islam and Judaism; and female genitalia are modified in accordance with customs prevalent in some regions of Africa, the Middle-East and South-East Asia. All of these modifications are legal, even in minors, except the last, which is illegal even for consenting adults.

In England, Wales and Northern Ireland, FGM is legislated against via the FGM Act 2003, according to which 'for a person to excise, infibulate, or otherwise mutilate any part of a girl's labia minora, majora or clitoris' is an offense carrying a sentence of up to 14 years. Definition 6(1) of the Act states that 'Girl includes woman,' which means that the terms of the Act apply to adult women just as they do to children, despite the different consent capacities of these groups in almost all other circumstances. A functionally identical piece of legislation applies in Scotland – Prohibition of Female Genital Mutilation (Scotland)

Act 2005 – with the same maximum sentence, but without this worrying clause (I therefore refer to 'UK legislation', except when stated otherwise).

The existence of dedicated legislation is itself noteworthy, given that there is no legislation to protect against any of the other non-medical genital alterations just mentioned. A wide literature has unfolded over the last two decades in relation to the hypocrisy presented by the inconsistencies in legislation. If removing the tissue of a small child is so obviously egregious, why is male circumcision so widely legal? If modifying the genitals of an adult woman is so concerning, why is female cosmetic genital surgery permissible even when the tissue removal is identical? I will not consider these questions in detail here, but instead refer the reader to works that tackle these hypocrisies directly (Dustin 2010; Earp 2016; Ehrenreich & Barr 2005; Johnsdotter & Essén 2010; Shahvisi 2016b; Shahvisi & Earp, forthcoming; Sheldon & Wilkinson 1998).

There are other aspects of the FGM Act that provoke specific concern, and these will form the focus of this section. Consider the following extract from the Act, which provides a caveat to the unlawfulness of genital alterations in females:

> (2) But no offence is committed by an approved person who performs
> (a) a surgical operation on a girl which is necessary for her physical or *mental* health [...]
> (5) For the purpose of determining whether an operation is necessary for the mental health of a girl *it is immaterial whether she or any other person believes that the operation is required as a matter of custom or ritual* (FGM Act 2003, Section 1, my italics).

This needs some unpacking. We are told that genital alterations, whilst generally an offence, *can* be performed for reasons of physical health. This means, for example, that a person with a malignant vulvar growth can undergo surgery within the law; equally, a patient with abnormally long labia, causing irritation with movement or from clothing, is able to obtain a reductive labiaplasty. These cases seem straightforward.

We are also told that genital alterations can take place in response to mental health needs. In other words, the clitoris or labia can be altered in cases in which doing so is deemed to be beneficial to the mental health of the patient. Cosmetic genital surgeries are offered within standard National Health Service (NHS) treatment for these purposes and are occurring in increasing numbers. These procedures generally consist of clitoridectomy and/or labiaplasty. Note that these procedures are core elements of FGA as practised for reasons of custom or ritual.[3]

In the years 2010–2011, 1726 labiaplasties took place within the NHS (Health and Social Care Information Centre 2012), and there is reason to believe that a greater number still occurred in the private health sector, where most cosmetic procedures are performed. A fivefold increase in the number of requests for labiaplasty was recorded in the UK between 2001 and 2008 (Runacres et al. 2015). This is despite the fact that studies have found that the labia of women requesting reductions via labiaplasty are in almost all cases within normal limits (Crouch et al. 2011). In addition, 2105 labiaplasties were performed on children under the age of 15 years in the period 2005–2016 (Health and Social Care Information Centre 2012), a figure which stands in stark contrast to the fact that *adult* women cannot consent to FGA within the law.

There has been a paucity of research into the psychology of requests for cosmetic genital surgeries, but interestingly, an empirical study (Veale et al. 2014) examining those requesting labiaplasty did not demonstrate any increased depression or anxiety-related psychopathology with respect to controls. Further, less than 20% of those in the study group satisfied diagnostic criteria for body dysmorphic disorder. The common thread was instead a general dissatisfaction with the appearance of the genital area, a strongly held genital aesthetic ideal, and a subsequent reported reduction in quality of life when ideal and reality do not meet. In a detailed case study (Veale & Daniels 2012), a woman requesting clitoridectomy (having already undergone labiaplasty) was deemed to have no psychiatric or personality disorder. She reported low quality of life in relation to her (medically normal) genitalia since, by her own admission, she had very specific aesthetic standards. She was able to undergo the procedure regardless.

In other words, there is no compelling case that those requesting cosmetic genital surgeries for reasons of mental health have either (a) statistically abnormal genitals, or (b) poor psychiatric health. Rather, there is evidence that women requesting labial and clitoral reshaping and reduction do so for aesthetic reasons, under the pressure of conformity to particular genital ideals. Even if there *were* more evidence for poor mental health amongst these patients, it is not clear that carrying out genital modifications on healthy tissue would be helpful in tackling the root problem. This is not to criticise the implementation of the procedures *per se*, but to suggest that it is misleading to describe them as medically indicated.

Sudanese surgeon (and anti-FGA activist) Nahid Toubia describes the bafflement and resentment of women of FGA-prevalent communities when they 'look at the Western world and see women undergoing their own feminization rites intended to increase sexual desirability' (Toubia 1995, p. 232, paraphrased within Sheldon & Wilkinson 1998, p. 264). This hypocrisy is particularly evident since the ideals pursued by women seeking FCGS originate in pornography (Braun 2005, p. 413; Essén & Johnsdotter 2004, p. 612; Iglesia 2012) and are therefore bound up with other debates about the sexualisation of female bodies.

Dustin (2010, pp. 15–16) discusses the role of the powerful medical lobby in ensuring a caveat in the legislation in order that surgeons could continue to practice the (highly lucrative) work of cosmetically modifying female genitals. One wonders whether yet another parallel might be drawn with FGA, where an employment sector of 'cutters' has developed in symbiosis with the practice (Mgbako et al. 2010), providing an economic basis for its continuation. In a debate in the House of Commons in 1985, Conservative MP Marion Roe noted that FGA legislation must not interfere with a 'patient's right to receive legitimate or ethical surgery', (*Prohibition of female circumcision bill 1985*

(UK Parliament)), where 'ethical' and 'legitimate' remain undefined. In the same debate, Labour MP Jo Richardson worries that the mental health clause

> could be considered to have racial overtones as it forbids the use of mental stress as a reason for those who wish to have female circumcision for ritual or custom as against those who use mental stress as a reason because of difficulties with deformed or enlarged genitalia [...] However, I have been unable to find any other way of changing it.
>
> (*ibid.*)

Evidently, she was not alone in her lack of imagination (or perhaps she was alone in her reservations), as the clause survives into current legislation.

Clearly, there is a double standard at work in the legislation, which states that certain procedures *can* be performed in order to meet the aesthetic needs (as mandated by particular norms) of certain groups but cannot be performed in order to meet the (culturally mandated) preferences of other groups. This is a strange twist, given that the ability to consent to a procedure when one is suffering from reduced mental health is typically diminished by that fact if it is affected at all, rather than privileged by it. The law's double standard, and the racism that underwrites it, is lost on many. Psychiatrist David Veale defends the illegality of one and not the other, noting that the

> spirit of the legislation sought was to remove the barbaric practice of female genital mutilation based on custom. I do not think legislators were able to anticipate the demand for cosmetic surgery where the subject's motivation is to reduce self-consciousness, discomfort or enhance sexuality.
>
> (2013, p. 325)

One obvious response to this double standard is the claim that FGA entails severe health risks. It is true that FGA can cause health issues both in the short-term—including pain, infection, haemorrhage, and, in extreme cases, death—and in the long-term—problems with urination, sexual pleasure, menstruation, infections and obstetric difficulties (British Medical Association 2011, p. 4). Yet several points must be noted: first these outcomes are often worst case scenarios rather than typical effects (Dustin 2010, p. 9); second, there are many varieties of FGA, ranging from a mere 'nick' to full excision, and the effects of these vary enormously, and are rarely separated out (see, e.g., Shahvisi 2016a; Dustin 2010, p. 9); third, many of these issues are associated with the conditions under which the procedure is performed (e.g., an unsanitary environment and non-surgical instruments), which could be reduced by medicalisation. This last point is arguably most important: the most notable difference between labiaplasty in an FGA context and a FCGS context is that one is performed by an expert clinician in a clinical setting with clinical instruments with appropriate follow-up, and the other is not. As such, one would expect infection and complications to be minimal in one and not the other. Regardless, FCGS also entails complications.

Excessive post-operative bleeding, dyspareunia, healing issues, adhesion, infection and reduction in sexual satisfaction are all commonly noted (Committee on Gynecologic Practice 2007; Goodman et al. 2010, pp. 1571–1572).

13.3 Ritual, custom and cultural relativism

One can rephrase UK legislation while maintaining its sense, to proclaim that alterations to female genitals for reasons of 'custom or ritual' are forbidden, while all other cases are permissible. In 1983, Lord Kennet assured the House of Lords that FGA 'is without any religious justification anywhere in the world, including the countries where it is endemic. It is a customary practice and no more' (*Prohibition of female circumcision bill (H.L.) 1983* (UK Parliament)). One wonders what the fate of the practice would be if it *were* religiously mandated, and how this hierarchy of justifiable reasons is itself justified.

In order to make better sense of the legislation, 'custom' and 'ritual' must be defined and distinguished. The legislation itself remains silent on the meanings of these terms, but they are well-defined elsewhere. Anthropologists define custom as

> Habitual practices of an individual or culture, the traditional way of doing things or thinking about them, as passed down the generations. Custom is learned but often erroneously perceived as "natural," and affects decisions regarding all areas of social life.
>
> (Morris & Morris 2012, p. 59)

Ritual is defined as a 'formal, often religious, set of practices characterized by themes of celebration, renewal, or affirmation. Actions performed in ritual often have symbolic meaning. [...] Ritual can be seen as strengthening the status quo' (*ibid.*, p. 219).

Three questions arise. First, is FGA rightly classified as being motivated by ritual and/or custom? Second, is female cosmetic genital surgery rightly understood as being motivated by ritual and/or custom? Third, what is it about rituals and customs that renders them unfit to be motivations for consensual actions?

To answer the first question, it seems fairly uncontroversial to describe FGA as both customary and ritualistic. It is an important part of the culture of those who follow the practice and is usually performed as ritual entry into the community, or to adulthood within that community. Motivations for FGA, like the practice itself, are incredibly varied (Lyons 2007). As with male circumcision, reasons include, for example, purported health benefits, hygiene, aesthetics, resembling other adults within the community, reduction of promiscuity and sexual attractiveness (Svoboda 2013, p. 244). One notable motivation for FGA is the feminisation of the genitals. The clitoris is seen by some groups as a vestigial penis, and its removal permits the fulfilment of female identity (Shweder 2000, p. 219). FGA is therefore part of the creation of the female sex and of the reinforcement of the sex binary.

As for the second question, it is now axiomatic to describe gender as a dynamic process of continual collaborative construction, impelled by social pressure, rather than a static, essential property of what fe/male bodies can do or be in the world. The performativity of gender (Butler 1990), widely understood as an instructive and edifying way of understanding the construction and perpetuation of gender, provides a ready template for understanding gender across cultures as a ritual that is collectively undertaken to renew and affirm the reality of the binary. Both sex and gender are daily created. Gender is created by what one does with one's body, for example, particular bodily comportments and clothing. Sex is created by what one makes one's body *be*, that is: modifications to bodies which accentuate sex dimorphism. For example, males are encouraged to cultivate musculature, females are required to remove body hair and restrict their calorie intake.

With this in mind, just as FGA is seen as a ritual which feminises genitals and produces the sex binary, so too might FCGS be seen as a ritual (amongst others) which permits one to achieve the 'ideal' female body, largely for reasons of (perceived) acceptability within the sexual world. While it may not be accurate to call FCGS customary, since despite its growing popularity it is still a marginal procedure, it falls squarely into a category of modifications to the female body (selective hair removal, make-up, dieting) that *are* customary within many cultures, and are performed repetitively, *ritualistically*, as ways of maintaining membership within the tribe of the normative female/feminine, under undeniably patriarchal conditions. As such, the distinction made in section 5 of the FGM Act is baffling.

One might argue that the point about FCGS not being customary deserves greater consideration. Where FGA is performed, prevalence rates generally exceed 80% and within specific communities can reach 100% (UNICEF 2005). FCGS is performed by a small minority of women in the UK. One could say that what is different (and wrong) about FGA is that it is *necessary* for adult women, while FCGS is not. This has some force. But it seems counter-intuitive that something that is not very important to the people of one culture should be more permissible than something that is deemed essential to people within another culture. In other words, a woman requesting FGA would likely have a greater desire for the procedure than a woman requesting FCGS, and more to lose if the procedure were not performed (including in mental health terms!), yet *she* would be denied it.

Turning to the third question: what is it about 'ritual or custom' which renders them inadequate bases to be motivations for consensual actions? An obvious response is that rituals are undertaken in order to conform to social norms, in which case, the consent is not optimally voluntary. As such, it is the norm that forms the basis for, and force behind, the practice, rather than the consent of the individual. Yet this is to ignore the function and logic that underwrites rituals, which are not performed (only) to avoid social penalty but to bring about specific, desired changes, that is, to remove genital components that are considered to be male, to achieve a more attractive appearance, or to reduce sexual desire etc. To paint those performing rituals as blindly following orders is to present them as Other, the colonial subaltern, for whose actions no logic should be expected or sought. This misrepresentation is not benign but may be seen in biopolitical terms as engineered to serve the ends of particular sites of social power, and to justify neo-colonial discourses about cultural superiority (see e.g., Foucault 1990). This is important because

> everything turns on who counts as a fellow human being, as a rational agent in the only relevant sense – the sense in which rational agency is synonymous with membership of our moral community.
>
> (Rorty 1993, p. 124)

In other words, representing rituals as irrational, and describing only select cultures as following rituals, is a way of marginalising those people within the moral community, and excluding their values from those which must be collectively negotiated and accommodated. It is a form of ethnocentrism which views European culture, and European patriarchy, as so natural and superior as to be beyond critique. Unsurprisingly, racism is evident throughout the political debate which forms the legislation. Consider the following comments, made by Baroness Gaitskell in the House of Lords in 1983:

> It is, after all, enough that women from other countries can come and live in ours. We are doing very well by them in allowing them to live in this country. It is nice for them and it is nice of us to do it. But we do not have to import their kind of rules. The point is that such people are not in a position to teach us anything about sexual behaviour. What have they to teach us about intimate sexual matters? Absolutely nothing.
>
> (*Prohibition of female circumcision bill (H.L.) 1983* (UK Parliament))

13.4 A failure of intersectionality

In the case of the burkini and the case of FGA, we are asked to believe that those opposed to these practices are attempting to defend the human rights of the women and girls concerned. That is, resistance to FGA and Islamic dress is ostensibly intended to combat the patriarchal norms that perpetuate these practices. Yet it is not clear that the norms are always patriarchal, and it is even less clear that this is the foremost concern for those who enact such vehement opposition, since their concern for the well-being of women does not generally extend to other issues, or to other areas of the same women's lives.

As Shweder points out (2000, p. 221), FGA is not a good example of the oppression of women and girls via control over female bodies, since more or less all societies which customarily perform FGA also perform male circumcision, while there are many cultures within which genital alterations are *only* performed upon males (consider Judaism, Islam, for the most part, and the culture of male genital alteration in the US). In most cultures with high prevalence of FGA, genital alterations are performed upon both sexes as intentionally equivalent initiation rites into adulthood. While FGA is often described as being intended to control and limit the sexuality of women, male circumcision is rarely described in this way, even though it has been shown to limit the sexual pleasure of men (Taves 2002). Further, FGA is almost exclusively discussed, performed and celebrated within women-only spaces, and there are examples of women defying the men of their communities in order to perform the practice (c.f. Thomas 1996), and young girls pursuing the practice while adults of all genders within their community repudiate it (c.f. Leonard 2000).

However, for the purposes of this section, let us assume that FGA is performed for reasons that *are* broadly patriarchal, and that critics' objection to the practice is authentically driven by this. After all, it is hard to explain away that fact that (say) a recent ethnography in Egypt, which has one of the highest prevalence rates of FGA globally, found that the principal motivation for performing clitoridectomy is 'to reduce and regulate girls' and women's sexual desires and sexual drive' (Fahmy, El-Mouelhy & Ragab 2010, p. 184). Even if one concedes that FGA is more generally an instance of the control of female bodies or sexuality, banning the practice would not necessarily be an appropriate response, either from a moral or a pragmatic position. In order to see this more clearly, consider the idea of intersectionality within feminist theory.

Coined by Black legal scholar Kimberlé Crenshaw (1991), 'intersectionality' builds on an operative concept dating back more than a century, originating in the work of Black feminists who recognised that the struggle for women's rights as an isolated cause would not be effective in attenuating the oppression of women of colour (c.f. Combahee River Collective 1983). Intersectionality emphasises that different forms of oppression interact with one another in complicated ways, so that feminists should not only be concerned with the oppression of women, who are manifestly not a homogeneous group, but should be concerned with how (say) racism, classism, homophobia and ableism jointly determine the experiences of women in ways that cannot be predicted simply by notionally combining these oppressions. Combating the oppression of any given group of women requires assiduous engagement with other pertinent marginal identities. This requires careful consideration of the positionality of the individual under question.

Those affected by FGA in the UK are women of colour who are asylum seekers, refugees, migrants (with or without documentation), or daughters or granddaughters thereof. Across the UK, there are over 86,000 first generation migrant women and girls who have experienced FGA in their countries of origin (Read 1998) and with rising numbers of refugees arriving from Sierra Leone, Somalia and Sudan, each of which has a prevalence of FGA exceeding 88% (UNICEF 2016), the numbers of women in the UK affected by FGA is increasing. A study based in South London noted that around 40% of those affected by FGA spoke little or no English (Momoh et al. 2001, p. 187). Further, while FGA is *not* an Islamic practice according to scripture (e.g., Rouzi 2013), many of those migrating to the UK from FGA-prevalent contexts are Muslims from Muslim majority countries where FGA is practised as a religious custom.

In other words, those who practice FGA are women of colour, often Muslims, migrants, refugees or asylum seekers, and may speak very little English. All of these factors are sources of significant vulnerability within the UK in the present context. Further, in the wake of increased scrutiny and complication around migrants using the NHS (Shahvisi, 2018), and new mandatory reporting and recording responsibilities for health care professionals regarding FGA (Amasanti, Imcha & Momoh 2016), those from FGA prevalent groups are likely to be further marginalised within health care settings. Data shows that migrants in general underuse health services (Steventon & Bardsley 2011) and have worse health outcomes (Jayaweera 2014; Raphaely & O'Moore 2010) with the current political climate raising particular concerns about health outcomes for Muslims in the UK (Laird et al. 2007).

Analyses of FGA tend to ignore, silence, or overwrite the lived experiences of the women of FGA-practising communities. Ahmadu criticises the way in which Western discourses on FGA tend to fixedly 'gaze between the legs of circumcised African women, rendering them "invisible" as individuals with their own dynamic histories, cultures, and traditions' (2007, p. 279). In particular, the vulnerabilities just mentioned are rarely foregrounded in discussions of FGA, even though it is likely that the threat and actuality of FGA to women of practising communities is less menacing than the threat and actuality of racism and social exclusion.

The criminalisation of FGA disregards the multiple interlocking vulnerabilities experienced by the women who are targeted by the legislation. People of colour, women of colour and even more so, *Muslim* women of colour, are made conspicuous and vulnerable by rising levels of racism within UK society. As Fernando points out 'police brutality and state racism are issues of everyday concern to Muslim and minority women, and therefore feminist issues' (Fernando 2016, p. 45). In the case of the burkini and FGA, the police are called upon to criminalise the body choices of consenting adult women, and state apparatus is called upon to codify racism into law. These are bans upon the ordinary lives of certain women, who are constrained by notions of criminality conveyed to them from outside their own culture to avoid sites of everyday existence (beaches and health services) in order to avoid being confronted by the violence of that criminalisation.

If one views FGA as a patriarchal restriction on the lives of women, to place additional restrictions on those lives through the threat of state violence seems no different to imposing bans on beachwear whose most likely outcome is the women in question remaining at home, debarred from public life by the joint effect of their own 'outsider' culture conspiring with the 'insider' culture to diminish possibilities for public participation which could offset the effects of racism and sexism. Bans on FGA and the burkini seem to follow the same farcical logic: criminalising the 'barbarism' of the act is given primacy over the welfare of those affected by the act; the vilification of the act and its symbolism trumps the rights of the people involved. This brings to mind colonial 'civilising missions,' and seems just as disingenuous.

This debate is a special case of a broader philosophical question about how to reify agency and understand its operation within the confines of the social world. The feminist literature on body modifications is instructive in this regard. Davis (1991) explores the concept of agency in relation to cosmetic surgery, asking how feminists should understand women's decisions to modify their bodies in response to patriarchal ideals. She recommends a feminist re-articulation of agency, which casts women as informed actors, and respects constrained choices as choices nonetheless. This is in spite of, and often in the awareness of, the fact that these decisions are harmful to women as individuals and as a whole. She contends that

> it is possible to view women who willingly choose and retrospectively defend cosmetic surgery for themselves as knowing what they are doing. Their decision may be a knowledgeable and rational one, even as it reproduces a complex of power structures that construct the female body as inferior and in need of change.
>
> (*ibid.*, p. 33)

So too must we recognise that one cannot 'save' women from the patriarchal aspects of FGA by beginning with the deeply problematic assumption of their lack of agency and proceeding with indifference to the many other constraints on their existence. One such constraint is racism, which is, either by accident or design, apparent in the double standard in the legislation. To fail to see an entire group of people as anything other than 'victims' of FGA, and to see fit to *punish* them for that, is a failure of intersectionality.

13.5 Conclusion

There has been a recent rise in nationalist populism across Europe, characterised by the perception of a 'civilizational threat' (Brubaker 2017, p. 3) posed by Islam, immigration, asylum seekers and the demand for multiculturalism and tolerance, which has fomented a staunch secularism which professes to privilege gender equality, LGBT rights, and the right to freedom of expression, as these are believed to be antithetical to the values of Islam. It is against this backdrop that those supporting the banning of FGA and the burkini claim to be acting in the best interests of women, and it is precisely because of that context that we should be suspicious of their claims. Even where concerns about the social meanings of FGA and the burkini are not disingenuous, banning these practices constitutes a failure of intersectionality, as it ignores the lived experience and subjugates the agency of those subscribing to these cultural practices.

In the case of FGA and the burkini, the intimate world of women is deemed to be a threat to Western culture. Both bans are bound up with ideals about the presentation of the female body. Opposing the burkini, which broke no French laws outside of the beach context, was just as much about promoting the bikini, and other forms of swimwear which expose the female body. As such the opposition was centred on the idea of the unclothed female body and its relationship to female sexuality. Opposing FGA, which breaks no UK laws when equivalent practices are described as FCGS, is a way of suggesting that particular women's body ideals are more acceptable than other women's body ideals, even if the realisation of those ideals is essentially the same.

To finish, I suggest that policy-makers and interlocutors in these debates consider FGA in its rightful place: as part of an intelligent, sensitive and collaborative dialogue about cultural pluralism and intersectionality that is led by women of FGA-prevalent communities, without fear of judgement or reprisal. To be swayed by the tide of populist sensationalism at a time when tolerance is needed more than ever is to commit particular groups to fear, danger and dehumanisation. After all:

> Tolerance means setting aside our readily aroused and powerfully negative feelings about the practices of immigrant minority groups long enough to get the facts straight and engage the "other" in a serious moral dialogue. It should take far more than overheated rhetoric and offended sensibilities to justify a cultural "eradication" campaign.
>
> (Shweder 2000, p. 227)

Notes

1 This is an inaccurate descriptor, but I use it here to be consistent with the wider literature. The burkini is a loose, but fitted, whole body swimsuit (often in two parts) with an in-built hood, akin to a sports hijab; a burqa is shapeless whole-body covering whose defining feature is a face-veil. 'Burkini' seems an apt term due to its closeness to 'bikini', but its inaccuracy only adds to the homogenising of varied Muslim practices and beliefs, and the sensationalising of this swimwear choice given the controversial relationship the French state has to the burqa.

2 Those interested in comparing the law and ethics of male circumcision and FGA may find the author's recent work with Brian Earp informative (Shahvisi & Earp, forthcoming).

3 Note that only 10% of women who undergo FGA endure the most extreme kind of alteration, 'infibulation', in which the clitoris and labia minora are excised, and the vulva sewn together, leaving only a small opening for urine and menstrual blood (Yoder & Khan 2008, 15).

References

Ahmadu, F. 2007, 'Ain't I a woman too? Challenging myths of sexual dysfunction in circumcised women', in Y. Hernlund & B. Shell-Duncan (eds.), *Transcultural bodies: female genital cutting in global context*, Rutgers University Press, New Brunswick, NJ, pp. 278–310.

Ahmadu, F. 2016, 'Why the term female genital mutilation is ethnocentric, racist and sexist – let's get rid of it!', *Hysteria*, 16 October, viewed 12 April 2017, www.hystericalfeminisms.com/voices1/2016/10/16/why-the-term-female-genital-mutilation-fgm-is-ethnocentric-racist-and-sexist-lets-get-rid-of-it.

Amasanti, M.L., Imcha, M., & Momoh, C. 2016, 'Compassionate and proactive interventions by health workers in the United Kingdom: a better approach to prevent and respond to female genital mutilation?', *PLoS Medicine*, vol. 13, no. 3, p. e1001982.

Braun, V. 2005, 'In search of (better) sexual pleasure: female genital 'cosmetic' surgery', *Sexualities*, vol. 8, no. 4, pp. 407–424.

British Medical Association. 2011, *Female genital mutilation: caring for patients and safeguarding children. BMA Ethics*, viewed 17 September 2017, www.bma.org.uk/-/media/files/pdfs/practical%20advice%20at%20work/ethics/femalegenitalmutilation.pdf.

Breedan, A., Blaise, L. 2016, 'Cannes, citing security risks, bans full-body 'burkinis' from its beaches', *The New York Times*, 12 August, viewed 10 April 2017, www.nytimes.com/2016/08/13/world/europe/cannes-muslims-burkini-ban.html.

Brubaker, R. 2017, 'Between nationalism and civilizationism: the European populist moment in comparative perspective', *Ethnic and Racial Studies*, vol. 40, no. 8, pp. 1–36.

Butler, J. 1990, *Gender trouble. Feminism and the subversion of identity.* Routledge, New York and London.

Combahee River Collective, 1983, 'A black feminist statement', in B. Smith (ed.), *Home girls: a black feminist anthology*, Kitchen Table: Women of Color Press Inc., New York.

Committee on Gynecologic Practice. 2007, 'ACOG committee opinion No. 378: vaginal "rejuvenation" and cosmetic vaginal procedures', *Obstetrics and Gynecology*, vol. 110, no. 3, p. 737.

Crenshaw, K. 1991, 'Mapping the margins: intersectionality, identity politics, and violence against women of color', *Stanford Law Review*, vol. 43, no. 6, pp. 1241–1299.

Crouch, N.S., Deans, R., Michala, L., Liao, L.M., & Creighton, S.M. 2011, 'Clinical characteristics of well women seeking labial reduction surgery: a prospective study', *BJOG: An International Journal of Obstetrics & Gynaecology*, vol. 118, no. 12, pp. 1507–1510.

Davis, K. 1991, 'Remaking the she-devil: a critical look at feminist approaches to beauty', *Hypatia*, vol. 6, no. 2, pp. 21–43.

Dustin, M. 2010, 'Female genital mutilation/cutting in the UK challenging the inconsistencies', *European Journal of Women's Studies*, vol. 17, no. 1, pp. 7–23.

Dustin, M., & Phillips, A. 2008, 'Whose agenda is it? Abuses of women and abuses of culture' in Britain', *Ethnicities*, vol. 8, no. 3, pp. 405–424.

Earp, B.D. 2016, 'In defence of genital autonomy for children', *Journal of Medical Ethics*, vol. 42, no. 3, pp. 158–163.

Ehrenreich, N., & Barr, M. 2005, 'Intersex surgery, female genital cutting, and the selective condemnation of cultural Practices', *Harvard CR-CLL Rev.*, vol. 40, p. 71.

Essén, B., & Johnsdotter, S. 2004, 'Female genital mutilation in the West: traditional circumcision versus genital cosmetic surgery', *Acta obstetricia et gynecologica Scandinavica*, vol. 83, no. 7, pp. 611–613.

Fahmy, A., El-Mouelhy, M.T., & Ragab, A.R. 2010, 'Female genital mutilation/cutting and issues of sexuality in Egypt', *Reproductive Health Matters*, vol. 18, no. 36, pp. 181–190.

Farrington, R., Saleh, S., Campbell, S., Jundi, A., & Worthington, E. 2016, 'Impact of proposal to extend charging for NHS in England', *The Lancet*, vol. 388, no. 10043, p. 459.

Female Genital Mutilation Act. 2003 (Government of the UK), viewed 11 April 2017, www.legislation.gov.uk/ukpga/2003/31/pdfs/ukpga_20030031_en.pdf.

Fernando, M. 2016, 'Liberté, egalité, féminisme?', *Dissent*, vol. 63, no. 4, pp. 38–46.

Foucault, M. 1990, *The history of sexuality: an introduction, volume 1* [Trans. Robert Hurley], Vintage, New York.

Goodman, M.P., Placik, O.J., Benson III, R.H., Miklos, J.R., Moore, R.D., Jason, R.A. et al. 2010, 'A large multicenter outcome study of female genital plastic surgery', *The Journal of Sexual Medicine*, vol. 7, pp. 1565–1577.

Health and Social Care Information Centre. 2017, viewed April 11 2017, http://content.digital.nhs.uk/article/2021/Website-Search?q=labiaplasty&go=Go&area=both.

HM Government. 2016, *Multi-agency statutory guidance on female genital mutilation*, viewed 15 April 2017, www.gov.uk/government/uploads/ystem/uploads/attachment_data/file/512906/Multi_Agency_Statutory_Guidance_on_FGM__-_FINAL.pdf.

Iglesia, C.B. 2012, 'Cosmetic gynecology and the elusive quest for the 'perfect' vagina', *Obstetrics & Gynecology*, vol. 119, no. 6, pp. 1083–1084.

Jayaweera, H. 2014, *Health of migrants in the UK: what do we know?*, The Migration Observatory, viewed 13 April 2017, www.migrationobservatory.ox.ac.uk/resources/briefings/health-of-migrants-in-theuk-what-do-we-know/.

Johnsdotter, S., & Essén, B. 2010, 'Genitals and ethnicity: the politics of genital modifications', *Reproductive Health Matters*, vol. 18, no. 35, pp. 29–37.

Laird, L.D., Amer, M.M., Barnett, E.D., & Barnes, L.L. 2007, 'Muslim patients and health disparities in the UK and the US', *Archives of Disease in Childhood*, vol. 92, no. 10, pp. 922–926.

Leonard, L. 2000, 'Interpreting female genital cutting: moving beyond the impasse', *Annual Review of Sex Research*, vol. 11, no. 1, pp. 158–190.

Lyons, H.D. 2007, 'Genital cutting: the past and present of a polythetic category', *Africa Today*, vol. 53, no. 4, pp. 3–17.

Mgbako, C., Saxena, M., Cave, A., & Farjad, N. 2010, 'Penetrating the silence in Sierra Leone: a blueprint for the eradication of female genital mutilation', *Harvard Human Rights Journal*, vol. 23, p. 111.

Momoh, C., Ladhani, S., Lochrie, D.P., & Rymer, J. 2001, 'Female genital mutilation: analysis of the first twelve months of a southeast London specialist clinic', *BJOG: An International Journal of Obstetrics & Gynaecology*, vol. 108, no. 2, pp. 186–191.

Morris, M., & Morris, M.A. 2012, *Concise dictionary of social and cultural anthropology*, John Wiley & Sons, Malden: MA.

Ogan, C., Willnat, L., Pennington, R., & Bashir, M. 2014, 'The rise of anti-Muslim prejudice: media and islamophobia in Europe and the United States', *International Communication Gazette*, vol. 76, no. 1, pp. 27–46.

Pech, M. 2016, *Une majorité de français opposée au port du burkini sur les plages*, viewed 10 April 2017, www.lefigaro.fr/politique/2016/08/24/01002-20160824ARTFIG00276-une-majorite-de-francais-opposee-au-port-du-burkini-sur-les-plages.php.

Prohibition of female circumcision bill 1985 (UK Parliament), HC Deb, vol 77 cc583–8, 19 April 1985, viewed 17 September 2017, http://hansard.millbanksystems.com/commons/1985/apr/19/prohibition-of-female-circumcision-bill.

Prohibition of female circumcision bill (H.L.) 1983 (UK Parliament), HL Deb, vol 444 cc990–1003, 10 November 1983, viewed 17 September 2017, http://hansard.millbanksystems.com/lords/1983/nov/10/prohibition-of-female-circumcision-bill#S5LV0444P0_19831110_HOL_193.

Quinn, B. 2016, 'French police make woman remove clothing on Nice beach following burkini ban', *The Guardian*, viewed 10 April 2017, www.theguardian.com/world/2016/aug/24/french-police-make-woman-remove-burkini-on-nice-beach.

Raphaely, N., & O'Moore, E. 2010, *Understanding the health needs of migrants in the South East region: a report by the South East migrant health study group on behalf of the department of health*, viewed 17 September 2017, www.imiaweb.org/uploads/docs/Dept_of_Health_Understanding_needs_of_migrants_report_2010.pdf.

Read, D. 1998, *Out of sight, out of mind*, FORWARD, London.

Rorty, R. 1993, 'Human rights, rationality and sentimentality', in S. Shute & S. Hurley (eds.), *On human rights*, Basic Books, New York, pp. 112–134.

Rouzi, A.A. 2013, 'Facts and controversies on female genital mutilation and Islam', *The European Journal of Contraception & Reproductive Health Care*, vol. 18, no. 1, pp. 10–14.

Rubin, A.J. 2016, 'French 'burkini' bans provoke backlash as armed police confront beach-goers', *The New York Times*, viewed 10 April 2017, www.nytimes.com/2016/08/25/world/europe/france-burkini.html?_r=0.

Runacres, S., Hayes, J., Grover, S., & Temple-Smith, M. 2015, 'Exposing the hidden truth about the need for adolescent labiaplasty', *Journal of Pediatric and Adolescent Gynecology*, vol. 28, no. 2, p. e60.

Shahvisi, A., 2018. Health worker migration and migrant healthcare: Seeking cosmopolitanism in the NHS. *Bioethics*, Vol. 32, no. 6, pp. 334–342.

Shahvisi, A., Earp, B. D. forthcoming. 'The law and ethics of female genital cutting.' In: Creighton, Sarah and Liao, Lih-Mei (eds.) *Female genital cosmetic surgery: interdisciplinary analysis and solution*. Cambridge University Press.

Shahvisi, A. 2016a, 'Cutting slack and cutting corners: an ethical and pragmatic response to Arora and Jacobs' 'Female genital alteration: a compromise solution'', *Journal of Medical Ethics*, vol. 42, no. 3, pp. 156–157.

Shahvisi, A. 2016b, 'Why UK doctors should be troubled by female genital mutilation legislation', *Clinical Ethics*, vol. 12, no. 2, pp. 102–108.

Sheldon, S., & Wilkinson, S. 1998, 'Female genital mutilation and cosmetic surgery: regulating non-therapeutic body modification', *Bioethics*, vol. 12, no. 4, pp. 263–285.

Shweder, R.A. 2000, 'What about 'female genital mutilation'? And why understanding culture matters in the first place', *Daedalus*, vol. 129, no. 4, pp. 209–232.

Steventon, A., & Bardsley, M. 2011, 'Use of secondary care in England by international immigrants', *Journal of Health Services Research & Policy*, vol. 16, no. 2, pp. 90–94.

Svoboda, J.S. 2013, 'Promoting genital autonomy by exploring commonalities between male, female, intersex, and cosmetic female genital cutting', *Global Discourse*, vol. 3, no. 2, pp. 237–255.

Taves, D.R. 2002, 'The intromission function of the foreskin', *Medical Hypotheses*, vol. 59, no. 2, pp. 180–182.

Thomas, L.M. 1996, ''Ngaitana (I will circumcise myself)': the gender and generational politics of the 1956 ban on clitoridectomy in Meru, Kenya', *Gender & history*, vol. 8, no. 3, pp. 338–363.

Toubia, N. 1995, 'Female genital mutilation', in J. Peters & A. Wolper (eds.), *Women's rights, human rights: international feminist perspectives*, Routledge, London, pp. 224–37.

UNICEF. 2005, *Female Genital Mutilation/Cutting: A Statistical Exploration*, viewed 15 September 2017, www.unicef.org/publications/index_29994.html.

UNICEF. 2016, *Female Genital Mutilation/Cutting Country Profiles*, viewed 13 April 2017, http://data.unicef.org/resources/female-genital-mutilation-cutting-country-profiles/.

Veale, D. 2013, 'Reply to Bewley (2012)', *Archives of Sexual Behavior*, vol. 42, no. 3, p. 325.

Veale, D., & Daniels, J. 2012, 'Cosmetic clitoridectomy in a 33-year-old woman', *Archives of Sexual Behavior*, vol. 41, no. 3, pp. 725–730.

Veale, D., Eshkevari, E., Ellison, N., Costa, A., Robinson, D., Kavouni, A. et al. 2014, 'Psychological characteristics and motivation of women seeking labiaplasty', *Psychological Medicine*, vol. 44, no. 3, pp. 555–566.

Yoder, P.S., & Khan, S. 2008, *Numbers of women circumcised in Africa: the production of a total*, viewed 13 April 2017, http://dhsprogram.com/pubs/pdf/WP39/WP39.pdf.

14 Integration, identity and elite migrants

Capturing the perspectives of overseas-trained South Asian doctors in the UK

Yasmin Ghazala Farooq

14.1 Introduction

In recent years, community cohesion in Britain has been an issue of concern, in which the role of established migrant communities and new immigrants to the UK has been scrutinised in the context of how well the migrants have integrated into British society. However, much of the existing literature in this area relates to the experiences of low or unskilled labour migrants.

This chapter is based on a study undertaken with highly skilled or so called 'elite' migrants, specifically, overseas-trained South Asian doctors in the UK. It is important to investigate the experiences of this understudied group as they form a significant part of the National Health Service (NHS) workforce. For example, in the late 1970s, 40% of hospital doctors and 20% of General Practitioners (GPs) in the UK were born overseas (Smith 1980). In 2008, overseas-trained South Asian doctors were described as the second single largest group of doctors working in the NHS after UK qualified doctors (Hann, Sibbald & Young 2008). It is also notable that the NHS is seen as a key aspect of so-called British Culture and was celebrated as part of the London 2012 Olympic Opening Ceremony.

The term 'overseas-trained South Asian' here refers to those doctors who obtained their basic medical degrees in India, Pakistan, Sri Lanka and Bangladesh. One of the key research questions related to how overseas-trained South Asian doctors perceive their own identities and view the communities around them and how such experiences fit in with the expectations of the 'Community Cohesion Framework' which applies to migrants. Only overseas-trained South Asian doctors who practised as general practitioners (GPs) were included in the analysis, as GPs have a unique role in terms of their close relationships with patients and the local communities of their practice population.

In the next section, I will briefly discuss the Community Cohesion Framework, and how it became a policy concern in multicultural Britain.

In 2001, some of the UK's northern towns experienced violence, involving clashes between hundreds of white and Asian youths and widespread damage to property and businesses. 'Community cohesion' consequently became a subject of significant interest and a focus for major policy intervention by the last Labour government when it was defined, in its simplest form, as the extent to which people feel part of a community. The government definition, adopted in 2003, reads as follows:

> A cohesive community is one where there is a common vision and a sense of belonging for all communities, the diversity of people's different backgrounds and circumstances are appreciated and positively valued, those from different backgrounds have similar life opportunities, strong and positive relationships are being developed between people from different backgrounds in the workplace, in schools and within neighbourhoods.
>
> (Home Office 2003, p. 7)

Following the 'race riots' as they were described by some (Worley 2005), the Cantle Report (2001) was the first published report that pointed out that high levels of segregation between Asians and whites existed in schools and neighbourhoods which significantly contributed to the riots. Economic deprivation and racism did not surface in such debates, rather, lack of community cohesiveness was held responsible in the report for the riots (Worley 2005). Integration was described as a key contributor to cohesion.

Since then, the question of migrant identities has become more pertinent than ever because in the government's community cohesion agenda identities are perceived to be necessary for community cohesion (Khan 2007). It is argued that our identities are socially produced and that they determine our relationships with the external world. Norton describes identity as

> [...] how people understand their relationship to the world, how that relationship is constructed across time and space, and how people understand their possibilities for the future.
>
> (Norton 1997, p. 410)

Jenkins (1994) and Nagel (1994) argue that studying immigrant identities is central to our understanding of their integration into mainstream British society. Transnational ties have generally been assumed to represent a challenge to migrants' successful integration (Snel, Engbersen & Leerkes 2006); these are ties that extend beyond the territorial borders of the country (Schiller & Fouron 1999).

Welzel, Inglehart and Deutsch (2005) contend that an individual's level of involvement in the community is determined by his or her personal attributes as well as being conditioned by the level of opportunities to which they are exposed. This implies that contextual factors need to be considered alongside socio-economic background when analysing the differences between individuals and how well they integrate into the communities as migrants; those with different social statuses may have different identities and integration experiences in different contexts. It is vitally important to develop an understanding of the dynamics that impact on cohesion in order to ensure effective policy interventions (Jayaweera & Choudhary 2008).

By drawing on the empirical evidence, I illustrate how the doctors in the study negotiate belonging and integrate with the wider society. The evidence shows that multiple identities are not considered by the doctors in the study to conflict with the obligations placed by domestic policies, and that their roles are not confined to within the narrow remit of the community cohesion policy framework.

14.2 Methodology

In order to investigate the process of sociocultural integration experiences and perspectives of overseas-trained South Asian doctors in the UK, this study was undertaken in three case study areas, with the expectation that localities are likely to have an impact on individuals' identity and community cohesion experiences (Commission on Integration and Cohesion 2007; Holy & Stuchlik 1981). The study included 27 in-depth interviews with overseas-trained South Asian doctors practising as GPs in the UK. The interviews were conducted between 2011 and 2012. Guidance notes for in-depth interviews were developed through informal discussions with GPs from the targeted research population. The topic guide used during the interviews included questions that related to the driving forces for migration, experiences and working conditions in the NHS, negotiating entry into general practice, entrepreneurial activity and innovation within general practice, how the interviewees navigate their multiple identities in different geographical contexts, experiences of racism and coping strategies and sense of belonging to Britain.

Case study areas with contrasting features were selected. For example, Manchester is a large urban area with high ethnic density, Sheffield is an urban area with ethnic density that equates to the national average and Barnsley is an ex-mining town with rural characteristics and very low ethnic density. The sample was selected by use of the snowballing method and a thematic analysis was undertaken using the computer software NVivo. The strategy I employed in the data analysis was an inductive analysis and I looked for patterns and categories emerging from the data (Patton 1990). The themes developed included reasons for migration, experiences in the NHS, entrepreneurship, identity, experiences of racism and coping strategies, the doctor-patient relationship and transnationalism. Each theme included subcategories, for example, the subcategories for migration included reasons for migration, processes for migration and networks.

The interviewees were aged between 50 and 76 years of age. The majority of doctors were concentrated in the age band of 60–75 years. Table 14.1 shows the ethnic, gender and religious breakdown of doctors interviewed in each of the case study areas. As can be seen, there are no overseas-trained doctors of Bangladeshi or Sri Lankan origin, which relates to fieldwork access issues in the case study areas.

Formal ethical approval was obtained from the University of Manchester's *Committee on the Ethics of Research on Human Beings*. In relation to the methodological considerations, some limitations should be taken into account when

Table 14.1 Ethnic, gender and religious attributes of participants related to the case study areas

Areas	*Sheffield*		*Barnsley*		*Manchester*		*Religion*	
Gender	*Male*	*Female*	*Male*	*Female*	*Male*	*Female*	*Hindu*	*Muslim*
Ethnic Origin								
Indian	7	1	2	1	6	1	14	4
Pakistani	3	0	4	1	1	0	0	9
Total	11		8		8		14	13

Note: The table shows absolute numbers divided into areas, and gender or religion in relation to ethnic origin

interpreting the results of this study. For example, the findings are contextually unique and the qualitative analysis is based on interviews with doctors of Indian and Pakistani origin only and females were under-represented in the sample.

14.3 Identity, community cohesion and perceptions of the doctors

A key government approach to community cohesion within the Community Cohesion Framework relates to the notion of 'Britishness' and having 'common values' for successful integration of migrants. McGhee (2003, p. 382) refers to such an assumption as a 'highly problematic political project'. Gilchrist, Bowles and Wetherell (2010) explain the significance of one's identity in the community, contending that it is important to recognise how people 'define, resist or adapt' their identities so as to enhance our own understanding of their engagement with their fellow citizens and with government.

In the following section, I will explore the empirical evidence about how the doctors perceived their identities and how their experiences relate to the debates of Community Cohesion Framework. Brah (2007) asserts that individuals are situated across various processes of identification, which change and lead to configuration into a specific pattern in a particular set of both social and psychological circumstances, making a particular identity prominent at a given time. The doctors' accounts showed that multiple identities were in process. Examples include the practicing of various identities such as religious, cultural, linguistic and professional identities, as well as how one's phase of life impacts on identity. In this chapter, I mainly focus on their responses to the sense of belonging to Britain, and hybrid and transnational identities.

14.4 Findings and discussion

14.4.1 Identity with British values

All the interviewees expressed a strong identification with British identity and the reasons for this identification were complex. Part of the explanation relates to their pre-migration exposure to British education from an early age. Their medical education model mirrored that of the UK, and their more positive reception in the UK compared with the South Asian community in general has had a long-lasting effect on their perceptions of Britain. The interviewees felt a deep affiliation with the UK, despite an acknowledgment that they had experienced inequalities within the structure of the NHS. For instance, all the interviewees described their motivation to come to the UK as a desire to become specialists through their postgraduate training. However, they could not progress in the specialities to which they had originally aspired, and consequently entered into General Practice, where it was slightly easier to secure employment as this was considered a less desirable speciality at the time. The following account was a typical response concerning a sense of belonging to Britain:

> When I came, I only had £8 on me and now with God's grace, I have achieved so much, my children have done well, I have a nice house, status in the community; medicine and Britain have been good for me.
>
> (gp7s)

Almost all of the interviewees used their own cultural framework to reflect and give meaning to their experiences, as is evidenced in the following account:

> There is a saying in our culture that you should be 'namak halal' which means one should be loyal to the benefactors, even if you have only had a pinch of salt from them.
>
> (gp5s)

Another doctor stated:

> We believe that Jis thali mein khao, us mein ched mat karo [translation: don't make holes in the plate that you eat out of, it implies that you take care of it because it is providing you with food].
>
> (gp3m)

The daily encounters with the society at large described by the doctors appear somewhat different from the well-documented experiences of their less privileged counterparts. This may be attributable to their particular type of social and cultural capital. Several of the interviewees mentioned being members of local rotary and golf clubs and attending elite social events. The following interviewee talked about his deep pride when he received his Officer of the Most Excellent Order of the British Empire (OBE) from the Queen:

> In 2009, I was given OBE, yes this is the picture at Buckingham Palace, you feel very proud, out of the whole country, including Wales and Scotland,

> I was the only GP in this year given an OBE. I was the community hero for my contribution to public services.
>
> (gpm4)

Others talked about their admiration of the ethos of the NHS, and also adapting to British values in their lives:

> I think queues are good, whether it's queuing in the railway station or cinema or wherever, queue is a queue it doesn't matter. There are a lot of things that are good about Britain and we all need to learn from it, and adopt those values, in particular, the National Health Service, which I think is admirable. Other nice things are punctualities and discipline.

He was quick to point out that his adaptation to Britain does not mean giving up his Indian identity:

> I do feel British, I feel happy that I have learnt a lot of good British values, and that doesn't mean I don't feel Indian, I know I'm an Indian I feel Indian, because I grew up, my whole formative years were in India, but of course, I do feel British as well.
>
> (gp2m)

The British values of fairness and tolerance cropped up in many interviewees' accounts, which one can argue is ironic given that their own accounts reveal that they did not always experience these. The images of Britain being fairer and more tolerant are partly based on the conditioning to which people from ex-colonies have been exposed (Sayyid 2004), and partly due to personal positive encounters with individuals. For some, Britain also offered a sense of security that they did not have in their countries of origin because of cultural, religious and linguistic tensions:

> My brother had already been to the UK, he said; go to Britain, the living conditions there are good, there is no discrimination on class basis there, if you are clever, you will make it
>
> (gp6s)

The interviewees were often keen to point out that they did not believe they had to give up their Indian or Pakistani identities to become part of the British society:

> […] that doesn't mean for even a second that where my warmth to my own country is concerned is lessened, that is even more, I would really want to do something for my society as well.
>
> (gpm4)

The processes by which doctors became woven into the social fabric of the local communities were described at length. The following account shows how the support of local communities helped them to achieve contextual embedding:

> There was a lot of community activities that I and other Asian doctors used to go to, there might be a dance, there might have been a pea and pie, whatever, small things, you know.
>
> (gp2)

The above account shows the interaction of an overseas-trained South Asian doctor with low- and high-class strata that includes participation in community activities such as dancing and attending 'pea and pie' parties, which specifically relate to the culture of a working-class mining community. Other accounts also provide evidence of overcoming social hierarchies:

> I had a patient [white male] who was always cleaning the outside area of my medical centre. I did not even know this until one day, he came in to see me, his hands had scratches all over and were bleeding. I said to him, 'what have you done to your hands', he said oh nothing much, it was then that I found out that it was him. He said I was just cleaning the bushes; actually I want to keep your place tidy.
>
> (gp4s)

The doctors' account below also suggests reciprocity in some of the doctor-patient relationships:

> He died [the above patient] two weeks after, I found out that his wife was struggling a little after he died, I employed her as a cleaner, she became very friendly with my wife, it was like a mother-daughter relationship. I had many more positive relationships with local patients.
>
> (gp4s)

14.4.2 Colonial and post-colonial identities

Bhabha (1994) describes hybridity as a fusion resulting from two relatively distinct cultural forms, styles and identities creating a discursive space that he regards as a third space. It is within this space that competing representations of identities such as 'local-global' are constantly negotiated.

The relationship of post-colonial people to Britain is often assumed to have commenced only at the point when they or their ancestors embarked on their journey to Britain, which fails to take into account their exposure and conditioning under the colonial rule (Sayyid 2004). The doctors talked about being educated in independent English medium schools and their medical education being based on the British model. The doctors' frequent code-switching between English and their first language is one example of their sociolinguistic hybrid identities (Bhatt 2013). Almost all the interviewees talked about the ease that they felt with their hybrid identities:

> I am proud to be Indian of my roots, but I am equally proud to be British and to be in England. I am a Hindu, but not a strict one; I pray at home and celebrate Hindu festivals.
>
> (gp2b)

It appears that the specific UK contexts served as spaces where the identities of doctors and patients were simultaneously negotiated against a backdrop of the legacy of Empire. The following account shows that the nature of doctor-patient encounters had been shaped by the historical colonial context:

> [...] some would show their arrogance by their body language that they were superior than us. You see they feel superior because they have ruled over you for hundreds of years or more, you know, they feel they are superior than all over the world not just us, they have colonised every part of the world. We did not think of the white working class as coming from lower strata because before us, they were English first.
>
> (gp10s)

In relation to integration into British society, the responses of this elite group of migrants were distinctive in that the majority of the doctors believed in having a 'public conforming identity' with few distinguishing aspects and did not approve of some of the visible performative acts exhibited in the behaviour of other South Asians, in particular Muslims dressing in so-called ethnic clothes. The class identities of the interviewees were exposed in their accounts regarding Asian people, in particular Asian women, as evidenced in the following quotation:

> I've seen women from lot of other Muslim countries, I think they are much more conservative here or have become over the last 10 years, than people in your Pakistan or in India, even Muslims there in India they don't dress like this here and that's why you feel more different, I think you have to, you just can't have a very rigid appearance or your ideas so you'll never mix up with anybody. Sometimes I get female patients and it's really difficult to even examine their ears as they are so fully covered.
>
> (gp3s)

Ballard (1979) and more recently Ang (2003, p. 141) contended that a powerful strategy adopted by those who are marginalised or excluded from white structures or western hegemony is that of claiming one's difference and turning the re-adopted cultural identity into symbolic capital.

The above account illustrates that the interviewee had little comprehension that this adaptation of Muslim women may be a coping strategy, and a reaction to the rejection experienced in British society. Interestingly, the interviewees' own strategy revolved instead around adopting a symbolic identity of their medical profession rather than their cultural identity. Although they wished to distance themselves from such behaviour, and the majority did not believe in affirming their ethnic identities symbolically by way of dress, the evidence shows that they achieved this by means of belonging to medical diasporas, which positively affirmed their ethnic identity. This shows how elites' strategies differ from non-elites while dealing with racism.

14.4.3 Entrepreneurship, bidirectional transmission of ideas and activities

Ballard (1994) regards migration itself as an entrepreneurship activity, whereas Bygrave and Hofer (1991) define an entrepreneur as someone who perceives an opportunity and creates the organisation for its pursuit. Although the concept of entrepreneurship has traditionally been discussed in relation to the lesser skilled sectors of the labour market, this study endeavoured to expand the concept of entrepreneurship to the skilled sector and build on the work of Raghuram, Henry and Bornat (2010). Those authors discuss the clustering of South Asian doctors in geriatrics medicine in their research, which they argue is related to the disadvantaged positions of both older people and the migrant doctors. The findings of the current study also confirm that the entry of the doctors into General Practice related to their strategies of self-employment to circumvent the system that blocked their mobility in the NHS. The doctors talked about the significance of their own networks in their extensive entrepreneurial activities in the UK, in which they set up and revitalised GP practices, equipping them with modern facilities and introducing many new initiatives. The scarcity of resources in the rural environments went hand-in-hand with the entrepreneurial spirit of the interviewees and such contexts provided them with perfect places in which to grow.

Determination to improve services for the most needy was stated as the main reason for innovation by many of the interviewees. Many of the overseas-trained South Asian doctors discussed their frustrations about their inability to implement their vision in their country of origin as a result of financial and governmental constraints. The following interviewee's account sums up the push factors for his migration, which include poor working conditions, lack of training opportunities and medical training not being geared to meet the needs of physicians and patients. It would appear from his account that he sees the UK system as superior:

> There was no improvement in the system, no changes, there is corruption, in hospitals, in all fields including NHS, everywhere, there are no facilities, there is no educational training programmes, we have got NHS service in Kashmir but it could be better if there were other facilities and educational programmes e.g. when I came here I had to go for GP training for three years, The system here is so well developed. Over there we were trained for something that we didn't have, the equipment, the training, the whole system.
>
> (gp8s)

Many in the study had a clear idea as to what an excellent health care model should look like, as they had several years of experience in the country of origin working in remote villages with very few resources, as well as in the UK. The experiences in the origin country may have informed a different perspective on health care provision and use of resources, as well as the experience of migration that may have encouraged risk taking and innovation.

The following interviewee, like many others, explained that the transformations they envisioned in general practice were attributable to making the best use of their capabilities (which were greater than is typical for UK-qualified GPs) and resources while offering enhanced primary care services and saving the establishment money:

> We came here not to become GPs, we came to become specialists, we had enthusiasm and we had capability. Most of us had years' experience before we came to the UK. I did around 300 vasectomies on my table in my practice. I did fair amount of circumcision of Pakistani babies, probably 150, ok in addition, I was the first doctor who started doing vasectomy under local anesthetic. It's because I was able to do it. We made a huge contribution in that sense.
>
> (gp9s)

Levitt (1998) refers to the role of social remittances in promoting immigrant entrepreneurship. Social remittances are ideas, behaviours, identities and social capital related to democracy, health and community organisation that migrants bring with them from their home countries and then culturally diffuse within the new settings. The doctors' accounts in this study provide evidence of bi-directional transmission of ideas and activities.

The interviewees in their accounts emphasised 'we' when talking about innovations and frustrations. Their accounts show that they functioned collectively and called upon their own cultural resources in problem-solving and creative thinking techniques, such as the collective reciting of Urdu poetry, and used idioms from their own languages from which they drew strength at times when no formal support system existed. An example is when an interviewee was talking about losing half of his patients' list when he took over his practice from a white doctor. He believed that race had played a significant part in this process. He explains how he coped with the challenges involved with this situation, reciting the following verse in Urdu:

> Baad e mukhalif se na gabra e eqab
> Ye to chilti and tujey uncha uraney kaliey
>
> [Translation: Oh bird, don't get troubled by the strong wind blowing from the opposite direction, It blows only to make you fly higher].
>
> (gp5s)

Erdal and Oeppen (2013) make a valid point that race and racism are often not acknowledged in debates about migrant integration. The findings of this research show that, despite having a privileged position in British society as health care professionals, the doctors were not immune from experiences of racism and they often talked about having 'imperial encounters'. For example, it is worth repeating the aforementioned account of experiences in inner city GP practices:

> [...] some [white patients] would show their arrogance by their body language that they were superior than us. You see they feel superior because they have ruled over you for hundreds of years or more, you know, they feel they are superior than all over the world not just us, they had colonised every part of the world at one point.
>
> (gp10s)

The degree of intensity of both overt and covert racism varied in different localities. The doctors were more likely to describe experiences where white patients demanded to see a white doctor at the reception desk in ethnically dense inner-city practices.

14.4.4 Towards an understanding of how integration and transnationalism interact

Brah (1996, p. 190) argues that one subtext embodied in the diaspora is that of 'home' and while home continues to be a mythical place of desire in the diaspora imagination, it remains a myth and place of no return. On the other hand, 'home' is also about the lived experience of a place, a locality, and it is deeply linked with how the processes of inclusion or exclusion operate and the subjective experiences that occur in particular localities. The findings related to place identity in this study support Brah's argument and showed that, where the local structures were less inclusive, transnational identities were more salient than in more inclusive places. Barnsley, an ex-coal mining town, for example, was described as a place that did not appear to cater for the cultural and religious needs of its small-sized Asian community. The interviewees from Barnsley articulated a sense of belonging more to Britain than to the place itself. Some of the doctors referred to looking forward to attending events such as the 'Chelsea Flower Show' and 'Royal Ascot'. The doctors in Barnsley were less likely to experience overt racism. Low ethnic density and rural characteristics of the place with its own health care needs and scarce resources were among the most common reasons quoted by the doctors:

> In the village the community is very close-knit. The only non-white persons in Barnsley in the 1960s were Asian doctors and if the locals saw you in that time, they will think that you are a doctor and would respect you.
>
> (gp3b)

> I know several generations of same families and I know them all for long enough. I know families; their children and then their children. They all come here. I had several five generation families.
>
> (gp2b)

The interviewees in Manchester were more likely to experience overt racism; the changing demography of the patient population did not appear to foster the same close bonds with patients and community that the interviewees from Sheffield and Barnsley talked so passionately about. The fact that they were the only group who mentioned their extensive involvement in transnational social entrepreneurship activities in their country of origin may relate to achieving social recognition elsewhere. This viewpoint has been argued by various scholars such as Vertovec (2002), Schiller, Basch and Blanc-Szanton (1992) and Vertovec and Cohen (1999), who refer to attachments that migrants maintain with persons, customs and interests which do not relate to the interests cultivated in the new place of migration. Basch, Schiller and Blanc-Szanton (1994) also add that the racialisation of migrants in the USA, which labels and disciplines them as such, leads them to seek alternative identities by means of cultivating transnational ties.

The interviewees discussed at length social entrepreneurship activities in the country of origin. This involvement shows the social impacts of migration in both countries. They talked about being able to leverage the prestige and professional status and financial resources they had acquired in the UK to their advantage in their countries of origin, by setting up various initiatives within the state-run hospitals, for example. One such initiative involved the integration of the deaf babies of poor families into mainstream society in India. The following interviewee explains how the programme involved screening babies from birth with the help of auto-acoustic screening machines purchased from the UK and provision of funding collected by charitable work in the UK to support staff such as speech therapists and the provision of hearing aids:

> Me and my husband are involved in charity, my husband's background is in ENT, so we started a hearing camp in India, for younger children, erm... we went to villages and did hearing tests, and gave them hearing aids, we gave them the hearing aids so that the children could be orally rehabilitated, they could integrate into normal society by going to a 'normal' school rather than to a deaf school.
>
> (gpm3)

She talks about her duty of care and concern for these children that extends beyond borders:

> We wanted children to have normal society ... they were already poor and on top of that they were deaf, they immediately became bottom of the social ladder ... if you can't hear, you can't speak either, so you're not integrating into the society, you won't get a job, you won't be able to learn, there are so many problems, so that's why we started the hearing aids charity.
>
> (gpm3)

The account below suggests that there are other overseas-trained South Asian doctors involved in such charitable work:

> Other doctors… there are a few doctors who have their own specialities, there is one who is in rehab medicine, he runs a charity for that.
>
> (gpm3)

She stated that she intended to use her networks to replicate this project in other cities and countries as she believes that the sustainability of this unique model is necessary to provide long-term support for social justice and economic development for the most vulnerable. Other doctors also talked about organising eye camps where they treated the poor. The account below describes in detail other charitable activities:

> You see your general practice is so busy that you don't have time to do anything else. I do have some voluntary role in Pakistan. I collect money for kidney dialysis for Noor Foundation and send over donations that I collect in the Ramadaan month which I have continued for several years. There are 21 centres that we support financially, mostly us [Asian] doctors in UK, though there are other community members as well and we provide 4 dialysis machines and funding for their maintenance. We carry out around 8,000 dialysis per year. Some of the older machines now need more maintenance.
>
> (gpm5)

Another doctor talked about his extensive involvement as follows:

> I have links with Nagpur medical association, there are about 200–250 of us from the same college and every two years we get together. We do some charity work in India, me and my wife [also doctor]. We raise funds, my wife is a very good collage artist and I do reasonably good photography, so together we make things and raise funds by selling them which we then send the money to India. We raised £3000 which we used to buy six scooters for paraplegics in India, this enables paraplegics more independence. I made some calendars of my wildlife photography and raised money by selling them. Two years ago, we ran a charity show and raised £1500 which we sent for a charity that is working with children living in slums. We support another charity which is involved in recycling in India. We (a few Asian doctors) have formed an organisation here which supports a charity hospital in a rural place in India.
>
> (gp1m)

Erdal and Oeppen (2013, p. 868) suggest that rather than considering transnational ties as a significant marker of difference per se, we need to consider how such ties impact on processes of integration. Both transnational activities and integration processes entail opportunities and demands and the focus should be on how migrants manage the coexistence of both processes in the balancing act. The doctors' accounts show that they did not envisage any potential conflict between their transnational roles and their community roles. A common response in this area was cited as follows:

> We only had a few pounds in our pockets; we owe it to this soil and people. (gp1s)

The ones who were more involved in transnational activities were just as likely to talk about their positive sense of 'Britishness' as others in the study. Vertovec (2009) argues that a definite causal relationship is difficult to identify as the correct reasons for individuals' greater or lesser involvement in transnational activities. However, both these processes of transnational activities and integration are not mutually exclusive and engagement in any social interaction, regardless of whether this is local or transnational, provides individuals with the ability to confidently interact and engage with others.

Racism is a continuing challenge in the lives of visible minorities and how individuals experience racism has been linked to the process of colonisation and the subsequent social contact that has been reproduced in the postcolonial relationships (Rex 1970). For example, more recently, in an ethnographical study, Tyler (2012) found that older white people have memories of working in colonial institutions which confirm that relics from the empire remain dormant in the UK landscape. Given that racism continues to play a significant part in British society, it is important to understand its implications for migrants who are human beings and are likely to act within the context of their feelings about their sense of security and self-esteem, which are important elements within human relationships, locally or transnationally (Ho 2008). The findings of this study lend support to Lucassen's (2006) perspective that integration and transnationalism are compatible if integration is seen as a process rather than a 'programme' into which migrants are shoved with an expectation that they will achieve the goal of integration within a given timeframe.

14.5 Conclusion

This chapter set out to investigate the sociocultural integration experiences and perspectives of an elite group of migrants, specifically, overseas-trained South Asian doctors in the UK, in order to contribute to contemporary community cohesion debates. These debates revolve around cohesion, integration and Britishness. Since the question of studying immigrant identities is stated as central to our understanding of their integration into mainstream British society, the focus of the study in this chapter was on the doctors' perceptions of their identities.

The evidence showed that in all three areas in which they were based, the interviewees had been accepted by their neighbourhoods and were aware that their elite status had afforded them symbolic capital that had facilitated integration.

The interviewees' accounts showed that personal experiences, such as exposure to western education in their country of origin, had also contributed towards their integration in British society, and they were more likely to be accepted by the wider society than their low/unskilled counterparts, being a member of an elite club. The specific characteristics of the place, such as whether it is a rural or urban context and its need to sustain health care provision, may have also facilitated the integration process.

The findings show an intersection of privilege and marginalization for this elite group of migrants. While many Asians in the UK may affirm their ethnic identities symbolically by way of dress, the responses of this elite group of migrants were distinctive in that the majority of the doctors employed practices of invisibility in the micro-politics of their everyday encounters, in response to perceived fear of racism.

Their accounts strongly point to their cross-cutting affiliations, which do not conflict with their allegiance to the UK. It is important to recognise that the Community Cohesion Framework suggests limited identities (one national identity, one national language and British values), even though elite migrants could hold multiple transnational identities, including those that strongly support community roles and activities in the UK and their countries of origin. The findings lend support to Gilchrist, Bowles and Wetherell's (2010) argument that it is important to recognise how people 'define, resist or adapt' their identities in order to enhance our own understanding of their engagement with fellow citizens and with the government.

References

Ang, I. 2003, 'Together-in-difference: beyond diaspora, into hybridity', *Asian Studies Review*, vol. 27, no. 2, pp. 141–154.

Ballard, C. 1979, 'Second-generation South Asians', in V. Saifullah Khan (ed.), *Minority families in Britain: support and stress*, Macmillan, London, pp. 109–129.

Ballard, R. (ed.) 1994, *Desh pardesh: The South Asian experience in Britain*, Routledge, London.

Basch, L., Schiller, N.G., & Blanc-Szanton, C. 1994, *Nations unbound: transnational projects, postcolonial predicaments, and deterritorialized nation-states*, Gordon & Breach, Langhorne, PA.

Bhabha, H. 1994, *The location of culture*, Routledge, London in New York.

Bhatt, R.M. 2013, 'Unravelling post-colonial identity through language', in N Coupland (ed.), *The handbook of language and globalization*, Wiley-Blackwell, UK, pp. 520–539.

Brah, A. 1996, *Cartographies of diaspora: contesting identities*. Psychology Press, Hove.

Brah, A. 2007, 'Non-binarized identities of similarity and difference', In: Wetherell, M., Lafleche, M. & Berkeley, R. (eds.) identity, ethnic diversity and community cohesion. London: Sage Publications, London, pp. 136–145.

Bygrave, W.D., & Hofer, C.W. 1991, 'Theorizing about entrepreneurship', *Entrepreneurship Theory and Practice*, vol. 16, no. 2, pp. 13–22.

Cantle, T. 2001, *Community cohesion: a report of the independent review team*, Government of the UK, Home Office, viewed 5 July 2018, http://dera.ioe.ac.uk/14146/1/communitycohesionreport.pdf.

Erdal, M.B., & Oeppen, C. 2013, 'Migrant balancing acts: understanding the interactions between integration and transnationalism', *Journal of Ethnic and Migration Studies*, vol. 39, no. 6, pp. 867–884.

Gilchrist, A., Bowles, M., & Wetherell, M. 2010, *Identities and social action: connecting communities for a change*, Community Development Foundation, London.

Hann, M., Sibbald, B., & Young, R. 2008, 'Workforce participation among international medical graduates in the National Health Service of England: a retrospective longitudinal study', *Human Resources for Health*, vol. 6, no. 9, pp. 478–449.

Ho, E.L.E. 2008, 'Citizenship, migration and transnationalism: a review and critical interventions', *Geography Compass*, vol. 2, no. 5, pp. 1286–1300.

Holy, L., & Stuchlik, M. 1981, *The structure of folk models*, Academic Press Incorporation, London/Oxford/Boston/New York/San Diego.

Home Office. 2003, *Building a picture of community cohesion: a guide for local authorities and their partners*, Government of the UK, London.

Jayaweera, H., & Choudhary, T. 2008, *Immigration, faith and cohesion: evidence from local areas with significant Muslim populations*, Joseph Rowntree Foundation, UK.

Jenkins, R. 1994, 'Rethinking ethnicity: identity, categorization and power', *Ethnic and Racial Studies*, vol. 17, no. 2, pp. 197–223.

Khan, O. 2007, 'Policy, identity and community cohesion: how race equality fits', in M. Wetherell, M. Lafleche & R. Berkeley (eds.), *Identity, ethnic diversity and community cohesion*, Sage Publications, London, pp. 40–57.

Levitt, P. 1998, 'Social remittances: migration driven local-level forms of cultural diffusion', *International Migration Review*, vol. 32, no. 4, pp. 926–948.

Lucassen, L. 2006, 'Is transnationalism compatible with assimilation? Examples from Western Europe since 1850', *IMIs-Beiträge*, vol. 29, pp. 11–31.

McGhee, D. 2003, 'Moving to 'our' common ground: critical examination of community cohesion discourse in twenty-first century Britain', *The Sociological Review*, vol. 51, no. 3, pp. 376–404.

Nagel, J. 1994, 'Constructing ethnicity: Creating and recreating ethnic identity and culture', *Social Problems*, vol. 41, no. 1, pp. 152–176.

Norton, B. 1997, 'Language, identity, and the ownership of English', *TESOL Quarterly*, vol. 31, no. 3, pp. 409–429.

Patton, M.Q. 1990, *Qualitative evaluation and research methods*, Sage Publications, Thousand Oaks, CA.

Raghuram, P., Henry, L., & Bornat, J. 2010, 'Difference and distinction? Non-migrant and migrant networks', *Sociology*, vol. 44, no. 4, pp. 623–641.

Rex, J. 1970, *Race relations in sociological theory*, Weidenfeld and Nicolson, London.

Sayyid, S. 2004, 'Slippery people: the immigrant imaginary and the grammar of colour', in I. Law, D. Philips & L. Turney (eds.), *Institutional racism in higher education*, Trentham Books: London, pp. 149–159.

Schiller, N.G., Basch, L., & Blanc-Szanton, C. 1992, 'Transnationalism: a new analytic framework for understanding migration', *Annals of the New York Academy of Sciences*, vol. 645, no. 1, pp. 1–24.

Schiller, N.G., & Fouron, G.E. 1999, 'Terrains of blood and nation: Haitian transnational social fields', *Ethnic and Racial Studies*, vol. 22, no. 2, pp. 340–366.

Smith, D. J. (1980) Overseas doctors in the National Health Service. London: Policy Studies Institutes.

Snel, E., Engbersen, G., & Leerkes, A. 2006, 'Transnational involvement and social integration', *Global Networks*, vol. 6, no. 3, pp. 285–308.

Tyler, K. 2012, 'The English village, whiteness, coloniality and social class', *Ethnicities*, vol. 12, no. 4, pp. 427–444.

Vertovec, S. 2002, *Transnational networks and skilled labour migration*, University of Oxford, Transnational Communities Programme, viewed 5 July 2018, www.transcomm.ox.ac.uk/working%20papers/WPTC-02-02%20Vertovec.pdf.

Vertovec, S., & Cohen, R. 1999, *Migration, diasporas and transnationalism*, Elgar, Cheltenham, UK.

Welzel, C., Inglehart, R., & Deutsch, F. 2005, 'Social capital, voluntary associations and collective action: which aspects of social capital have the greatest 'civic' payoff?', *Journal of Civil Society*, vol. 1, no. 2, pp. 121–146.

Werbner, P. 2005, 'The translocation of culture: 'community cohesion' and the force of multiculturalism in history', *The Sociological Review*, vol. 53, no. 4, pp. 745–768.

Worley, C. 2005, "It's not about race. It's about the community', New Labour and community cohesion', *Critical Social Policy*, vol. 25, no. 4, pp. 483–496.

15 How to support migrant physicians in navigating through an unfamiliar health care system

Findings from a qualitative interview study

Corinna Klingler and Georg Marckmann

15.1 Introduction

In the last decade, Germany has seen the steepest increase of foreign-trained[1] physicians among member countries of the Organisation for Economic Cooperation and Development (OECD), which are typically considered receiving countries of the global medical brain drain (OECD 2015). Numbers of migrant physicians have long been low in Germany – 5% in 2006 (Ognyanova & Busse 2011). One reason might be that the country had not considered itself an 'immigration country' and restricted labour market access to high-skilled migrants, including physicians (Fellmer 2008). This changed primarily because the physician associations in the 2000s warned about a physician shortage (Hoesch 2009), which was backed by various studies (Blum & Löffert 2010; Kopetsch 2010). In 2016, approximately 11% of all practicing physicians were foreign nationals, coming mainly from European countries like Austria, Greece or Romania but also increasingly from politically unstable countries outside Europe, like Syria (Bundesärztekammer 2017).

From the international literature, we know that migrant physicians face various challenges due to the (cultural) differences between the system in which they were trained and socialized and the system in which they now work (Hall et al. 2004; Michalski et al. 2017; Pilotto, Duncan & Anderson-Wurf 2007). Migrant physicians, for example, have repeatedly shared that they have struggled with concepts like patient-centred care or individual-oriented – instead of family-oriented – approaches to decision-making (Michalski et al. 2017). In Germany, academics have also become increasingly interested in understanding the possibly problematic experiences of migrant physicians having to navigate an unfamiliar health care system (Jansen, Hänel & Klingler 2018; Jansen, Schnepf & Hänel 2015; Klein 2016; Klingler & Marckmann 2016; Klingler et al. 2018; Kovacheva & Grewe 2015). Participants in these studies have pointed out similar intercultural challenges, as described in the international literature, but have also addressed further difficulties, ranging from limited command of skills needed in the new context of practice (e.g. limited language capacity or insufficient experience with taking blood, as this task was considered a nurse's task in their country of training) to difficulties with accessing the health care system (e.g. complicated and lengthy licensure procedures), as well as interpersonal conflicts in the workplace (e.g. disrespectful and discriminatory comments as well as conflicts arising from colleagues' misunderstanding of limited knowledge as limited motivation).

Given the described difficulties and their possible consequences for patient safety, physician well-being and job retention, it will become more important in the future to implement comprehensive support structures to improve professional integration of migrant physicians. These support structures should be targeted to the needs of migrant physicians. In this regard, it is interesting that while migrant physicians have shared what they experienced as challenges and barriers to practice in Germany, no study has yet investigated what kind of support they actually desire and need. We, therefore, conducted an interview study with migrant physicians working in German hospitals to describe what kind of support they would consider helpful for foreign-trained doctors who plan to or are beginning to practice in German hospitals. The results can contribute to the development of concrete support measures for migrant physicians.

15.2 Methods

The results presented here are part of a larger research project investigating the experiences and expectations of migrant physicians working in German hospitals. Some of the results describing problematic experiences in medical practice have already been published (Klingler & Marckmann 2016). The description of methods draws on this earlier publication.

15.2.1 Study design

We chose a qualitative, explorative research design, as neither the experiences of migrant physicians in Germany nor their perspectives on support needs had been described at the time of study implementation. 'Migrant doctors' were defined as physicians born and trained outside of Germany who are now working in the German health care context. We conducted semi-structured interviews based on an interview guide, which was constructed in accordance with Helfferich (2009). The interview guide contained questions about (problematic) experiences in and with the German health care system, support received from various stakeholders, as well as support they would have liked to have received. The interview guide was discussed with experienced researchers and was pilot tested.

15.2.2 Sampling and recruitment

To capture a broad spectrum of perspectives, a maximum variation sampling strategy was chosen (Patton 2001). We identified the source country (where the physician was born and trained) and specialty as relevant characteristics that might likely influence the perspectives and experiences of participants.[2] Doctors from the source countries most represented among migrant physicians in Germany were included. However, no data on country of birth and training of physicians are available in Germany. We therefore used data on nationality as the closest estimate. At the time of data collection, Russia, Greece, Poland and Romania were the most important source countries. Austria, being among the greatest source countries, was excluded, as we assumed that – due to linguistic, cultural, and organizational proximity – Austrian-trained physicians would have had very similar experiences to German-trained doctors and thus no need for special support structures. Additionally, we wanted to include a non-European source country. At the time of data collection, the largest group of non-European doctors was Iranian doctors, whom we included. We constructed a sample plan in accordance with Schreier (2012). However, we had to adapt the sample plan and include physicians from other non-European countries, as it proved difficult to find Iranian participants. Regarding medical specialty, the two largest specialties – internal medicine and surgery – as well as psychiatry were included for sample construction. Four State Chambers of Physicians approached potential participants on our behalf via a written request sent out by mail. In addition, snowball sampling was used. Participants were asked to approach potential further candidates after the interview. Five participants were recruited via this strategy.

15.2.3 Data collection and sample

Face-to-face interviews were conducted by CK (a female researcher with experience in qualitative research and no prior relation to the participants). The setting was chosen by the participants (eight in hospital ward; eight in public spaces, like restaurants; and four at home). Interviews were conducted in German and lasted between 20 and 80 minutes (mean 54 minutes). All interviews took place between April 2013 and January 2014. A professional transcription service (audiotranskription.de) transcribed the recorded interviews using the simplified rules of Dresing and Pehl (2015). Transcriptions were controlled and anonymized by CK.

In total, 20 interviews were conducted. Of those 20 participants, six were born and trained in Romania, five in Poland, four in the Russian Federation, two in Greece, one in Iran, one in Libya and one in Syria. The participants worked or had worked in internal medicine ($n = 9$), psychiatry ($n = 7$) and surgery ($n = 4$). Some of the participants had already been in Germany for more than ten years ($n = 7$), and others had just started to practice a few months ago ($n = 3$). For a full overview of the sample, see Table 15.1.

Table 15.1 Description of the sample

	Internal medicine	*Psychiatry*	*Surgery*
Country of birth and training/specialty			
Romania	3	2	1
Poland	2	2	1
Russian Fed.	2	1	1
Greece	1	1	0
Libya	1	0	0
Iran	0	1	0
Syria	0	0	1
Gender			
Female	12		
Male	8		
Years practiced in Germany (at time of interview)			
>10 years	7		
5–10 years	7		
1–5 years	3		
<1 year	3		

Note: The table shows absolute numbers ($n = 20$)

15.2.4 Data analysis

CK analysed the data using qualitative content analysis adapted from Schreier (2012). The coding frame presenting the various wishes for support was developed inductively from the data. The construction of a preliminary coding frame was based on the analysis of ten interviews. Interviews were first coded independently, and codes were then compared across interviews to construct a preliminary coding frame (this strategy is called progressively summarizing). The remaining interviews were coded using the strategy of subsumption (Schreier 2012). Passages of the interviews discussing support wishes were compared against the coding frame, and new codes were added where necessary, that is, where the preliminary coding frame could not capture interview material. Relevant passages were translated into English for this article by CK.

15.2.5 Research ethics

The research ethics committee of the Medical Faculty of the Ludwig-Maximilians-Universität München (LMU Munich) approved the study conditional on anonymization of the data. No full review was required. Anonymization is a strategy to protect participants from potential harm (e.g. stigmatization), which might occur if published interview passages can be associated with them. When anonymizing the data, we had to ask ourselves to what degree interview data should be anonymized (only names, cities or even country of birth and training) (Saunders,

Kitzinger & Kitzinger 2014). In accordance with some participants' wishes, we anonymized quite extensively, including country of birth and training. Passages, which might indirectly reveal country of birth and training but could not be deleted without losing important context information for analysis, were not used in this publication. CK fully informed study participants about the study goals, methods and data protection both orally and in writing. Participants were given time to ask questions. Then, they were asked to sign an informed consent form.

15.3 Results

Participants perceived several support strategies as helpful in overcoming various difficulties[3] that they experienced when starting medical practice in Germany (see Table 15.2 for a full overview). In the following, we do not provide a full overview of difficulties experienced, which is provided in a separate paper (Klingler & Marckmann 2016), but we do mention difficulties for which management strategies were proposed as necessary background information.

15.3.1 Strategies addressing the licensure process

Participants found the licensure process to be particularly cumbersome because it was difficult to access relevant information and took a lot of time. They thought that it would have been extremely helpful if someone had provided them with condensed information on where to apply and what paperwork is needed to become a licensed physician in Germany.

> People need help with where one should do what. You need to register here. You need those certificates. One needs a little support if there are no recruitment agencies doing it for you.
>
> (Physician 8)

Participants furthermore wondered whether it would be possible for the future employer to coordinate the process, as it is easier for the hospital than for the migrant physician to navigate the (well-known) system and communicate (in German) with relevant agencies:

> Well, you can do it maybe, but it is difficult, so to say. It takes quite some time and those documents, if nobody supports you. [...] These bureaucratic and legal things, it is of course better if the hospital handles them. That would always be better.
>
> (Physician 1)

15.3.2 Strategies addressing limited setting-specific competencies

Participants also shared that they were struggling because they had to acquire setting-specific competencies needed for managing patient care in Germany. In this regard, they referred to verbal and written language, understanding organizational aspects of the German health care system and the specific hospital environment as well as knowledge about the dominant cultural paradigm, and certain clinical competencies that they had not needed in the system in which they were trained (e.g. taking blood). The participants suggested various strategies that would help them in acquiring relevant competencies.

Many participants suggested that a period of work-shadowing before starting to work would be particularly helpful in getting to know the system and practicing relevant skills without being fully responsible for the patient.

> Maybe I should have taken the time just for one to three months to observe and not from the start take on all the responsibility of this work. It was way too early in my perspective with regards to language. I think one needs around three months to settle into a system, not just professionally but also socially and as a human being.
>
> (Physician 3)

Participants suggested different time frames as necessary, at a minimum, to spend work-shadowing, with one person suggesting more than a year.[4] Additionally, participants suggested that financial support of some kind (e.g. scholarships or loan schemes) would be necessary to allow physicians to sustain themselves and possibly their families during these times of generally unpaid internships. One physician who was work-shadowing in a clinic that offered him free meals and housing during that time expressed a desire for some additional pocket money. He argued that it would have provided him with the opportunity to socialize and become part of the community:

> I think, if someone does an internship working as physician, it is good if he earns some money, for example pocket money, not too much, because it helps with knowing and getting to know the culture, with having a friend, with improving the language. If one sits in a café, for example, you can meet new people and that helps a lot.
>
> (Physician 17)

Most participants, furthermore, agreed that language courses offered before clinical practice are of high importance as a precondition for safe practice but also because there is no time to learn the German language once one starts working full-time:

> That is too late. When one joins a hospital, as junior doctor or relies on getting a job position, a language course is inappropriate. [...] Either one has already done one before or not. Well, language classes, that is just not happening. There is just no time.
>
> (Physician 16)

Participants also pointed out the importance of language courses that are targeted to their particular needs, such as covering the vocabulary required in a clinical context. Some participants took language classes without a specific focus on medical jargon and were disappointed with how little the classes prepared them for clinical work. Participants also pointed out that language classes should be offered in more places because there were often no nearby opportunities for learning. Others argued that there should also be scholarships or loan schemes to finance language classes and the daily life of physicians who generally had no opportunity to generate income while preparing for licensure.

Interestingly, a few participants also considered an exam that tested preparedness for practicing in Germany as helpful and found that it reassured them that they were ready to enter medical practice:

> But that one has to take the equivalency exam,[5] really, that was not bad. [...] I mean, it does not have to be a hard exam, but that one checks whether the man or the woman can cope in the medical field that should be the case.
>
> (Physician 10)

The preceding strategies would have to be offered before the physicians begin to practice as full members of the care team. Other strategies were proposed for the time after having started to practice as a licensed physician. Mentoring was mentioned as a potentially very helpful measure. Ideally, mentors should be from the same background (in terms of the system they were trained in) and be able to give explanations in the mother tongue to ensure understanding at the beginning. Some participants emphasized the importance of having mentors who are patient and who do not perceive mentoring as a burden. In cases where mentoring was assigned as an unwelcome task, participants felt unable to approach their mentors and ask questions or were uncomfortable doing so:

> For me, it would have been important to just have someone to go to, like a mentor, or, I don't know, someone who would really be there for me, really and honestly helpful for me. Not only because the superiors have assigned him, have told him you need to, you should.
>
> (Physician 9)

Furthermore, many participants expressed the importance of an induction phase for an adequate length of time with increasing responsibility and decreasing supervision over time.

> Ideally, we would just start working, when we start, we do not have immediately, we can just observe. Just go to work, try to do your job and if there are problems, ask, ask, ask. But without all the pressure and the expectations: If you have to immediately, why have you only written one referral letter and not six. Just so we can learn in peace.
>
> (Physician 2)

Many had to take on full responsibility for a whole ward without having been given any time to get to know the system or get accustomed to practicing in the German language. Such situations have been experienced as overwhelming.

Some participants proposed further strategies. One participant said that it would have been helpful if certain routine processes were explained in writing. In this way, superiors can ensure that relevant information is provided to the physician. Furthermore, one can reread relevant information and does not have to process everything all at once.

> And there are just so many things which nobody, you have to just write it down somewhere somehow because it happens all the time. And you cannot explain everything at once and tell someone who is new: You need to do this, you are not allowed to do that.
>
> (Physician 13)

One could, for example, imagine a booklet giving an overview of the most important rules and routines. Another participant pointed out that a training course introducing the electronic system used for patient management – which often differs even between hospitals in Germany – would have been quite helpful. Another participant imagined that using interpreters at the beginning to bridge communication difficulties would be helpful but argued that it would be difficult to implement and possibly not financially viable.

15.3.3 Strategies addressing interactions within the care team

Participants also said that interactions with various members of the care team were sometimes problematic, as they were faced with an unwillingness to help, unfriendliness and lack of patience. Some believed that co-workers were expecting them to hit the ground running and were accordingly unnerved that migrant physicians needed time to become accustomed to various aspects of the German health care system in general and the organizational specificities of the individual hospital. The participants thought that it would be helpful to educate colleagues about difficulties associated with working in an unknown system to avoid conflicts arising from wrong expectations:

> Nursing staff, other co-workers that they are prepared that now foreign physicians are coming. They are physicians, but there are problems with the language. That they learn to cope with this and not because they have such high expectations, you know, these were always there, I always experienced these [high expectations].
>
> (Physician 18)

Furthermore, participants sometimes felt socially isolated and not really accepted by the care team. One participant told us enthusiastically about various social activities that had acquired the status of rituals in the hospital where he first worked. He had experienced these activities as highly beneficial in helping new colleagues to become part of the care team – also on a social level. For example, during Christmas time, new colleagues were asked to prepare and serve a specific type of burnt punch (Feuerzangenbowle) for the whole team:

> All physicians and psychologists that started that year, we are talking 2004, we all had to – at no costs to ourselves – but we had to, we were obligated to prepare burnt punch for all physicians and psychologists. [...] Really cool integration, really. Like all the new ones, you know, all are going shopping together. And those cone-shaped sugars, we bring to the pharmacists because she bathes them for a week in alcohol just so that it all burns well later and yes like that. She provided us with the recipe and then we had to do the shopping. [...] And at the end we were all handed certificates that we had made excellent burnt punch and we are now allowed to work in the hospital.
>
> (Physician 15)

The participant felt that this activity helped immensely with truly becoming a team and stated team-building measures like this would also be helpful in other settings.

15.3.4 Strategies addressing further practical difficulties

Participants also repeatedly mentioned that support with non-work-related aspects of daily living would be highly desirable. First of all, some participants had problems with finding accommodation – sometimes because landlords were sceptical of their limited language abilities or displayed xenophobic attitudes. Participants would have appreciated if hospitals either supported them in flat-hunting (e.g. with support letters or financial guarantees) or offered accommodation. The participant who provided the following quote recounted that she was not successful in finding a flat until her colleague offered her his apartment, which he had been renting out:

> Otherwise I would not have found a flat. I am curious, we have a new Turkish colleague now who is searching a flat. I am curious whether he can find one alone. Maybe if the hospital would vouch for you at the beginning maybe it would be faster.
>
> (Physician 12)

Other practical difficulties complicate daily living, and physicians would have appreciated support in the form of a person explaining administrative peculiarities to them. Examples of such difficulties include opening a bank account or getting a cell phone.

> One needs a bank account and there should be a person that says: Wait, you need your passport, this certificate, this certificate, this certificate. Now we chose a bank. This, this, this. Now we go there together, I help you.

> Because very often the people just do not understand what they are supposed to fill out, what they are supposed to sign. You would need a person who accompanies you and that would be helpful.
>
> (Physician 8)

15.3.5 No specific support measures for migrant physicians requested

Interestingly, some participants found it difficult to formulate wishes for specific support structures. One participant pointed out that it is difficult to make generalizing statements because migrant physicians are all different, have different preferences and experiences and therefore need different kinds and levels of support. He argued that for physicians working in Germany only for a short period to earn money, for example, measures to facilitate social integration in the care team will be of less interest:

> I don't know. Really this, I think, it is simply – there is just the question of everybody having different experiences, attitudes of what one wants to do. I also know four physicians who came here [...] They save all their money for some kind of goal and they move on. I could not do this somehow, you know? Therefore, for me a little bit of integration is something positive.
>
> (Physician 15)

One participant argued that support after having started clinical practice is altogether unnecessary or even unhelpful – although it should be pointed out that she thought work-shadowing as preparation for clinical practice was highly desirable. She argued, on the one hand, that it is the responsibility of the physician to acquire relevant knowledge and that waiting for others to help would prove a destructive attitude. Furthermore, she argued that the differential treatment of migrant physicians could complicate the relationships within, instead of further integrating these physicians into, the care team:

> And I think if a hospital, it does not matter which one, says to this person 'You have those duties and those rights' and the other one is treated a little differently that it will just not all grow together somehow. I was from the start part of the team. And if the hospital does something especially for foreigners, it will just not work out, I think.
>
> (Physician 7)

15.4 Discussion

This is the first study to describe what measures migrant physicians would consider helpful in overcoming various integration difficulties. Although this is the first study conducted in the German context, some studies have posed similar questions to physicians migrating to other countries (Curran et al. 2008;

Table 15.2 Desired support strategies for migrant physicians

Before starting clinical practice	
Strategies addressing bureaucratic barriers in the licensure process	Provide information on where to apply and what paperwork is needed Future employers should organize licensure process
Strategies addressing limited setting-specific knowledge	Work-shadowing Offering language courses Subjecting migrant physicians to an exam to check preparedness for practicing in Germany
Upon starting clinical practice	
Strategies addressing limited setting-specific knowledge	Mentoring schemes Structured induction phase of adequate lengths Involving interpreters Devising a booklet containing the most important information about organization of hospital/ health care system Offering a training course in the computer system used within hospital
Strategies addressing interaction within the care team	Educate co-workers with regards to potential difficulties migrant physicians might experience during transition Joint social activities should be organized
Strategies addressing further practical difficulties	Hospital should support flat-hunting or offer accommodation upon arrival Hospital should offer administrative help with difficulties of daily living
No specific support measures requested	
Support needs depend on personal preferences and experience, and therefore, no generalizing statement possible	
No support requested	It is the responsibility of the migrant physicians to ensure they acquire the necessary competencies Special treatment is destructive to becoming a trusted member of the care team

Hawken 2005; McGrath, Henderson & Phillips 2009). Many measures were also identified as helpful in those studies, corroborating our findings, for example, language courses, work-shadowing or mentoring. Some strategies had not been identified by those studies, for example, the proposal to have employers organize the licensure process and support flat-hunting, introducing exams for all migrant physicians to check professional competencies, or the importance of financial support allowing sustenance of a family during periods of work shadowing or preparatory courses. At the same time, participants in these studies identified strategies aimed at fostering integration that had not been formulated by the participants of this study. In a study in the Australian context, participants saw a need to reduce difficulties with passing the licensure examination (McGrath, Henderson & Phillips 2009). This result demonstrates that a balance might have to be struck in terms of the difficulty of these exams, as the licensure exam can be experienced as helpful, by letting physicians know where they stand with regards to necessary competencies, but it can also become an insurmountable barrier. Support groups where migrant physicians could share their experiences and support each other were also perceived as helpful in another study (McGrath, Henderson & Phillips 2009). Additionally, it was seen as highly desirable to support the whole family in settling in, for example, by helping spouses to find jobs and organizing tours of the area to foster community links (Curran et al. 2008; McGrath, Henderson & Phillips 2009). Furthermore, participants found that preparatory courses could address more than language, for example, cultural issues, organization of the system or introduction to the specific local population (Curran et al. 2008; Hawken 2005). Moreover, some participants wanted to relax rules on where and when a migrant physician can practise – as in these contexts, a precondition for licensure is an agreement to practice for a certain amount of time in an underserved region (McGrath, Henderson & Phillips 2009). Some of those strategies – like the last one presented – are only relevant in specific health care systems because they target a rule that does not exist in Germany. However, some strategies, such as support groups, might also prove effective in easing the transition into the German health care system.

While we think knowing about the needs and support wishes of migrant physicians is important, we want to point out that just because something is desired by a certain group does not necessarily imply it should be implemented. The proposed strategies should be seen as a starting point for further investigations and deliberations. There are two questions that have to be answered when thinking about how the institutions and people constituting the German health care system should support the integration of migrant physicians. First, it needs to be shown that the proposed strategies are truly effective in easing the transition to the 'new' system. In a systematic review of educational interventions for migrant physicians, Lineberry et al. (2015) showed that the evaluation of many of the approaches developed and described in the literature is insufficient to non-existent. Attempts at proving effectiveness should accordingly be strengthened.

In addition, a normative question is raised: What responsibility do the various actors within the health care system have with regard to enabling integration? One participant displayed a clear attitude towards this question: he thought that the receiving society has no responsibility but that the responsibility for managing the transition and acquiring relevant knowledge rests solely with the migrant physicians. This does not seem plausible to us, as the health care system benefits greatly from foreign-trained physicians. Following other authors, we think that integration should be a two-way process, where both the receiving society and the migrant must make an effort (Raghuram 2007). In the context of medical migration, the receiving health care system and the migrant physician will have to work together – for example, the one offering courses and the other making the best of it – to manage challenges effectively. However, from a normative perspective, it is unclear how much support the receiving society owes to the migrant physicians and vice versa. Because this is not the place to provide a full normative argument, we want to constrain ourselves to raising a few pragmatic points: in many cases, it will simply be in the self-interest of receiving health care systems to provide extensive and structured support measures. Where physicians are left alone to acquire relevant knowledge and skills, even the most diligent and responsible physicians will need time to learn and without adequate guidance will learn via trial-and-error methods. This approach will be to the detriment of patient safety and cannot be in the interest of the German health care system. Obviously, one option would be to increase licensure requirements, such that migrant physicians must acquire all relevant knowledge on their own before they enter medical practice.[6] However, this approach will be a waste of human resources, especially when no financial support that would allow physicians to sustain families while preparing for exams is offered. It is questionable whether Germany can afford such 'brain waste' – particularly in times of physician shortages.

In Germany, so far, no structured approach to integrating migrant physicians has been implemented. In two interview studies with stakeholders in hospitals, participants have described support measures for migrant physicians that were implemented in the respective clinics (Klein 2016; Kovacheva & Grewe 2015). Support was provided in acquiring setting-specific competencies (e.g. in-house German classes or mentoring) and with managing practical issues (e.g. flat-hunting or opening a bank account). Both studies, however, showed that often no specific support was offered, and that 'migrants are not perceived as a special target group for personnel policies' (Kovacheva & Grewe 2015, p. 19). Another survey study conducted in the state of Bavaria also showed that only few (25%) hospitals have implemented support structures understood as training opportunities to acquire language and further setting-specific competencies (Schmidt & Gresser 2014). One study argued that hospitals in rural areas, especially, provide support measures in an attempt to retain physicians in a presumably less attractive environment, but support is more rarely offered by institutions in urban, presumably more attractive, areas (Klein 2016). In addition to hospital-based support structures, various private institutes[7] offer training that prepares migrant physicians for clinical practice, often including teaching of the language and medical knowledge, helping with job applications and the organization of internships. These initiatives are often focused on migrants from non-European countries who must take an exam to prove equivalency of their education. Such training, unfortunately, is not offered on a large scale (Ognyanova et al. 2014). Although support is still limited, political actors are slowly realizing the importance of adequate integration of medical personnel into the German health care system. The German Medical Assembly of 2017, for example, formulated clear political demands for more educational opportunities for migrant physicians and also demanded from policymakers a change in licensure procedures (including making preparation for licensure exams financially viable) (Deutscher Ärztetag 2017).

A national goal should be to implement structured and nationwide support for migrant physicians, although it is not yet clear how exactly it should be designed and who should implement it. The measures presented above should be a starting point for further discussion; thereby, policymakers should also take into consideration the comments from participants that had a more sceptical outlook on targeted support measures for migrant physicians. Their comments point out ways that support measures – even if meant well – can go wrong: (a) If they do not take into account the variance in expertise and experience of migrant physicians and instead offer a one-size-fits-all approach. These approaches might end up being perceived as frustrating by the majority of concerned physicians and prove less effective. (b) Where support is not well communicated to receiving care teams or support is only offered to migrant physicians – while other junior doctors or ancillary care personnel are left to themselves in dealing with the various issues they face – implemented measures will prove destructive to team cohesion. It could well be perceived as preferential treatment and incite anger and frustration. Other groups that have been put under intensified pressure by the increasing economization of the health care system like nurses (Braun, Klinke & Müller 2010) should also be the subject of further research and support measures. Indeed, all junior doctors should be considered a group in need of additional support (Eidgenössische Technische Hochschule Zürich et al. 2011; Reiß et al. 2011). As these doctors also have to learn to navigate an unfamiliar system, the problems they struggle with will most likely not be different in kind to those migrant physicians face but only different in degree.

Lastly, one additional aspect that shines through these more critical comments will warrant further attention: by pointing out that migrant physicians are first co-workers with equal rights and equal duties, one participant refused the discourse driving this research, which paints migrants as first vulnerable and in need of support. The participant apparently felt that this discourse restrained her possibilities for meeting on an equal footing. It is an open question whether research that focuses on problems and vulnerabilities instead of benefits and resources of migrants – as well intentioned as it may be – impairs rather than improves the position of this group within the receiving society. Similar arguments will apply to studies focusing on the vulnerabilities of migrant patients. Further research on this question, especially from research ethicists, would be highly desirable.

15.4.1 Limitations

Due to the qualitative design of the study, we do not know whether what has been perceived as helpful by participants of our study will similarly be perceived by the majority of physicians. Further quantitative studies will be necessary to establish the generalizability of our findings. Furthermore, just because something is perceived as helpful, it is not necessarily effective in overcoming certain difficulties or more effective than other strategies. This point should be emphasized given the fact that participants often just imagined that certain strategies would have been helpful (sometimes because of reports from friends and family) but had not been offered that kind of support. This study can therefore only be a starting point for further evaluative research. Another limitation might have been that interviews were conducted in German, which might have led to misunderstanding. However, all but one participant had passed the language test required for licensure and were able to sufficiently express themselves in German; therefore, this risk should be considered marginal. Further interviews might have revealed additional, potentially effective support measures. As our sampling strategy was limited to specific specialties, different or additional support might have been found desirable in other settings (e.g. rehabilitative medicine).

15.5 Conclusion

This is the first study to investigate what measures are perceived as helpful by migrant physicians in overcoming the challenges of operating in an unfamiliar health care system. Proposed strategies target various aspects, like difficulties with licensure procedures, setting-specific competencies, interpersonal interactions and practical problems. Some physicians also expressed their reluctance to formulate support wishes and their reasons were presented alongside proposed measures. As, thus far, the support offered by institutions in the health care system is scarce, proposed strategies can be insightful for policymakers hoping to improve the integration of migrant physicians for the sake of patient safety, physician well-being and retention. However, policymakers should also take into consideration the critical comments, which warn about the effects of a focus on problems and support instead of on the benefits and resources of migrant physicians. As this study cannot establish effectiveness, but just desirability, from the perspective of participants, the findings should trigger not only further evaluative research but also normative investigations regarding the distribution of responsibility for efforts at integration. It would furthermore be highly desirable to investigate how research in the migration field should be framed, given its possible impact on the position of migrant physicians and patients in society.

Acknowledgements

Above all, the authors want to thank the study participants for devoting their time and sharing their sometimes very personal stories. We also wish to thank four Physician Chambers (Landesärztekammern Westfalen-Lippe, Sachsen–Anhalt, Rheinland-Pfalz und Bayern) for their help in recruiting the participants. Feedback from various researchers from different institutions of the Ludwig-Maximilians-Universität München (LMU Munich) has greatly improved the quality of this study. We would also like to thank the German Academic Scholarship Foundation (Studienstiftung des deutschen Volkes) and the Friedrich-Baur-Stiftung for their financial support of this project.

Notes

1 Germany does not collect data on physicians' country of birth or country of training but only on nationality. However, following the most recent report of the Organisation for Economic Cooperation and Development, we use these data as the closest estimate.
2 Obviously, there are further factors influencing experiences of migrant physicians (e.g. age). However, for pragmatic reasons, we had to limit the factors we varied to two.
3 Not for all difficulties experienced, however, could adequate support strategies be identified by participants.
4 However, when discussing the usefulness of work-shadowing, the participant referred to the time spent working as part of her 'Anpassungszeit'. Until the early 2000s, migrant physicians could be required to spend a certain time working unpaid in hospitals as a condition for licensure (this period was called 'Anpassungszeit'). During this time, doctors had more responsibilities than interns, but less than a fully licensed junior doctor.
5 Qualifications of physicians who have studied medicine in a country outside the European Union are subjected to formal equivalency testing. If the training is not considered equivalent in content, the physician needs to undergo an additional exam (generally the Kenntnisprüfung) as a precondition for licensure. Qualifications obtained within the European Union are automatically recognized, and licensure can be obtained without additional testing (with few exceptions).
6 This approach is chosen in the United States (Rabben 2013), but not in Germany, at least not for migrants from other countries of the European Union. As already mentioned above, their degrees are automatically recognized.
7 The physician advocacy group 'Marburger Bund' provides an overview of these institutions on their website: www.marburger-bund.de/mitgliederservice/auslaendische-aerztinnen-und-aerzte/faq-auslaendische-aerzte#frage16 (last accessed September 23, 2017).

References

Deutscher Ärztetag. 2017, *Beschlussprotokoll des 120. Deutschen Ärztetages vom 23. bis 26.05.2017 in Freiburg*, Bundesärztekammer, viewed 4 July 2018, www.bundesaerztekammer.de/fileadmin/user_upload/downloads/pdf-Ordner/120.DAET/120DaetBeschlussProt_2017-05-26.pdf.

Blum, K., & Löffert, S. 2010, *Ärztemangel im Krankenhaus: Ausmaß, Ursachen, Gegenmaßnahmen*, Deutsches Krankenhaus Institut e.V., Düsseldorf.

Braun, B., Klinke, S., & Müller, R. 2010, 'Auswirkungen des DRG-Systems auf die Arbeitssituation im Pflegebereich von Akutkrankenhäusern', *Pflege & Gesellschaft*, vol. 15, no. 1, pp. 5–77.

Bundesärztekammer. 2017, *Ärztestatistik 2016*, viewed 3 July 2017, www.bundesaerztekammer.de/ueber-uns/aerztestatistik/aerztestatistik-2016/.

Curran, V., Hollett, A., Hann, S., & Bradbury, C. 2008, 'A qualitative study of the international medical graduate and the orientation process', *Canadian Journal of Rural Medicine*, vol. 13, no. 4, pp. 163–169.

Dresing, T., & Pehl, T. 2015, *Praxisbuch Interview. Transkription & Analyse. Anleitungen und Regelsysteme für qualitativ Forschende*, audiotranskription.de, Marburg, viewed 3 July 2017, www.audiotranskription.de/audiotranskription/upload/Praxisbuch%206.%20Auflage_web.pdf.

Eidgenössische Technische Hochschule Zürich, Institute for Environmental Decisions, Consumer Behavior, Bundesärztekammer. 2011, *Ergebnisse der Evaluation der Weiterbildung, 2. Befragungsrunde 2011, Bundesrapport*, Bundesärztekammer, viewed 23 September 2017, www.evaluation-weiterbildung.de/data/Bundesrapport2011.pdf.

Fellmer, S. 2008, *Germany restricted the freedom of movement for polish citizens – but does it matter?* eumap.org – monitoring human rights and the rule of law in Europe, viewed 3 July 2017, www.opensocietyfoundations.org/sites/default/files/fellmer_0.pdf.

Hall, P., Keely, E., Dojeiji, S., Byszewski, A., & Marks, M. 2004, 'Communication skills, cultural challenges and individual support: challenges of international medical graduates in a Canadian healthcare environment', *Medical Teacher*, vol. 26, no. 2, pp. 120–125.

Hawken, S. 2005, 'Overseas-trained doctors' evaluation of a New Zealand course in professional development', *The New Zealand Medical Journal*, vol. 118, no. 1219, pp. 40–46.

Helfferich, C. 2009, *Die Qualität qualitativer Daten: Manual zur Durchführung qualitativer Interviews*, VS Verlag, Wiesbaden.

Hoesch, K. 2009, *Was bewegt Mediziner? Die Migration von Ärzten und Pflegepersonal nach Deutschland und Großbritannien*, LIT Verlag, Münster.

Jansen, E., Hänel, P., & Klingler C. 2018, 'Rehabilitation-specific challenges and advantages in the integration of migrant physicians in Germany: a multiperspective qualitative interview study in rehabilitative settings', *Public Health*, vol. 160, pp. 1–9.

Jansen, E., Schnepf, T., & Hänel, P. 2015, 'Divergierende berufliche Sozialisation von migrierten Ärzten', *Public Health Forum*, vol. 23, no. 2, pp. 116–118.

Klein, J. 2016, *Transferring professional knowledge and skills: the case of Central and Eastern European migrant physicians in German hospitals*, Budrich UniPress, Opladen.

Klingler, C., Ismail, F., Marckmann, G., & Kuehlmeyer, K. 2018, 'Medical professionalism of foreign-born and foreign-trained physicians under close scrutiny: a qualitative study with stakeholders in Germany', *PLoS One*, vol. 13, no. 2, p. e0193010.

Klingler, C., & Marckmann, G. 2016, 'Difficulties experienced by migrant physicians working in German hospitals: a qualitative interview study', *Human Resources for Health*, vol. 14, no. 1, p. 47.

Kopetsch, T. 2010, *Dem deutschen Gesundheitswesen gehen die Ärzte aus! Studie zur Altersstruktur- und Arztzahlentwicklung*, Bundesärztekammer und Kassenärztliche Bundesvereinigung, Berlin.

Kovacheva, V., & Grewe, M. 2015, *Workplace integration of migrant health workers in Germany: qualitative findings on experiences in two Hamburg hospitals*, viewed 4 July 2017, http://workint.fieri.it/wp-content/uploads/2014/09/National-Research-Report-Germany_EDITED-1.pdf.

Lineberry, M., Osta, A., Barnes, M., Tas, V., Atchon, K., & Schwartz, A. 2015, 'Educational interventions for international medical graduates: a review and agenda', *Medical Education*, vol. 49, no. 9, pp. 863–879.

McGrath, P., Henderson, D., & Phillips, E. 2009, 'Integration into the Australian health care system: insights from international medical graduates', *Australian Family Physician*, vol. 38, no. 10, pp. 844–848.

Michalski, K., Farhan, N., Motschall, E., Vach, W., & Boeker, M. 2017, 'Dealing with foreign cultural paradigms: a systematic review on intercultural challenges of international medical graduates', *PLoS One*, vol. 12, no. 7, p. e0181330.

OECD. 2015, *International migration outlook 2015*, OECD Publishing, OECDiLibrary, Paris, viewed 4 July 2017, doi: 10.1787/migr_outlook-2015-en.

Ognyanova, D., & Busse, R. 2011, 'A destination and a source: Germany manages regional health workforce disparities with foreign medical doctors', in M. Wismar, C.B. Maier, I.A. Glinos, G. Dussault & J. Figueras (eds.), *Health professional mobility and health systems: evidence from 17 European countries*, World Health Organization, Geneva, pp. 211–242.

Ognyanova, D., Young, R., Maier, C.B., & Busse, R. 2014, 'Why do health professionals leave Germany and what attracts foreigners? A qualitative study', in J. Buchan, M. Wismar, I.A. Glinos & J. Bremner (eds.), *Health professional mobility in a changing Europe: new dynamics, mobile individuals and diverse responses*, World Health Organization, Geneva, pp. 203–232.

Patton, M.Q. 2001, 'Purposeful sampling', in *Qualitative research and evaluation methods*, Sage, Thousand Oaks, CA, pp. 230–247.

Pilotto, L.S., Duncan, G.F., & Anderson-Wurf, J. 2007, 'Issues for clinicians training international medical graduates: a systematic review', *The Medical Journal of Australia*, vol. 187, no. 4, pp. 225–228.

Rabben, L. 2013, *Credential recognition in the United States for foreign professionals*, Migration Policy Institute, viewed 23 September 2017, www.migrationpolicy.org/sites/default/files/publications/UScredentialrecognition.pdf.

Raghuram, P. 2007, 'Interrogating the language of integration: the case of internationally recruited nurses', *Journal of Clinical Nursing*, vol. 16, no. 12, pp. 2246–2251.

Reiß, L., Reiß, S., Tinneberg, H.R., & Hackethal, A. 2011, 'Zur Zufriedenheit in der gynäkologischen Facharztausbildung. Evaluation durch Assistenten und Ausbildungsleiter', *Der Gynäkologe*, vol. 44, no. 8, pp. 647–652.

Saunders, B., Kitzinger, J., & Kitzinger, C. 2015, 'Anonymising interview data: challenges and compromise in practice', *Qualitative Research*, vol. 15, no. 5, pp. 616–632.

Schmidt, S., & Gresser, U. 2014, 'Entwicklung und Konsequenzen des Ärztemangels in Bayern', *Versicherungsmedizin*, vol. 66, no. 1, pp. 25–29.

Schreier, M. 2012, *Qualitative content analysis in practice*, Sage, London.

16 Migrants, pluralism and end-of-life decision-making for children with life-limiting illness

Perspectives on the case of Josip

Katja Kuehlmeyer and Monika Führer

16.1 Introduction

Decision-making about medical treatment can be difficult and emotionally challenging. It can be particularly difficult to make decisions about life-sustaining treatment when vulnerable patients' lives and well-being are at stake. Children with very severe life-threatening and life-limiting illnesses are especially vulnerable patients and most families struggle when they need to cope with a child's severe illness. The challenges then increase if the family is in a foreign environment and must navigate through a foreign health care system in a foreign language. Patients and their families might not be familiar with the procedures and measures that are suggested by the medical staff. Communication is a prerequisite for coming to a shared understanding of an illness and giving patients and/or their parents or other family members the opportunity to participate successfully in shared treatment decisions about the right treatment approach. Communication can obviously be extremely difficult if the parties are unable to speak the same language. If language interpreters are not readily available, either due to structural deficits or in emergency situations, misunderstandings can easily occur. Even if communication can be successfully established, cultural differences might be present, which require culturally competent handling. Furthermore, shared decision-making and advance care planning can raise meta-ethical questions about whether all the participants – regardless of their cultural identity or background – should be guided by the same principles and norms and about who has the last say in the decision-making process when value conflicts are at the heart of an interpersonal conflict.

In this chapter, we highlight some of these challenges by outlining a case involving an infant with a life-limiting illness whose family had recently migrated from Croatia to Germany. This is an anonymized case, based upon real cases arising in the provision of Specialized Paediatric Palliative Home Care (SPPHC) in Munich, Germany.[1] SPPHC is provided by multi-professional teams, for the most part consisting of paediatricians, paediatric nurses and social workers trained in palliative care. These teams deliver home care with a medical focus that includes regular home visits and a visiting 24/7 on-call service. In Germany, access to SPPHC (and SPHC for adult patients) has become a legally granted right for patients who suffer from a "progressive life-limiting illness in an advanced stage that requires complex and extensive support", which was granted for minors in 2007 (Bayerisches Staatsministerium für Umwelt und Gesundheit 2009; Bender et al. 2017; Groh et al. 2013;).

In this chapter, we first provide a structured summary of the case of Josip, an infant with a pontocerebellar hypoplasia. Three independent commentaries follow the case description, which reflect particularly on its ethical, legal and social implications.[2] In his commentary, Ilhan Ilkilic argues that the child's best interest should be the focus of (ethically defensible) decision-making. However, he acknowledges the barriers that prevent effective communication about Josip's best interest in this case, emphasising the important influence of cultural values and moral diversity. He advocates a dialogue, which respects intercultural aspects and ensures that the different parties' values and ideals are accounted for. Ilkilic suspects that a clinical ethics consultation, involving a consultant with the necessary intercultural competence, could prove helpful to establishing this kind of constructive dialogue.

Richard Huxtable also refers to the ethical and legal significance of the child's best interest, and offers three general prescriptions, which he relates to Josip's case. First, he argues that clinicians should focus on the case before them, including both its general and particular features, which will mean recognising that these parents are not only migrants, but also individuals. Second, he suggests that health services should be attentive to, and have some method for navigating, pluralism, which – like Ilkilic – leads him to argue for some form of clinical ethics support. Third, and again like Ilkilic, Huxtable suggests that everyone involved in a case like this should ensure that there is effective communication. In his discussion of some of the ethical models underpinning clinical ethics support, Huxtable critically refers to the widely known 'principlist' framework, which encompasses the principles of beneficence, non-maleficence, respect for autonomy and justice.

In his commentary, Georg Marckmann offers a defence of this approach to clinical ethics consultation, which he applies to the case of Josip. Marckmann notes that principlism has a strong universalist tendency but is not universal in a strict sense. Rather, the approach can accommodate different cultural values and contexts, both in the interpretation of the principles and in seeking to balance these in a synthesis to arrive at an ethical decision. Marckmann recommends prioritizing the interpretations of the patient or his or her family, but also suggests that a principlist approach can help to resolve the question of which interpretations should prevail in contested cases. He closes by observing how Josip's case contains some lessons for the future, such as the need to develop a strategy for addressing cultural and linguistic differences, which can carefully balance the obligations owed towards young patients and their parents.

Following the commentaries, we describe how the situation was resolved by the SPPHC team.

16.2 Case narrative: Josip

Josip was 11 months old when he was referred to SPPHC by a local University Hospital. After discharge from the hospital, Josip lived with his family in a small flat in Munich. The family contacted doctors and nurses via phone whenever they required palliative medicine and care. The multi-professional team made home visits on a regular basis to assess the medical condition of the child, as well as the stability of his care environment.

16.2.1 Medical situation

Josip suffered from pontocerebellar hypoplasia (PCH), which is a rare autosomal recessively inherited neurodevelopmental and neurodegenerative disorder with a prenatal onset and characterized by progressive atrophy of the cerebellar hemispheres, the pontine structures and varying involvement of supratentorial regions of the brain causing severe motor and cognitive impairments. So far 11 different forms of PCH have been identified, with varying courses of the disease, with, in some cases, almost absent developmental progress and early lethality (Dijk et al. 2018).

From birth onwards, Josip was not able to swallow and, as a consequence, a percutaneous endoscopic gastrostomy (PEG) tube had been inserted. The illness was advancing, affecting his brain functions. Because he suffered from seizures, anticonvulsive therapy had been started in the hospital. Nasal and oral suction of secretion was necessary several times daily. His oxygen saturation was monitored and, if necessary, he received additional oxygen through a mask. He showed recurrent episodes of oxygen desaturation and bradycardia associated with airway obstruction or seizures. There is no curative treatment for this type of illness. The medical treatment was focused on symptom control, foremost to manage his seizures and his mucous congestion to reduce suffering. Amongst other medications, morphine was prescribed to mitigate his dyspnoea. The palliative care team took care of his medication, organized medical aids like a special mattress and established a professional nursing service and physiotherapy.

16.2.2 Family situation

Both of Josip's parents were born in Croatia. Josip's mother had migrated to Germany a year earlier, his father six months later. Josip's mother spoke German fairly well. His father was taking language classes but was largely unable to communicate without an interpreter. The child had two healthy siblings, aged three and four years, respectively. His mother was Josip's primary caregiver. She also took care of the family's household and the two healthy siblings. She later accepted a job as a hairdresser to improve the family's tense financial situation, as the father had difficulties finding a job because of his poor German language abilities. The professional nursing service was a prerequisite for Josip's mother to be able to work. Yet, Josip's father rejected the service, insisting that his wife should care for their children. Recurrent conflicts with the professional nurses were reported from both sides. There were no relatives available to offer support to the family.

The situation was proving excessively demanding on Josip's mother. One day she experienced heavy headaches and was admitted to hospital to be examined for suspected cerebral bleeding, which fortunately was found not to be case. During her hospital stay, the palliative home care team visited the family's home, where they realized that, in the absence of his wife, Josip's father was having difficulty coping with taking care of his severely ill child. Both parents agreed to admit Josip to a children's hospital to ensure he was receiving adequate care while the family could recover.

16.2.3 Decisions about emergency medical treatment

Josip's parents expressed different expectations regarding further treatment for their son. Josip's mother rejected the option of further hospital stays. She had understood and accepted that he could die in the near future and wanted him to die peacefully at home. Language barriers made the father's position difficult to assess. One day, a guest doctor who spoke Croatian was accompanying the care team on a home visit. On that occasion, Josip's father showed the care team PET-scans and said: 'They betrayed us in the hospital. They gave us scans of different children'. The guest doctor attempted to dispel this misconception, explaining that the scans show different layers of the same brain. On another occasion, Josip's father stated that he was expecting Josip to grow and learn how to walk and talk.

The palliative care team began conversations about advance care planning in relation to probable future emergency situations but interpreters were often not available to support the discussions. Josip's mother therefore translated for her husband. Although she emphasized that other doctors had already explained the diagnosis and prognosis to her husband, the care team was unsure about his level of understanding. The mother stated that neither of them wanted any further hospital stays nor any life-prolonging treatments – even in life-threatening situations.

One day, the family's landlord called the SHPPC-team. Neither Josip's mother nor the professional nurses were at home. Josip's father was alone with his child and the monitor was sounding an alarm, indicating a deterioration in Josip's respiration. His oxygen saturation and his heart rate had dropped rapidly. The landlord explained that Josip's skin looked pale and the boy was no longer moving. He could not say whether Josip was breathing. His eyes were closed.

16.3 Commentary 1: The ethical implications of interculturality in paediatric palliative medicine

Ilhan Ilkilic

16.3.1 Introduction

The case description showcases a decision-making conflict, or rather a conflict of interest, concerning the palliative care of an 11-month-old child. The main context of this case is that those involved cannot speak the same language and thus are unable to adequately communicate with one another without the help of an interpreter. Not only language barriers, but also cultural differences make organizing and proceeding with palliative care at the end of a child's life substantially more difficult. The main question is how to provide for the child's well-being and act in the child's best interest in an intercultural context given these circumstances. This complex process contains many ethically relevant topics and questions, which will be discussed in the course of this commentary.

16.3.2 Normative conditions

The medical treatment of a minor almost always includes a third party in the classic patient-doctor relationship, namely the parents of the ill child or adolescent. Given that a sick infant or child cannot proclaim their right of self-determination because they are not (yet) able to give informed consent, it is the parents or appointed proxies that end up making the treatment decisions. Hence in paediatrics, it was the child's best interest and the child's well-being, which became the ethical normative focus, rather than patient autonomy.

When evaluating whether a therapeutic strategy is in the patient's best interest, the *President's Commission for the Study of Ethical Problems in Medicine and Biomedical and Behavioral Research* (1983) recommends applying the following criteria: "the relief of suffering, the preservation or restoration of functioning, and the quality as well as the extent of life sustained" (President's Commission for the Study of Ethical Problems in Medicine and Biomedical and Behavioral Research 1983, p. 135). In its Convention on the Rights of the Child, the United Nations also declares that in every situation, which also includes being in a state of illness, the child's best interest has to be taken into consideration: "In all actions concerning children, [...] the best interests of the child shall be a primary consideration" (UN 1989, Art. 3, Abs. 1). It is internationally approved and accepted to take this ethical norm into consideration in the medical treatment of a child.

16.3.3 Interculturality in health care

Intercultural situations in health care involve encounters in which the individuals involved belong to and identify with different cultures. As a result, people with different, culturally defined concepts and values regarding medical care come together. However, it is not an intercultural doctor–patient relationship until both doctor and patient, and/or the patient's relatives, understand themselves as a member of another culture. This entails that interculturality in a doctor–patient relationship cannot be determined externally but has to be established within a given context.

Interculturality by itself cannot change the constitutional characteristics of the health care system. The reasons are clear: subjective systems and patterns of interpretation that have been influenced by culture can either strengthen or, circumstantially, weaken the asymmetry and valuation difference that is present in a doctor–patient relationship. Additionally, misunderstandings and misinterpretations can result from language and cultural barriers, which rarely occur in the intracultural doctor–patient relationships. It is also important to keep in mind that diverging moral values and their corresponding pluralism are considered a constitutive characteristic of modern society. This moral diversity plays an important role in the development of interculturality in pluralistic societies' health care systems. It even has greater normative meaning with regard to ethical conflicts in an intercultural context than language barriers and cultural practices. These phenomena are linked to the meta-ethical question of the universality of normative concepts and their implications, which include the patient's well-being and the patient's best interest. Thus, language barriers as well as moral diversity are starting to play an increasingly important role in determining the patient's best interest.

16.3.4 Interculturality in paediatrics

Although ethicists and lawyers around the world have come to a general consensus regarding the significance of a child's well-being, there is still controversy among experts concerning the criteria and definition of this ethical norm (Fleischmann 2016; Stuhlinger 2005). As an example, experts have criticized the absolute prioritization of medical facts as the deciding criteria concerning the child's best interest (Dörries 2003, pp. 122 ff.; Glannon 2005; Schulz-Baldes 2006). The focus on medical parameters permits objective criteria, but at the same time it is also redundant in that it omits important facts that furthermore pertain to the child's well-being. Rightly so, it is argued that psychological, emotional, social and cultural needs and their implementation need to be taken into consideration in the decision-making process (Dörries 2003, pp. 124 ff.).

Even if, from an ethical perspective, there are good reasons backing the consideration of comprehensive criteria that include cultural values, it is important to keep in mind that this amplification will bring subjective evaluations and decisions with it. On the one hand, the child's well-being will benefit from this comprehensive catalogue, but on the other hand, it will cause the choice of criteria to become more subjective and allow more scope for varying interpretations. Thus, it will become increasingly more complex and difficult to find a solution among conflicting parties. It will then become necessary to implement a hierarchy and a consensus concerning prioritization, in order to ensure the flawless application of these criteria. However, in a pluralistic society, it will not be possible to establish this procedure without conflict. For example, how does one act if the consideration of cultural values conflicts with the medical criteria of a pluralistic society? (British Medical Association 2001)

16.3.5 Case analysis and discussion

The health care professionals and the doctors in this case felt overwhelmed not only because of the language barrier, but also because of the cultural differences. Communication barriers in an intercultural decision-making conflict can have various dimensions. An interpreter can translate medical information in order to eliminate comprehension difficulties between a terminally ill child's father and the medical staff, if the communication barrier is solely due to language. One can hope that this would dissolve the dissent between the conflicting parties. However, the dissent in the presented case seems to be more complicated, in that the father declined to have the outpatient medical team administer palliative care to his son and also claimed that the x-rays were swapped and did not belong to his son. These allegations may result from misinformation or from distrust and scepticism towards the medical staff. Thus, a constructive conversation between all parties is necessary. The goal of this conversation would be to find out whether this allegation is based on factual misinformation or if it is a sign of distrust. In the case of the latter, it is important to find the reasons for this distrust and to try and resolve these.

Other aspects of an intercultural communication process also need to be taken into consideration. It is often ignored that the meaning of normative terms in everyday practice cannot be adequately explained through simple translation in that they are often open to interpretation and culturally predefined. Thus, they might be normatively divergent for each conflicting party. In this context, various clinical-ethical questions arise: Is the child's best interest the focus of each party's ethical orientation? Is the moral relevance of the child's well-being identical for all conflicting parties? Do all the participating parties choose a course of action that caters to the child's well-being? Does the definition of 'suffering', 'life', 'quality of life', etc. mean the same thing to each party? Can these definitions be objectified and made accessible to each party within an intercultural communication process?

Even though these questions are vital in understanding and solving the conflict at hand, it cannot be expected that the medical staff or the parents can communicate or reflect on these in a structured way. Thus, an outpatient clinical ethical consultation can play an important role in these types of situations. The goal of this ethical consultation should be to establish an understanding of the ethical problems among the conflicting parties. This understanding should not only be on a factual level, but also on a moral level. It also needs to be emphasized that the ethical consultants need to have intercultural competence (Ilkilic 2017).

In addition to communication barriers, cultural practices and the corresponding cultural barriers also played an important role in the presented case. The family had been in a 'foreign country' for quite some time, which is socially very different from their home country. The everyday routine and lifestyle, as well as the family members' role allocations and expectations and their corresponding cultural image are still foreign. Perhaps, a woman acting as the wage earner of the family is not necessarily self-evident. Her new role might not accommodate the father's self-perception and expectations and he might not consent to the fact that his role as head of the family is socially and psychologically challenged. Whether or not leaving treatment decisions about his child up to his wife has to do with these culturally influenced role reversals could be resolved in an open conversation.

There are also other reasons that could explain the father's wish to have his wife care for their child. For example, it might be important to the mother to follow certain cultural rituals at the end of a child's life. The intention of the family to collectively bid farewell to their beloved child may also be a reason for this wish. The palliative care team may not be welcome in that the family might assume that they will prevent these cultural practices from taking place.

The mother's values and how she interprets the situation are not mentioned in the case description. However, we can decipher from the case analysis that the situation is putting an enormous physical and psychological strain on her and that she is against her son's hospitalization. Her opinion about her husband's wish remains unclear. Does she agree with her husband's wishes or would she prefer the provision of professional care? What are the reasons behind this decision? How does she assess the current conflict? To what extent is she able to choose a course of action? Her terminally ill child's end-of-life treatment may be important to her. But how free is she in making that decision? Staying at home means not going to work and forfeiting an income that is necessary in supporting the family financially.

The effect that the absence of a mother's attention towards her child and the professional care has on the terminally ill child should also be taken into consideration in the given case. To what extent does the child perceive how much attention he is getting from his mother and could this have a positive effect on his quality of life? What effect would the omission of professional palliative care have on the child's quality of life?

16.3.6 Conclusion

Many points in the presented case were left open, meaning that our ethical analyses and evaluations remain hypothetical, as was to be expected. Yet, it should nevertheless be advocated that in this case the child's best interest should remain the focus of an ethically justifiable decision. However, there are many barriers that prevent a shared understanding of the child's best interest in this case. Language as well as cultural barriers are important challenges to the decision-making process. In addition, the normative terms presented in this case are influenced by cultural values and characterized by moral diversity. A dialogue which respects intercultural dimensions is necessary in order to ensure the accessibility of the parties' values and ideals. An outpatient clinical ethical consultation that has the necessary intercultural competence could be an important aid in establishing this kind of constructive dialogue.

16.4 Commentary 2: Migration, bioethics, pluralism

Richard Huxtable

16.4.1 Introduction

The UK's National Health Service (NHS) was (and is) aimed at providing care for everyone, based on need (Department of Health 2015; NHS Choices 2018). Soon after its launch in 1948, questions arose about whether 'everyone' was to include migrants. In 1952, Aneurin Bevan, who pioneered the service, suggested that 'the sheep' should not be 'separated from the goats', for reasons of both 'generosity and convenience' (Bevan 1952).[3] As Bevan appreciated, practical and ethical obstacles prevent the separation of migrants from non-migrants, although such questions continue to be asked, both in the UK and elsewhere. Bevan's observations inform this commentary on Josip's case, in which I briefly offer three general and connected prescriptions for those implicated in, and dealing with, such a case. I therefore argue, first, that clinicians should focus on the case before them, including both its general and particular features, second, that health services should be attentive to, and have some method for navigating, pluralism, and third, that everyone involved in the case should ensure that there is effective communication.

16.4.2 Migration and pluralism

The first prescription is that clinicians should look to the case in question, and in doing so be mindful of both its *general and particular features.*

Getting ill, getting access to health care and getting appropriate health care can all be challenging for migrants, as well as for non-migrants. First, various studies show that migrants can and will get ill: they may be in vulnerable positions, taking on dangerous jobs, and enduring psychosocial difficulties (Akinola, Krishna & Chetlapalli 2014; Chen et al. 2012; Dwyer 2009; Jolivet et al. 2012). As such, migrants – like everyone else – will have need of health services.

Second, despite this, migrants will not necessarily get access to the health care that they need, for example, due to their unfamiliarity with the receiving country's health service or policies which deny or diminish their eligibility (Sargent 2006; Supanchaimat et al. 2015). Sometimes, however, the reasons for not accessing services are less apparent: for example, Chinese people in the UK reportedly make less use of cancer and specialist palliative care services, although 'the reasons for this are unclear' (Payne et al. 2005, p. 111).

Yet, third, even if access is secured, migrants might not receive appropriate care. There are reports of migrants experiencing unjust discrimination (Fang et al 2014; Lauderdale et al. 2006; Worth et al. 2009), struggling to surmount communication and cultural barriers (Lauderdale et al. 2006; Supanchaimat et al. 2015), and a lack of 'fit' between the values of migrants and the values of the receiving health service (Supanchaimat et al. 2015). The aforementioned UK study noted how trends in palliative care – such as valuing individual autonomy and disclosure to the patient not the family – 'are based on assumptions which may not be shared by the Chinese community' (Payne et al. 2005, p. 111).

These various findings suggest there are *general* considerations pertaining to the health care of migrants, regardless of who they are or from whence they came. Yet, excessive reductionism should be avoided. To return to Bevan's metaphor, goats are heterogeneous, as are sheep (Pfalzbot 2018; Sheep101. Info 2018), and so too are migrants and non-migrant inhabitants of a territory (if we can even identify such people). Migration is a multi-faceted phenomenon, not reducible to nationality, since it comprises (for example) migration, return migration and 'internal' migration, and its effects can persist across generations, even after nationality or residence are secured (IOM, WHO & UN OHCHR 2013, pp. 13–14). The UK study recognized, for example, that 'the term "Chinese people" is problematic because it represents a heterogeneous group of people' (Payne et al. 2005, p. 111). Even membership of a particular faith group is no guarantee of uniformity: for example, Roman Catholic parents have reached radically different decisions about whether their conjoined offspring should be separated, despite their shared faith and the apparent similarity of the situations (Huxtable 2002).

Given the plurality of migration and migrants, Wild and Dawson argue for a case-based approach to tackling the challenges arising in and from migration, which is:

> sensitive to the diversity of migrant experiences while also being able to discuss more general considerations. This can be tackled through an explicit effort to consider many different circumstances and phases of migration, including a special focus on the individual 'vulnerabilities' according to each case.
>
> (Wild & Dawson 2018, p. 69)

Their attention is on public health ethics, but their observations apply just as well to dilemmas arising in clinical ethics and therefore to Josip's case. As such, our first prescription is that the clinicians should focus on the case in question, attending to any general considerations, but never losing sight of its particularities.

In Josip's case, there might be general considerations arising from the fact that Josip and his parents are migrants: for example, there are likely to be generic questions of justice and of access to health care to consider. However, there will also be considerations particular to *these* migrants. Some of these might also be fairly general, for example, involving the family's socio-economic situation, ethnicity, culture and values. Here, for example, we might need to account for the family's Croatian heritage or (although this is not revealed in the case report) the religious faith of the parents. But some such considerations will not be peculiar to migrant families. We might well find that a migrant family is not, or not entirely, populated by 'moral strangers' (Engelhardt 1996, p. 7). Indeed, many of the themes arising in Josip's case will be familiar from cases involving families that have long (perhaps always) been resident in the relevant territory: socio-economic hardship, parenting roles for mothers that are assumed to differ from those of fathers, discomfort with (or distrust of) professionals, and different understandings of what will be best for a child. But we will also need to be even more particular, looking specifically to *this* patient and *this* family. We should not assume that the family's nationality, route into the receiving country, faith and so on will mean that there is an 'off-the-peg' solution which will neatly fit this particular family in this particular situation. In short, we should avoid reductionism and be alert to pluralism.

16.4.3 Bioethics and pluralism

The second prescription is that health services should be attentive to, and have some method for navigating, *pluralism*.

The field of bioethics should be able to help here as it is alert to pluralism, not least because the field itself is unavoidably pluralistic in various senses, since it encompasses a plurality of people, perspectives and values. Bioethics is a multi- and inter-disciplinary endeavour, which – importantly – has regard not only for ethical arguments and justifications, but also for practical perspectives and experiences. Sheehan and Dunn summarize bioethics' goal as addressing practical 'ought' questions, which they argue involves making *convincing* claims that actually serve to *convince* the relevant stakeholders (Sheehan & Dunn 2013, p. 57). Whether or not one favours Sheehan and Dunn's precise formulation, bioethics essentially echoes Bevan's reference to 'generosity and convenience', as it is concerned with both the ethical and the practical (cf. Brownsword 2008, pp. 15–17; Wild & Dawson 2018, p. 68).

Given these twin concerns, pluralism is part of the bioethical condition. Plurality is present not only at the surface level of the two domains (the ethical and the practical), but also beneath the surface, as bioethics provides a meeting place for a vast variety of people, disciplines and perspectives, which are themselves heterogeneous (Silber 1982, p. 24). There are diverse ethical schools of thought, as well as diverse practical perspectives, which emanate from clinicians, patients and many others. The diversity is apparent wherever bioethics work is undertaken. Indeed, despite suggestions to the contrary, there are not necessarily or exclusively *particular* bioethical values and approaches operating in *particular* territories (Huxtable 2018b). Like – and with – migrants, ways of thinking and being will travel in and out of territories. As such, there is a recognizable field, bioethics, which is concerned with issuing practical 'oughts', but it is a pluralistic field.

Clinical ethics, as a subset of bioethics, has long appreciated the need to attend to and navigate such pluralism, and it is here that bioethics might best support clinicians (and, indeed, health services, patients and families) in their dealings with cases like Josip's. Clinical ethics support services are available in many countries in different forms, but clinical ethics committees appear particularly promising, given their apparent commitment to recognising and working through pluralism. Committees are usually diverse in their composition, encompassing various health care professionals, lay members, chaplains, lawyers and clinical ethicists (who might be drawn from an academic setting). Such a broadly constituted group therefore pools pertinent knowledge and skills, with everyone bringing something valuable to the committee's work (Huxtable 2012). Committees can be involved in education, policy work and, of most relevance here, case consultation, where the latter role involves issuing advice to clinicians about ethically difficult cases, that is, issuing the aforementioned practical 'oughts'.

Such services' commitment to pluralism is also apparent in the different methodologies and approaches used in the formulation of their ethical advice. Some approaches, such as 'moral case deliberation' deliberately blur the lines between the ethical and practical, seeking a 'fusion of horizons', which generates some sort of consensus about what should be done (Stolper, Molevijk & Widdershoven 2016). Other models, such as the 'four quadrants' approach, involve some separation of the practical – such as 'contextual features' and 'indications for medical intervention' – from the ethical – 'preferences of the patient' and 'quality of life' – but they nevertheless aspire to bring these elements together to arrive at a recommendation (cf. Dunn 2014; Jonsen, Siegler & Winslade 2006; Knox 2014; Sokol 2008). Others focus more on the ethical side, albeit again in a pluralistic fashion, as is evident, for example, in the use of the four principles approach by some clinical ethics services (Beauchamp & Childress 2013; Hurst, Chevrolet & Loew 2006).

Clinical ethics support services, and committees particularly, therefore appear well-equipped to advise on cases like Josip's, provided that they – like the clinicians directly involved – attend to the general and particular features of the case in question. However, procedural questions continue to surround these services (e.g. Huxtable 2012, 2018a). Can a committee be sufficiently responsive, where, as appeared to be the case for Josip, advice is needed urgently? Who should be entitled to seek a committee's advice – should this only be the clinicians, rather than patients or family members? Who should be entitled to sit on a committee and in what capacity? And what sort of methodologies and processes are needed?

An answer to the last question requires engagement with the pros and cons of different pluralistic models. The chosen model will need to be sufficiently pluralistic, particularly if it is to respond appropriately to cases involving migrants. For example, the principlist model has been charged with imperialism, since it 'not only advances a distinctively Western (Anglo-American) position but also fails to recognise the multiplicity of traditions and perspectives that exist even within the societies it purports to reflect, i.e. in contemporary pluralistic communities' (Huxtable 2013: p. 40). Some suggest that Beauchamp and Childress' model is sufficiently accommodating of, and applicable to, countries other than the USA and those with diverse values and commitments (Aksoy & Elmai 2002; Gillon 2003; Tsai 2005). However, some territories and some faiths appear to be committed to quite different principles or values, which suggests this will not always be a sufficiently 'open' model (Rendtorff 2002; Westra, Willems & Smit 2009). Perhaps, then, what is needed is a more pluralistic model, which does not specify in advance the precise ethical principles or values which are to be negotiated.

Of course, whichever ethical values enter the picture, some methodology will be needed for working through these values, as well as the relevant practical insights, in order to arrive at a practical 'ought'. Here particular questions arise about the weight that is to be accorded to different considerations and how these are to be combined. Where migrants are concerned, to return to Bevan's metaphor, complex questions might arise about the extent to which the concerns of 'sheep' should give way to those of 'goats', or vice versa. Whoever is implicated, an account will certainly be needed of how purported 'facts' and 'values' should be brought together. Progress is being made here, at least in relation to normative 'empirical bioethics' research (Ives, Dunn & Cribb 2017). Similar progress is probably also needed in the field of clinical ethics, as existing methodologies are not always clearly specified or readily comprehensible. Principlism, for example, involves specification of the principles and balancing between them, via a process of 'reflective equilibrium' (Beauchamp & Childress 2013; Rawls 1971, see commentary of Marckmann, p. 272). This is a process which is also often used in empirical bioethics research, but which nevertheless remains somewhat mysterious.

16.4.4 Ethics and communication

The third prescription is that everyone involved should ensure that there is *effective communication.*

A truism I often relay to medical students is that good ethics needs good facts and good communication. The facts will come from different sources: patients and families will know their situation and what treatment can (or cannot) work for them; clinicians will know the diagnosis, prognosis, treatment options, risks and benefits; lawyers will know what is legally permissible; and so on. Kant instructs us that 'ought' implies 'can' and different stakeholders will have different insights into what can be done, which will have a bearing on what should be done.

Of course, good communication is also essential, not only in working out the facts – the known, unknown, unknown unknowns, and so on – but also in working out the ethical way forward. As such, the protagonists – principally the family and professionals in this case – will need to ensure that the lines of communication are open. Furthermore, the ethical deliberation process also entails a commitment to effective communication. I have elsewhere argued for a process of 'principled compromise', which requires participants to be reliable, reflective and respectful in their negotiations with one another (Huxtable 2012). The relevant participants might be the aforementioned protagonists or, for example, the members of and participants in a clinical ethics support service, such as a committee.

These (admittedly brief) observations have implications for Josip's case. Where migrants are concerned, then, at a minimum, the receiving health service should have adequate translation services available and access to relevant sources of advice, at least where these are needed in the particular case. Without wishing to be critical of the conscientious professionals involved, this is a troubling aspect of Josip's case: the professionals certainly appeared committed to communicating with his parents, but everyone appeared to be let down by a lack of suitable translators. Reliance on the mother or on a visiting doctor appears inadequate, as they might have conflicting interests, which might mean that the father's voice is not adequately heard. Better, it seems, to have a sufficiently funded and independent service, which can facilitate effective communication between the different protagonists. Thus equipped, the family and the team can then seek to air their respective opinions, perhaps embarking on some form of 'shared decision-making' or at least some process of 'advance care planning', in which all the relevant stakeholders are heard.

There are also implications for the ethical deliberation process. Dialogue appears to be needed not only between the protagonists, but also between the different values in play. This returns us to the question of methodology and the challenge of ensuring that different 'voices' are heard and these are somehow brought into harmony (cf. Chadwick 2015). The voices might be those of the different stakeholders, but might also, metaphorically, be those of the different values – how are the different perspectives and values to be combined in order to arrive at a 'solution'? Should the emphasis be on consensus or coherence or something else entirely?

16.4.5 Conclusion

There are, therefore, numerous questions raised by Josip's case, some of which might be specific to his situation, but others of which have wider relevance and import. Hopefully, in bioethics, we will continue to search for answers to these questions, to enable us to deliver on bioethics' goal of issuing practical 'oughts'. In these modest reflections, I have argued that a case like Josip's requires those involved to be alert to its general and particular features, have some means of attending to and navigating pluralism and be committed to effective communication. Resolving the dilemmas arising from such a case will not always be straightforward, but I hope that continued attention to these 'oughts' might help everyone involved to work together to plot a way forward.

16.5 Commentary 3: universalism versus particularism in clinical ethics: a coherentist perspective

Georg Marckmann

16.5.1 Introduction

In some respects, medical ethics is as almost old as medicine itself. Already in the fourth century B.C., a group of Greek physicians working with Hippocrates developed a code for physicians' appropriate behaviour, the famous Hippocratic

Oath. This early document of professional self-obligation points to the fact that medicine is intrinsically a moral endeavour. The deeper reasons for this lie in the asymmetry of the physician-patient relationship: a vulnerable patient, often in severe distress and threatened by death, is seeking help from another person, the physician, who has – potentially – the power to help the patient by curing the disease or at least alleviating her suffering. The moral self-obligation binds the physician's power to the interest of the patient and thereby constitutes a crucial source of patients' trust. With the increasing possibilities of modern medicine and the high value of patient autonomy in pluralistic societies, medicine has become more challenging, both for physicians and patients. Deciding what is in the best interest of the patient has become more difficult, especially in patients with severe diseases. In reaction to the resulting moral issues and dilemmas, ethical reflection in medicine has become increasingly sophisticated, and medical ethics has developed into a flourishing discipline, both in the clinical context – often referred to as clinical ethics – and as biomedical ethics in academia. In my commentary, I will elaborate the normative foundations of clinical ethics and then apply the resulting normative framework to arrive at an ethically justified decision in the acute crisis of Josip. I will especially discuss the extent to which a coherentist approach to medical ethics can accommodate the tension between universalism and particularism, both in the realm of ethical theory and in (pluralistic) societies.

16.5.2 Coherentist justification of clinical ethics

In clinical ethics, the guiding question is usually: Which course of treatment should be chosen from an ethical perspective? Clinical ethics consultation offers physicians and other health care professionals support in making difficult ethical decisions about patient care. In these situations, clinical ethics makes *normative* claims about what is morally right or wrong, good or bad, just or unjust. As it involves normative ethics, clinical ethics requires a justification by an ethical theory. However, clinical ethics is challenged, like other fields of applied ethics, with a multitude of different, often conflicting ethical theories. Depending on which theory is chosen, the results of ethical arguments will be quite different. For example, it is quite obvious that a utilitarian consequentialist will arrive at different conclusions regarding life-sustaining treatment in a patient with severe cerebral trauma compared to a Kantian deontologist. In the tradition of contractarian ethical theories, John Rawls developed an approach to ethical justification, which does not refer to one of the fundamental ethical theories, but rather starts with our everyday morality (Rawls 1971). From considered moral judgements, we derive prima facie binding mid-level ethical principles which give us guidance for making evaluations in challenging ethical situations. These principles are tested against theoretical assumptions and judgements in single cases and have to be refined until we reach a 'reflective equilibrium', that is, coherence between judgements, principles and theoretical assumptions.

16.5.3 Principlism: universalistic or particularistic?

Based on this coherence theory of justification, four principles have been proposed by Tom L. Beauchamp and James F. Childress in the 1970s in their seminal book *Principles of biomedical ethics*: beneficence, non-maleficence, respect for autonomy and justice (Beauchamp & Childress 2013). These principles cannot be considered universal in a strict sense, as they are derived from considered judgements, which may vary depending on the cultural background. De facto, there is a wide agreement across different cultures that the four principles are the ethical cornerstones of medical practice. Especially in modern, industrialized societies, the four principles therefore can be considered 'quasi universalistic'. However, particular moralities or cultural contexts may influence the application of the principles considerably. In the first step, the *interpretation* of the principles can be influenced by culturally specific aspects. In some societies, for example, the family plays a more important role than the individual in the decision-making about medical treatment and therefore the family becomes the focus of respect for autonomy. In the second step, when conflicting principles have to be *balanced*, the weight of the principles may vary according to the cultural background of the protagonists. In Western societies, for example, respect for autonomy frequently takes (relative) priority over the beneficence-based obligations. Thereby, the coherentist approach to medical ethics is open to varying cultural interpretations and the balancing of moral principles. Ideally, interpretation and balancing of the principles should be sensitive to the patient's cultural background – and the answers to ethical conflicts may vary with cultural backgrounds. Difficult situations and conflicts can arise if the cultural values of the care team diverge significantly from the values of the patient or the patient's family. While care teams should try to respect the patient's (or their surrogates) specific interpretations as far as possible, there will be limits to what patients can demand from the care team, for example, continuation of futile medical treatment.

16.5.4 Principle-based model of ethical case discussion

In ethically challenging cases, the four principles can give normative guidance and structure the workup of the case, especially in a team case discussion on the ward (Marckmann & Mayer 2009; McCullough & Ashton 1994; cf. Box 16.1 for overview).

At the beginning, any ethical case discussion requires a thorough medical workup of the case (step 1), which includes a collection of all available information about the patient's situation (a) and an analysis of the available management strategies (b). The ethical evaluation (step 2) then starts with the beneficence-based obligations (a): Which is the best strategy for the patient from the perspective of the care team? Then it has to be clarified which strategy the patient prefers after having received all relevant information (b). The third evaluation element looks to obligations towards third parties, like

BOX 16.1 Principle-based model of ethical case discussion (cf. McCullough & Ashton 1994; Marckmann & Mayer 2009)

Step 1: Analysis → medical workup

a Medical situation of the patient (history, symptoms, findings, diagnoses, etc.)
b Management strategies with outcome (prognosis) of each strategy (benefits and burdens/risks)

Step 2: Evaluation → Specification of moral obligations

a Beneficence and non-maleficence ('best interest perspective')
b Respect for autonomy (patient perspective)
c Justice (obligations to third parties)

Step 3: Synthesis → balancing conflicting obligations

- Obligations converge → good ethical reasons to choose the strategy
- Conflicting obligations → balancing based on case-specific reasons

Step 4: Critical review → Objections? Preventions?

families or other patients (c). In step 3, the synthesis, what must be assessed is whether the obligations resulting from the four principles converge or diverge. If they converge, there are good ethical reasons to choose the respective management strategy; if, however, there are conflicting obligations, these have to be balanced, based on good, case-specific reasons. Step 4 finally consists in a critical review of the ethical decision elaborated in the synthesis: What is the strongest objection? Could the conflict have been avoided? In the last section, I will demonstrate how we can arrive at an ethically justified decision in the case of Josip.

16.5.5 A principle-based discussion of the case of Josip

Step 1 (medical situation): Josip, an 11-month-old patient with a progressive neurodegenerative disorder (pontocerebellar hypoplasia) suffers from an acute crisis at home, when neither his mother as primary caregiver nor the nurse is present. There are two different management strategies in this situation: (1) Life-prolonging emergency treatment, including cardio-pulmonary resuscitation (CPR) if necessary. The prognosis is difficult to assess in the acute situation, but the underlying disease will progress and Josip will have an increasingly diminished quality of life (e.g. mucous congestion, dyspnoea, bradycardia with airway obstruction and seizures). (2) No CPR, comfort measures only. Josip will most likely die within the next minutes to few hours.

Step 2 (ethical evaluation):

1 *Beneficence, non-maleficence*: At best, life-prolonging therapy (strategy 1) can postpone the inevitable death of Josip. In light of the deteriorating quality of life with burdensome symptoms, strategy 2 – comfort measures only – could be the better option for Josip because it does not prolong his suffering.
2 *Respect for autonomy*: Josip has no decision-making capacity, so the parents have to act as substitute decision makers. The mother wants Josip to die peacefully at home, which would correspond to strategy 2 (comfort measures only). However, she is currently away and would not be able to comfort her son during his last phase of life, so she would perhaps prefer, one could speculate, that Josip's life be stabilized, enabling her to be with him during the last phase of his life. The position of Josip's father is even more difficult to assess due to language barriers. He mistrusts the hospital and expects Josip's positive development. According to Josip's mother, he agreed to forgo life-sustaining interventions, however, his level of understanding is unclear. From the case description, we have no information about the current wishes of Josip's father. Overall, there are no clear arguments for one of the two strategies based on the principle of respect for autonomy.
3 *Obligations to third parties*: Both for the mother, who is not present at the moment, and for the father, it could be better if Josip were to overcome this acute crisis and then die (if he does not recover quickly) under more controlled circumstances in which both of his parents are present. Therefore, strategy 1 would be favourable according to the obligations towards third parties.

Step 3 (synthesis): While the beneficence-based obligations point towards strategy 2 (comfort measures only), obligations towards third parties appear instead to be inclined to strategy 1 (life-sustaining therapy). The autonomy-based obligations are not really clear. Therefore, we have at least an ethical tension between the beneficence-based obligations and the obligations towards third parties. That the wishes of both parents with respect to this concrete situation (life-threatening crisis with the mother present, rather than the father being alone with Josip) are not really clear, could be an additional argument to start with strategy 1, stabilize Josip (if possible and not too burdensome), help the father with an interpreter to make an informed decision, together with the mother. This could result in a firmer ethical basis to forgo life-sustaining treatment in the next life-threatening crisis.

Step 4 (critical review): The strongest objection against choosing strategy 1 is that it may prolong Josip's suffering, including a prolonged treatment in the intensive care unit (ICU). Therefore, optimal palliative care is crucial, and the decision must be reviewed if Josip remains in a critical, burdensome situation. In addition, the decision to forego life-sustaining treatment may be more difficult for the parents if Josip remains on the ICU with continuous invasive ventilation. Could the conflict have been avoided? Apparently, it was not possible to get a clear position from the father regarding life-sustaining treatment in the event of life-threatening crises – which would have been a help in reducing the ethical tensions in the situation a little bit.

16.5.6 Conclusion

The coherentist approach to biomedical ethics, which is based on the four mid-level ethical principles beneficence, non-maleficence, respect for autonomy and justice, has a strong universalist tendency, but is not universal in a strict sense. It is open for particular cultural values and contexts, first, in the interpretation of single principles and, second, in balancing conflicting obligations. Care teams should be sensitive to the patient's culturally specific interpretations of the resulting obligations (e.g. the patient's understanding of autonomy). Thereby, the patient's or her family's interpretations can come into conflict with the interpretations of the team. While the patient's or her family's perspective respectively should have priority, in contested cases a principle-based case discussion among the team should be conducted in order to determine whose interpretation should prevail. The application of the approach to the case of Josip tried to illustrate how, in cases of ethical uncertainty or conflict, a structured principle-based workup can help to arrive at an ethically justifiable decision. The different cultural backgrounds and language difficulties contributed in this case to the complexity of the decision and may require a strategy that carefully balances the obligations towards the young patient and his parents.

16.6 Case resolution

The SHPPC decided to call the emergency doctor and left their base to drive to the family's home. On the phone, they informed the emergency physician about the condition of the child and the current situation. By the time the emergency doctor and the SHPPC team had arrived, Josip's heart had already stopped beating in the presence of his father, who felt helpless and overwhelmed by the situation. Given the severity of his neurologic condition and the estimated duration of the hypoxia, the emergency physician assumed that it was highly unlikely that CPR would have been successful in this case. Thus, he decided not to initiate CPR. Josip's mother was not present during the situation, which made her feel guilty afterwards, since she could not comfort her son as he died.

Notes

1 We are grateful to Dr. Kathrin Knochel (MD at the Center for Peadiatric Palliative Medicine, Munich University Hospital) who helped with the case description. We also appreciate the contribution of Maria Ruhfass (Research Assistant at the Institute of Ethics, History and Theory of Medicine at Ludwig Maximilians Universität (LMU) Munich) who contributed to an early draft of this manuscript. We thank the participants of the panel discussion, which was part of the international workshop on ethical, legal and social implications of health care for migrants at LMU Munich (March 16, 2016). We furthermore thank the German Ministry for Education and Research for funding the workshop in which the discussion took place (01GP8413).

2 The commentators had participated in a public panel discussion of this case during an international workshop in Munich (March 16, 2016). Commentators were free to reflect on the themes or dilemmas they perceived, plus any recommendations they might have. Questions to consider included whether emergency services should be called, the patient should be transferred to an intensive care unit, and generally how health care professionals and health services should seek to navigate pluralism in such cases.

3 I am indebted to Robert Hughes, a then medical student at the University of Bristol, for bringing this passage to my attention and, indeed, for spurring my interest in this topic, through our joint research presentation, 'Separating Sheep from Goats? (Denying) Access to Primary Healthcare for Overseas Visitors' (Centre for Ethics in Medicine Research Seminar, March 2008, Bristol, UK). My thanks also to Simon Jenkins, who undertook a literature review, which informed part of Section 16.4, and to Giles Birchley and Zuzana Deans for helpful discussions during the writing of this commentary.

References

Akinola, A.B., Krishna, A.K.I., & Chetlapalli, S.K. 2014, Health equity for internal migrant labourers in India: an ethical perspective, *Indian Journal of Medical Ethics*, vol. 11, no. 4, pp. 232–237.

Aksoy, S., & Elmai, A. 2002, 'The core concepts of the "four principles" of bioethics as found in Islamic tradition', *Medicine and Law*, vol. 21, pp. 211–224.

Bayerisches Staatsministerium für Umwelt und Gesundheit. 2009, *Palliativversorgung von Kindern und Jugendlichen in Bayern*, viewed 2 July 2018, www.stmgp.bayern.de/gesundheitsversorgung/sterbebegleitung/palliativversorgung.

Bender, H.U., Riester, M.B., Borasio, G.D., & Führer, M. 2017, "Let's bring her home first': patient characteristics and place of death in specialized pediatric palliative home care', *Journal of Pain and Symptom Management*, vol. 54, no. 2, pp. 159–166.

Beauchamp, T.L., & Childress, J.F. 2013, *Principles of biomedical ethics*, Oxford University Press, New York, Oxford.

Bevan, A. 1952, *In place of fear*, Heinemann, Portsmouth, NH.

British Medical Association. 2001, *Consent, rights and choices in health care for children and young people*, BMJ Books, London.

Brownsword, R. 2008, 'Bioethics: bridging from morality to law?', in M. Freeman (ed.), *Law and bioethics: current legal issues 2008, Volume 11*, Oxford University Press, Oxford.

Chadwick, R. 2015, '"Getting ethics": voices in harmony in bioethics', in R. Huxtable & R. ter Meulen (eds.), *The voices and rooms of European bioethics*, Routledge, Abingdon.

Chen, L., Li, W., He, J., Wu, L., Yan, Z., & Tang, W. 2012, 'Mental health, duration of unemployment, and coping strategy: a cross-sectional study of unemployed migrant workers in eastern china during the economic crisis', *BMC Public Health*, vol. 12, no. 1, p. 597.

Department of Health. 2015, *The NHS constitution*, Department of Health, London, viewed 3 July 2018, www.gov.uk/government/publications/the-nhs-constitution-for-england.

Dijk, T van, Baas, F., Barth, P.G., & Tien Poll-The, B.T. 2018, 'What's new in ponto-cerebellar hypoplasia? An update on genes and subtypes', *Orphanet Journal of Rare Diseases*, vol. 13, no. 1, p. 92.

Dörries, A. 2003, 'Der Best-Interest Standard in der Pädiatrie – theoretische Konzeption und klinische Anwendung', in C. Wiesemann (ed.), *Das Kind als Patient*, Campus, S, Frankfurt, pp. 116–130.

Dunn, M.C. 2014, 'Toolbox for ethical thinking', in D. Anantham et al. (eds.), *Making difficult decisions with patients and families: a Singapore casebook*, National University of Singapore, Singapore, viewed 22 May 2018, www.bioethicscasebook.sg/making-difficult-decisions-with-patients-and-families/.

Dwyer, J. 2009, 'When the discharge plan is deportation: hospitals, immigrants, and social responsibility', *Bioethics*, vol. 23, no. 3, pp. ii–iv.

Glannon, W. 2005, *Biomedical ethics*, Oxford University Press, New York.

Engelhardt, H.T. 1996, *The foundations of bioethics*, 2nd edn, Oxford University, New York.

Fang, M.L., Malcoe, L.H., Sixsmith, J., Wong, L.Y.M., & Callendar, M. 2014, 'Exploring traditional end-of-life beliefs, values, expectations, and practices among Chinese women living in England: informing culturally safe care', *Palliative and Supportive Care*, vol. 13, no. 5, pp. 1261–1274.

Fleischmann, A.R. 2016, *Pediatric ethics: protecting the interests of the children*, Oxford University Press, New York.

Gillon, R. 2003, 'Ethics needs principles – four can encompass the rest – and respect for autonomy should be 'first among equals'', *Journal of Medical Ethics*, vol. 29, no. 5, pp. 307–312.

Groh, G., Borasio, G.D., Nickolay, C., Bender, H.U., Lüttichau, I von, & Führer, M. 2013, 'Specialized pediatric palliative home care: a prospective evaluation', *Journal of Palliative Medicine*, vol. 16, no. 12, pp. 1588–1594.

Hurst, S.A., Chevrolet, J., & Loew, F. 2006, 'Methods in clinical ethics: a time for eclectic pragmatism?', *Clinical Ethics*, vol. 1, no. 3, pp. 159–164.

Huxtable, R. 2002, 'Separation of conjoined twins: where next for English law?', *Criminal Law Review*, pp. 459–470.

Huxtable, R. 2012, *Law, ethics and compromise at the limits of life: to treat or not to treat?* Routledge, Abingdon.

Huxtable, R. 2013, 'For and against the four principles of biomedical ethics', *Clinical Ethics*, vol. 8, no. 2–3, pp. 39–43.

Huxtable, R. 2018a, 'Clinic, courtroom or (specialist) committee: in the best interests of the critically ill child?', *Journal of Medical Ethics*, vol. 44, pp. 471–475.

Huxtable, R. 2018b, 'On the open seas: pluralism and bioethics in Europe', in T.C. Chuan, R. Huxtable & N. Peart (eds.), *Healthcare ethics, law and professionalism: essays on the works of Alastair V. Campbell*, Routledge, Abingdon (forthcoming).

IOM, WHO, & UN OCHCR. 2013, *International migration, health and human rights*, IOM, Geneva.

Ilkilic, I. 2017, 'Interkulturelle Kompetenz als Schlüsselqualifikation für Gesundheitsberufe', *Gesundheit Gesellschaft Wissenschaft*, vol. 17, no. 2, pp. 24–30.

Ives, J., Dunn, M., & Cribb, A. (eds.) 2017, *Empirical bioethics: practical and theoretical perspectives*, Cambridge University Press, Cambridge.

Jolivet, A., Cadot, E., Florence, S., Lesieur, S., Lebas, J., & Chauvin, P. 2012, 'Migrant health in French Guiana: are undocumented immigrants more vulnerable?', *BMC Public Health*, vol. 12, no. 1, p. 53.

Jonsen, A., Siegler, M., & Winslade, W. 2006, *Clinical ethics*, 6th edn, McGraw-Hill, New York.

Knox, J.B.L. 2014, 'The 4C model: a reflective tool for the analysis of ethical cases at the neonatal intensive-care unit', *Clinical Ethics*, vol. 9, no. 4, pp. 120–126.

Lauderdale, D.S., Wen, M., Jacobs, E.A., & Kandula, N.R. 2006, 'Immigrant perceptions of discrimination in health care: the California Health Interview Survey', *Medical Care*, vol. 44, no. 10, pp. 914–920.

Marckmann, G., & Mayer, F. 2009, 'Ethische Fallbesprechungen in der Onkologie: Grundlagen einer prinzipienorientierten Falldiskussion', *Der Onkologe*, vol. 15, no. 10, pp. 980–988.

McCullough, L.B., & Ashton, C.M. 1994, 'A methodology for teaching ethics in the clinical setting: a clinical handbook for medical ethics', *Theoretical Medicine*, vol. 15, no. 1, pp. 39–52.

NHS Choices. 2018, 'Principles and values that guide the NHS', viewed 22 May 2018, www.nhs.uk/NHSEngland/thenhs/about/Pages/nhscoreprinciples.aspx.

Payne, S., Chapman, A., Holloway, M., Seymour, J.E., & Chau, R. 2005, 'Chinese community views: promoting cultural competence in palliative care', *Journal of Palliative Care*, vol. 21, no. 2, pp. 111–116.

Pfalzbot, G. 2018, 'Goat facts (from various resources)', viewed 22 May 2018, www.goatworld.com/articles/goatslife/goatfacts.shtml.

President's Commission for the Study of Ethical Problems in Medicine and Biomedical and Behavioral Research. 1983, '*Deciding to forego life-sustaining treatment. A report on the ethical, medical and legal issues in treatment decisions*', Government Printing Office, Washington, DC.

Rawls, J. 1971, '*A theory of justice*', Harvard University Press, Cambridge, MA.

Rendtorff, J.D. 2002, 'Basic ethical principles in European bioethics and biolaw: autonomy, dignity, integrity and vulnerability – towards a foundation of bioethics and biolaw', *Medicine, Health Care and Philosophy*, vol. 5, no. 3, pp. 235–244.

Sargent, C.F. 2006, 'Reproductive strategies and Islamic discourse: Malian migrants negotiate everyday life in Paris, France', *Medical Anthropology Quarterly*, vol. 20, no. 1, pp. 31–49.

Schulz-Baldes, A. 2006, 'Therapiebegrenzung in der Neonatologie: Entscheidungen im besten Interesse des Kindes?', in J. Schildmann et al. (ed.), *Entscheidungen am Lebensende in der modernen Medizin: Ethik, Recht, Ökonomie und Klinik*, Lit Verlag, S, Berlin.

Sheehan, M., & Dunn, M. 2013, 'On the nature and sociology of bioethics', *Health Care Analysis*, vol. 21, no. 1, pp. 54–69.

Sheep101.Info 2018, *Counting sheep*, viewed 22 May 2018, www.sheep101.info/sheeptypes.html.

Silber, T.J. 1982, 'Bioethics: an interdisciplinary enterprise', *Journal of Religion and Health*, vol. 21, no. 1, pp. 21–28.

Sokol, D.K. 2008, 'The "four quadrants" approach to clinical ethics case analysis: an application and review', *Journal of Medical Ethics*, vol. 34, no. 7, pp. 513–516.

Stolper, M., Molewijk, B., & Widdershoven, G. 2016, 'Bioethics education in clinical settings: theory and practice of the dilemma method of moral case deliberation', *BMC Medical Ethics*, vol. 17, no. 1, p. 45.

Stuhlinger, M. 2005, 'Das Kindeswohl als zentrale ethische Norm in der Pädiatrie', *Zeitschrift für Medizinische Ethik*, vol. 51, no. 2, pp. 153–165.

Supanchaimat, R., Kantamaturapoj, K., Putthasri, W., & Prakongsai, P. 2015, 'Challenges in the provision of healthcare services for migrants: a systematic review through providers' lens', *BMC Health Services Research*, vol. 15, no. 1, p. 390.

Tsai, D.F. 2005, 'The bioethical principles and Confucius' moral philosophy', *Journal of Medical Ethics*, vol. 31, no. 3, pp. 159–163.

UN. 1989, *Convention on the rights of the child*, viewed 22 June 2018, www2.ohchr.org/english/law/pdf/crc.pdf.

Westra, A.E., Willems, D.L., & Smit, B.J. 2009, 'Communicating with Muslim parents: "the four principles" are not as culturally neutral as suggested', *European Journal of Pediatrics*, vol. 168, no. 11, pp. 1383–1387.

Wild, V., & Dawson, A. 2018, 'Migration: a core public health ethics issue', *Public Health*, vol. 158, pp. 66–70.

Worth, A., Irshad, T., Bhopal, R., Brown, D., Lawton, J., Grant, E., Murray, S., Kendall, M., Adam, J., Gardee, R., and Sheikh, A. 2009, 'Vulnerability and access to care for South Asian Sikh and Muslim patients with life limiting illness in Scotland: prospective longitudinal qualitative study' *BMJ*, vol. 338, b183, pp. 1–11.

Index

FSC
www.fsc.org
MIX
Papier | Fördert gute Waldnutzung
FSC® C083411

Kolibri 360 GmbH
Ferdinand-Jühlke-Straße 7
99095 Erfurt, Deutschland
produktsicherheit@kolibri360.de